A HISTORY OF GREEK LITERATURE

A HISTORY OF
GREEK LITERATURE

BY *Moses Hadas*

Jay Professor of Greek

Columbia University

COLUMBIA UNIVERSITY PRESS

New York and London

PREFACE

CHAPMAN AND POPE, LANG, LEAF, AND MYERS, MADE ARTISTIC TRANSLATIONS of Homer, each a proper representation of the Greek for its own generation. For Pope, Chapman was antiquated; for Lang, Leaf, and Myers, Pope was antiquated; and today the quaint archaism of Lang, Leaf, and Myers obtrudes a needless obstacle between Homer and his reader. Each generation requires its own versions of the classics, and similarly each generation requires its own interpretation of them. What interested the philologians of Alexandria or of our fathers' day interests only a handful among us, and if our learning has grown thin in some places our interest has grown wider in others. Things in the Greek, by design or accident, to which our predecessors were blind or indifferent have moved into the center of interest. There is one sufficient reason for writing a new history of Greek literature, and that is that the year is 1950.

But to say new or different things about Greek literature is neither easy nor safe. Greek literature has been studied widely and intensely for many centuries, and if a man says something that has not been said before there is a strong probability that he is wrong. And a book like this dare not be wrong too often. Its author hopes, as all authors hope, that it may find its way to many shelves, to some where it will have no support from other works in its own field and where it may therefore be consulted for a name or a date or a trustworthy interpretation; and a book that may be so used may not flaunt its author's idiosyncrasies. But even a compiler's mind inevitably affects the materials which pass through it, if only by a different distribution of attention. The Greeks were especially concerned with men as members of society. I have wished to understand them, not merely as creators of Beautiful Letters, but as thoughtful men who had and expressed an attitude toward their fellow men. In so doing I have not knowingly distorted the truth.

In two matters I have distorted truth. One falsehood is in the apportionment of space. If some authors are to be mentioned at all they must have enough sentences to make them somehow meaningful, and the inevitable result is that some third-raters have a great deal more than a third of the space given first-raters. But reducing works of literature to a common scale of mensuration is an absurd enterprise at best, and so I have made my criterion usefulness. The reader is likely to require only to be reminded of certain matters concerning Homer or the tragedians or Thucydides, whereas Menander or Apollonius or the Greek romances may be outside his range. In any case, I have sought to mention every author down to the Hellenistic age of whose works there are remains considerable enough to be read (and not too many of whom there are no such remains). For the Hellenistic and following periods treatment has perforce been selective, but I believe that nothing of permanent worth as literature written before the age of Justinian has been overlooked.

The other distortion is in the spelling of proper names. To continue using Latin forms when Latin is no longer the universal language of scholarship is absurd, but all English books of reference and virtually all English translations use the Latin forms, and it would only confuse the unwary to say Aias or Hekabe, Alkaios or Aischylos, when he is used to Ajax and Hecuba and Alcaeus and Aeschylus. In other matters also the convenience of the nonspecialist reader has been consulted. Brief outline of certain longer works are included because they are convenient to have; outlines of the plays, to be meaningful, would require disproportionate space. In the text, reference is made only to passages in the ancient authors; further bibliographical information, again with the English reader in view, is provided in the Bibliographical Note at the end. The works there mentioned, whether or not specific acknowledgment of indebtedness is made, are the source of most of the information in this book.

Adequate acknowledgment of indebtedness is impossible in such a work as this. Frequently, not only an idea but a felicitous expression of it finds its way into a teacher's notebook without inverted commas, and from the notebook to the printed page. If I have appropriated another's work I shall trust that his principal purpose in writing it (as I make bold to avow that mine is in writing this book) was not so much to serve his glory as to propagate interest in one of man's most precious legacies, and that he may even join me in hoping that our combined efforts may be serviceable to that cause.

Specific and grateful acknowledgment is due to the Oxford University Press for quotations from their *Oxford Book of Greek Verse in Translation* and from Lionel Pearson's *Early Ionian Historians;* to the Harvard University Press for various passages from the Loeb Classical Library; and to the University of Chicago Press for a quotation from Richmond Lattimore's version of Pindar.

Moses Hadas

Columbia University in the City of New York

CONTENTS

A HISTORY OF GREEK LITERATURE

Chapter 1. THE NATURE OF GREEK LITERATURE

BEGINNING WITH THE GREEKS THEMSELVES AND UNTIL TODAY A KNOWLEDGE OF Greek literature, however imperfect or derivative, has been indispensable to educated men; more scholars in more countries and for more centuries have studied that literature than any other secular subject. But the kind of interest which Greek literature has held for educated men has not always been the same. At some stages new appreciation of classic form has provoked imitation or emulation; at others, significant aspects of content or spirit have been noticed and advertised. Frequently, as in the renascences of the second, sixteenth, and early nineteenth centuries, these new appreciations were suggested by, and helped promote tendencies in, contemporary thought: Greek literature furnished a pattern for civilized behavior, it taught that the proper study of mankind is man, it exemplified untrammeled naturalism, it embodied the only true theory of art. In the thirteenth century the Greeks were looked to merely as the authoritative repository of all secular knowledge, as the Scriptures were the repository of all sacred knowledge. And when knowledge expanded and came to be divided among specialists, the study of Greek literature became the science of philology, which operated, in imitation of other sciences, by minute classification and definition, with only limited concern for spirit or content. But in the various humanist revivals of interest in Greek literature, particularly in the sixteenth century and in our own, it has been the content and the spirit which has engaged men's attention; how the Greeks said a thing was regarded as less important than the thing they said.

Humanist interest in Greek literature is no accident. Despite its long history—longer than that of any other European literature—Greek literature is sufficiently homogeneous for certain generalizations concerning it to be ventured, and of these the first is that Greek literature is to a peculiar degree anthropocentric. Its preoccupation is with man, and it seeks to help man understand himself and adjust himself to the demands of the world. It is informed by the social, political, and philosophical currents of its day, and it consciously seeks to guide opinion on these matters. From Solon to Alexander any citizen who stood aloof from public concerns was condemned as useless, and the writers of Greece looked upon themselves and were looked upon as performing a peculiarly important public function. Poets, says Aristophanes in *Frogs,* are the teachers of men, and in that play the palm is given to Aeschylus because his poetry is the more edifying and because he offers the better political advice for the welfare of the state. The poets, generally speaking, made poetry their profession; the orators, paradoxically to our feeling, seriously considered themselves the successors to the poets, and not only because they attended to elaborate refinement of form, but also because they took over the function of providing instruction. Plato, with whom specialization of function and caste is a principle, expresses the view, in *Ion* and elsewhere, that the poet is inspired. But Plato gives the fullest recognition to the poet's teaching function by excluding from the ideal state poets whose teaching may not coincide with the program of a controlled state. The Olympian detachment, the concern with only the eternal verities of pure art, which an earlier generation of critics attributed to the Greeks, are wholly imaginary. Even Sophocles, the most Olympian of them all, is definitely concerned to promote certain views on contemporary questions. Without exception the writers of Greece are reformers or rebels.

This does not mean that Aeschylus wrote tragedies merely to approve certain innovations in theology or Aristophanes, comedies to condemn innovations in politics or philosophy. They were primarily artists, and to consider them merely or primarily as advocates of rebellion or reform is to do violence to their function as artists. But they wrote, not in or about a vacuum, but in a period of intellectual ferment and about things of immediate import. Only the euphuistic Alexandrian poets, sheltered from the world by Ptolemy's Museum, produced art for art's sake. Yet if it is understood that Greek literature possessed artistic beauties that are difficult for our alien perceptions to apprehend, and that disproportionate attention to a single aspect is consequently a distortion, then it is not unreasonable, as it is indeed inevitable, that we turn to what is within our scope, to what we can relate to other thought—in a word, to the content which is relevant and meaningful for us. The Greeks themselves would have it so; for it is in thought and speech, they insisted, that man is pre-eminent over the animals, and the record of thought and speech they regarded as the highest form of art.

The high earnestness of Greek literature was attended by the rigid discipline of conservative formalism. Precisely as in their architecture each species (and the Greeks invented virtually all the species of literature that Europe knows) developed its proper form, which was strictly adhered to.

Epic is written only in hexameter and in a certain vocabulary; the associations of the hexameter are aristocratic. Admonitions on politics or manners are elegiac. Choral poetry, substantive or in tragedy, retains Doric coloring and stylization. Iambic is the verse of the people; dialogue is in iambic, and the iambic of tragedy is easily distinguished from the iambic of comedy. When the matter associated with a certain form ceases to be written, that form goes into abeyance. The range of subjects in tragedy is limited, most being derived from a fixed body of myth. It was not that the Greeks could not conceive of other themes, for we know of a handful of plays on historical and other subjects; but these only serve to show that, as in architecture, once a form was found correct for a species, deviations were not acceptable. Formalism and stylization descend even to the comedy of manners, and explain the narrow range of plots which seem to modern readers practically identical. Not unrelated to this formalism, another aspect of discipline is worth mention, and that is an almost Victorian observance of the decencies. The Old Testament is far more outspoken than anything in classic Greek—always excepting Aristophanes, where there is a religious sanction for indecency; the nearest approach to Old Testament in this respect is the most Old Testament-like of Greek books, Herodotus. The view of Byron's contemporaries, expressed in such lines of *Don Juan* as,

> And thus they form a group that's quite antique
> Half naked, loving, natural, and Greek

is callow nonsense.

The somberness suggested by reticence, rigid observance of forms, and earnestness of purpose would seem to be accentuated to grimness in such fatalistic tragedies as *Oedipus,* compared to which the prophets of the Old Testament who thought they might avert doom by exhorting the people seem wildly and frivolously optimistic. But Greek literature is, in fact, ebullient in spirit as it is agile in wit. Plato and Euripides have been misunderstood for generations because people with more sluggish blood thought a man dealing with high themes must be consistently grim or else a clown. It is a related paradox that so grim a play as *Oedipus* leaves spectator or reader happy, and if there are plays that leave him sad they are the comedies. The explanation of the paradox is that Greek literature is thoroughly adult, thoroughly civilized. To speak of even Hector or Achilles as belonging to the childhood of a race is nonsense, and the nonsense becomes ludicrous for the literature of Athens. Greek literature is valuable not merely as a museum piece or the record of an interesting phase in the spiritual history of mankind. Loves, hates, aspirations, have not changed essentially, and the quest for truth which was the paramount concern of the Greek writers concerns us no less. Not only Thucydides and Plato but Hesiod and Solon can share in our councils, and not only to recite the minutes of a previous meeting but to participate in the deliberations.

But before these voices are heard the reader must bear one consideration in mind, a consideration, indeed, that may have a part in explaining the persistence of forms and the observance of proprieties. The Greek literature which we have is almost uniformly conservative, even when it derives from a period when conservatism was in retreat. Only occasionally is the voice of demos heard, only rarely does a Thersites speak up in the assembly of the lords, and then he cuts a ridiculous figure. Homer, Theognis, Pindar, Sophocles, patently uphold the aristocratic tradition. Aristophanes is violently opposed to all the innovations which are associated with the rise of demos. Thucydides and Xenophon, Plato and Aristotle, are all in greater or less degree opposed to what they rightly or wrongly regard as the excesses of democracy. Pericles, indeed (himself an aristocrat), enjoys literary approbation—after his death; and it may be, though the question can be argued, that after his death the democracy did go to unmanageable extremes. Yet it was the democracy which gave appreciative hearings to, and bestowed prizes upon, its critics, and after Demosthenes, the last great defender of that democracy, was crushed by Macedon, both the critics and the special qualities of Greek literature vanished. The quest for truth persists, but its direction is now individual salvation or scientific knowledge. But the littérateurs of the Alexandrian period write, not because there is something compelling for them to say, but because it amuses them to write and their patrons expect it; and they write, not for the welfare of their city, but to display their learning and ingenuity to their peers. The audience grows enormously with the spread of Greek education, but the relatively homogeneous public of the polis now becomes two publics, with specialist readers at one pole, and at the other, people who move their lips as they read.

But even with this deflection, and with the rise of Rome and the advent of Christianity, the course of Greek literature is recognizably consistent; at every transformation it retains something of the old as it admits the new. Though periodic aberrations submerge they never wholly destroy the qualities which make Greek literature of the great period unique. Chief among these qualities, perhaps, is a miraculously consistent good taste, hardly perceptible because of its apparently effortless perfection. Only the Parthenon, whose exquisite refinements only an engineer with micrometers can measure, can provide an analogy. And as in the Parthenon, an aspect of good taste is functional honesty. Every line is artistic, but every line has its function; there is no decorative sham, no distortions to suit a special theory. In the sparing communication of intelligent mind to intelligent mind there is no room or need to make explicit subordinate currents of intimate emotions or vague fancies.

The forthrightness and virility, large monumental style, sensual plasticity, crystalline clarity, of Greek literature are due in part to circumstances of presentation which are different from ours. In the first place, the appeal is always to the ear rather than the eye. And not only was much of the literature recited, but it was recited outdoors, in broad daylight, before a large and predominantly masculine gathering. Furthermore, poetry had a public and official character, and was customarily presented in contests at the national religious festivals and at funeral games. The Pythian games in particular were known for their contests in poetry and music, and drama was always presented in prize contests at the Dionysiac festivals. Poetry was regarded as a profession; like other crafts it tended to be hereditary, and its practitioners were associated in guilds, possibly on a family basis. Outdoor oral presentation under official auspices by professional craftsmen responsible to a large and informed audience preserved, not only the formalism, but the economy and spaciousness of Greek literature. Its emotions are written large and plain for all to understand.

Chapter 2. ORIGINS AND TRANSMISSION

THE GREEKS WE KNOW WERE A MIXED STOCK, CHARACTERIZED BY PASSIONATE suspicion of coercion and remarkable assimilative powers, formed by union of the natives with invaders who descended from the north, bringing their language with them, about the end of the third millennium B.C. The original invaders came in two groups: one down the Vardar Valley into mainland Greece, and the other across the Dardanelles into Asia Minor. The western group formed an amalgam (Mycenaean) with the natives ("Pelasgian," Helladic) who had already been touched by the ancient and advanced Minoan civilization whose center was Crete. Tablets recently discovered at Pylos show that Minoan language was used at least for bookkeeping, but the language of the Mycenaeans was Greek and their rulers, Achaeans. In Asia Minor the invaders became subject to, or formed principalities within, the Hittite empire. At Troy, one such principality seems to have flourished for many years, until its power was broken by a united effort of the principalities in mainland Greece under the leadership of Agamemnon.

After the events which form the background of the Trojan War, about the twelfth century B.C., a new wave of immigrants, kindred to the first but culturally less advanced, caused upheavals in Greece. They descended into the Peloponnese, where Sparta became their chief center, and also gained dominance in Crete and in other centers of mainland Greece, from which they displaced their kinsmen of the earlier migrations. Those displaced, chiefly of the Ionian stock whose principal center was Attica, migrated to the coast of Asia Minor, where they formed a chain of settlements collectively called Ionia. These Ionians (the Javanites of Scripture), already highly civilized and now occupying a much richer country and one directly exposed to the influences of the ancient civilizations of the East, rapidly attained a brilliant culture. In Greece proper the poverty of the soil and the constraint of a rude dominating class retarded development.

The earliest artistic productions of the Greeks were Ionian, and Ionia provided incentive as well as artists for development in Greece proper.

The Ionians (of whom the Athenians subsequently came to be the acknowledged representatives) were traditionally individualist and enterprising, speculative and imaginative, and in all things curious innovators. The Dorians, of whom the Spartans were the acknowledged leaders, were amenable to discipline and in all things conservative. The contrast between the two strains was accentuated by changes in their respective polities in the historical period. In the sixth century a sudden change in Sparta made it into a corporate state which exercised complete control over the lives of its citizens, whom it reduced to the status of a permanent military garrison. Before the revolution, as artifacts show, the Spartans were no less interested in the luxuries of culture than other Greeks; after it autarky and xenophobia discouraged intercourse with the outer world, and military discipline limited education to the horizon of petty officers. In Athens, on the other hand, commerce and navigation made a large urban population restive against the domination of a governing group, and when, in the sixth century, power was assumed by a series of individual "tyrants," these made it a principal objective to encourage arts and letters.

Diversity in their economies thus exaggerated and crystallized the rivalry between the two strains, which continued for centuries and could easily be exacerbated to the point of war. But within the limits of individualism which Greek political units maintained throughout their history, all Greeks were conscious of their essential affinity, and could sometimes be brought to undertake combined action against non-Greek enemies. Their religious concepts were virtually identical, their usages showing only normal local variations, and certain local festivals soon acquired a pan-Hellenic character; their language similarly showed only dialectical variations.

Of the Greek language, because it is the material of which their literature is made, a word must be said. Greek is singularly fluid and musical and extraordinarily rich and supple, suited for expressing with economy and clarity as well as with beauty all the refinements of thought of which the mind is capable. Today Greek can claim the longest uninterrupted history as a recognizable continuum of any language used in Europe, and though the modern naturally differs from the ancient tongue, the difference is not nearly so great as, let us say, that between the earliest and latest forms of English, which are separated by a much shorter span. By far the greater portion of Greek literature is in the dialect of Athens, called Attic. It was Attic from which the *koine* or "common language" developed; this continued to be the principal language of civilization for many centuries after Athens lost its importance.

Attic itself is a variant of Ionic, of which the great prose monuments are Herodotus and Hippocrates. Its differences from Attic are slight and can be mastered in a few minutes; it combines adjoining vowels differently, and substitutes *k* for *p* in certain classes of words. The Homeric or epic dialect is usually (but not entirely correctly) cited as a branch of Ionic, with which it has marked affinity. Its most noticeable characteristic (besides, of course, archaism and a certain artificiality in vocabulary) is archaism in grammatical endings. Doric elements occur in all poetry intended to be sung, but chiefly in choral lyric, and so most copiously in the choral portions of tragedy. Its most noticeable characteristic is the use of broad *a* for Attic *e* (*mater* for *meter, Athana* for *Athena*); its effect is to give the dignity of archaism. We have virtually no Doric prose and none at all in Aeolic, which is represented chiefly by Alcaeus and Sappho. Besides variations in morphology Aeolic is peculiar in its fuller retention of the digamma (*w*), which was completely lost in Attic. In addition to the recognized literary dialects, Aeolic, Doric, Ionic, and Attic, there were many other nonliterary local variations for which inscriptions furnish evidence. The literary dialects soon became associated with their appropriate literary genres, and do not necessarily reflect the origin of a writer.

With their language the invaders brought meter, which, whatever it may have originally been, was reduced, before Homer wrote, to a quantitative pattern of long (−) and short (˘) syllables, so that a long syllable is metrically equivalent to two shorts, with substitution of metrical equivalents being permitted where the verse scheme allows. Modern adaptations of classical meters substitute stress accent for quantity. The Greeks also differentiated pitch accents—acute (′), circumflex (^), and grave (`)—which moderns are incapable of reproducing but which must have formed a kind of counterpoint in Greek verse. In poetry intended for recitation, chiefly hexameter, elegiac, and iambic, verses are all qualitatively equivalent and are not divided into strophes; variety is achieved by variations within the pattern and in the use of the caesura, or pause within the line. Poetry intended to be sung (and normally also danced) shows great variation in verses, though a basic "foot" usually recurs; but the correspondence between strophes is generally very exact.

How much of the substance of literature the invaders brought with them, in addition to its vessels of language and meter, it is difficult to say. Doubtless they had certain folk tales, as the appearance among other Indo-European branches of motifs known in Greece demonstrates. On the other hand, the great myths and the cycles of saga which are the basis of early Greek literature are associated with places where Mycenaean culture flourished and seem to have reached their perfect form in the Mycenaean age. The organization of the gods is like the organization of a Mycenaean court.

How soon these sagas were written down is not known. Writing in ideographs (each symbol representing a word rather than a letter or syllable) was long known in the eastern Mediterranean, and pre-Greek inscriptions have been found on Crete and in Pylos in the Peloponnese, but the Achaean and Dorian invaders had no writing of their own, and we cannot say whether the ideographic writing was used for literature. But by the eighth century the Greeks had borrowed the North Semitic alphabet, which they called Phoenician letters. Like the Hebrew, with which it was identical except for variations in the forms of letters, this alphabet had a symbol for each consonant but none for vowels. The Greeks improved it by making certain consonant characters which they did not need represent vowels and inventing or adapting others. Directly or through its Latin adaptation the Greek alphabet is the ancestor of all the alphabets of Europe.

Even after the art was learned writing was used only by the professional makers and reciters of literature. It was long before a reading public in our sense came into being, and even after books became relatively common the writer's appeal was always to the ear rather than the eye. It was possible to be literally illiterate and yet possess the close familiarity with texts which Aristophanes' parodies of tragedy premise. Books were made of strips of papyrus (hence *biblos,* the word for book) pasted together into a long roll, which was then written upon in columns perpendicular to the length. Rolls were awkward to handle, especially to locate passages, a circumstance which incidentally determined the division of long works into "books."

The customary division of Greek literature into periods is meaningful if it be remembered that the literature always retained the continuity of a living organism. Significant turning points in Greek history are naturally reflected in the literature. Of these the first that can be marked with certainty is the repulse of the Persian invasion about 480 B.C. But surely there were earlier turning points; for Hesiod, though he knows Homer, belongs to a different intellectual and economic climate, and the Ionian lyric writers of the following century differ as widely from Hesiod. After 480 and until the death of Alexander (323 B.C.) Greek literature is almost exclusively Athenian, and little written under the authoritarian Dorian regimes has survived. The beginnings of drama, history, and philosophy had been laid before the rise of Athens to economic and cultural supremacy, but the efflorescence of the latter half of the fifth century when the greatest works in all these fields, as also in architecture, sculpture, and painting, were produced in rapid succession remains an astonishing phenomenon in the history of civilization. When Athens was left impoverished by its failure in the Peloponnesian War its brilliance was rapidly dimmed.

An even sharper stage is marked by Alexander, whose conquests reorganized the world into large geographical units and emasculated the city-states. The citizen of Athens had participated directly in his government by sitting in the ecclesia (there were no representatives), and he took as direct and active an interest, according to his tastes and abilities, in questions of art and philosophy. Now his political life was ordered from above, and his own stature in consequence reduced; he was as ready to accept the dogma of the schools in matters of the spirit also. Literature, as exemplified by Menander, who was acknowledged its leading exponent, is reduced to comedy of manners, and bourgeois problems of marriage and proper settlement in life are his subject matter. Contemporary philosophers were mainly engaged in teaching accommodation, by one route or another, to the stern exigencies of life in a society in which men were dwarfed. In Alexandria, which was the wealthiest city in the Hellenistic world and its cultural leader, literature grew precious. Learned poets produced allusive and highly polished jewels for each other's delectation, and scholars labored upon the texts and biographies of the great writers of the past. But erudition, polish, and ingenuity have their legitimate place in literature, and none can deny the title of poet to Callimachus and Apollonius and especially Theocritus and to certain poets of the *Anthology*.

Rome, like Greece itself, was culturally a province in the Hellenistic empire, and though rich philhellene Romans afforded Greek teachers of philosophy and Greek poetasters a remunerative audience, the influence in the opposite direction was practically nil. The Roman period (conveniently dated from the sack of Corinth in 146 B.C. to the foundation of Constantinople in A.D. 330) produced many useful compilations. Lucian represents the age's wit and polish, Marcus Aurelius its moral earnestness, and Plutarch, by virtue of his catholic reading, his copiousness, and his sensibility, provides the most useful single guide to what the Greco-Roman world knew and thought.

Nor did Christianity revolutionize attitudes to Greek literature, for so much of Christianity was Greek in origin and so many of the Greek Fathers were men of culture. The concept of the "classics" had long been fixed, and literature was regarded as an integral part of ordinary life. St. Augustine was hostile to the pagan classics; Clement of Alexandria preferred to use them in the interests of Christianity. In the period following, to the suppression of the pagan schools of philosophy by Justinian in A.D. 529, thoroughly secular works of high merit were written by believing Christians; best known among these are Quintus of Smyrna's long hexameter poem which continues the story of *Iliad,* Heliodorus' prose romance called *Aethiopica,* and many of the epigrams in the *Palatine Anthology.*

Byzantine scholars retained a continuous knowledge and appreciation of the ancients, and much of the information in our own commentaries depends on their work. They kept alive a creative tradition also, though the theological preoccupation of much of their work limits its interest for ordinary students. It may be remarked, however, that such productions as the *Homilies* of Photius are immeasurably more learned and urbane than similar productions in the West. But the period preceding the fall of Constantinople in 1453, the dark centuries to the recovery of Greek independence in 1821, and the subsequent renascence of Greek literature fall outside the scope of this book.

It remains to say a word concerning the preservation and transmission of our Greek texts. What we have is but a fraction of what once existed, and that we have as much as we do is doubtless due to the concept of "classics" which itself originated in classical times. We have complete texts of Homer, Herodotus, Thucydides, Xenophon, Plato, Isocrates, Demosthenes, and Aeschines; our greatest loss is in lyric poetry. Before the establishment of the Library at Alexandria there were no large public collections of books, though the state did preserve a "standard" Homer and copies of prize-winning tragedies. Works left by the wayside by changes in taste, like those rejected in public competitions, were simply not copied. Rhetoric made a conscious effort to supplant lyric, and the ethical philosophies, whether they advocated Epicurean ataraxy or Stoic apathy, discouraged subjective lyric. Scholars of the Peripatetic school composed large systematic works on various subjects, using and weakening the chances for survival of older works. These processes were operative even in the fourth century, and the losses due to changes in taste and to epitomizing and anthologizing continued. If the anthologist's selection practically assured the loss of the rest of an author's work, it did preserve something, and in the judgment of the anthologist what was most valuable. Aeschylus, because of the difficulty of his language and his moral problems, soon fell out of favor; and we might have had nothing but for the schoolmasters' selections. It is difficult to assess the responsibility of authors of secondary works, like Strabo's on geography or Apollodorus' on mythology, for the loss of the original works which they used. In the case of scissors-and-paste authors like Diodorus Siculus or Diogenes Laertius we should rather be grateful for what we have.

The librarians of Alexandria devoted scrupulous and competent attention to the books in their care, but their foundation, though supported by the Ptolemies, was in effect a private association depending on wealthy patronage, served by, and serving a clique of, specialists whose learning and literary conventions made wider participation impossible. When Egypt's wealth was siphoned off to Rome there was no room for such a luxury, and only books whose claim upon the attention of ordinary men made them independent of patronage could maintain themselves. What survived antiquity was preserved in Constantinople, though the fourth, fifth, and sixth centuries had ancient works no longer extant. The last wholesale loss was occasioned by the adventurers of the Fourth Crusade (A.D. 1204). The preservation, and basic interpretation, of most of what we now have is due to the Byzantine scholars. In addition to whole texts the Byzantines have given us many excerpts, especially from such writings as those of the cyclic poets, and many a line of poetry to illustrate a rare word or usage.

To the stock of manuscripts preserved by the Byzantines and propagated in Western Europe there have been added, especially since 1890, a number of papyri recovered from the sands of Egypt, dating from the Hellenistic and Roman periods. The most significant discoveries of new material are Aristotle's *Constitution of Athens,* considerable portions of three plays of Menander, the epinician odes of Bacchylides, the orations of Hyperides, the mimes of Herodes, the *Ichneutai* of Sophocles, and new fragments, still disappointingly few, of Alcaeus and Sappho. Fragments of works already known tend to testify, especially in the case of Homer, to the remarkable fidelity of our manuscript tradition. Charred copies of Epicurean authors, especially of Philodemus, have been recovered from Herculaneum.

Besides works preserved in independent manuscript tradition, or newly recovered, we have a large stock of fragments, collected from citations in extant authors. Herodotus gives us a number of epigrams of Simonides; Demosthenes quotes a whole poem of Tyrtaeus; Dionysius of Halicarnassus, one of Sappho; and Plato, practically a whole one of Simonides. Plutarch has many quotations, especially from the dramatists, and Athenaeus gives us most of what we know about Middle and New Comedy. Diodorus Siculus' history preserves long passages of his sources practically unaltered. Other authors of the Roman period perform similar services. The nature of the Hellenistic philosophical works he employs is clearly indicated in the essays of Cicero, and it has been practically established that Lucretius is based on the "longer catechism" of Epicurus.

The work of the scholars who have assembled, preserved, and tended our legacy of Greek literature has a legitimate interest for students of that literature but is itself not a part of it and so cannot be treated here. The Bibliographical Notes at the end of this volume will mention modern books in which such information may be found.

Chapter 3. HOMER

IN THE FOREFRONT OF GREEK AND THEREFORE OF EUROPEAN LITERATURE STAND the supreme creations of *Iliad* and *Odyssey*. "Poetic genius" receives its ideal and complete meaning by reference to Homer; and the only reasonable definition of "epic" is a poem that somehow resembles *Iliad*. The immediate and burning beauty of *Iliad* can only derive from the white heat of genius, but it is clear that its author had behind him a long tradition of poetry similar to his own. He assumes that his hearers are familiar with the great common pool of stories from which he drew, and the main traits of his principal characters seem to have been fixed. Only strange characters or novel incidents, like the episode in which Chryses figures at the beginning of the poem, are introduced or explained or underscored. Language too and style are patently the products of a school. There is nothing primitive or childish about Homer's language; it is copious and clear and capable of describing any situation, expressing any mood. And yet it is a language that was never spoken but invented for the use of poetry and brought to perfection before Homer wrote. The metrical skill and the facility in accommodating patterned phrases to the metrical scheme, the recurring formulas and the standing epithets, all posit generations of practice and the tradition of a school. But *Iliad* is not a compilation; if the stories and the methods are traditional, they have been subordinated to an artistic purpose, and the masterpiece which has emerged, as a whole and in its parts, bears the impress of the poet's personality.

The subject of *Iliad* moves in two planes. One is the Tale of Achilles, or *Achilleid,* which is concerned with the genesis of the Wrath and its issue; the other is the Tale of Troy, or *Iliad,* which forms a background for *Achilleid* but retains its independent interest. *Achilleid* is essentially a moral tragedy, the legitimate forerunner of the great dramas of the fifth century which treat of great souls who are caught in the grip of circumstances and are made to suffer from the defects of their own high qualities. Achilles' temper, which is in the nature of a tragic flaw rather than a vice, leads to disaster and to his own moral deterioration. The balance of right and wrong is depressed on the side of wrong when he rejects Agamemnon's bid for reconciliation. He rehabilitates himself and asserts the victory of civilization when he overcomes his own passionate impulse to abuse the body of Hector and returns that body to Priam. But the tragedy of Achilles is integrated with the epic of *Iliad*. Its meaning is enhanced by the events of which it is a part, and it enhances the meaning of those events in turn. We are shown how one great soul, privately and in relation with other great souls, confronted large problems and overcame them, and his victory communicates a vicarious satisfaction to hearers whose souls are less great. Nothing in the story nor in its characters is puny, and the manner of its telling is rich and full; there is no exaggeration, no theatricals, no moral falsetto.

Passion is the keynote of *Iliad,* but passion made to conform to and to serve civilization, and the result is authentic and unparalleled nobility. The story moves with swiftness, and its rapidity is only heightened and given savor by calculated retardations which lend spaciousness. The story is direct but not childlike, for the poet is a mature man addressing mature men for whom psychological subtleties do not have to be spelled out. The poet's truth cannot be questioned, nor his judgment in selecting incidents or portraying character. These are the people who figured in the history, and this is what they did—there can be no doubt. When Achilles thought to attack Agamemnon in the assembly it was Athena who bade him desist, and when we are told that he later wept we know that it was so, and are not embarrassed. When a mighty hero is confronted by a dangerous enemy and has spent spear and sword, he lifts a boulder to hurl that two—but only two—men of the present generation could scarcely lift. When Helen appears before the Trojan elders on the wall they acknowledge in their grasshopper voices that such beauty is worth fighting for, though it was their sons who were being killed for her sake and their city that was being destroyed. But romance cannot carry more than its proper weight: "Even so," they say, "let her go upon their ships, and not stay to vex us and our children." When on the battlefield Glaucus and Diomedes discover that their fathers were friends they forego fighting and decide upon a courteous exchange of weapons, and Glaucus accepts Diomedes' bronze armor in return for his gold. But chivalry cannot carry more than its proper weight, and the poet tells us that Zeus bereft Glaucus of his wits, in that he accepted the value of nine oxen for the value of a hundred. When Hector communes with his heart before finally confronting Achilles, he ponders, like the sober and care-burdened leader he is, on his responsibilities to Troy, and the images he uses reflect the dusty sweetness of a long ago: "No time is it now to dally with him from oak-tree or from rock, like youth with maiden, as youth and maiden sport with one another." Hector runs thrice about the walls of Troy, but his dignity is undiminished; and the sympathy which his plight evokes is grave rather than sentimental. The indignities visited upon Hector's body arouse no revulsion but give the heroic measure of Achilles' passion and of his victory over that passion when for civilization's sake he restores the body to Priam.

Achilles is a passionate man, who deliberately chose a short life illuminated by glory when he was offered the alternative of a long and humdrum one. Agamemnon's affront was therefore particularly grievous, for it cheated him of the thing for which he had bargained away his ease. Now his honor demands that he insult Hector's body, but when the test comes he can subordinate his passion to the requirements of a noble code. Hermes' advice to Priam not to linger after he has received the body shows how hard won was the victory. The poem is filled with battle glee, but its heroes have pondered life, and their drama is not without philosophy. To the reader it communicates a vicarious pride in man's achievements in adjusting himself to life, first in hearty enjoyment of the details of glorious weapons and splendid garments and good food, and then in confronting the gods and fate, and finally in achieving nobility. Its lessons of fate and man's response are enhanced by its grandeur, and its ornaments of simile and epithet and subtle metrical skill are not meretricious adornment but reflect the same civilized refinement of brute nature as the heroes and their moral exemplify.

For though raw nature is close to the surface in the flaming, stark warrior, he can reflect on the meaning of life, show great courtesy to his peers, amuse his leisure with song. Gallant Diomedes is a lesser Achilles, brave enough to confront the gods in battle, courteous always, respectful even when criticizing his superiors' timidity. Ajax has stubborn strength without subtlety, he cannot see why a return of seven women for one should not satisfy Achilles. Odysseus is his opposite; he is the shrewdest and most ingenious of the Greeks. Although he was awkward in figure and in posture when he arose to speak, his words covered his auditors like snowflakes. He is the prototype of the man who devotes a cunning mind to the general cause when his private ethic might rebel at such practice. Agamemnon is overbearing and unimaginative, timorous in making decisions but distinguished in presence and brave enough in fight. Old Nestor is a Polonius-like character whose function is to assuage the passions of younger men, usually by reminiscing of his youth until their fury dies. The Trojans are not essentially different from the Greeks; though because they are at home, while the Greeks are on a foreign expedition, they are more luxurious. Their leader, man-slaying Hector, is an awesome enough warrior with his helmet's waving plumes, but he is a care-burdened prince and husband and father, with a heavier feeling of responsibility than any of the Greeks. He shows great tenderness to his family and compassion for his people. Paris, whose seduction of Helen was the first cause of the war, is a silken young man, but he is the favorite of Aphrodite, and his pre-eminence in his own domain is acknowledged and respected. It is natural that we see more of the women of the Trojans: Helen herself, who is justified in her beauty; Andromache, the peerless wife and mother, noble and affectionate; Hecuba, the aged queen, doomed to heroic bereavement. But among the Greeks too Briseis shows her own perceptiveness and Patroclus' fine sensibility when at Patroclus' funeral she speaks of the gentle solace he used to offer her.

Just as Aphrodite cherishes her protégé and shields her favorites, especially her own son Aeneas, so do the other gods, some favoring the Trojans and some the Greeks. Yet they never so manipulate the characters as to reduce their stature as thinking and acting men. The superiority of the gods consists only in their immortality and in their eternal youth; they are as impotent as men to avert the decrees of fate, and their passions and ethics are completely human. For what they are, with their limitations and shortcomings, the heroes' belief in them is quite real, but there is a curious lightness in the poet's attitude. We should expect of a gallant society of cultured nobles impatience alike with brooding orthodoxy and with grim denial of orthodoxy, and the tone in *Iliad* is, in fact, one of banter rather than ridicule. There is intentional fun but no thought of atheistic propaganda when Zeus and Hera indulge in a conjugal spat in the first book or when Hera entices Zeus from his work by her physical charms in the fourteenth. Only an anachronistic piety could wish to delete Zeus' preamble to his love-making in which he itemizes a long list of previous conquests, and only a later rationalism could find more than humor in the loves of Ares and Aphrodite. These two deities actually join in the fighting and are wounded, and though they bleed ichor instead of blood they howl with pain. Only once is the intervention of a god essential to the story, and that is when Apollo takes up his priest's cause at the beginning. Elsewhere, the gods are used, and with great skill, either to point up or resolve a crisis, or as a pendant to the mortals. Thus at the end of the first book the council on Olympus is a counterpart to the assembly of the Greeks; in each, the characters are introduced and their roles indicated. The polity of the gods is like that of the mortals. Like Agamemnon, Zeus is only *primus inter pares;* his authority is by no means unqualified, and he must sometimes bluster. The family lines of the gods and their functions are not so definite as Hesiod later made them; but systematization has clearly been at work, and some order has been introduced into what must have been chaos.

The poet stands outside his story, with his audience. He does not visibly manipulate the tale, does not strive to create suspense; on the contrary, coming events are frequently foreshadowed. Very seldom does he intrude (as a spectator might) to express a judgment or draw a parallel. It is in such parallels that the poet's personality is most clearly to be apprehended. Though the similes are in form as objective as the narrative, they are yet the poet's only medium for commenting on the story for whose telling he is an impersonal instrument. Whereas the narrative consistently adheres to a remote heroic age with its aristocratic society and viewpoints and avoids flagrant anachronisms in the material objects it mentions, the similes reveal the viewpoint of common people and refer to material objects contemporary with the poet rather than with his story. They speak of farming and sheepherding, pursuits which the nobles scorned; of trumpets and stained ivory, objects which the heroes were ignorant of; they mention iron, whereas the warriors knew only bronze; riding horseback, whereas the warriors harnessed their horses to a chariot. Sometimes the similes extend for several lines, like a mounted ornament, almost but never entirely independent of the thing they illustrate. They are frequently used to mark pauses or changes in action or to end a scene. In the fighting over the body of Patroclus, which is the last great battle piece, as many as five similes are used. They afford a change and relief from the concentration required of the reader in tenser passages. Spaciousness and a similar relief are afforded by the ritual-like solemnity of the repeated lines and the ornamental, but not merely ornamental, epithets. Out of 27,853 lines in *Iliad* and *Odyssey,* 9,253, or one third, are repeated or contain repeated phrases.

The long battle pieces seem repetitious—to a reader who is impatient of battles, as reports of football or bridge games seem repetitious to hearers whose interests are elsewhere. The battle pieces are not perfunctory, as they sometimes are in Virgil, who seems to include them under constraint and with his face turned away, but are written by an expert and for experts. The thing to notice is the extraordinary variety in these battle pieces, not only in the details of action, but in the backgrounds of the personalities involved. Things as well as men have their genealogies and histories—the scepter of Agamemnon, the shield of Ajax, the bow of Pandarus. The robing of a warrior, the serving of a feast, is recounted in detail with no sense of condescension to triviality, no impairment of dignity. The story has truth and stature, and the least detail has its dignity.

But dignity and large seriousness must not be confounded with utilitarianism. The poet's motive is the motive of the literary man, to give the pleasure which literature is capable of giving. His verses are not a device to propitiate hostile spirits or to preserve sacred statistics. On occasion he includes utilitarian poetry, when it is relevant to his story and of interest to his readers. That is the explanation of the long catalogue in the second book; details of the catalogue are, in fact, inconsistent with his own plot, yet there is no need to assume that the catalogue is a later "Hesiodic" insertion. Its data are, on the whole, relevant, and it is placed where it belongs. Other passages also seem disproportionate or inconsistent with the over-all plan of the poem; the poet had many things to tell, and he wrote a poem so long that it could be recited only in portions. Nevertheless, the main threads are always kept well in hand, and the story marches steadily to the end which is foreshadowed at the beginning.

But this is not to deny that a good or indeed a tighter story than the one we have might result from using only part of the material. For example, Book 11, where Agamemnon does well without Achilles but not well enough, might logically follow Book 1. Agamemnon's willingness to dispense with Achilles and Achilles' belief in his own indispensability would thus both be justified, the fighting about the wall (whose existence does, in fact, come as a surprise) would be eliminated, Achilles would at once be drawn into battle by the death of Patroclus, and prove his worth by slaying Hector. Blemishes in individual books have been held to demonstrate the structural weakness of the whole. Book 2 is criticized for its long catalogues; Book 3, because the duel between the two men most concerned for Helen and Helen's identification of the Greek heroes for Priam should come in the first and not the tenth year of the war; Book 4, because it is merely an appendage to Book 3; Book 5, because Diomedes' exploits quite make us forget Achilles; Book 6, because Hector's farewell should precede his death immediately and does not; Book 7, because its duel makes it a doublet of Book 3; Book 8, because it has the highest proportion of lines used elsewhere; Book 9, because the amends offered Achilles are more than he bargained for, and his attitude thereafter is difficult to explain; Book 10, because it is "insulated," having little connection with what precedes and follows and because its long night requires too many meals. The books after Book 11 are even more vulnerable.

In addition to apparent flaws in structure, other inconsistencies have been adduced to prove disparate and piecemeal composition. These have chiefly to do with simultaneous use of materials (iron and bronze), weapons (round shield and "tower" shield), social customs (bride price and dowry), divinities (Ares and Athena as war gods) which belong to diverse stages of civilization. To explain these difficulties, numerous

theories of composition by accretion, combination, or expansion have
been put forward. The expenditure of industry, ingenuity, acumen, and
paper on the so-called "Homeric question" is appalling in retrospect, and
carries a lesson of humility for scholarship. The various critical criteria
showed little consonance, so that in the end the test of genuineness remained taste; and here scholars were at complete variance, there being
practically no considerable section which one scholar condemned which
another did not consider genuine and indispensable. Taste being the
ultimate criterion, more confidence may be placed in the judgment of
poets than of scholars, and poets who have spoken on the subject agree
that *Iliad* as we have it is due to the conception and execution of one
supremely great poet. Indeed, poets have been more willing than other
critics to accept unity of authorship for both *Iliad* and *Odyssey,* though
skepticism here has a sounder basis and a longer history.

Most critical difficulties recede—if they do not vanish—when it is
realized that the poem is an Iliad as well as an Achilleid, the story being
told, as it were, in two planes; that the poet is dealing with an age in
the remote past and so must inevitably commit anachronisms; that most
of the anachronisms occur in similes, where the poet is speaking in his
own person; and, finally, that the poet is dealing, like the later tragedians,
with traditional materials, which might be given new meaning by re-
distribution of emphasis and by newly invented circumstances but which
would not allow violent distortions or omissions. All the parts whose
genuineness has been questioned have their function. The catalogues in
Book 2 are a kind of Domesday Book, in keeping with epic interest in
genealogy, and could not be omitted. The identifications and duel in the
third book come as early as they can, within the framework of the poem.
These and similar "displaced" or "insulated" episodes provide relief
and sustain interest by offering a possible escape from disasters to come.
Hector's farewell and other "detachable" encounters vary and enrich the
whole. The ninth book is not only in itself one of the finest but is highly
important to the drama. So far, Achilles has been in the right, and Agamemnon in the wrong; now the stage is set for the ideal tragic conflict, Achilles
having spoiled his case and Agamemnon having improved his. The
successful night raid in Book 10 dispels the gloom among the Greeks
by retarding the action as well as making the combatants appear more
equal, and it gives greater meaning to the battles in Book 11. Similar defense may be offered for the sections in the latter half which have been
questioned. This is not to say that Homer started with a clean slate and
wrote down the whole poem precisely as we have it out of his head. He
was heir to a long tradition, and certainly used existing materials and

techniques. On the other hand, after the poem had been composed interpolations of lines and whole passages doubtless crept in, as the Alexandrian scholars who purged the text were well aware. Plausible cases may be made against a number of passages, not only the catalogues and the Dolon episode, but such incidents as the fighting at the river in Book 21 and the latter half of the games in Book 23. But it is harder to believe that a work which shows the hand of genius at every turn and is dominated by a single grand concept can be the product of accident or of a syndicate or of a compiler than to accept it as the work of a single poet, and there is no reason to doubt that that poet's name was Homer.

By reason of its primacy in Greek literature the influence of *Iliad* was incalculably great. Throughout their history the Greeks were as closely familiar with its text as Puritans with the text of the Bible. Its influence on the tone and much of the substance of subsequent literature is plain. But its influence in other directions was no less significant; one need only think of Alexander the Great carrying his *Iliad* about in a jeweled casket and consciously making Achilles his pattern. It becomes important to notice, then, that *Iliad* is a thoroughly aristocratic poem, devoted to the glorification of the aristocratic view of life. Glory is the driving force and the object of existence, and honor is the paramount code. Birth, wealth, and prowess in arms confirm a man's title and give him the right to whatever his strength, qualified by a feeling of *noblesse oblige,* can win him. There is no other law, human or divine. The law is confirmed in Book 2 by the episode of Thersites, the only man in *Iliad* who questions it. Thersites (though later criticism made him a cousin of Diomedes) is represented as repulsive in appearance and given to ranting, and there is universal applause when Odysseus, who represents the interests of organized society, belabors him. But the Thersites episode demonstrates that the aristocratic tone of the poem (the only toilers we see are those figured on the shield of Achilles) is intentional, and that Homer envisaged, and ridiculed, precisely the type of demagogue who plagued the aristocrats of Athens centuries later. But Homer was read and venerated, not only under aristocracies, but under democracies and tyrannies as well. Only Plato realized the enormous political influence he could exert and proposed to remove him (but not for his aristocratic bias) from his ideal state.

Many of the personages of *Iliad* reappear in *Odyssey,* but they have settled down to domestic respectability. Caste is no less important, but it is now achieved and demonstrated, not by prowess in arms (the memory of the Trojan War is ever present but curiously remote), but by impressive mansions elegantly appointed and inhabited by calm and gracious gentlefolk. A man makes his mark by undertaking long voyages, associating on terms of equality with the great of the earth, and bringing home valuable possessions. There is new concern for the details of the management of great households and a corresponding interest in their chatelaines, Helen and Arete, Penelope and Calypso. The Helen who launched a thousand ships and burned the topless towers of Ilium is matured into a gracious matron whose servants carry her silver workbox and golden distaff, the merely decorative emblems of her dignity. She is a majestic hostess who makes her young guest comfortable, and when the men's conversation grows melancholy she puts nepenthe in their drink. Courtliness is exalted over chivalry, and mind over circumstances. The standing epithets attached to the three leading characters are "wise" (*polymetis*) for Odysseus, "heedful" (*periphron*) for Penelope, and "discreet" (*pepnumenos*) for Telemachus. Orderliness in society and administration is important, and among the gods Zeus is grown more masterful and the lesser deities tend to become agents of his will. On the other hand, the simple acceptance of such a deity as Athena is less easy, for her readiness to transform Odysseus' appearance for relatively minor ends and herself to assume various guises, including a bird's, suggests magic rather than religion.

Many of the marvels encountered by Odysseus are similarly in the realm of a magic fairyland. Phaeacia is somewhere between the simple country mansion of Ithaca and Circe's demonic ménage on Aeaea. But in each case the reader effortlessly and unconsciously adjusts the quality of his belief to the requisite pitch. Even in the more romantic settings the essential truth noticed in *Iliad* is present also in *Odyssey*. Not only is there domesticity, a swineherd's steading, an old dog dying on his dung heap (at the front door of the palace!), but Odysseus himself shoots venison for his men, carries the carcass down to the seashore, and dresses it for them; Virgil, copying the passage (*Aeneid* 1.184–194), has Aeneas shoot seven lordly stags, which are then transported and dressed by nameless powers.

Fidelity to recognizable situations is especially apparent in the first four books, which deal with Telemachus' travels. Here is a theme almost unique in Greek literature—the education of a hero; but the role for which he is being educated is not that of a glorious warrior but of a peaceful prince whose estate rests upon the profits of far-flung voyagings. In Calypso's isle, similarly, at Phaeacia, and in the reunion with Penelope the core of familiar human relationships and problems is patent, but in each case the situation is enhanced by an aura of brilliant circumstance and the play of the supernatural. The figure of Odysseus himself, who has become a symbol of restless questing, is a combination of the weary traveler making his toilsome way home and the insatiable seeker driven by a demonic urge.

The intermingling of distinct elements of "history" and fancy is characteristic of the difference between *Iliad* and *Odyssey*. *Odyssey* is frankly intended for entertainment, and its artfulness is easier to sense since it is more sophisticated. "The song which men most heartily applaud," Telemachus says to Penelope (1.351), "is that which comes the newest to their ears." The story consists of many strands, which are not drawn together into a single skein until Book 17. Progress is by zigzag and by the skillful use of the flash back. More careful intellectual, though perhaps less intense spiritual, attention is required of the hearer. The poet's use of existing materials and techniques is more patent than in *Iliad,* and the conglomerate is nearer a mechanical than a chemical compound. But the disparate materials have been artistically shaped to the poet's design. The result is not only one of the most stirring and enduring tales of adventure ever fashioned by man, but a tale so artistically constructed that a closely knit arch reaches from the situation made clear on the first page to the conclusion at the end, with the members between not only decorating the structure by their individual beauties, but each contributing to the support of the whole.

If, as students of the genre suggest, genuine epic must offer a serious demonstration of how man by exertion of hand and brain may adjust himself to the hard conditions of life imposed by a hostile environment, and if *Iliad* is accepted as the gauge by which to define the genre, then *Odyssey* is either the first example of decline from the epic ideal or, as epic, implies a different set of requirements for adjustment to environment. Over and above whatever else it may be, *Iliad* is a reflective poem, setting forth a way of life and offering men assurance of their kind's capacity to assert themselves and their values. The actors and presumably the audience are all nobles, but their glory is achieved by their hands and feet and words, and the rest of humanity can look on and be edified. The aristocracy of *Odyssey* is perhaps surer of itself, but its basis is wealth and acquired courtesy. A chief purpose of the first four books is to show how Telemachus learned to comport himself properly in great houses and how he was well received by exalted personages. The swineherd Eumaeus and Euryclea who washes Odysseus' feet had princes for parents, but now they feed swine and wash feet notwithstanding. If Achilles is the pattern for an Alexander, Odysseus is the model for the hungry Greekling who lived by his wits in Rome. If the distinction between *physis* and *nomos,* nature and convention, which later led the Cynics to deny the validity of class differences as being due only to *nomos,* be applied to the epics, men's position in *Odyssey* would appear to derive more plainly from *nomos*. In social background, then, as well as in its new attitude toward the gods, at once more and less reverent than *Iliad's,* and in its use of intrigue as against the straightforward account of *Iliad, Odyssey* is to *Iliad* as Euripides to Aeschylus.

But none of these differences—in the concept of what is to be desired by men, in technique of narrative, in indulging or avoiding excursions into fairyland—necessarily implies that the poems were written in different ages or by different poets. If we bear in mind the diversity of theme, none of the differences is so great as to preclude the possibility of their composition by the same poet, at different periods or in differing moods. Their resemblance, not only in language, meter, and style generally, but in the superlative creativeness, largeness of scope, and easy mastery, suggest unitary authorship. Before the Alexandrians, Homer's authorship of both *Iliad* and *Odyssey* seems not to have been questioned; but the ancients may have been gullible, for they also accepted some of the Cyclic poems as Homeric. Aristotle was the first to limit Homer to *Iliad* and *Odyssey,* yet even he refers to the dubious *Margites* as Homeric. The Alexandrian chorizontes or "separatists" first mooted the question whether the two poems were the work of a single author, and many, perhaps most, scholars today who reject the wholesale dismemberment of the individual poems (from which *Odyssey* has suffered as much as *Iliad*), which was usual in the nineteenth century, believe that the two poems cannot be the work of the same man. The nature of the problem can perhaps best be suggested by the solution of Dionysius of Halicarnassus, an astute critic in the age of Augustus, to wit, that *Iliad* is the work of Homer's youth and *Odyssey* of his old age.

For dating Homer our earliest literary statement is Herodotus', who says (2.53.2) that both Homer and Hesiod lived some four hundred years before his own time, or approximately 850 B.C. It is hardly conceivable that works of such compass could be composed without the aid of writing, and the introduction of the Semitic alphabet is dated to the ninth century. On the other hand, there is every indication that Homer was a classic when Hesiod wrote. Herodotus' tradition is not to be rejected summarily; perhaps his date is somewhat high for Hesiod, or even a trifle low for Homer. The ancient tradition which dates the Trojan War to the twelfth century is substantiated by archaeology. Some considerable period must have elapsed before its events could be transmuted to legend and its personages and ways of life regarded as belonging to a vanished heroic age. These considerations and the rather tenuous archaeological material available make the ninth century a not improbable date.

The earliest mention of a text of Homer is the enactment into law by Hipparchus, son of Pisistratus, or, alternatively, by Solon, of the custom of reading Homer complete at the Panathenaic festival which took place every four years at Athens. The text had been, and continued to be, transmitted by rhapsodes, who were professional reciters. The tradition that Pisistratus *fixed* the text is taken by some scholars to mean that the poems were actually first put together in the sixth century, but the tradition is late and untrustworthy. Doubtless the state preserved an official text, as it did of the tragic poets. Zenodotus of Ephesus, the first librarian at Alexandria, an epic poet and the inventor of textual criticism, expunged many lines of Homer and marked others that he suspected with an *obelos,* or upright stroke. Aristarchus of Samothrace, a century later, was a much more conservative critic, and his text is the basis of our vulgate Homer.

Chapter 4. CYCLIC POEMS, HOMERIC HYMNS, OTHER HOMERICA

ILIAD AND ODYSSEY TELL THE STORY OF ONLY A FEW WEEKS IN THE Trojan War and the homecoming of only a single hero, and it was natural that there should be attempts to fill out the story with similar epics. Our knowledge of these poems (all definitely post-Homeric) comes chiefly from the lost *Chrestomathy* of Proclus (a second-century grammarian rather than the fifth-century Neoplatonist) who had himself probably used an anthology; extracts from Proclus are carelessly cited in the *Bibliotheca* of Photius and in other Byzantine writers. The Alexandrians—probably Zenodotus of Ephesus—arranged the works chronologically, and it was doubtless at that time that they received the name "cyclic." The word seems equivalent to "Ring," as in Wagner's usage, but it also bears the connotation of "long-winded" and "trivial," as in Callimachus (*Greek Anthology* 12.43) and Horace (*Ars Poetica* 136). The so-called *Tabula Borgiaca* gave the canon of the *Cycle* with the names of the authors and the length of the poems, but only part of the stone is intact. The number 44,400, presumably the total number of lines, appears at the end. The names of the authors were attached later and are sometimes inconsistent and always unreliable; better writers who mention the *Cycle* do not name its authors. Herodotus (2.117 and 4.32) disagrees with the belief that Homer wrote *Cypria* and *Epigoni*. Aristotle's references to *Cypria* and *Little Iliad* indicate that he regarded the authorship as unknown. The most obvious difference between these and the Homeric poems (not enough is available for subtler comparisons) is the scale; whereas *Iliad* deals with some fifty days, these poems gave full accounts of what happened both before and after the Trojan War.

Their remains being so slight we need do little more here than name the ten poems. Pre-Trojan matters were dealt with in *Titanomachy* and the *Theban Cycle: (a) Titanomachy,* variously ascribed to Arctinus of Miletus and Eumelus of Corinth (both eighth century B.C.), told of the offspring of Heaven and Earth and the accession of Zeus to dominion. Athenaeus (7.277d) has a passage from the second book. The *Theban Cycle* comprised three poems. (*b*) *Oedipodea* is stated by the Tablet to have been composed by Cinaethon of Lacedaemon (eighth century B.C.) and to have run to 6,600 verses. Practically nothing is known of its contents, but since Athenaeus (7.277e) tells us that Sophocles followed the *Cycle* closely, it may have had the story of Oedipus the King. (*c*) *Thebais,* 7,000 lines, told the story of Eteocles and Polynices and the Seven against Thebes. The Theban War, Hesiod says, was the greatest before the Trojan, and sons of the Seven were heroes in the Trojan War. The poem was long ascribed to Homer, and Pausanias (9.9.5) rates it next after *Iliad* and *Odyssey*. Only *Thebais*, but without great probability, has been claimed as antedating *Iliad* and *Odyssey*. (*d*) *Epigoni* ("the after-born"), ascribed to Antimachus of Teos (eighth century B.C.), recounted the expedition of the sons of the Seven against Thebes and the sack of the city.

Six epics, together with *Iliad* and *Odyssey,* made up the *Trojan Cycle*. (*e*) *Cypria,* later divided into eleven books, recounted events from the apple of discord and the judgment of Paris to the early battles at Troy and the assignment of Chryseis and Briseis to Agamemnon and Achilles as prizes. It included incidents such as the desertion of Philoctetes on Lemnos, which were used by the tragedians. Its authorship is quite uncertain. (*f*) *Aethiopis* was a sequel to *Iliad* in five books, beginning with the arrival of Penthesilea and her Amazons to help the Trojans after the death of Hector. Achilles slays her, and then Thersites for mocking his grief for her. He then slays Memnon and is himself slain by Paris and Apollo, whereupon Odysseus and Ajax quarrel over his armor. The poem was assigned to Arctinus. (*g*) *Little Iliad* told of the award of the arms to Odysseus, the consequent madness of Ajax, and the introduction of the wooden horse into Troy. The author was said to be Lesches of Mitylene (seventh century B.C.). (*h*) *Iliupersis* or *Sack of Ilium,* ascribed to Arctinus, told of the capture of the city, the departure of the Greeks with their booty, and Athena's plan for their destruction at sea as punishment for the rape of Cassandra. *Little Iliad* and *Sack of Ilium* are more or less parallel to *Aeneid* 2 and appear to have overlapped. (*i*) *Nostoi* or *Returns,* in five books, was ascribed to Agias of Troezen, of whom nothing is known. Various heroes meet various adventures on their return from Troy; Agamemnon's death is told, as is Orestes' vengeance on Aegisthus. Menelaus' return is the last mentioned, and thus events are brought up to those in *Odyssey*. (*j*) *Telegony,* in two books by Eugammon of Cyrene (sixth century B.C.), told what happened to Odysseus after his return. He is eventually killed by Telegonus, his son by Circe, who then marries Penelope, and Telemachus marries Circe.

As far as may be judged from their fragments these poems still leave Homer without peer. Some of the incidents, as those of the Amazon and black Memnon in *Aethiopis,* are apparently creations of the poet's fancy, without basis in tradition, and the marriages at the end of *Telegony* also seem sophisticated preciosity. But the main interest of the *Cycle* for the student is in the use later writers made of them, especially in quarrying plots for tragedy. Indeed, the currency of the stories in more attractive forms of tragedy and choral lyric must have been largely responsible for the loss of the originals. A continuous account, in Homeric style, of events between the close of *Iliad* and the sack of Troy, probably but not surely based upon the Cyclic poems, is given in the *Posthomerica* of Quintus of Smyrna, who lived in the fourth century A.D.

Neither in antiquity nor in modern times have scholars given the group of poems called *Homeric Hymns* the attention they deserve. Subject matter and language are of the sort that scholiasts revel in, yet the *Hymns* are not cited even where the context in *Iliad* or *Argonautica* would clearly be clarified by such citation. This and the circumstance that in the manuscript tradition these poems were associated with Alexandrian works led scholars in the past to suspect a late date. Closer study demonstrates that none of the principal poems in the group can be dated lower than the sixth century B.C. Thucydides (3.104) quotes thirteen lines from *Hymn to Apollo* as from Homer, referring to them as a "Prelude" (*prooimion*). This designation raises the question of the intended use of the poems. Several close with the formula: "And now I will remember you and another song also," which suggests that they are introductory to a longer hymn appropriate to a given deity and festival. But the longer pieces, which run to 500 or more lines, are clearly substantive works, too long for mere introductions. Presumably like the term in modern music, "prelude" was used for independent compositions which bore a technical resemblance to that form.

The poems are all in hexameter, following Homeric language and usage quite closely, though they have far fewer epithets and no extended similes in the Homeric manner. Their narrative is more supple and easy flowing. More significant than the difference in style is an urbane maturity in dealing with the myths relating to certain of the gods. The collection contains thirty-three pieces, of which the hymns to Demeter, Apollo, Hermes, Aphrodite, and Dionysus are of considerable length.

No. 1, *To Dionysus,* was probably of the long type, but all but twenty-one lines are lost. These deal with the birthplace of the god and the establishment of his festival. No. 2, *To Demeter* (495 lines), extant only in a manuscript found by Matthaei in Moscow in 1777, and dated to the seventh century B.C., is the finest in the collection and one of the most winning pieces in Greek literature. The hymn describes the seizure of Persephone by Hades, the grief of her mother Demeter which she assuages by caring for a mortal infant at Eleusis; her vengeance on gods and men by causing famine, which induces Zeus to bring Persephone back from the lower world during the growing season of each year; and the establishment of the Eleusinian mysteries to commemorate her sorrows. The fragrance and gentleness which pervade the poem, the successful fusion of human warmth and divine majesty in Demeter herself, especially in her relations with the charming daughters of Celeus, give us a new insight into the emotional possibilities of a pagan cult. The Eleusinian mysteries themselves, based on the annual rebirth of vegetation, suggested that for man too life might be renewed if the proper ceremonies were performed, and the step from the notion that ritual participation would assure continued existence after death to the concept of salvation by ethical and spiritual endeavor was easy.

Most editors have believed that the two parts of No. 3, *To Apollo* (546 lines, seventh century B.C.), 1–178 dealing with Delos and 179–546 dealing with Delphi, were originally distinct and reflected a rivalry between two centers of Apollo worship. But the best modern opinion sees no necessity to deny the unity of the poem, the author's progress from Delos to Delphi being natural and the joint being no more awkward than similar joints in Homer. The hymn is a prime source for the cult of Apollo and seems to have been better known than the others. Thucydides' quotation from it has been noted; Aristophanes' *Knights* 1016 seems to expect the audience to recognize an echo of line 443.

No. 4, *To Hermes* (580 lines, seventh century B.C.), describes the colossal roguery and inventiveness of the infant Hermes, as exemplified in his contriving the lyre, stealing the cattle of Apollo with heroic cunning, and brazenly confronting both Apollo and Zeus. Two millennia of more puritanical religion make it difficult to realize that the hymn is in fact a devout celebration of the qualities characteristic of a deity with functions important for humanity, and few have resisted the temptation to see in it either a burlesque, like *Batrachomyomachia* or a rationalist's scoff, like those Lucian indulged in a millennium later. Others, with somewhat better perspective, seek to interpret it in terms of Aristophanes, to which the edition of Allen, Halliday, and Sikes properly retorts (p. 269): "There is an element in common between the temper of the hymn and that of Old Comedy, but it consists in the circumstance that both were written by Greeks." The hymn is what it professes to be, but this does not preclude its being gay (the gaiety is delightfully rendered in Shelley's version) nor the possibility that social criticism of a kind is involved.

Hermes is a humble sort of god, and the insistence on his contributions and his acceptability to the greater Olympians may reflect an attitude of the disinherited among his worshipers. The *Ichneutai* of Sophocles, a satyr play of which some four hundred lines were discovered in Oxyrhynchus, seems to tell the same stories of Hermes, but in a slightly different order.

In No. 5, *To Aphrodite* (293 lines, seventh century B.C.), the recognition of Aphrodite's province is as candid as is that of Hermes in the preceding hymn. The sensual description of the seduction of Anchises is not meant to be titillating, nor the discomfiture of the goddess a mockery. All creatures, the poet begins, are subject to Aphrodite, save only the goddesses Athena, Artemis, and Hestia. To humble her pride of power Zeus caused Aphrodite to love a mortal, whom she proceeds to seduce after elaborate preparations. When she has accomplished her design she reproaches her victim; and here we may see a complaint against the capricious and unjust treatment of a humble shepherd by a greater power. But she feels her own humiliation and grief keenly also, and here we perceive a decided ethical advance over the superficially similar episode concerning Ares and Aphrodite sung by Demodocus in *Odyssey* 8.266 ff.

No. 6, also *To Aphrodite,* tells, in twenty-one lines, of the adornment of the goddess by the Horai. No. 7, *To Dionysus* (59 lines, seventh or sixth century B.C.), tells how Dionysus was seized by pirates, the miracles he performed on their ship, and how its sailors were transformed into dolphins. The story was a favorite for later poets, and is illustrated in the sculptures on the choregic monument of Lysicrates. No. 8, *To Ares* (15 lines), belongs to the Hellenistic period, and its inclusion in the collection is something of a puzzle. It has a decided Orphic character and it seems to be addressed to the planet Mars rather than to Ares. The remaining hymns are, with one exception, very slight, and are addressed, in that order, to Artemis, Aphrodite, Athena, Hera, Demeter, the Mother of the Gods, Heracles the Lionhearted, Asclepius, the Dioscuri, Hermes, Pan, Hephaestus, Apollo, Poseidon, Zeus, Hestia, the Muses and Apollo, Dionysus, Artemis, Athena, Hestia, Earth the Mother of All, Helios, Selene, and again the Dioscuri. No. 19, *To Pan* (fifth century B.C.), tells of Pan's merry frolics among woodland scenes, and is almost unique in older Greek literature for its fresh and spontaneous delight in wild natural scenes.

Sundry minor works to which the name of Homer has been attached remain. Aristotle (*Poetics* 1448b) declares that *"Margites* [which he had ascribed to Homer] stands in the same relation to our comedies as *Iliad* and *Odyssey* to our tragedies." Only six lines are extant, and we know only that Margites was a blunderer who "knew all things, but knew them all badly," that he did not know whether his father or mother was his parent, nor what a man did with his wife. The inclusion of iambic verses with the hexameters points to a date after Archilochus. *Cercopes* tells of a pair of knavish brothers who were punished by Heracles, apparently by being turned into monkeys. *Batrachomyomachia* (303 lines) parodies the warlike epic with an account of a war between frogs and mice, humorously named and fantastically armed, complete with divine machinery, Zeus sending crabs to end the struggle. It is ascribed (along with *Margites*) to Pigres, brother of the Artemisia who fought at Salamis. The possibility of satire is not exploited. There is no wit, except in the original concept, and no fun except in the names and equipment of the warriors, yet the Byzantines found it diverting, as numerous late interpolations show.

The *Life of Homer* falsely ascribed to Herodotus contains seventeen short hexameter pieces (some of which occur elsewhere), around which the *Life* seems to have been written. These pieces are called the *Homeric Epigrams,* but they are certainly not Homer's. Only Nos. 14 and 15 have any extent or interest. The first promises to call blessings down on some potters if they are generous, threatening a plague of gremlins if they are not. The second, called *Eiresione,* is a spring song for children who beg from house to house.

The *Contest of Homer and Hesiod,* extant in twelve pages, dates from the age of Hadrian, but along with its late material it makes use of an earlier comparison made by the sophist Alcidamas some five hundred years before. *Contest* deals with the descent and dates of the poets, their match at Chalcis, their works, and their death. It is of little value either as history or criticism. We now turn to Homer's rival in the *Contest.*

Chapter 5. HESIOD AND HESIODIC SCHOOLS

THE CONTEST BETWEEN HOMER AND HESIOD IS A CONTEST BETWEEN THE BRIGHT splendor of godlike heroes and the dour sobriety of a Boeotian farmer, between the right of might and blood and the right of law, between the poetry of warriors, as a Spartan king said, and the poetry of helots, between the world which Don Quixote tried to recreate and the world Sancho Panza lived in. An eminent Victorian critic actually speaks of Hesiod's rules as revealing "the spirit of a prudent clown" with "sordid aims in life." In fact, Hesiod is the prophet of that righteousness which makes it possible for men to live together. Though Hesiod's influence is far less striking than Homer's, Hesiodic quotations and allusions are surprisingly frequent, and whereas a Homeric tag is frequently introduced merely as ornament, Hesiod is usually cited for his substance. That substance was of prime importance in shaping the ethics of Greece, and also of Rome. A people educated only in Homer would not be nearly so ready to accept Christian ethics as one informed by Hesiod. Homer is the classics of the ancients; Hesiod their Bible.

Opposition to the Homeric ideal was conscious on Hesiod's part. To him the Muses of Helicon had asserted that they could tell many true things as well as pleasant and plausible falsehoods; surely this is a formal declaration of departure from heroic poetry, perhaps intended as a direct refutation of such a line as *Odyssey* 19.203:

> Thus in the likeness of truth he related a tissue of falsehood.

And posterity was clearly aware of the opposition. *Contest of Homer and Hesiod* (§ 322) quotes the epigram which Hesiod allegedly inscribed on the tripod which he himself says (*Works and Days* 654 ff.) he won as a prize for song at a contest in Chalcis, and which in any case probably dates from the sixth century: "This tripod Hesiod dedicated to the Muses of Helicon when at Chalcis he overcame divine Homer in song." Hesiod recognized the incompatibility between the predatory ideals of the heroic lords and the interest of humbler folk, and it was sympathy with hard-pressed shepherds and peasants that loosed his tongue and emboldened him to challenge a degenerate aristocracy. A new vocabulary of epithets of approval and disapproval appears in Hesiod: truthful, never-lying, oath-keeping, law-abiding, righteous, unjust, sinful. It is even more significant that attributes which are complimentary in Homer—proud, strong-spirited, having prowess in arms—take on a pejorative sense in Hesiod. It is the quest for righteousness in Hesiod that gives him the first title of *vates,* sacred bard.

This quest and the social consciousness out of which it grew are not Hesiod's only substantive contributions to the Greek spirit. He was an innovator both in theology and in science. Homer's gods are immortal, and there is no suggestion that a change in their nature or function is ever contemplated. The thought that a different generation of gods had once held sway and had been supplanted by force is vague, and the logical inference that the current gods might fare similarly is never drawn. That thought is put into the foreground by Hesiod. But more important, Hesiod is the first to emphasize the relationship, in the Prometheus story and elsewhere, between sin and retribution. The prime function of Zeus, and therefore of human kings who are his vicars, is to guard over justice and morality. Zeus begets his first offspring not by Metis (Cleverness) but by Themis (Law), and his first-born are the Horai—Eunomia, Dike, Eirene (Order, Justice, Peace). Hesiod creates many personifications, not only of places and powers, such as Gaia, Uranus, Pontus (Earth, Heaven, Sea), but also of conditions, moods, actions, such as night, dark, love, old age, forgetfulness, hunger, pain, fear, blindness, sleep, dreams, murder, battle, deceit, reproach. His systematization and his presentation, so to speak, of a process of reasoning rather than a statement of conclusions make him a significant pioneer in the field of Greek science.

Hesiod's verse is Homeric and his dialect epic; it is clear that he was thoroughly acquainted with Homer, and indeed he implies, in the story of the competition at Chalcis, that he traveled about reciting heroic poetry as well as his own. But a significant difference is that Hesiod speaks in his own person, not as the impersonal instrument of the Muses. He repeatedly addresses his brother Perses, with whom he apparently engaged in a lawsuit concerning their inheritance, but it is a mistake to regard *Works and Days* as intended for Perses' admonition; the name is hardly more significant than is that of Memmius in Lucretius. Hesiod tells us of his father also, that he came from the Aeolian Cyme, driven by poverty, and settled in Boeotian Ascra, a village near Helicon, "bad in winter, wretched in summer, good at no time" (*Works and Days* 640). He tells us too that he was a shepherd and that the Muses taught him song as he was tending lambs under Mount Helicon (*Theogony* 22-23). Unlike Homer, then, of whose personality we know nothing, Hesiod tells us a good bit about himself—enough, at least, for later authors to embroider. But none of the details derived from external sources has any degree of reliability. The one useful point is Herodotus' dating of Hesiod to a period 400 years before his own day, and modern scholars are inclined to think that date somewhat early.

Individuality is revealed, not only in autobiographic details and in direct admonitions delivered in the first person, but in Hesiod's style. The conscious and effective art in which his admonitions are clothed are peculiarly Hesiod's. His descriptions of the turns of the seasons and his allusions to the Muses have a special beauty which grows out of their sincerity. His apothegms have epigrammatic neatness. He has many charming rustic expressions: the snail is "the house-carrier"; the snake, "the hairless one"; the burglar, "the day sleeper." The cuttlefish in the winter sea is "the boneless one gnawing his foot by his fireless hearth in his cheerless house"; cutting one's nails is "severing the withered from the quick on the five-branched"; and a shrew "roasts her man without fire." A description of what a man wears, as told respectively in *Iliad* and *Works and Days,* will illustrate Hesiod's quality. This is how Patroclus was armed in *Iliad* (16.130–138):

Patroclus harnessed him in shining bronze. His goodly greaves, fitted with silver clasps, he first girt round his legs, and next did on around his breast the well-dight starry corslet of the swift-footed son of Aeacus. And round his shoulders he cast a sword of bronze with studs of silver, and next took the great and mighty shield, and on his proud head set a well-wrought helm with horsehair crest, and terribly nodded the crest from above.

—Lang, Leaf, and Myers

And this is how Hesiod advises a man to dress for winter (*Works and Days* 536–546):

Put on, as I bid you, a soft coat and a tunic to the feet to shield your body,—and you should weave thick woof on thin warp. In this clothe yourself so that your hair may keep still and not bristle and stand upon end all over your body. Lace on your feet close-fitting boots of the hide of a slaughtered ox, thickly lined with felt inside. And when the season of frost comes on, stitch together skins of firstling kids with ox-sinew, to put over your back and keep off the rain. On your head above wear a shaped cap of felt to keep your ears from getting wet.

—H. G. Evelyn-White

But though Hesiod had not Homer's delight in splendid apparel and food and society, and his theme is how best to survive in a grim world, he is neither clod nor clown. Nature gives him delight, and song, and the esteem of his fellow men, and he knows how to take his ease, when the cicada chirps, under a shady rock, with wine and curds and barbecued veal and kid.

Works and Days starts with an invocation to Zeus (whose name Hesiod uses almost interchangeably with "the gods") and a promise that he will tell true things (1–10). The Muses' declaration (*Theogony* 26 f.) that they can tell true things as well as plausible falsehood makes this promise seem like a formal declaration of an anti-Homeric program. Strife is of two sorts: overreaching is bad, emulation good (*Works and Days* 11–41). The fall of man was caused by the curiosity of a woman—the story of Pandora and her jar—in consequence of which man may no longer lead an easy life but is doomed to toil (42–105). Humanity has descended from a Golden Age through a Silver, Bronze, and Heroic to the present Iron Age, in which might is right and the sense of mutual obligation is relaxed; soon Aidos and Nemesis, scruple and righteous indignation, will leave the earth (106–201). A hawk says to a nightingale that only a fool laments the power of the stronger, for might makes right; but men must pursue righteousness, for righteousness brings blessings, and violence brings retribution, if not upon themselves, upon their houses. Zeus has innumerable spirits watching over the deeds of men, and whenever Justice is abused she reports to Zeus. Beasts and birds may devour one another, but for men justice is ordained (202–285). Work is no disgrace, but idleness is; prosperity gained by honest industry gives a man prestige, but property must not be acquired dishonestly, nor must one injure a stranger, violate a brother's bed, wrong orphans, or rebuke parents; rather must the gods be propitiated (286–341). There follow proverbs chiefly prescribing prudent but fair relations with neighbors and closing with another admonition to work (342–380). Here begins a farmer's year, various tasks being recommended for various periods. There is work even for winter: do not loaf with the gossips in the smithy. But in the heat of summer there is time for a picnic in the shade (342–617). Hesiod dislikes navigation and frowns on trading, but gives a calendar for sailors also (618–694). There follow precepts on marriage, relations with fellow men, decency in manners, and certain superstitions (695–764), and then a calendar of lucky and unlucky days (765–928).

The similarity of many of the precepts in *Works and Days* to those in *Proverbs* (which, in turn, has analogues in Egypt and Babylonia) is striking. But more significant is the general tone of moral earnestness and the close parallels in theology with pre-exilic Judaism. Hesiod too has a Fall, and if a man himself escape divine retribution for wrongdoing, yet his house (but not himself in another life) will pay the penalty. Men have a moral responsibility which animals do not. They must be governed by

law, which protects the weak and restrains the strong, but under this
law free enterprise is the rule. It is a fine thing for a man to get ahead of
his neighbors, but not by overreaching them.

It is no longer necessary to refute those who would discerp *Works and
Days,* nor even those who deny *Theogony* to Hesiod. This longer work is
of much less general interest than *Works and Days,* though it is unique
as an organized account (the systematization being most likely Hesiod's)
of the gods of Greece. The poem presents a genealogy of the gods from
Chaos to the establishment of their definitive hierarchy, and thus constitutes a basis for, and an introduction to, universal history. The poet
first tells of his own inspiration by the Muses, declares his program of
adhering to truth, and invokes the Muses, describing and naming them,
to assist his enterprise of celebrating the race of the gods (1–115). First
was Chaos, then Earth and Eros, who constitutes an indefinite force of
attraction and reproduction. Earth produces Heaven, to whom she bears
Titans, Cyclopes, and hundred-handed giants (116–153). At Earth's in-
stigation the Titans, under the leadership of Cronos, revolt against Heaven,
mutilating and severing him from Earth. The marriages and offspring of
the Titans are enumerated (154–410), special space being given to Hecate,
who is particularly favored by Zeus and brings men blessings (411–452).
Cronos, knowing that he is to be supplanted by one of his children, swal-
lows each as it is born, until Zeus, saved by his mother, Rhea, overcomes
Cronos and forces him to disgorge his children (453–506). The Titan
Prometheus deceives Zeus (who permits himself to be deceived) in ap-
portioning a sacrificial victim between gods and men, and steals fire from
heaven. Zeus sends Pandora, the primal woman, to plague men, and
Prometheus is bound (507–616). The children of Cronos, under the
leadership of Zeus, defeat the Titans in a great battle (617–819), and Zeus
also blasts Typhoeus, the latest-born child of Earth, whereupon the gods,
at Earth's prompting, make Zeus king (820–885). Zeus' marriages and
begettings are enumerated, as are those of the other Olympians and of
their offspring (886–962). Lastly, the sons born to goddesses of unions
with mortals are named, and the poem closes with an appeal to the Muses
to sing of the tribe of women (963–1022).

There is piety here, as well as concern for order and interest in genealogy,
though the piety is of a priestly type. Nor can the prophetic aspect be
overlooked. The Zeus-Prometheus story, where Hesiod's material must
have shown Prometheus hoodwinking Zeus by playing upon his greediness,
is elevated into cosmic significance and Zeus is raised in wisdom and
power. The traditional gods appear to retain their prerogatives, but when
they are supplemented by such abstractions as Strife, Toil, Forgetfulness,

Famine, and the like (*Theogony* 226 ff.), one wonders just how precise Hesiod's concept of the gods was. Eros, who was quite a concrete local god, is abstracted into the great cosmic force of Love (120 ff.). Illuminating, in this connection, is the deification of Rumor: "Rumor never wholly dies away when many people voice her; surely it also is a god" (*Works and Days* 763–764).

Connected with *Theogony* (though not necessarily by Hesiod) were five books of *Eoiai,* in which the famous women of legend, with their offspring, were treated. The title is the plural of the expression "or such a woman as," which was used to introduce each new section. The best of our fragments is the fifty-six-line introduction to *Shield of Heracles,* the remaining extant work in the Hesiodic corpus. These lines tell of Alcmena's marriage to Amphitryon, how her husband and Zeus both visited her in the same night, and how she bore their respective sons, Iphicles and Heracles. The remainder treats of Heracles' encounter with the brigand Cycnus, son of Ares. There is a long (lines 139–317) description of Heracles' shield, in obvious imitation of Achilles' in *Iliad* 18. There are other obvious, and rather poor, imitations of Homer, notably in the accumulation of similes. But the story is lively and it is well told. With the help of Athena, Heracles kills Cycnus and wounds Ares. Cycnus was buried by his father Ceyx, but Apollo caused his tomb to be washed away, because he used to waylay pilgrims en route to Delphi.

Of lost works ascribed to Hesiod *Divination by Birds* was attached to *Works and Days* and *Astrology* (properly *Astronomy*) attached to *Divination. Precepts of Chiron* apparently contained moral and practical ethical precepts, and *Great Works* apparently gave instructions on farming. *Idaean Dactyls,* probably dealing with metalworking, was connected with *Great Works.* As *Shield* was connected with *Eoiai,* so probably were other relevant episodes, such as *Epithalamium to Peleus and Thetis, Descent of Theseus to Hades, Circuit of the Earth* (on aspects of the Argonaut legend), *Suitors of Helen, Daughters of Leucippus,* and *Marriage of Ceyx,* many of which were undoubtedly interpolated into the original poem. Two other books were ascribed to Hesiod, *Aegimius,* dealing with the war against the Lapiths (also ascribed to Cercops of Miletus), and *Melampodia,* dealing with famous seers.

Dubiety concerning the Hesiodic authorship of all but *Works* and *Theogony* ranges from strong suspicion to virtual certainty. They are mentioned because they provided the mythico-historical material which later writers used and subsequently incorporated into handbooks, which insured the loss of the original works. For the same reason, mention may be made of a number of similar pre-sixth-century works associated with other names. *Corinthiaca,* ascribed to Eumelus, contained the Medea story. Cinaethon of Sparta, variously credited with authorship of *Little Iliad, Oedipodeia,* and *Telegony,* may have produced other things also. *Naupactica,* ascribed to Carcinus of Naupactus, dealt with the Argonauts. Asius of Samos, better known for elegy, wrote heroic genealogies; his best known fragment deals with Samian customs. Chersias of Orchomenus, said to be a contemporary of Periander, is the only Boeotian poet named with Hesiod. Hegesinus is said to have written an *Atthis* (on Attica). There must have been a number of epics on Theseus and on Heracles. The poems of Pisander the Rhodian and Panyasis, the uncle of Herodotus, on this subject were so excellent that ancient critics included them in a canon of five epic poets (Homer, Hesiod, Pisander, Panyasis, Antimachus). Fragments of all these and similar productions are too slight and allusions too equivocal to allow much that is definite to be said about them. Criticism, perhaps too imaginative, detects the influence of Hesiod as well as Homer, even to the point of noting the emergence of the common man.

The emergence of the common man and his restiveness under aristocratic misrule which comes to light in Hesiod is reflected also in a religious movement in the seventh and sixth centuries (which have been called the *saeculum mysticum* of Greek history) which itself had important repercussions in literature. Apollo of Delphi was an old established Olympian who was concerned for religious conservatism and for the maintenance of ancestral usages in cults of heroic ancestors, loyalty to the traditions of the state, and the like. In its function as oracle the cult of the Delphian Apollo was in touch with the ruling classes in the cities, which it supported and by whom it was in turn supported. In the seventh century the peasant god Dionysus, a stranger to Olympus, makes his way into Greece, offering religious satisfactions to the common people which they were denied in the cult of Apollo. The rivalry of the two gods is reflected (as we can see in the literature) in different standards of approved conduct, the followers of Apollo (among whom almost all our writers are found) always counseling temperance, moderation, restraint—in a word, conservatism in all things—as against the nervous, emotional, innovating tendencies of the followers of Dionysus. The religious rivalry was naturally an aspect of, and an instrument in, political unrest. The "tyrants" who rose to power by championing the cause of the common people against the aristocrats regularly patronized the religion of Dionysus. It was something in the nature of an eclipse for Apollo and a victory for Dionysus when under the Athenian "tyrants" dramatic performances were made part of the Dionysiac festivals. Though Apollo retained his antidemocratic character (he Medized in the Persian war and Laconized in the

war against Sparta), Dionysus became respectable in the Athenian democracy, and his votaries never felt bound as a sect. But Orphism, in which
emotionalism and release were even more prominent than in the religion
of Dionysus, did constitute a sect, and lasted, with transformations, as
long as paganism itself. The Orphics were sincere devotees and used what
means they could to propagate their views, but they were also religious
obscurantists, and if they had prevailed would have thwarted the intellectual awakening in Athens.

Hesiod had shown that a man who has something to say on religion and
ethics might do so in hexameter verse, and the Orphics followed in his
footsteps, regarding themselves in a sense as the propagators of his tradition. Much of their literature was pseudepigraphic, being ascribed to
Orpheus and Musaeus, of whom nothing can be said with certainty. Orphics had a theogony of their own, in which Zagreus, son of Zeus and
Persephone and an important figure in Orphism, was devoured by Titans,
who were then slain by Zeus' thunderbolts and from whose ashes rose
man. Orphism thus had something like original sin and something like
Manichaeism, and its asceticism gave it common traits with Pythagoreanism. The first holdfast in a morass of conjecture is a passage in Herodotus
(7.6.3-4) which tells us that at the court of the Pisistratids, Onomacritus
of Athens, an oracle expert, arranged the prophecies of Musaeus, and that
he was banished because his attempt to foist a forged prophecy into the
collection was detected by Lasus of Hermione, who is known as a lyric
poet and teacher of Pindar. Other Orphic works alluded to or extant in
fragments include eschatological hymns on gold leaf, an adaptation of the
Homeric *Hymn to Demeter* in a papyrus, and the *Hieroi Logoi* or "sacred
legends."

Just as the Orphic use of the name of Musaeus proves that genuine
Musaeus material must have existed, so does Jewish and Christian use
of the Sibyl (who is mentioned by fifth-century authors) prove that collections of Sibylline oracles existed. The collection, in fourteen books, which
goes under that title was obviously put together to promote Jewish and
Christian propaganda. A similar intent is apparent in the 230 verses of
the *Pseudo-Phocylidea,* attached to the name of Phocylides, who wrote
maxims in the style of *Precepts of Chiron* in the seventh or sixth century.
Fifth-century writers attribute a large number of prophecies in hexameter verse to Bacis, of whom nothing is known.

To these misty theological figures we may add three who used hexameter verse for the transition to rational philosophy, whose doctrines as
well as personalities are easier to apprehend. Xenophanes of Colophon
(in Asia Minor) spent most of his long life, which practically covered the

sixth century, in the West and is spoken of as the father of philosophy at Elea, the south Italian school. Hesiod had criticized the ethics of Homeric heroes; Xenophanes criticizes the gods: Homer and Hesiod attributed to the gods everything that is disgraceful and blameworthy among men; very many lawless deeds have they sung of the gods, theft and adultery and mutual deceit (7, Diels). These gods are no gods, but the petty imaginings of unreasoning minds: "If oxen and lions had hands to draw and make things as men do, they would draw the shapes of the gods and fashion their bodies like the forms they themselves have, horses like horses and oxen like oxen" (6, Diels). Looking up to universal heaven, says Aristotle (*Metaphysics* 986*b*), Xenophanes proclaimed that unity is god. Not only the theology of the heroic age but practices associated with that theology are criticized. One elegiac poem (which belongs in the next chapter) objects to the honors paid to athletes for their own or even their horses' strength when intellect is what gives a man his value (2, Diels). But Xenophanes is not puritanical. The longest of his elegies (1, Diels) describes a festive party, where men drink no more than they can carry home without the aid of a servant and the entertainment does not deal with fictional encounters of Titans, giants, and centaurs.

Parmenides, a younger contemporary of Xenophanes and the central figure in the Eleatic school, is more the abstract thinker. He distrusted sense perceptions as yielding only opinion, and is several times mentioned with respect in the Platonic dialogues, but he is a philosophical versifier rather than a poet. What Aristotle said of Empedocles, that he and Homer "have really nothing in common apart from their meter" (*Poetics* 1447*b*) applies in greater measure to Parmenides. Empedocles of Agrigentum in Sicily (and so a Dorian) who lived during the middle of the fifth century deserves a high place both as thinker and as poet. Extraordinary tales in Diogenes Laertius make him seem very theatrical if not an absolute charlatan; on the other hand, Lucretius, though he disagrees with his scientific opinions, shows nothing less than reverence for him (1.726 ff.) and modeled his *De Rerum Natura* on Empedocles' *Peri Physeos*. The world, according to Empedocles, is composed of the four elements, earth, air, fire, and water, sometimes personified as Aidoneus (Hades), Hera, Zeus, and Nestis, which are everlastingly combined and separated by Love and Hate, or attraction and repulsion. Empedocles was also concerned with medicine and politics as well as with philosophy, and he was the teacher of the rhetorician Gorgias of Leontini. Empedocles' other great work, besides *Peri Physeos*, was *Catharmoi* or *Purifications,* which seems to have recommended Pythagorean asceticism and the doctrine of reincarnation. These three are mentioned here because each shows some kinship with the Hesiodic schools and employed hexameter verse. Their prose confreres will be considered in another place. Meanwhile we must return to the seventh century, to look at poetic forms which followed upon Hesiod's.

Chapter 6. LYRIC

OF ALL THE PRODUCTS OF GREEK GENIUS WHICH ARE LOST TO US THE LOSS IN lyric poetry is among the most grievous, certainly in literature. In prose —philosophy, history, oratory—we have what the Greeks themselves regarded as their best. Homer was pre-eminent in heroic poetry, and we have Hesiod's best work. In tragedy, nine tenths of the work of even the Great Three has perished. Of other classic poetry only Theognis and Pindar have come down in independent manuscript tradition, and only Bacchylides has been restored by finds of papyri. Perhaps the greatest single loss in all literature is the work of Sappho, whose meager fragments are only enough to give credit to the ancients who esteemed her the greatest of the lyric poets.

Devotion to poetry is as truly a Greek trait as is the pursuit of reason. It is Greek devotion to poetry as the normal vehicle for artistic expression rather than inability to speak in prose that makes our history of Greek poetry five hundred years older than our history of Greek prose. If interest and proficiency in poetry had not been so widespread, Greek theaters need not have been so capacious. The main content of the education of Greek children was poetry and song. The educational and character-shaping function of music (which included poetry) was taken for granted throughout Greek history. Only in the age of the sophists was this function questioned; and doubts were refuted by the "scientific" explanation that movement of the soul was directly affected by music. It is only in the light of the importance attached to music as an agent for shaping character and even political attitudes that the schism precipitated by the introduction of flute music as a rival to stringed instruments becomes intelligible. The flute was Dionysus' instrument, and like Dionysus himself a newcomer from the East, characterized by emotional excitement and the negation of the conservative qualities of temperance and restraint inculcated by the religion of Apollo. The legends of the musical contests between Apollo with his lyre and Marsyas with his flute and of Athena's disgust when she found that the flute distorted her cheeks reflect this rivalry. Just as official recognition of the cult of Dionysus was in effect a plebeian victory so was the eventual acceptance of the flute by Apollo himself. Yet long after it was so accepted, preference for the lyre and objection to the flute are a sure index of a writer's political conservatism.

The new forms that came in with the new music are even more eloquent of social change, and the meters themselves reflect the change. Hexameter demands stateliness in vocabulary and utterance, and its effect is almost liturgical. In the elegiac couplet the second line or so-called "pentameter" is really two separate units of two and a half dactyls each; these do not admit many of the mouth-filling phrases of hexameter, and the language of elegy is less ornate, as the periods are shorter. The next step is iambic, which accommodates itself perfectly to the language of common speech; ordinary prose frequently falls into iambic rhythm automatically. In solo lyric, furthermore, dialectical differences brought the poetry nearer an ordinary audience. The social implications of these forms continued definite because the Greeks were careful to retain the form found appropriate to a given content. The change in content corresponds generally to the change in form. In elegy a poet in his own person gives utterance to all manner of thought, counsel on politics or manners, reflections on life, tribute to the dead, or the like. Iambic is subjective in the modern sense of lyric. A poet speaks of his own experiences and voices his personal views, which are apt to be in opposition to traditional views. Generally, lyric poetry was intended, not for the entertainment of the gentry, but for all people. The displacement of heroic poetry by lyric in the seventh century, in a word, may reflect a defeat of the aristocracy and the emergence of the common man.

But the history of lyric poetry goes far back of the seventh century. Greek legend preserved the names of ancient bards, such as Orpheus, Linus, Musaeus, Pamphus, Eumolpus, Thamyris, Amphion, Olen, Philammon. The mythical character of most of these is transparent, but it is clear that lyric poetry was known before Homer. As *Iliad* and *Odyssey* presuppose much antecedent heroic poetry, so do our extant fragments of the seventh and sixth centuries presuppose a long lyric tradition. In the decorations on the shield of Achilles, which represent all phases of life, remarkable prominence is given to song and dance (which originally regularly accompanied song). A whole section is given to a choral dance (*Iliad* 18.590–606):

Also did the glorious lame god devise a dancing place like unto that which once in wide Cnosus Daedalus wrought for Ariadne of the lovely tresses. There were youths dancing and maidens of costly wooing, their hands upon one another's wrists. Fine linen the maidens had on, and the youths well-woven doublets faintly glistening with oil. Fair wreaths had the maidens, and the youths daggers of gold hanging from silver baldrics. And now would they run round with deft feet exceeding lightly, as when a potter sitting by his wheel that fitteth between his hands maketh trial of it whether it run: and now anon they would run in lines to meet each other. And a great company stood round the lovely dance in joy; and among them a divine minstrel was making music on his lyre, and through the midst of them, leading the measure, two tumblers whirled.

—Lang, Leaf, and Myers

Elsewhere on the shield a wedding song (490–496) and a dirge (569–572) are described. Besides wedding songs and dirges we hear of other varieties. The general term for the cult song is "hymn," performed solo or by a chorus, to the accompaniment of the cithara. Each god has his appropriate cult song; Dionysus' was the dithyramb, Apollo's the paean. In addition there were *threnoi,* dirges; *epithalamia* and *hymenaeoi* for weddings; *encomia,* in praise of great men, of which those for victors in the athletic games were called *epinicia; embateria,* or war songs; *skolia,* or table songs, usually with an aristocratic bias; love songs, generally addressed to a member of the same sex; proverbs; and work songs, to accompany grinding, weaving, baking, water-drawing, children's begging, and the like. Not all these categories are represented in our surviving specimens. What we do have it is usual, and convenient, to classify according to verse form, which itself suggests the nature of the subject.

A common but rather loose classification is to call all poetry other than hexameter lyric. Lyric would then be divided into two principal categories, elegy and iamb, and melic or true lyric. The distichs of elegy and the lines of iamb were at first chanted, the elegy to the flute and the iamb to the lyre, but afterward recited. Melic or true lyric, in which the lines are not of uniform length, was sung or danced and sung. Though the lines within strophes are of varying length, the strophes as a whole follow an absolutely identical pattern, and the basic foot is usually persistent. Melic is in turn divided into two classes, monody or solo lyric, of which the supreme example is Sappho, and choral lyric, of which the supreme example is Pindar. In solo lyric all the strophes are equivalent; in choral lyric the strophes are arranged in triads (strophe, antistrophe, epode), and the triads are repeated.

Elegy comes first, and its earliest representative is from Asia Minor. The first elegiac poet in our anthologies is Callinus, whose one considerable fragment is a spirited exhortation, apparently to his fellow Ephesians, to fight bravely against the Cimmerians who were invading Asia Minor early in the seventh century. The poem starts (1.1–4):

> How long, young men, unsoldiered, disregarding,
> Laze you, scorned by neighbors round about?

> Slack to the bone, on peace resolved, supinely
> Careless in a land where all is war?
> —*T. F. Higham*

A similar martial tone fills some half dozen extant pieces of Tyrtaeus, who was summoned to Sparta for the Second Messenian war (which makes him contemporary with Callinus), possibly from Lesbos, but, according to a late legend shaped by Athenian-Spartan rivalry, from Athens, where he was said to have been a lame schoolmaster. Each of Tyrtaeus' pieces is an exhortation to the Spartans not to shirk but to fight for their country, pointing out the glory and the practical advantages of courage and the practical disadvantages and disgrace of cowardice. His poems became a kind of sacred literature which young Spartans learned by heart. If at first glance the respect for war-like prowess seems Homeric, a significant change is to be noted from the Homeric ideal. Tyrtaeus' soldier is concerned for his own place in the city, but he is a citizen before he is a hero. He fights, not in single combat, but in a line with his fellow citizens; his reward is not abstract glory but the esteem of his countrymen and security for his city and himself. War is a grim necessity, not a blazing adventure; yet even so Greek concern for the beautiful appears in a line (6.30) urging young men to fight in the forefront on the ground that they make handsomer corpses than old men.

Mimnermus of Colophon, who lived later in the seventh century, illustrates the luxurious temper of Ionia as Tyrtaeus does the ruggedness of Sparta. He too admired military prowess, but he loved pleasure, especially the pleasure associated with shining youth, which he looks back upon with wistful regret, and he abhors the dry discomforts of old age and poverty. His most familiar fragment (#1) begins with the line: "What is life, what pleasure is there, apart from golden Aphrodite?" Mimnermus wrote a long poem called *Nanno* after a girl he loved; if certain fragments really come from that poem it dealt with a variety of themes, some mythological. There is mention of the story of Jason's quest, and a fine piece on the labors of the sun. In grace and technical skill Mimnermus' mastery makes both Tyrtaeus and Solon, to whom we now turn, seem primitive.

It is appropriate that the first poet of Athens should be one of the great statesmen of Europe, and a merchant, student, and lover of good living to boot. At a time when tension between the greed of the rich and the consequent restiveness of the poor threatened to prostrate the state Solon, who was himself of aristocratic birth, restrained the excesses of both extremes (as a tool of the rich, radical critics say, to make the minimum concessions that would prevent revolution) and by finding a middle ground laid the foundations for Athenian democracy. The introduction of coined money and the expansion of foreign trade had impoverished small land-holders. Farms were mortgaged at ruinous rates, and when borrowers could not pay they were enslaved. Even so, the exploiting class was so feeble that they lost Salamis, which was vital to their commerce, to the Megarians. Solon presented himself to the Athenians as a herald from Salamis and said that he would liefer be known as a man of Pholegandrus (an insignificant island) than as an Athenian "of the letters-go of Salamis" (#2). The usual pattern of Greek reaction to aristocratic oppression was for popular indignation to have recourse to a "tyranny" for protection against the aristocracy, and even Athens, despite Solon's efforts, had its tyranny some thirty years later. Solon sought to make democracy viable by canceling mortgages (by the *seisachtheia,* or "disburdening ordinance"), forbidding enslavement for debt, and admitting the lowest class of citizens to the ecclesia. Solon's poems, of which about 250 lines are extant, are a kind of commentary on his life and program. As in Hesiod, but now with specific application to a busy metropolis, the ideal is equality under the law, with neither class overreaching the other. Solon is an Athenian patriot, confident of divine protection and desirous of national aggrandizement. An attractive poem (#3, quoted by Demosthenes in *On the Embassy*) speaks first of the gods' care for Athens, points to social unrighteousness of the Athenians themselves as the city's greatest danger, and closes with a doxology to Eunomia or Good Order:

This it is that my heart biddeth me tell the Athenians, and how that even as ill government giveth a city much trouble, so good rule [Eunomia] maketh all things orderly and perfect, and often putteth fetters upon the unrighteous; aye, she maketh the rough smooth, checketh excess, confuseth outrage; she withereth the springing weeds of ruin, she straighteneth crooked judgments, she modifieth proud deeds; she stoppeth the works of faction, she stilleth the wrath of baneful strife; and of her all is made wise and perfect in the world of men.

—*J. M. Edmonds*

Solon's love of learning new things and his delight in the works of Aphrodite, Dionysus, and the Muses is perfectly consistent with his ideal of Athenian citizenship. He influenced the course of literature in Athens, not only by example, but also by precept, for it was probably he that legislated for the systematic reading of Homer at the Panathenaic festivals. In later Athenian tradition Solon assumed superhuman stature. He is one of the Seven Sages (the earliest list, as given by Plato, in *Protagoras* 343*a,* includes Thales of Miletus, Pittacus of Mytilene, Bias of Priene, Solon of Athens, Cleobulus of Lindus, Myson of Chen, and Chilon of Sparta). Plato thought (*Timaeus* 21*b*) that Solon was not only very wise in other respects, but that of the poets he was the most independent; Plato's approval doubtless had a political basis and suggests that Solon's program was essentially conservative.

Theognis of Megara is the only early poet whose work has come down in an independent manuscript tradition, but his book presents a puzzle, for among its 1,400 lines are recognizable quotations from other poets as well as verbatim repetitions of passages in the book itself. Evidently, the book grew by accretion, perhaps as a repository for gnomic wisdom, though the section dealing with pederasty seems odd for an educational work. Perhaps it is rather a song book (didactic poetry, in the Greek view, being perfectly suitable for song) embodying the code of aristocratic conduct at a period when aristocracy was threatened by rising democracy and "tyranny." It is impossible to find a rational explanation for the arrangement of the work or the limits of Theognis' own part in it. Those passages which bear the name of Cyrnus, whom the author frequently addresses, are very probably Theognis'. The views they present are consistent, and generally characteristic of the tone of the whole work, which is truculently aristocratic. In Theognis, "the good" means the aristocrats and "the bad," the lower classes. Blood and breed are paramount, and the effect of wealth in obliterating class distinctions is deplored. Why, when such care is exercised in choosing livestock for breeding, are aristocratic lines permitted to degenerate for the sake of profitable marriages? No other book in Greek literature, with the possible exception of the *Old Oligarch*, is so outspoken in class prejudice. It is of interest to note that a youthful work of Nietszche exalted Theognis above the herds of vile democracy. But despite its overtones of abuse and self-pity and its didacticism there is an earnestness of conviction, which can only be regarded as admirable in a man of his class, and a grace of expression that makes his work poetry. No offense can be taken (as offense may be taken in the case of Roman poets who borrowed the conceit) when he asserts that his song has given Cyrnus immortality (237–252):

I have given thee wings to fly with ease aloft the boundless sea and all the land. No meal or feast but thou'lt be there, couched 'twixt the lips of many a guest, and lovely youths shall sing thee clear and well in orderly wise to the clear-voiced flute. And when thou comest to go down to the lamentable house of Hades in the depths of the gloomy earth, never, albeit thou be dead, shalt thou lose thy fame, but men will think of thee as one of immortal name, Cyrnus, who rangeth the lands of Greece and the isles thereof—crossing the fishy un-harvestable deep not upon horseback mounted but sped of the glorious gifts of the violet-crowned Muses unto all that care to receive thee; and living as they shalt thou be a song unto posterity so long as earth and sun abide.

—*J. M. Edmonds*

Elegiac meter continued to be used for centuries, but chiefly for epigrams, some of which will be noticed under Simonides. Now we turn back to the seventh century for the iambic tradition, which opens with the vivid figure of Archilochus of Paros, who wrote in both forms. Elegy marked a relaxation of heroic poetry's conservatism in form and matter; the supple iambic form eliminated all constraint on vocabulary, and its matter was as revolutionary as its form. Archilochus was the bastard son of an aristocratic father and a bondwoman mother, and his poetry runs the gamut of scorn, hatred, sarcasm, resignation, and vindictiveness. His program, if it can be dignified as such, is purely one of negation, but he is the most articulate, as well as the most gifted, opponent of the aristocratic ideal. He is proud of his prowess with the spear, which wins him his bread and his wine; but he can jest at having thrown his shield away in retreat, a cardinal sin in the chivalric code. For general, he wants no well-groomed dandy but a tough little man who stands firm on his bow legs:

> Not for me the general renowned nor the well-groomed dandy,
> Nor he who is proud of his curls or is shaven in part;
> But give me a man that is small and whose legs are bandy,
> Provided he's firm on his feet and is valiant in heart.
> —*A. Watson Bain*

When Lycambes thought that Archilochus was not good enough for his daughter Neobule to marry, Archilochus so lampooned the family that they could only hang themselves. He is moved by the death of a relative at sea, but condemns excessive grief as womanish. Archilochus' importance as an innovator, in spirit as well as form, continued to be recognized, and especially by the Romans; it was doubtless the tone of his poems that gave iamb the connotation "vulgar."

The tone of Semonides of Amorgos is rather bourgeois than anti-aristocratic. He is represented chiefly by a 120-line poem comparing various types of women to such creatures as sows, vixens, bitches. Here is the sow:

> At the creation God made women's natures
> various. One he made from a bristly sow:
> and all her household welters in confusion,
> lying aground in miscellaneous muck,
> while she unwashen in unlaundered clothes
> reposes in her pigsty, fattening.
> —*Gilbert Highet*

Only the type which resembles the bee is well spoken of; she resembles the virtuous woman of *Proverbs* 31.

A complete break with the heroic tradition is marked by Hipponax of

Ephesus (sixth century B.C.), who is credited with the invention of the choliamb, or scazon, an iambic verse in which a trochee or spondee is substituted in the last foot. Hipponax' scanty fragments are enough to justify his reputation as a scurrilous, whining cynic from whom all trace of the heroic has departed. He attacks the sculptor Bupalus, apparently for making a caricature of him, he begs for a coat and shoes, he says that a woman gives her husband pleasure on only two days, the day he marries her and the day he buries her. Practically nothing is known of Hipponax' rival Ananius, one of whose very few fragments has the strange oath, "By the cabbage." With this development of iambic the Achilles ideal has vanished; Thersites has come into his own. The scazon retained its antiheroic implications; it was used in later ages by the Cynic Phoenix of Colophon and by Herodes for his *Mimes*. Catullus refined it for his own uses in Latin, and in the second century A.D. Babrius versified Aesop's fables in it.

We come now to melic poetry, and first to the solo lyric, and to the greatest poetess of whom the world has knowledge. The prodigious volume of modern comment and speculation on Sappho is in inverse ratio to the pitiful handful of her work that remains, and much of it is a completely misdirected effort to assimilate Sappho with the critics' own notions of feminine propriety. So far as they can be ascertained the facts of Sappho's life are these: She was born at Eresos on Lesbos of good family about the middle of the seventh century B.C., when a series of popular leaders was overthrowing the aristocracy. To escape the turmoils on her native island she went to Sicily, where she lived long enough for her hair to whiten, and after her death was honored with a statue which Verres stole from Syracuse five hundred years later. She was married and had a daughter named Cleis. In Lesbos, Sappho was the leader of a group of younger associates, probably formally organized into a cult thiasos. The comparison which later antiquity drew between her work and Socrates' is not without point. Some of Sappho's poems would be appropriate for occasions when one or another of her girls left the group to be married, or when they communicated with Sappho from their new homes. In any case the poems involve only women, and breathe a deep personal affection. They are altogether personal, dealing with Sappho herself and her friends and their feelings for one another. There are no speculations on life and society, but only the poetess's own experiences, and while these experiences are not broad they have unparalleled depth and intensity and delicacy. Sappho wrote the dialect she spoke, and owed nothing to a formal poetic tradition. With no trace of effort she raises what looks like ordinary speech to the highest level of melody and expressiveness.

The secret of her poems' power is in their truth. The meter is perfect, but perfectly suited to the matter. The language is simple, with no meretricious adornment. There can be no suspicion that these poems are other than they seem to be, the perfect and perfectly sincere utterance of an exquisite soul. The only certainly complete poem is the first in our collection, preserved by Dionysius of Halicarnassus:

Aphrodite splendor-throned immortal, wile-weaving child of Zeus, I pray you:
Do not overwhelm my heart, Lady, with suffering and sorrow,
but come here, pray, if before this you have heard my voice and marked my cry, and stepping from your father's golden house you came,
harnessing your chariot, and fair swift sparrows brought you to dark earth, whirring their strong wings, from heaven through middle air;
swiftly they came, and you, Blessed One, with a smile on that immortal face, asked me what ailed me, and why I called,
and what I specially wished in my troubled heart to be brought about, and "Whom shall I persuade and bring to your love; who is it, Sappho, that wrongs you?
Even if she flees, she shall soon pursue, if she does not accept gifts she shall give them, and if she does not love, she shall soon love, even if she wills it not."
Come to me now again, release me from sore trouble, fulfil what my heart desires fulfilled; yourself be my ally.

The power of this invocation derives from the obvious but highly un-common circumstance that Aphrodite is here not a poetic conceit but a present deity to whom, as to her special patroness, Sappho offers sincere and confident prayer. She has no doubt that in a previous crisis Aphrodite came to her assistance with power and grace, and she envisages the benison of that visit and petitions for another. If the agitation of modern critics on the question of Sappho's morality is to be noticed at all, this poem would seem sufficient demonstration of an utterly pure spirit, at once childlike and intense.

Plato himself is credited with an epigram (*Greek Anthology* 9.506) suggesting that Sappho be added to the canon of nine Muses. Others sug-gested, without hyperbole, that the Boeotian poetess Corinna be added to the canon of nine lyric poets. Corinna, like her countrywoman Myrtis, was an elder rival, perhaps a teacher of Pindar. This circumstance and the fragments (slightly augmented by papyri) indicate that Corinna dealt with mythological themes. Other poetesses of the early period who are known by name or reputation are Telesilla of Argos, who armed the women of Argos and turned back a Spartan attack; Praxilla of Sicyon, who celebrated Dionysus; and a certain Clitagora, whose songs are men-tioned in a fragment of the comic poet Cratinus.

Roughly contemporary with Sappho and like her a native of Lesbos was Alcaeus, the model of the fighting, loving, drinking, but withal sensitive and patriotic poet. A typical drinking song begins:

> Zeus rains; a storm comes in its might
> From heav'n, and freezes rivers tight . . .
> Put down the storm! Pile up the fire,
> Mix the sweet wine to your desire,
> And round your forehead set
> A dainty coronet.
> —*C. M. Bowra*

In another, Alcaeus refuses to wait for lamplighting time to begin his potations. And the fighting man's joy in good weapons is gloriously expressed in the praise of an armory:

> Splendid burns the huge house with bronze; rich is the ample roof
> with radiant helmets; overhead each helmet lets a horsehair plume
> droop, the warrior's ornament. Plates of armour hang on the pin,
> greaves of radiant bronze, defense against the sturdy javelin.
> Curved shields and cuirasses of new linen bestrew the room;
> here are blades from Chalcis; here is many a cincture and kilt of proof.
> These are things we must remember now our duty shall begin.
> —*Gilbert Highet*

Horace, who had much more of Alcaeus to read than we and was much influenced by him, even borrowing his characteristic meter, says of him (*Odes* 1.32.5 ff.) that he was fierce in battle but that even in war and when saved from shipwreck he sang of Bacchus, the Muses, Venus, Venus' lad Cupid, and a certain fair boy named Lycus. But Horace's summary seems to stress the roisterer disproportionately. The figure of the ship of state which Horace uses comes from Alcaeus (along with the Alcaic meter), and Alcaeus' political fragments fit into the course of the turbulent civil disorders in Lesbos. His view is at once aristocratic and individual; his chief objection to the popular leaders Melanchrus, Myrsilus, and then Pittacus (who had helped overthrow the others, and was subsequently counted one of the Seven Sages) is their low birth. Alcaeus has not the quiet strength of Sappho; he raises his voice in anger or exultation, he is impulsive and temperamental. But like Sappho he raises ordinary speech, effortlessly, to perfect expression and achieves the perfect harmony of substance and form.

Of Ionia, Herodotus (1.142) says that its air and climate are the most beautiful in the whole world and that no other region is so blessed. In culture Ionia had reached its zenith long before peninsular Greece, and it was already in decline before it was subdued by the Persians, whose defeat caused the rapid rise of Athens. In the departments where they excelled no other Greeks surpassed them. One was in hard speculative thought, in which the so-called Ionian "physicists" were supreme. The other was in elegant and luxurious living, which the Ionians elevated to an art. Because Ionian voluptuousness was natural and not reaction against the constraints of puritanism it was never truculent or offensive. Anacreon of Teos (born approximately 572 B.C.) is a true representative of Ionia. His fragments show a graceful and urbane poet who celebrates wine, women, and song with as much sincerity as Sappho celebrated Aphrodite, though of course without Sappho's intensity, and with no sense that indulgence constituted a lark for which Nemesis would inflict a hangover. A new note in Anacreon, and his special quality, is wit; his emotions are not the less real because he deals with them urbanely, but he has a civilized readiness to laugh at himself. In lines like "again I am in love and not in love, am mad and not mad" (#79) he stands outside himself and looks on at the spectacle with amusement. Capacity for detachment from self and the novel combination of lyric and wit is illustrated in a piece made familiar by its Horatian adaptation (#88):

Thracian filly, why do you look askance at me with your eyes and cruelly fly me and think that I have no sense? Know that I could nicely put a bridle on you and hold the reins and turn you about the limits of the course. But now you graze over the meadows and skip lightly in your play; for you have no skilled horseman to mount you.

—C. M. Bowra

A number of his pieces express his distaste of the frailties of old age and look back wistfully on a hearty youth. Such is the poem (#44) beginning, "My temples are already hoary and my head is white. No longer is graceful youth with me, and my teeth are old." Such pieces are the basis of the caricature of Anacreon as a bibulous old lecher which appears in a number of epigrams in the *Anthology*. In fact, Anacreon was a serious poet, dealing maturely with an important if circumscribed sphere of human experience. Anacreon's note is so distinctive that his name has been associated with his kind of poetry throughout antiquity and in modern times. In modern times his reputation has been based on a group of sixty short poems, called *Anacreontics,* which were appended to Cephalas' anthology. Some of these are very charming, but the collection cannot be older than the Hellenistic age, and the bad Greek and bad versification of some suggest authorship late in the Byzantine period.

Choral lyric seems a peculiarly appropriate art form for a beauty-loving people who demanded full participation in a society governed by law. A visible manifestation of a similar mutually sustaining harmony is the

Doric temple, and it is interesting that choral lyric was shaped by the Dorians (being, indeed, the only literary form in which they pioneered) and always retained certain Doric linguistic peculiarities. But though the institution was first given official recognition in Sparta, its great masters, Stesichorus, Simonides, Pindar, Bacchylides, to say nothing of the Attic tragedians, were from other parts of Greece, and Terpander and Alcman, who instituted choral lyric in Sparta, were newcomers there. "If ever the Spartans required the aid of the Muses," says Aelian (12.50), "their custom was to send for foreigners. For instance they summoned Terpander, Thales [or Thaletas, the Cretan poet], Tyrtaeus, Nymphaeus of Cydonia, and Alcman." Plutarch's systematic treatise *On Music* says (1134*a*) that "the first establishment of music at Sparta was due to Terpander."

Though we have certain statements regarding Terpander's musical career his actual remains amount only to seven lines. Alcman is in better case, for besides the usual snippets we have about a hundred continuous lines in a papyrus brought to Paris in 1855 by Mariette. This fragment constitutes the greater part of a *partheneion,* or chorus for girls. It opens with a conventional myth of Heracles, suitable for Sparta whose royal line he founded, and then proceeds to banter between two groups of the girls, Hagesichora and Agido comparing themselves and their rivals to cows or race horses and the like. The tone is of a family party rather than a public festival, for which the poem must have been composed. Alcman's fragments give the impression of an old and amiable grumbler. In one he is concerned with a dish of pease porridge, and in another he wishes he were a halcyon—because the female of that species was supposed to carry the decrepit male pick-a-back.

Of the successors of Alcman who are only names mention must be made of Arion, if only because of Herodotus' story (1.23–24) of his rescue by a dolphin and his invention (more properly formalization) of the dithyramb, the choral song to Dionysus. A figure of first-class importance in Greek literature is Stesichorus of Himera in Sicily, in the beginning of the sixth century. Data on his life are so confused and the range and volume (twenty-six books) of his work so great that it has been suggested there were two men by the same name; the name itself is really a title, signifying "arranger of choruses." His principal contribution was to give new relevance and new life to the mass of legend in the heroic epos, and so to make it available to the tragedians. Quintilian spoke of him as *epici carminis onera lyra sustinentem* ("sustaining the burden of epic poetry with his lyre"). In his hands the stark stories of the heroes acquired meaning for ordinary humanity; he was apparently the first, for example, to see the tragic implications in the passion of love. The titles of his works (his poems seem the first to have been given names, like those of Greek tragedies) cover almost the entire range dealt with in tragedy, in particular stories growing out of the Trojan War, such as the murder of Agamemnon and the vengeance of Orestes. When he wrote a poem that was disrespectful to Helen (whom western Dorians regarded as a goddess) she blinded him; he then wrote a *Palinode* or recantation, declaring that Helen had not gone to Troy but had spent the war years in Egypt (a version followed by Herodotus 2.113–120 and used by Euripides in *Helen*), whereupon his sight was restored to him. His *Daphnis* told of a shepherd who was loved by a nymph and blinded because he was unfaithful; it is interesting that so early an example of the amatory shepherd derives from Sicily.

Ibycus of Rhegium, in southern Italy, is most familiar because of his association with the legend of the cranes, celebrated in Schiller's poem. He belonged to a ruling family in southern Italy, and we are told that he was offered and refused the dictatorship. Of his poetry little was known until an anonymous Oxyrhynchus papyrus of the first century B.C. was declared to be his by the unanimous judgment of competent scholars. This piece, whose technical interest is that it shows the rudimentary triadic structure perfected by Pindar, hymns the praise of the young Polycrates, tyrant dictator of Samos, in ornate and sensual language, using the Greek expedition to Troy as a vehicle. Ibycus' other considerable fragments include poetic addresses to love and to the spring as the harbinger of love. In erotic and in praise of nature Ibycus strikes a new note. His treatment of heroic saga seems to have been after the manner of Stesichorus, and he too contributed to the stock used by the tragedians.

His couplet on the heroes of Thermopylae has made Simonides known, if only through Cicero's version, to every literate European since his own day. Besides

> Tell them in Lacedaemon, passer-by,
> That here obedient to their word we lie

Herodotus (7.228) gives another of Simonides' epigrams, and additional ones are derived from other sources. At the time of Thermopylae Simonides was already an old man, having been born (in Ceos) in 557, and he already enjoyed a great reputation as a poet and had received many lucrative commissions to compose occasional pieces. He is, indeed, the first substantial figure known to us who prospered materially by his poetry. Cultivated men in the centuries following assumed familiarity with Simonides as with no other poet; in Plato's *Protagoras* Socrates uses the poem beginning

> Hard it is wholly to win worthy manhood,
> With hand and foot and heart alike to be foursquare

to arrive at a definition of virtue. This poem, of which twenty-one lines are extant, was part of an epinician ode for Scopas son of Creon, tyrant in Thessaly; it is to be noted that Pindar, the great master of epinicia, has nothing so thoughtful as this poem, nor indeed so gay and festive as other fragments of Simonides show him to be. Besides his mature thoughtfulness and gaiety Simonides is master of pathos (as may be seen in the *Danae* fragment) and of sensual representation. Plutarch (*On the Glory of the Athenians* 3) credits him with the dictum: "Painting is silent poetry, and poetry painting that speaks." Besides epigrams and epinicia Simonides wrote all other forms for which there was a demand, especially dirges and encomia. Among his hundred or so fragments several are long enough to give a fair idea of Greek lyric at its best. The nine lines on the Greek dead at Thermopylae reach as high nobility as patriotic poetry is capable of:

Of those who died at Thermopylae glorious is the fate and fair the doom; their grave is an altar; instead of lamentation they have endless fame; their dirge is a chant of praise. Such winding-sheet as theirs neither rust nor all-conquering time shall bring to nought. But this sepulcher of brave men hath taken for its habitant the glory of Hellas. Leonidas is witness, Sparta's king, who hath left a mighty crown of valor and undying fame.

Equally supreme of its kind is the fragment of a dirge that depicts Danae afloat upon the waves at night:

> When, in the carven chest,
> The winds that blew and waves in wild unrest
> Smote her with fear, she, not with cheeks unwet,
> Her arms of love round Perseus set,
>   And said: O child, what grief is mine!
> But thou dost slumber, and thy baby breast
> Is sunk in rest,
> Here in the cheerless brass-bound bark,
> Tossed amid starless night and pitchy dark.
>   Nor dost thou heed the scudding brine
> Of waves that wash above thy curls so deep,
> Nor the shrill winds that sweep—
> Lapped in thy purple robe's embrace,
> Fair little face!
> But if this dread were dreadful too to thee,
> Then wouldst thou lend thy listening ear to me;
> Therefore I cry: Sleep babe, and sea be still,
> And slumber our unmeasured ill!
>   Oh, may some change of fate, sire Zeus, from thee
> Descend, our woes to end!
> But if this prayer, too overbold, offend
> Thy justice, yet be merciful to me!
>   —*J. A. Symonds*

If sheer devotion to beauty, free from the tyranny of the subject, may
be credited to any of our authors, Pindar is that author. If there is similar
detachment from current problems and consequently similar timelessness in Sophocles, yet the problems of man and fate in Sophocles are so
perennial as to have permanent relevance. But the subject matter of the
Pindar we have is trivial—victories in boxing and mule racing and other
athletic contests—and to us, therefore, Pindar's achievement is in the realm
of pure art.

Pindar was devoted to beauty, but for him beauty must be associated with
brilliance and solidity, which could be fostered only by a hereditary aristocracy. Blood and breed alone give distinction to men and bloom to civilization. Agile and probing wits are as suspect as they are disturbing. Pindar
was born at Cynoscephalai at the gates of Thebes in 520 B.C., and his maturity therefore fell in the stirring times of the Persian wars. But Thebes
Medized, that is to say, collaborated with the invader; Pindar never realized
the implications of the invasion nor the magnitude of Athens' service in
repelling the Mede. It is significant that when, a century and a half later,
Alexander the Great, another invader who stoutly believed in the prerogatives of birth, destroyed Thebes he took special pains to spare the house
of Pindar. Rightly or wrongly, later antiquity credited Pindar with encouraging Medizing. Polybius, who wrote two centuries after Alexander
and was himself hostile to democracy, remarks (4.31.5):

That war is a terrible thing I agree, but it is not so terrible that we should sub-
mit to anything in order to avoid it. For why do we all vaunt our civic equality
and liberty of speech and all that we mean by the word freedom, if nothing is
more advantageous than peace? We do not indeed praise the Thebans because
at the time of the Persian invasion they deserted Greece in the hour of peril and
took the side of the Persians from fear, nor do we praise Pindar for confirming
them in their resolution to remain inactive.

                                                          —W. R. Paton

Polybius errs in citing lines of Pindar which refer in fact to civic strife
rather than foreign war, but on Pindar's attitude he is surely right. Pindar
distrusted democracy and was suspicious of the new ideas, social and
philosophical, to which democracy gave rise. Pindar did write in praise of
Athens, notably the famous "Oh, the gleaming and the violet crowned and
the sung in story, the bulwark of Hellas, famous Athens, city divine!" In
the parabasis of *Acharnians* (636 ff.) Aristophanes remarks how susceptible
the Athenians were to praise of this sort, noting that "gleaming" was in
fact an epithet more appropriate to sardines. For his eulogy the Athenians
rewarded Pindar richly, and his native Thebes fined him. The incident
only proves that devotion to beauty can be indifferent to politics; it does

not alter Pindar's rooted conviction that capacity for beauty, like prowess in the games, is the hereditary prerogative of the aristocracy. It is hard to realize that Pindar was actually younger than Aeschylus and surely saw his plays, so different are the intellectual climates of the two men.

The main fact in the life of Pindar is his association with the princely houses, especially of Aegina, Syracuse, and Cyrene, from which he received commissions for poems. *Pythia* 5.72 ff. says: "Mine it is to sing of the dear glory that cometh from Sparta, whence sprang the Aigeidai, my own forefathers." It is doubtful in the context whether these lines are to be attributed to the chorus or the poet; but if he did not claim Dorian descent, his sympathies were clearly with the Dorians. He was proud of his Theban birth and training (*frg.* 198). At Thebes, where that instrument was perfected, he learned the flute from his uncle Scopelinus. He studied the technique of lyric composition at Athens with Agathocles and Apollodorus, and probably also with Lasus of Hermione, who is credited with bringing the dithyramb to its highest perfection. Still in his teens, Pindar returned to Thebes to practice the career of poet. His earliest effort is said to have neglected the use of myth, and the omission was pointed out by the Boeotian poetess Corinna, fellow pupil or teacher of Pindar. He then crowded his next poem with myths, and was admonished by Corinna "to sow with the hand, not with the sack." A fragment of Corinna (#21) reproaches the poetess Myrtis for competing with Pindar, by whom she was defeated.

In pursuing his career of poet Pindar composed all the various forms which were customarily commissioned. The *Life* in the Ambrosian manuscript lists seventeen books of his poems: one each of *hymns* and *paeans,* two each of *dithyrambs, prosodia* (processional songs), and *parthenia,* another of *parthenia,* two of *hyporchemata* (dance songs), one each of *encomia* and *dirges,* and four *epinicia.* The order is from works celebrating gods to those celebrating men. In the epinicia the order follows the foundation dates of the four festivals: *Olympia* (776 B.C.), *Pythia* (582 B.C.), *Isthmia* (581 B.C.), and *Nemea* (573 B.C.). At the end (*Nemea* 9, 10, 11) are three odes connected with Sicyon, Argos, and Tenedos. Within each book of epinicia the order of odes is horse or chariot races, boxing or wrestling, running. Only the epinicia have come down in ordinary manuscript tradition. The usual meager stock of fragments of the remainder was greatly augmented at the beginning of the present century by papyri finds, none of which, however, contained a complete work. They do contain enough to show that a greater amount would not change a judgment of Pindar based upon the forty-four epinician odes we have complete. The epinicia appear to have been Pindar's favorite form, and even in antiquity his reputation was based upon them.

Much greater religious and patriotic significance attached to the Greek festivals than to any athletic meets in modern times. They were pan-Hellenic in character, and all Greeks whether from the motherland or the colonies were welcomed; on the other hand, all non-Greeks were excluded. For the duration of the festival a sacred truce was proclaimed. The Olympian and Pythian festivals each fell at intervals of four years, the Pythian always falling in the third year of the Olympiad. From 220 to 216 B.C. (for which specific details are available), and probably from the beginning, each Olympian and Pythian festival was followed by a Nemean and Isthmian festival. All fell in the summer. The four festivals together formed a *periodos* or circuit, and a victor in all the festivals is described as a *periodonikes*. In horse and chariot races, not the jockey or driver, but the owner was regarded as victor. The prizes were wreaths, respectively of wild olive, bay, dry celery, and fresh celery.

The glory won by a victor in the games was greater than that bestowed today upon a movie star or champion athlete or Nobel prizeman. Upon his return from the games the victor was received with great ceremony by his townsmen, the walls being breached for his entry; he remained an important personage in the community, and dined at the town hall at public expense. At his first reception a traditional "Hail the conquering hero comes" was sung; subsequently, a chorus performed a lyric which a professional poet had composed for the occasion. Even by Pindar's day philosophers like Xenophanes objected to the excessive honors paid to athletic prowess, especially when exhibited vicariously by a horse, and Euripides echoed these sentiments. But there was something glorious and Greek, something at which a barbarian would be utterly puzzled, in undergoing long toil and expense (Pindar's *ponos* and *dapane*) for the sake of a prize of a few leaves. When Alcibiades' aristocratic extravagances were thrown up to him he judged (rightly) that he could sway the democrats in the Athenian ecclesia to give him the command against Syracuse by boasting of the glory he had brought Athens by entering seven chariots at Olympia (Thucydides 6.16). The possibility of political abuse was one of the arguments against glorifying athletic victors; it is to be noticed that Pindar's patrons are mostly "tyrants." It is easy to see that such a man as Pindar would regard the games as the culminating splendor of civilization and would give his wholehearted best to glorifying them in the odes he was commissioned to write.

That best is very great. Majestic and radiant language intertwined in exquisite rhythms are built up into magnificent architectural structures. The onlooker with limited sympathy is very greatly impressed; those whose full sympathy allowed participation must have been deeply stirred.

The pattern of the odes is fairly but not absolutely regular. Certain elements had to be included—the name of the victor, including mention of members of his family (which may have been stipulated in the contract); the place and the appropriate deity; more or less relevant episodes from heroic legend; and such other matter as may have been desired by the patron or suggested by the poet's fancy. Such an arrangement seems inevitable, and not much help is given by the traditional divisions, to which, indeed, many of the odes cannot be made to conform. These are prelude (*proimion*), beginning (*arche*), first transition (*katatrope*), center (*omphalos*), second transition (*metakatatrope*), conclusion (*exodion*), and seal (*sphragis*).

The openings are regularly imposing and elaborate. Some fact or reflection given expression in the opening makes the transition to the myth, which may be brief or of almost epic proportions, as the story of Jason in *Pythia* 4. The conclusions are frequently abrupt to the point of awkwardness. Progress is made, not by a steadily moving picture, but by a series of leaps, contrasting rather than chronological, from picture to picture and from peak to peak. Pindar's language is soaring, dazzling, drenched in color. The logic which unifies the disparate elements in a poem is not reason, but aesthetic emotion. He perceives some symbol about which the various factors can crystallize, and all are then seen in terms of this symbol, which may then attract new images. Where communication rests on combinations of overtones made meaningful by exquisite elaboration of form, translation is helpless. Pindar is proof that pure lyric is essentially untranslatable, yet some notion of his manner may be conveyed by a line-for-line version of the opening of the First Olympian:

> Best of all things is water; but gold, like a gleaming fire
> by night, outshines all pride of wealth beside.
> But, my heart, would you chant the glory of games,
> look never beyond the sun
> by day for any star shining brighter through the deserted air,
> nor any contest than Olympia greater to sing.
> It is thence that the song winds strands
> in the hearts of the skilled to celebrate
> the son of Kronos. They come their ways
> to the magnificent board of Hieron,
>
> who handles the scepter of dooms in Sicily, rich in flocks,
> reaping the crested heads of every excellence.
>   —*Richmond Lattimore*

It is to be expected that a man of Pindar's conservative temper would be religious, and his attitude is indeed one of reverence. Each of the odes is filled with present deities, and in *Olympia* 1 he specifically rejects a version of a myth which attributed cannibalism to the gods. Yet it is a mistake to regard Pindar as an original religious thinker. From Hesiod onward sober Greeks were refining the myths, and Pindar's ethics, like his theology, conform to the contemporary norm. *Olbos, koros, hybris, ate* retain their traditional succession: the prosperity that produces satiety culminates in insolence and brings upon itself mischief. The one spiritual concept for the expression of which Pindar must be given priority is of the divine origin and destiny of the soul. In a dirge (*frg.* 96) he says: "While the body of all men is subject to overmastering death, the image of life remains alive, for it alone comes from the gods."

Pindar had strong conviction of his divine mission as a bard; we have the usual story of the gods dropping honey upon his lips while he slept as an infant. His consciousness of his own dignity as artist kept his relations with the grandees who were his patrons on a footing of equality. Frequently in the poems he speaks of his work in his own person. He obviously regarded the glory of his own achievement as equal to that of the athletes he celebrated. The task which the Muses have given him he calls (*Paean 7b*) immortal. This conviction of the poet's own immortality, of becoming, in a word, a classic, though held by Theognis, is in Pindar a new thing. It was eagerly seized upon, especially by the Romans, and is the unmistakable ancestor of such things as the Horatian *non omnis moriar* and *exegi monumentum aere perennius* and of claims to bestow immortality upon those whom the poet deigns to name.

Pindar's recognition as a classic came long before the Alexandrian critics put him at the head of their canon of nine lyric poets. So rapidly did his world change that after him and his journeyman rival, Bacchylides, the genre fell into virtual desuetude, and there was no occasion for ideological opposition to depreciate his work. Pindar was especially admired by the Romans. Horace (*Odes* 4.2) calls him inimitable and speaks of his sweeping force and his variety. Quintilian (10.1.61) echoes and confirms Horace and calls Pindar *novem lyricorum longe princeps*. Humanists valued Pindar for his ethical content. In his translation of the poet (A.D. 1558) Melanchthon quotes, but with protest, Politian's judgment that Pindar deals with the same subjects as *Psalms* but with greater sweetness and more brilliant examples. Later, and before Pindar's prosody was understood, the apparently anarchical form of his torrential utterances attracted Ronsard and a host of followers to write "Pindaric odes," which eventually elicited from Voltaire a scornful reference to *galimatias pindarique*. Pindar's area of tangency with contemporary interests is less than that of any other Greek classic, and this combined with the real difficulties of language, meter, and allusiveness make him the least read (if not the least discussed) of the classic Greeks, as he is the most difficult to present in translation. But in the art of pure poetry he remains pre-eminent, and it is from the aesthetic point of view that he must be approached by modern critics.

The poet of the lyric nine who was Pindar's closest competitor for commissions was Bacchylides, nephew and protégé of Simonides, born some dozen years earlier than Pindar and, like Simonides, on the island of Ceos. Until the discovery in 1896 of a papyrus containing thirteen epinicia and six dithyrambs by this poet he was the least known of the nine. The new poems prove Bacchylides a poet, indeed, but prove more abundantly how much greater a poet was Pindar. The first-rate critic who wrote the treatise *On the Sublime* ascribed to "Longinus" compares the two as follows (33.5):

In lyric poetry would you prefer to be Bacchylides rather than Pindar? And in tragedy Ion of Chios rather than Sophocles? It is true that Bacchylides and Ion are faultless and entirely elegant writers of the polished school, while Pindar and Sophocles, although at times they burn everything before them as it were in their swift career, are often extinguished unaccountably and fail most lamentably. But would anyone in his senses regard all the compositions of Ion put together as an equivalent for the single play of the *Oedipus*?

—*Rhys Roberts*

Modern criticism must agree with "Longinus." Comparison is easy, for the scope and manner of Bacchylides are roughly the same as Pindar's. Bacchylides is smooth and correct and builds with deftness, but the power is gone. One feels that he is well trained and follows the rules, but far inferior to his originating master; a student fresh from the difficulties of Pindar almost resents the ease with which he reads Bacchylides. Bacchylides learned from Simonides, and it was doubtless the direct influence of the veteran Simonides that procured his nephew assignments at the Syracusan court over Pindar. It is almost certain that Pindar is comparing himself to Simonides and Bacchylides when he says (*Olympia* 2.86 ff.): "The true poet is he who knoweth much by gift of nature, but they that have only learnt the lore of song, and are turbulent and intemperate of tongue, like a pair of crows, chatter in vain against the god-like bird of Zeus." Bacchylides, on the other hand, makes no claim to be an eagle but calls himself (3.98) the nightingale of Ceos. Bacchylides uses as many epithets as Pindar, but unlike Pindar's they are expected, like a conventional rhyme, and do not startle; and there is more about flowers and more women. The stories too are told chronologically and are not splinters from a blazing symbol. Bacchylides' fifth ode, with its finely imagined ghosts in Hades, is perhaps the best specimen of his work.

The poems labeled "dithyrambs" are puzzling, for in style they differ little from the epinicia, showing none of the extravagance of language and meter associated with that form and practically ignoring the god Dionysus whom the dithyramb was supposed to honor. It may be that by the fifth century the dithyramb, like tragedy, which also originated as worship of Dionysus, had given up any perceptible relationship to that god; the expression, "What has this to do with Dionysus?" became a common way of characterizing irrelevance.

Pindar's latest work is dated to the middle of the fifth century B.C. Bacchylides, if a statement in Eusebius is correct and correctly interpreted, was "well known" in 431. The new masters embedded their choral lyrics in tragedies, and those who would instruct or edify or titillate wrote prose philosophy or history or oratory. Aside from the dramatic poets the only poet before the Alexandrian age of whom we have considerable remains is Timotheus of Miletus (end of fifth and early fourth century B.C.) of whose *Persae* 253 continuous lines were found in 1902. This was a *nome,* or solo composition to be performed to musical accompaniment, extravagant in language and meter. A drowning Persian addresses the sea as follows:

"Bold as thou art, ere now thou hast had thy boisterous throat bound fast in hempen bonds [alluding to the bridge over the Hellespont]; and now my king —aye mine—will plow thee with hill-born pines, and will encompass thy navigable plains with his far-roaming rays. O thou frenzied thing, hated from of old, who treacherously embraces me, while the breeze sweeps over thy surge!" So spake he, panting with strangled breath, as he spat forth the grim sea-dew, belching from his mouth the brine of the deep.

—*R. C. Jebb*

If this turgidity is a fair sample of what was being produced it is little wonder that poetry went into retirement. Now we shall glance briefly at the beginnings of prose before turning to tragedy.

Chapter 7. PROSE BEGINNINGS: THE RISE OF ATHENS

THE RELATIVELY LATE INTRODUCTION OF PROSE FOR LITERARY EXPRESSION IS not a phenomenon peculiar to Greece. It is self-evident that prose must have been used from the earliest times, not only for daily intercourse, but also for priestly or other records, whether written or, as the various words for "recorder" suggest, memorized. Our earliest datable Greek writing is a prose inscription carved by Psammetichus II's Greek mercenaries in 589 B.C. upon the legs of the colossus at Abu Simbel in Nubia. Poetry normally has priority, because its patterns facilitate memorization and because it is patently artistic; it is more difficult to give prose the requisite differentiation from ordinary speech. Prose came to be used for literature, not only because of sophistication in the use of language and ready availability of a practicable writing material, but also as a result of certain historical factors.

In the sixth century B.C. the Ionians, who were in the van of Greek civilization, were absorbed in the Persian Empire, either directly or through previous subjugation by Lydia. Thus while Athens was making national heroes of great figures from Solon to Miltiades the Ionians could only look to the remote past for their heroes, and their appreciation of epic was therefore of a different quality than Athens'. Herodotus declares that his purpose is to preserve the memory of great deeds of the past—what Homeric bards called *klea andron*. His first sentence is: "These are the researches of Herodotus of Halicarnassus, which he sets forth to preserve what men have done from oblivion and to prevent the great and wonderful achievements of Greeks and Barbarians from losing their due meed of glory." Epic, of which national pride is the lifeblood, could not survive in a subject people. Writers of epic migrated to free Greece, poets who remained turned to subjective lyric, and where conditions permitted and their interest was political such poets as Alcaeus bitterly castigated tyranny. History, then, was looked to for the kind of record of the past which epic had provided, and compilers of the Alexandrian and later periods cite Homer and the chroniclers indifferently for early history and geography.

Possibly because there could be no political objection to a transcript of official records, early chronicles were sometimes called "Annals" (*Horoi*, an old Greek word for years). The foundation or colonization of cities must have been dealt with in such works as Cadmus' *Ktisis Miletou*, Ion of Chios' *Khious Ktisis*, or Hellanicus' *Peri Khiou Ktiseos*. Such works as *Aeolica, Persica, Aegyptiaca, Scythica*, all attributed to Hellanicus, dealt with particular peoples. Many dealt with mythical subjects. There being two sources of information, legend and official records, it would be a writer's object to present as interesting a story as he could without too much violence to recorded fact. Such titles as Hellanicus' *Phoronis, Deucalionea, Asopis, Troica*, and others suggest an epic content.

The *locus classicus* for these historians is the fifth chapter of Dionysius of Halicarnassus' essay on Thucydides:

Before I begin to discuss the work of Thucydides I want to say a few words about the other historians, his predecessors and contemporaries, which will throw light on the method of the man, thanks to which he was able to excel those who went before him, and his genius. Now of earlier historians before the Peloponnesian War there were a great number in a great many different places; among them may be mentioned Eugeon of Samos, Deiochus of Proconessus, Eudemus of Paros, Democles of Phigalia, Hecataeus of Miletus, the Argive Acusilaus, Charon of Lampsacus, and Amelesagoras from Chalcedon; and among those who go back a little way before the Peloponnesian War and extend down to the age of Thucydides, Hellanicus of Lesbos, Damastes of Sigeum, Xenomedes of Ceos, Xanthus the Lydian, and numerous others. These men all adopted a similar method as regards the choice of themes and in talents did not differ very widely from one another, some of them writing Hellenic histories (as they called them), others barbarian histories; but instead of coördinating their accounts with each other, they treated of individual peoples and cities separately and brought out separate accounts of them; they all had the one same object, to bring to the general knowledge of the public the written records that they found preserved in temples or in secular buildings in the form in which they found them, neither adding nor taking away anything; among these records were to be followed legends hallowed by the passage of time and melodramatic adventure stories, which to the modern reader seem very naïve indeed; the language which they used was for the most part similar (as many of them adopted the same dialect of Greek), clear, simple, unaffected, and concise, appropriate to the subject-matter, and not revealing any elaborate art in composition; there is nevertheless a certain charm and grace which runs through their writings, to a greater degree in some than in others, thanks to which their works still survive.

—Lionel Pearson

It is singular that Athenian writers of the fifth and fourth centuries are silent about these writers and that knowledge of them seems to date only from the Alexandrian age. But it is not necessary to suspect, as some scholars have done, that Alexandria produced forgeries to associate with ancient names. The Ionian historians never made their way to Athens because they could not compete with Athenian dramatists, philosophers, and poets and with the histories of Thucydides and of Herodotus who made Athens his home. The Ionian historians therefore came to Alexandria directly, not through the medium of Athens. It is from the Alexandrians and their successors that our fragments derive. Herodotus surely made free use of his predecessors, especially of Hecataeus; he mentions him four times, always to criticize him, and it is a safe assumption, in view of the known literary usage of the historians, that he used him in many places where he does not mention his name.

Because of Herodotus' testimony Hecataeus is a clearer figure than the others in Dionysius' list. Two works are ascribed to him, *Genealogiae* (otherwise referred to as *Herologia* or *Historiai*) and *Periegesis* or *Periodos ges*. The latter, one among a number of travel books, was a geographic and ethnographic guide to the countries around the Mediterranean and was accompanied by a map. Herodotus certainly used this book, though it is apparently Hecataeus whom he has in mind when he scornfully says (4.36):

I cannot but laugh when I see numbers of persons drawing maps of the world without having any reason to guide them; making, as they do, the ocean-stream to run all round the earth, and the earth itself to be an exact circle, as if described by a pair of compasses, with Europe and Asia just of the same size.

Besides Hecataeus the important figures in the Ionian school are Xanthus the Lydian, Charon of Lampsacus, and Hellanicus of Lesbos, who was most prolific. The scant fragments of all are in the Ionic dialect, and deal chiefly with mythological matters. This is as might be expected. As historians they were superseded, partly by Herodotus, more so by Thucydides, and entirely by the fourth-century writers of universal history such as Ephorus and Theopompus. They were quoted for mythological lore, in which the fifth and fourth centuries were little interested, by Alexandrians, who were antiquarians rather than historians or literary men.

These writers, and others too, made large use of the great body of unwritten popular literature which was surely current in Ionia from the earliest times. Among the authors we have, freest use of stories and fables is apparent in Herodotus, though Hesiod's apologue of the hawk and the nightingale (*Works and Days* 202 ff.), Solon's use of the fox to exemplify cunning (*frg.* 11), and Archilochus' *ainos* (the Ionian word for fable) of a fox and an ape (*frg.* 86, cf. 89) show that these beast fables were known and used earlier. Herodotus himself (2.134) mentions "Aesop the fable writer" as a fellow slave of the courtesan Rhodopis, contemporary with Croesus. Aesop became, as Julian (7.269) later called him, "the Homer or Thucydides or Plato of fables." Aristophanes cites him (*Peace* 127), and Socrates awaiting execution obeyed a divine behest to write poetry by versifying fables of Aesop (*Phaedo* 61*b*). It is exceptional that a fable is mentioned without Aesop's name being attached to it. There must surely have been a *Life of Aesop* and a collection of his fables in the fifth century, but it was inevitable that both should have been constantly altered. How tenuous is their connection with Aesop was shown by Richard Bentley in an appendix to his *Dissertation upon the Epistles of Phalaris* (published in 1699). Phaedrus, a freedman of Augustus, wrote five books of "Aesop's fables" in Latin verse, and some two centuries later Babrius used an Aesopic collection as the basis for his much-quoted *Mythiambics*. The Byzantines made several recensions of the *Aesopea,* and they have thoroughly penetrated European literature. The fables constitute the one genre in which the Greeks seem to have acted as intermediaries between the ancient East and ourselves. It is worth noticing that the Ionians who fashioned the purely intellectual structures which will be mentioned in the following paragraphs also hold primacy in the more earth-bound exercise of the intellect involved in the manipulation of fabliaux.

Ionia's greatest contribution to Greece, and the world, was its rational philosophy. The gift was the more important because it was a timely antidote to the Orphism which had grown apace in the West. It was Ionian reason, culminating in metaphysics, which rescued Greece from a religion interpreted by priests and ensured free political and social progress. It is to the Ionian physicists, as much as to any single factor, that we owe the free and uncompromising spirit of inquiry which is the hallmark of Greek civilization. What might have taken its place is suggested by the cosmology of Cosmas Indicopleustes (cited at the end of Ch. 16), developed after the Ionian impulse had spent its force. Popular stories of Thales, first in the Ionian succession, suggest a speculator in olive oil rather than on the nature of the universe, but he must have been the latter, for Aristotle credits him with the theory that the universe is composed of water. Anaximander's book, extant in Theophrastus' day, may well have been the first in Greek prose. In Anaximander's view the world is a series of opposites, "separated out" of an as yet undifferentiated mass; since that is spatially boundless, it is natural to assume that other worlds than ours arise in it also. Anaximander held that all life came from the sea, and that the present forms of animals were an adaptation to a fresh environment. Anaximenes, who also wrote a book, thought of the world as breathing air from the boundless mass outside it, and spoke of this air as a god. Heraclitus of Ephesus (about 540 to 480 B.C.), justly called the Obscure, is the first of these thinkers whose personality we can sense. He had a haughty contempt for the crowd (*frg.* 114): "The Ephesians would do well to hang themselves, every grown man of them, and leave the city to beardless lads; for they have cast out Hermodorus, the best man among them, saying, 'We will have none that is best among us; if there be any such, let him be so elsewhere and among others.'" Nor did he hold his predecessors in high regard (*frg.* 16): "Much learning does not teach one to have understanding; else it would have taught Hesiod, and Pythagoras, and again Xenophanes, and Hecataeus." Heraclitus wrote in a difficult style for the few; his manner is oracular and his thought profound. His doctrine was that all things, including the percipient being, are in constant flux (*panta rhei*), but that nevertheless the world is governed by fixed law. He insisted on the reality of soul, but without theological implications; he remains in the secular and pantheist tradition of the Ionians.

Pythagoras, who taught in the West about the middle of the sixth century, must have been a powerful thinker and teacher, but he wrote nothing. Much of what is called Pythagoreanism is later accretion, but such familiar Platonic concepts as metempsychosis, the tripartite soul, and the purgation of the soul surely derive from Pythagoras; his influence was in the direction of mysticism rather than rationalism. Xenophanes' attacks on anthropomorphic polytheism, based on contemporary science, have been noted. Parmenides at sixty-five conversed with the youthful Socrates, and so belongs to the middle of the fifth century. Interesting from the literary point of view is the poetic device of his *Proem* (he wrote in hexameters) which represents his ascent on a chariot, attended by sun-maidens, to the home of the goddess, who is supposed to speak the remainder of the verses. Parmenides is concerned for the relation of thought and being. What *is* is a finite, spherical, continuous body, with nothing beyond it. Coming to be and ceasing to be are mere "names," as are motion, color, and the like. They are not even thoughts, for thought must be of something that *is,* and none of these can *be.* Empedocles was a physician and democratic politician in Acragas in the middle of the fifth century. He assumes the existence of the four elements (fire, air, earth, water), and the forces of Love and Strife which attract or separate. Empedocles has greater vigor of poetic expression than clarity in his cosmology and his explanation of the rise of mortal beings. Anaxagoras of Clazomenae is dated by his friendship with Pericles, whom old-fashioned Athenians thought probably tainted by Anaxagoras' "atheism." In fact, he was rather, in a sense, a theist, for whereas even Empedocles had called his Love and Strife gods, Anaxagoras appears to have called only the source of motion god. This source is Mind (*nous*), which is the source of knowledge as well; Mind was not conceived of as an incorporeal force, however, but as a sort of "fluid." The book of Leucippus, the senior originator of the atomic theory which was to be popularized by Epicurus and later by Lucretius, seems to have been incorporated with that of his junior confrere Democritus. Democritus, born at Abdera about 460 B.C., was an effective writer as well as a scientifically imaginative thinker. He conceived of the world, and of man and his soul, as composed of atoms, alike in quality but different in size and weight, existing in void. This consistently materialistic explanation of the universe as the result of a fortuitous concatenation of atoms left no room for interference by the gods nor for a future existence. Democritus was also concerned with ethics, and advocated the pursuit of happiness by cultivation of reason and moderation in desires. Diogenes Laertius (9.46 ff.) enumerates fifteen tetralogies of works, in philosophy and science, attributed to Democritus. Of these the one which expounded the atomic theory is supposed to have been the *Great Diacosmos.* Most of the fragments are ethical apothegms; one (*frg.* 191) is long enough to show that his style was clear and persuasive. Democritus lived until well into the fourth century; the reported death date would make him more than a hundred years old.

The second half of the fifth century was an age of technical treatises. Various branches of knowledge were made the objects of methodical study and systematization. One of the impressive monuments of the age is the body of medical treatises associated with the name of Hippocrates, not the father (for there are practicing physicians in Homer), but the first systematizer of medicine. Hippocrates was born in 460 B.C. and belonged to the Asclepiad guild on the island of Cos; though Hippocrates and his island were Dorian his books are all in Ionic, proof of Ionic primacy in scientific prose. Plato's *Protagoras* shows that Hippocrates was well known at the fictive date of that dialogue, which is about 435 B.C.; and *Phaedrus* (270c) seems to show that he wrote treatises. More than seventy are in the Hippocratic corpus, many doubtless from other hands and many of Hippocrates' own doubtless revised, as is natural for scientific works. Though these books belong to the literature of knowledge rather than the literature of power there is much good reading in them. Perhaps the most interesting for the layman is *Airs, Waters, Places,* in three books. This treatise discusses the relative healthfulness of various climates and speculates on the causes of epidemics. On the basis of their physical constitution Hippocrates decides that men are equal, differences among them being due to climate and convention; the ethical implications of this doctrine, not necessarily on the basis of Hippocrates, were first driven home by the Cynics and Stoics; Aristotle, though a biologist, denied human equality. The *Sacred Disease* is a fine protest against those who claim that epilepsy, or any other disease, is supernatural in origin. *Prognosis* makes the point that the patient will give the physician his full confidence, necessary for successful treatment, if the physician can foretell symptoms in advance. *Ancient Medicine* provides an interesting history of the art, and the *Art* is an eloquent defense of it. Throughout there is evident a real consideration for the welfare of the patient that is refreshing in technical treatises of this category.

Science had done what it could to explain the world, but its explanations seemed to have little bearing on more immediate problems of human conduct, of relations of men to one another and to society. If even scientists rejected views other than their own, then surely law too, *nomos,* was a set of conventions, not absolute like nature or *physis.* The "goodness" of the citizen could be a matter of varying interpretation and practical instruction. In the fifth century we see the rise of a group of men who did not indeed constitute a school but who professed to teach "goodness" (*arete*), which was explained to mean the power of directing states and families aright. These men were called Sophists, but in the fifth century the term had not yet acquired the connotation of conscienceless quibbling which was attached to it in the fourth century and which it still carries. But some prejudice attached to the word from the beginning. Being "too clever" was always an offense, and even in the *Apology* Socrates seeks to absolve himself from the imputation of being a "wise man." The Sophists, moreover, were "professionals," a thing abhorrent to aristocratic Athenians. Actually, the Sophists naturally taught people who could pay them, and these were generally the prosperous and well-born, who were the natural prey of the democracy. What they taught, then, was largely the art of succeeding in a democratic state, to persons who did not belong to the ruling democracy, and the art of getting off from attacks in courts of law. Furthermore, the Sophists were subject to Athenian prejudices against foreigners. And finally, when sophistic ideas and techniques came to be associated with socially radical doctrines and behavior, the ring of prejudice against the class was made complete. But there is no reason to doubt that the best of the class looked upon themselves sincerely as teachers of "goodness," and were as eager to differentiate their subject matter from the impracticalities of philosophy as the philosophers were to differentiate theirs from sophistry.

The most highly esteemed and most influential of such teachers, and apparently the first to give himself the professional title of Sophist (Plato, *Protagoras* 317*b*) was Protagoras of Abdera, who was about a generation older than Socrates. Writings of Protagoras are mentioned in Plato's *Theaetetus* (152*a*) and Isocrates' *Helen* (10.2); his central doctrine, of which the revolutionary implications cannot be exaggerated, is the famous "Man is the measure of all things, of things that are that they are, and of things that are not that they are not." If things are to one man as they appear to him, and to another as they appear to him, then it is possible to make two opposite statements both of which are "true," though one may be "weaker" and another "stronger." It is the business of the disputant "to make the weaker statement the stronger," and the art of so doing can be taught. The art in itself, it must be noticed, is not immoral; in a given case the better position may be the weaker, and it is the disputant's legitimate business to make it stronger as well as better. But it is the wider implications of the "man the measure" doctrine which revolutionized Greek thought; for, as man's views and interests change, all orthodoxies must be subject to constant re-examination and traditional authority must lose its force. Not only law and social relations (and Protagoras himself was essentially conservative in these matters), but myth and religion forfeit their external authority and become liable to alteration and adaptation. This is doubtless the basis for the story, improbable in itself, that Protagoras was judicially charged with impiety. Our single sentence from his *On the Gods* reads: "With regard to the gods, I cannot feel sure either that they are or that they are not, nor what they are like in figure; for there are many things that hinder sure knowledge, the obscurity of the subject and the shortness of human life." Greek orthodoxy was normally concerned with ritual, not with creedal affirmations. Other early Sophists who require mention are Hippias of Elis, who was a polymath or perhaps a sciolist; Prodicus of Ceus, who is associated with the apologue of the Choice of Heracles preserved in Xenophon (*Memorabilia* 2.1.21–34) and whose study of synonyms pioneered in grammar; and Gorgias of Leontini, whose proper place is with the orators.

Where the Hellenes of the West, if a loose generalization may be hazarded, from Hesiod down through the Orphics and Pythagoras, had sought means for accommodating themselves to the world, most of the writers mentioned in this chapter, embryonic historians as well as Milesian physicists and teachers of "goodness," sought to explain the world. All seem to have fresh curiosity and a blithe confidence that the world can, in fact, be explained. In a larger sense, divergences between philosophers and Sophists are only sectarian differences within the larger intellectual ferment which makes Athens at its fifth-century meridian the period of the most acute and fruitful rationalist questioning in the history of Europe.

Greek literature of the fifth century B.C. and to the end of the classic period, tragedy and comedy, history and oratory and philosophy, is, in fact, all informed by the seething currents of Athenian rationalism and is all Athenian. The efflorescence of Athens and its artistic primacy were favored by political and economic developments, which, in turn, affected its literature. When Ionia fell under Persian domination Athens soon replaced it as a commercial and intellectual center and quickly outstripped it. Coined money, as well as philosophers and their doctrines, was introduced from Ionia, and the new middle class which arose in consequence was able to arrest and then supplant the domination of the nobles. The democracy proved to be as eager in encouraging the arts as the "tyrants," who had enabled the democracy to arise, had been; and the empire it acquired opened broad horizons of power and wealth which contributed largely to the burgeoning of intellectual activity and artistic creation. The parallel afforded by sixteenth-century England is striking, and not least in the artistic forms taken by literary creation.

The sense of enlargement, of self-consciousness, of pride, which power and wealth brought, and the physical resources they afforded, the heightened tempo of urban life itself, the testing of old orthodoxies, in social problems no less than in religion, by the touchstone of the new speculation and the new natural science, all contributed to an intellectual ferment and a spiritual search to discover man's proper place in the world, his relations to society and to destiny. We now turn to a group of men who pondered long on life, perceived the tragedy implicit in it, and made that tragedy a thing of dignity with a beauty of its own.

Chapter 8. DRAMA

SURELY GREEK TRAGEDY MUST BE COUNTED AMONG MAN'S HIGHEST ACHIEVE-
ments. A happy conjunction of circumstances had evolved a democratic
society capable of receiving and eager to encourage great artistic production, had developed the several component arts to the point where they
could be fused into an organic whole, had produced a group of poets
with profound insight into the nature of man and the fundamental
problems of life who elevated the new creation to unsurpassed spiritual
and aesthetic greatness.

Of the elements which comprised Greek tragedy the reader is deprived
of music and dance and spectacle. To say that we are reading libretti
instead of witnessing operas is misleading (because of a different relationship between the words and music), but the comparison is nevertheless
suggestive. We can only regret what is missing and look at what we have,
the words, and even without imagining song and dance or envisaging
spectacle or transporting ourselves to a frame of mind we conceive appropriate for fifth-century Athenians, the words speak to us directly and
profoundly. It is a measure of the ultimate truth and the perennial mean-
ingfulness of Greek tragedy that, highly formal as it is and conventional
as all drama must be, a reader with an adult mind requires no commentary,
not even experience in the modern theater, to apprehend its essential matter.

That is because the Greek play tends to be single-minded, intense, clear
in outline; no line is superfluous, all somehow contribute to expounding
the theme. To the strangeness of the chorus, the myths, the god from the
machine, one soon grows acclimated. A Greek play is shorter than two
acts of *Hamlet,* for it has no fanciful overtones or bypaths, it deals only
with the aspects of a character that are relevant to the matter in hand, it
assumes adequate knowledge of life and imagination on the part of its
audience. At the core of all the tragedies is the struggle of man against fate,
though each poet's conception of the tragic is different. In Aeschylus, if
a generalization is valid, the interest is in the struggle itself. The agonists
meet in a vacuum like astral bodies; our attention is all on the surfaces as
they collide. In Sophocles the tragic interest is in the character of the
agonists; Sophocles' third actor enables us to see them in the round. In
Euripides the interest is again in the conflict, but there is fuller concern

for the effect upon the individuals, less for understanding or justifying fate. Sophocles works within the moral order as it exists; Aeschylus seeks to elevate our concept of it. But Aeschylus and Euripides as well as Sophocles were first and last artists, not theologians or moralists. They were full and thoughtful men, and their convictions are reflected in their plays and to some degree shaped their concept of the tragic. Because we have only the words (and those we feel as with thick mittens) it is natural that we feel safest in discussing the aspect of their art conveyed in words, more especially as interest and competence in such discussion are widespread.

For discussion and reflection there is always room, for Greek tragedy never presents a white hero opposed to a black villain. Where it may seem to do so, as in Sophocles' *Antigone,* we may be sure we are misreading the play, for the Greeks wrote tragedy, not melodrama. The spectacle of virtue always triumphant could only corroborate smugness; the spectacle of flawless virtue crushed to earth would only be shocking, as Aristotle points out. If in the elemental struggle against destiny man seems doomed to defeat, that is the way life looked to the tragedians. Their gloom is no fatalistic pessimism but an adult confrontation of reality, and their emphasis is not on the grimness of life but on the capacity of great figures to adequate themselves to it. The tragedy is accentuated by the large stature of its persons. The little man's woes may be pathetic, but not tragic. Merely by naming Agamemnon the poet has his grand figure, and needs waste no space to build him up. Usually (but not always) he has another asset, which a modern playwright would hardly regard as such, the audience's probable familiarity with the outlines of the story. They came to see, not how the story would turn out, for the heroic legends were conned in childhood, but how the heroes came to do what it was known they did, and what the meaning of it might be. Everyone knew that Orestes murdered his mother; but under what pressure could a son be brought to do such a thing, and what is its meaning? Greek tragedies are not mysteries (unless in the medieval sense). The "recognition" or "change of fortune" is not, as it is likely to be with us, at the end, but nearer the middle of the play. Generally the play ends on a note of calm, all passion purged.

The primal origins of the elements of tragedy, into which scholars with an anthropological flair have delved deep, need concern us here no more than they did the tragedians and their audiences. What they knew was that tragedy had evolved from the dithyrambic choruses performed in honor of Dionysus, whose early irregularity had been reformed and given a fixed character by Arion in Corinth. If it be remarked that the plays show little concern with the god and the ancient objection be raised, "What has this to do with Dionysus?" the answer may be suggested by the dithyrambs of Bacchylides, the only specimens of the genus we have, which, as we have noted, have little to do with Dionysus. In any case, our tragedies were performed as part of the service to Dionysus, during his festival, and on ground sacred to him. The religious association affected the nature of the plays, the manner of their presentation, and the attitude of the audience. The conservatism of religion contributed (but only contributed, for the Greeks habitually adhered to their artistic forms) to the constant form of tragedy, from which there are no important deviations. The subjects were practically limited to the existing body of myth, many of whose themes had been used and made ready for tragic treatment by Stesichorus and his fellows. The actors were persons of high dignity, in a sense priests of Dionysus (as contrasted with the slave actors in Rome). They wore masks and rich and elaborate costumes calculated to enhance their impressiveness. Their performance was dignified and stylized, though scope was afforded for high individual artistry. Violence was eschewed (though here again sound taste rather than religion may have been the controlling factor); acts of violence were supposed to take place offstage, and were reported in long messengers' speeches. The audience, as is appropriate to a religious function, were participants rather than spectators; and the fact that the performance was in the nature of a prize contest heightened their interest. The level of intelligence and taste must have been high indeed to make an audience enthusiastically appreciative of the difficult style and matter of an Aeschylus—or of the parodies of that style and matter in an Aristophanes.

The dignity imparted by the use of stories out of a hagiographa and by the stateliness of the performance was supported by the formalism of the chorus. The chorus was the central nucleus out of which tragedy had developed, and it always retained its formal importance and its traditional dialect, even when the spoken parts came to be written in plain Attic, grown virtually colloquial in Euripides' plays. From its first entry in the parodos the chorus remained in the orchestra (except where there was a change of scene, as in Eumenides and Ajax) until the play closed, and its failure to prevent catastrophe by active intervention (as in Agamemnon) or by revealing its knowledge (as in Hippolytus) creates a certain awkwardness. But the superb use made of what might seem to be an intolerable incubus shows how a strait pattern may enlarge rather than fetter art. Sometimes, as in Aeschylus' Suppliants and Eumenides, the chorus is a central figure in the tragedy. Sometimes, as with the elders in Agamemnon or the captive Trojan Women, they are the ones most nearly affected by the doings of the principal actors. Sometimes, as in the Oedipus plays, they are "ideal spectators," whose reactions clarify in terms of ordinary humanity the powerful emotions of the chief personages. Very frequently they weave a psychological background for the action, either directly by recalling a relevant passage of history, as when the *Agamemnon* chorus sing of the sacrifice of Iphigenia, or, as in *Antigone,* by singing the high prowess of mankind when Antigone makes her decision or of the power of love when Haemon makes his. They introduce new arrivals (there were no handbills), encourage or dissuade an actor in a certain course, or point up the significance of his utterances. Always their *stasima* or fixed odes serve as a sort of curtain to set the episodes apart and, where necessary, to indicate the passage of time. In much of Euripides the latter are indeed their only functions, if we choose to forget the meaning of the music as such. Possibly by Euripides' day ornate music (introduced by Timotheus) had made words as useless as they sometimes are in opera; in the earlier tragedians the words certainly dominated the music. Of the choral music and dancing we know little, except that the metrical schemes, practically never repeated from play to play, indicate considerable intricacy. The proportion of lyric to spoken lines tends to decrease with time, and the meaning of the plays becomes more explicit; of a play like Aeschylus' *Suppliants* we must remember that it is a lyrical drama, with music being the chief vehicle for conveying the author's meaning. Sometimes there are passages of lyric dialogue (*kommos, kommoi*), when the actors and audience must be brought to a high emotional pitch for some extraordinary action; the best example perhaps is in *Choephoroe,* where Electra, Orestes, and the audience must be steeled to the horror of the matricide.

Not religion alone but the authority of the state enhanced the dignity of tragedy and made it a national concern. The chief magistrates of the state, the Archon Eponymus for the Great Dionysia in the spring and the Archon Basileus for the Lenaea in the fall, supervised the performances. The archon chose three among the playwrights who submitted their work, to whom he "gave a chorus." The duty and expense of mounting the play were assigned to a rich citizen as a liturgy, or form of income tax; another liturgy was to fit out a battleship. The archon also assigned each poet a protagonist, or principal actor, who provided his own subordinates. Each poet competed with a tetralogy, consisting of three tragedies, not necessarily related in subject, and a satyr play. Judges were chosen by lot from a large panel previously selected. The names of the victorious choregus, poet, and actor were inscribed on tablets, on remains or abstracts of which our knowledge of the facts is based.

Of the numerous theaters in Greece that at Athens, which seated some seventeen thousand persons, is the most interesting, though much altered from its original form, and that at Epidaurus, which seated some forty thousand, the best preserved. All theaters afford a pleasant outlook, usually to the sea. The theater has three elements: a flat circular space called the orchestra, where the chorus and probably the actors performed (the question of a raised stage for the actors has been almost as much vexed as the Homeric question); an auditorium, built against a hillside which permitted the action to be seen in the round rather than frontally; and a *skene,* or booth where the actors retired to change masks, the front of which, after the time of Sophocles, was painted. But neither in such scene painting nor otherwise was realism sought. A number of stage devices are mentioned, of which only the "machine" is clear or important; this was a crane used for the appearance of gods.

The arrangements here described represent the developed form; they were doubtless very rudimentary when Thespis, according to the Parian Marble, which is the source of much of our literary chronology, won the prize at the first official presentation of tragedy in Athens in 534 B.C. Thespis, whom Aristotle does not mention and of whom Horace (*Ars Poetica* 275 ff.) strangely knows more than any Greek, was said to have "discovered" one actor (*hypokrites,* literally "answerer"), that is, to have been the first to have a speaker impersonating a character perform with the chorus. His successor, Choerilus, is said to have produced 160 plays between 524 and 484 B.C. Pratinas, who competed with Choerilus and Aeschylus in the 70th Olympiad (probably 499 B.C.), invented the satyric drama. Of his fifty plays thirty-two were said to be in this form; either the regular proportions (one satyr play with each trilogy) had not been fixed, or he wrote satyr plays for others. Of Phrynichus, who won his first victory between 512 and 509 B.C., we have more knowledge. Aristophanes praises him for his songs in two affectionate passages (*Wasps* 220, *Birds* 748 ff.; cf. *Frogs* 689); and he was the first to employ female characters (always played by men). His *Phoenissae,* produced in 476 with Themistocles himself as choregus, celebrated the victory of Salamis. Another historical play was his *Capture of Miletus* (the city was taken by Darius in 494 B.C., when the Athenians had refused petitions for help). When this play was acted, says Herodotus (6.21), "the whole theater burst into tears and the people sentenced him to pay a fine of a thousand drachmas for recalling to them their own misfortunes. They likewise made a law that no one should ever again exhibit that piece."

AESCHYLUS

And now the curtain rises upon Aeschylus, son of Euphorion, who was born at Eleusis in 525 B.C., who fought as a hoplite at Marathon in 490, and who died in Sicily in 456 when, it is said, an eagle mistook his bald head for a stone and dropped a tortoise upon it to crack its shell. Aeschylus is credited with a number of technical innovations, such as devising the elaborate costumes of actors and chorus. Far the most important of these was his introduction of the second actor, which made drama in a full sense, the clash of will between two characters, possible. But his greatest contribution was in imparting to tragedy the high intellectual tone which his successors maintained. In poetry of lavish grandeur that rivals Pindar's, Aeschylus probed deep into the springs of human conduct and the ethical truths by which men live. Of the some eighty or ninety plays which Aeschylus wrote, seven have come down to us.

Suppliants is the oldest, and therefore the earliest play in Europe; though its date is unknown, 491 B.C. is a plausible suggestion. *Suppliants* is of interest, not only as showing the early structure of the drama, but also for manifesting the concept and treatment of a tragic theme which Aeschylus was to pursue in his later plays. To a point on the seashore near Argos there have come the fifty daughters of Danaüs, fleeing from Egypt to avoid marriage with their cousins, the fifty sons of Aegyptus. They claim a hereditary right of asylum, and the King of Argos is confronted with the problem of either refusing or being involved in a war with the Egyptians, whose herald appears to demand extradition. That same day his world had been all serene, and now through no fault of his a tragic flaw has developed in the universe to destroy his happiness. A democratic king, he goes to consult his citizens about the choice. Just when his daughters' danger is most acute Danaüs goes off to speak to the Argives; Aeschylus had not yet acquired deftness in the use of his second actor, and the man who played Danaüs was needed to return in the person of the Egyptian herald. The Danaïds themselves, who express their consternation and their threats to hang themselves from the sacred images in elaborate lyrics which take up the main part of the play, are the chief "actor." Why they were so horrified at marrying their cousins is not clear, but need not concern us, for like the improbabilities in *Oedipus* it is a matter *exo tou dramatos,* outside the action. What is clear is that they were somehow partly in the wrong in preferring Artemis to Aphrodite; we have lyrical drama, not melodrama, and a prefiguring of *Hippolytus* as well as *Oedipus.* The dramatist's surest touch is in his lyrics, which convey the main effects of the piece. Besides being the most lyrical, *Suppliants* is also the most spectacular (with the possible exception of *Eumenides*) of our extant tragedies. The gyrations of the fifty maidens with their dark masks and vivid costumes, possibly attended by fifty hand-maidens in addition, must have been eye-filling.

Persians, the only Greek historical tragedy extant, comes later after an interval of some twenty years, being part of a prize-winning trilogy in 472 B.C. for which Pericles served as choregus. The theme is the defeat of the Persian expedition by the Greeks, the magnificent messenger's speech describing the battle of Salamis being clearly an eyewitness account. Though the basis of the play is the greatest victory in Greek history, the tone is one of solemn piety: "Not unto us, O Lord, not unto us, but unto thy name give glory." Not a single Greek is named, though many Persian grandees are; not Greek virtue, but Xerxes' sin, the familiar procession of *koros* ("satiety") which leads to *hubris* ("wanton insolence") and re-sults in *ate* ("destruction"), was the cause of the outcome. Susa as the scene of action substitutes remoteness in space for remoteness in time, and affords opportunity for Aeschylus' skillful use of spectacular effects. Darius is the first ghost to rise on a European stage. The entry, in a carriage, of the bedraggled Xerxes and the long silence of Queen Atossa (another favorite Aeschylean effect) must have heightened the thrill.

Seven against Thebes (467 B.C.) takes up the story of Oedipus' sons, Eteocles and Polynices, where their father's curse in *Oedipus at Colonus* was to leave them. When the news comes that Polynices with six Argive chieftains is approaching to attack the city, Eteocles quiets the chorus of terrified maidens, and proceeds to assign a champion to meet each of the attackers as the messenger reports his name and the devices on his shield. The chances that Eteocles will have to confront his own brother (he him-self does not know that Polynices will attack one gate) are inexorably in-creased to certainty when the sixth champion is chosen. The quality of the tragic idea is very like that of Sophocles' *Oedipus;* the hero doing his duty as a good but not a flawless man is more and more inextricably en-meshed, while first the audience, and then his interlocutors, and only at the end he himself becomes aware of his predicament. In *Oedipus* the tragedy is adorned by circumstantial plot and precise character delinea-tion; in *Seven* it is unrelieved in its starkness and absorbs our total in-terest. Surely to look only at Eteocles' victory over his brother at the end of the play and the interdiction of burial for Polynices (which sets the stage for *Antigone*) is to miss the heart of the drama.

Some critics find the intellectual premises of *Prometheus* so difficult to reconcile with the age of Aeschylus that they adopt the rather heroic solution of attributing the play to some unknown writer of the sophistic age, who wrote it, not for presentation, but as a philosophical pamphlet. There are indeed marked differences from the consistent views represented in the other six plays, but we have too small a fraction of Aeschylus' work and know too little of his other treatment of the myth involved to justify denying the tradition of Aeschylean authorship. If the play is Aeschylus' work it must antedate the trilogy, and internal evidence indicates that it comes later than *Seven*. In Hesiod the quarrel between Prometheus (who was little more than the patron saint of potters) and Zeus was over a paltry deception in regard to sacrificial meat; but Hesiod did make the story a vehicle for teaching divine retribution. Here the stature of Prometheus is raised to that of Satan in *Paradise Lost,* and the conflict is more real because, unlike Milton's God, Zeus is neither omniscient nor beneficent. Prometheus, who had helped Zeus to power but had subsequently incurred his ill will by bestowing fire and other blessings upon mankind, is by Zeus' command nailed to a desolate cliff in Scythia. A chorus of sea-nymphs, Oceanus, Io, comfort or counsel him and elicit his story. Hermes demands that Prometheus yield up his secret concerning Zeus' eventual overthrow, and when Prometheus remains defiant he is hurled into an abyss by a convulsion of nature. Our sympathy naturally goes out to a superior being who is being crucified for his benefactions to mankind, and it seems difficult to reconcile the tyrant Zeus (even though he is represented as being at the beginning of his reign, with much yet to learn) with the just Zeus whom Aeschylus depicts in his other plays. Structurally, the play is like the story of Job: a good man, rooted to one spot, is visited by friends with whom he discusses the justice of God; subsequently, it develops that all, in varying degrees, have failed to recognize the magnitude of God's strength and wisdom. Perhaps the answer in *Prometheus* is similar. Zeus, newly enthroned, had wished to abolish the puny and inadequate race of men and replace them with something better, but Prometheus had made it possible for them to struggle on in life. We are on Prometheus' side because we cannot separate our interests from our imagination; perhaps if we had the entire trilogy we could say with Job: "I have heard of thee by the hearing of the ear, but now mine eye seeth thee."

The *Oresteia,* which won the prize in 458 B.C., is our only surviving trilogy. The first play, *Agamemnon,* tells how that king returned to Argos after his victory at Troy, how he was fulsomely welcomed and then treacherously slain, along with Cassandra, by his queen Clytemnestra acting in collusion with his cousin Aegisthus. This play is surely one of the greatest in literature; it can bear any amount of criticism profitably, and it can be read profitably with none. It might be mentioned, for the sake of distinguishing Aeschylus' tragic idea from that of his followers, that whereas such minor characters as Watchman, Herald, and Aegisthus are drawn with considerable realism, only so much of the principals, Agamemnon and Clytemnestra, is indicated as is needful for their tragedy. Even when they confront one another in blood, across the red carpet and in the gory bath, there is no dramatic conflict in a true sense but rather two disparate tragedies, each proving itself in the other. The carpet scene itself is a magnificent piece of theater, Clytemnestra displaying her tragic fault of strength and Agamemnon his of weakness. The carpet is rolled up after him as he walks unshod across the orchestra and up the steps; and it wants but little imagination to see him wading through a sea of blood.

In *Choephoroe,* or *Libation Bearers,* the poet has the task of making one of the most heinous crimes in the Greek calendar endurable. At the bidding of Apollo, Orestes has returned to Argos to avenge his father by killing his mother. It is a hard deed, though Clytemnestra's guilt is clear and we have no sympathy for her. The audience, no less than Electra and Orestes, is lifted to the requisite emotional pitch by a long lyric scene between brother, sister, and chorus. Until after the murder is committed Orestes seems only a lay figure speaking appropriate sentences—not a living being to be thought of in connection with matricide. But afterward he quickens to astonishing sensitivity; when the blood-stained robe is shown he realizes how he has been caught between a divine command which might not be denied and a foul crime which might not be committed. He can only go mad, and he dashes from the scene, pursued by the Furies.

Sublime theology, noble patriotism, and stirring spectacle combine to lay the problem to rest in *Eumenides* (or *Kindly Ones,* a euphemism for the Furies). From Delphi, where he had sought asylum, Orestes is hounded by the Furies, in the most thrilling spectacle in tragedy, to Athens, where Athena institutes a court of Athenian jurors to adjudicate the case of Orestes. The Furies insist that if their ancient prerogative of exacting blood for blood is abrogated all bonds of order will be dissolved. Apollo's defense argument is no better than that of a smart Athenian lawyer; among other things he says that a mother is not the parent of a child but only the nurse of the father's seed. It may be noted that Apollo was never a favorite at Athens; in the Persian War Delphi Medized, and in Euripides' day it would favor the Spartans in the Peloponnesian War. The jury votes six and six, and Athena as president decides for Orestes. The mechanical vendetta justice of blood for blood is abolished, and the curse of the house of Atreus, which might have continued endlessly, is thus laid to rest. The Eumenides, retaining their chthonic character, are given new duties as blessers of earth's increase and are assigned a shrine on the Acropolis declivity. Order is now directed by reason; justice will be dealt by a human court under the patronage of Athens' patron deity, the goddess of reason. Man's freedom of will is vindicated, and punishment for guilt is thus rendered just. Every man is responsible for his own crimes, as the elders declared in the *Agamemnon;* the guilt of the fathers does not constrain the children to guilt, but only inclines them toward it, and this inclination they can and must defeat.

Besides these seven plays of Aeschylus names of seventy-two others are mentioned. There are some hundreds of fragments, and additions are made almost annually as papyri publications are issued. A relatively large number of the lost plays seem to have dealt with Dionysiac subjects. Recently published fragments of the *Dictyulci* (or "Net Drawers") are from a satyr play in which the chest containing Danaë and her infant is drawn up by fishermen. There are also fragments of another satyr play called *Isthmiastai*. None of the fragments alters the impression of majestic grandeur conveyed by the seven extant plays. Aeschylus is a difficult author, and cannot have been easy ever. His principal trait is a powerful virility, an enormous strength shaped by high artistry and turned to the uses of civilization. In lesser hands his ruggedness must have degenerated into bombast, and softer ages did consider him grotesque. Highly embroidered and allusive language which might be turgid or precious, fantasies which might be conceits, speculation which might be casuistry, spectacular effects which might be showy tinsel—all of these have in Aeschylus an honest virility which compels respect. He wrestles with language and images and character, and drains his readers' intellect and emotion in the process, but he achieves serenity in art and he communicates it to his readers. In religion his earnestness and loftiness set him on a level with the Hebrew prophets. Like the prophets he was revolutionary; it was not his aim to preserve the traditional sanctities, which were already being associated with political reaction, but rather to achieve and propagate a purer theology, which would necessarily not remain the prerogative of a class.

A characteristic of Aeschylus which is less likely to be noticed by the reader (as contrasted with the audience) is the rich exuberance of Aeschylus' spectacular effects: fifty Danaïds with handmaids and attendants in *Suppliants,* an exotic court and a ghost in *Persians,* a chorus of terrified women in *Seven,* a gigantic figure nailed to a mountain cliff overlooking a gulf in *Prometheus,* fires lighted at dawn on numerous altars in *Agamemnon,* swirling black-swathed and snake-haired Furies in *Eumenides,* entrances in strange chariots and a variety of sound effects. All of this is romantic or preclassic rather than classic, and was sharply pruned in Sophocles. Because Sophocles was aristocratic in his associations and outlook, and *sophrosyne,* restrained temperance, was a conscious principle in the aristocratic code, it is not too much to see in Aeschylus' more exuberant style another aspect of the democracy of the ebullient Themistocles, anti-Persian, anti-Spartan, and pro-democratic.

SOPHOCLES

There is a striking contrast between the stark hopelessness of his characters' struggles and Sophocles' own life, which is among the happiest of which we have record. He was of good family, handsome, wealthy, healthy, enjoyed the high esteem of his fellow citizens, held important public offices, won more prizes than his rivals, had a son who was a successful playwright. He retained his faculties to the end of his long life, which coincided with the period of his city's greatness, surely among the choice periods of the world's history, and he died, at ninety, just before his city's fall. If life looks grim to such a man it must be grim indeed; its compensation is in the nobility of the ideal, the gallantry of the struggle, the sheer beauty of the poetry, which is itself a victory over the terrifying things that happen to reasonably good men.

Sophocles was born in a well-to-do family at Colonus (now within Athens) in 496 B.C., educated in music by Lampros, the conservative rival of Timotheus who influenced Euripides' music, and as a youth led the chorus of thanksgiving for the victory at Salamis. This honor is proof of his good looks as well as of good family connections. His first production, in 468, won the prize over Aeschylus. Partisanship was so intense on this occasion, says Plutarch (*Cimon* 8), that the archon appointed Cimon (who was leader of the aristocratic party) and his brother generals to act as judges, and they awarded the prize to Sophocles. There is plausible, but not indisputable, basis for the conjecture that Sophocles was associated with the pro-Sparta group around Cimon. There is ancient evidence for Sophocles' piety, and we know that he several times served the state in positions of trust—bestowed upon him, it appears, in recognition of his merit as a poet, and not for political or military skill. The circumstances of his life, as well as his plays, suggest that Sophocles was a conservative, opposed to innovation in religion and politics. Yet such plays as *Trachinian Women* and *Electra* show that he learned from Euripides; and Oedipus' disclaimer of guilt in *Oedipus at Colonus* when he had acknowledged guilt in the earlier *Oedipus* shows that the Sophists had done their work. Indeed, scholars draw a line between his earlier plays (but all that we have come from his full maturity) and the later ones which reveal sophistical influence, but there is no unanimity on where the line is to be drawn. The general cast of Sophocles' thought appears to remain conservative to the end.

We say "appears" because it is much less easy to apprehend Sophocles' own beliefs from his plays than Aeschylus' or Euripides' from theirs. Aeschylus stands revealed in his plays; Euripides will even spoil a play in order to put some favorite doctrine in the mouth of a character. But Sophocles is almost Shakespearean in eliminating himself from his work. We speak of Hamlet, not Shakespeare, saying "to be or not to be"; similarly, we must speak of Oedipus or Antigone, not Sophocles, saying the things put into their mouths. Tragedy's elemental struggle between man and his destiny is clearest in Sophocles, but Sophocles' eye is single upon the human side of the equation, how men suffer and how they behave under the inexorable pressure of destiny. The moral order is subjected neither to the refining criticism of Aeschylus nor to the less revolutionary but more destructive criticism of Euripides. In Sophocles the premises of the moral order are accepted without question; he is concerned with examining the results of the impact of that order on the individual character, and all his technical refinements are calculated to exhibit character more fully and deeply. But without impugning Sophocles' purity as an artist it must be remembered that he wrote in a period of ferment, and that the Greeks always expected their poets to be teachers and did not confine their instruction to one corner of the curriculum. Sophocles did seek, with an art so perfect as to conceal itself, to promote one set of religious and political beliefs against another set. The ideas he opposed were those of the restive democracy, and those he set forth were the traditional ideal of the aristocracy.

If it be objected that Creon's speech in favor of a firm hand on the reins of government (*Antigone* 162 ff.), being dramatic, may not be used as evidence for Sophocles' beliefs, yet surely the next choral ode, celebrating the achievements of man and closing with reprobation of audacious thoughts, does represent the author's view:

Possessing in his resourceful skill a thing subtle beyond belief, he moves now towards evil and now towards good. When he honors the usages of the land and justice which is bound by gods' oath he stands high in the city. He is without city in whom what is not fair is habitual by reason of his audacity. May the man who behaves so not share my hearth, may his thoughts not be mine.

So too the words of the chorus at the end of the same play (1346 ff.):
"Being discreet is the chief part of happiness. One must not be irreverent
towards the gods. The big words of vaunting men pay a price of big blows
and teach discretion in old age." Even if the tone of the choral passages too
is dictated by dramatic considerations, yet the fact that such sentiments
are appropriate in so many of the plays shows that the author set a special
value on the noble virtues of piety, obedience, restraint. So with the oracles,
which Sophocles employs with such consummate skill as elements of intrigue, as foreshadowing doom, as a touchstone of character. The oracles
are abundantly justified dramatically, yet it cannot be accident that Sophocles
is specially concerned to vindicate Delphi. Apollo's prophecies are always
realized to the letter, and those who slight them always come to grief.
Apollo's oracle, we know from Thucydides (1.118), had promised the
Spartans that "invited or uninvited the god would take their part."

It has long been a commonplace of criticism that Sophocles is the perfect
artist, concerned exclusively with creating works of supreme beauty; his
works have been traditionally regarded as the absolute models, for which
Aeschylus was a preparation, and from which Euripides degenerated. His
plays are indeed excellently wrought, and constitute the best literary
pendant for the harmony and controlled strength of the Parthenon and its
sculptures. His innovations are all calculated to enhance dramatic effectiveness. The third actor was introduced because a dialogue with a spectator
or referee multiplies the number of facets that may be seen in a simple
dialogue. Minor normal characters are introduced to provide a scale for
measuring the complexity of their principals; Ismene and Chrysothemis
show us what has happened to Antigone and Electra. The element of intrigue and a sophisticated sense of theater appear; Chrysothemis has been
quite forgotten when news of Orestes' death has come, and when she returns to her grieving sister with news that Orestes must have arrived the
theatrical effect is stunning. Regularly before calamity strikes jubilant
hopes are raised. The tragic sense is heightened by foreshadowing which
is meaningful to the audience but unperceived by the victim. The plots
are both elaborated and tightened, and give the actor more opportunities
to reveal himself; revelation of the actor was not essential when attention
was focused on the conflict rather than on the participants.

When one considers that the themes of the Sophoclean theater are such
as to drain the passions—Oedipus, Antigone, Orestes on the rack, and the
screws inexorably tightened—the "serenity" which generations of critics
have found in the plays and their author becomes something of a paradox.
But if there is no restraint in the harrowing tales of blood and of agonizing
passions which Sophocles favors, yet in the manipulation of these passions

Sophocles remains the calculating artist; his is the emotion recollected in tranquillity. We are subjected to intense experience, as if by a psychiatrist's prescription, and are released when the desired purge has been effected, with some certificate of cure, as at the end of *Electra*. Aeschylus' solutions had been the attainment of a new level of insight, intellectual and theological; Euripides left the tragedy "most tragic," and contrived an artificial solution by a god out of the machine whom the audience might or might not accept. Sophocles is the mystagogue whose own emotional sympathies are detached but who leads the candidates for initiation through the degrees of the mystery and brings them out to light at the end.

In modern times (but not in Byzantine, when it was apparently a favorite) *Ajax* has been regarded among the least satisfactory of Sophocles' plays, because of apparent defects, and for want of external evidence it has accordingly been regarded as our earliest Sophoclean drama. Chief exception is taken to the fact that the hero dies at line 865, the remaining third of the play being taken up with a dispute as to whether he merits burial. But it is with the whole of Ajax' career, to which the decision on burial is integral, and not merely the lurid spectacle of his madness and suicide, which make burial questionable, that the play is concerned. Were Ajax' large deeds and large sufferings merely those of a sturdy braggart, or does he merit the title of "hero" in the technical sense of a *daimon* who receives annual offerings? The decision on burial is necessary to establish Ajax' stature, just as the canonization of a saint gives meaning to his career and shows that his martyrdom was not a piece of frivolous stubbornness. Yet though Ajax' heroization is ratified, his presumptuous self-assertion is not condoned. Even the reader who has learned not to associate gods with goodness is shocked at the fiendish gloating of Athena over her pitiful victim; but how else should the patroness of the Parthenon deal with independence of spirit and want of emotional restraint carried to so violent a pitch? Long ago Professor Paul Shorey (himself a Sophoclean) wrote that "objection to the role of Athena in *Ajax* is a sure index of a parlor pink." Nor are Menelaus' and Agamemnon's personal vindictiveness, in excess of their obligations as leaders, approved; proper sobriety and loyalty are exemplified in Odysseus, who comes to represent the interest of the state. Her patient humility and womanly strength makes Tecmessa one of the most appealing feminine characters in tragedy.

Antigone, dated by external evidence to 441 B.C., is the most misread of ancient plays, for if, as the latest book on Sophocles declares, Creon is the villain in the play and Antigone a noble saint, we should have not a Greek tragedy but a melodrama. The play is about Creon, who has almost twice as many lines as Antigone. Of the position each takes, the poet certainly, and almost as certainly the audience, thought Creon's, representing the authority of the state, was more right, and Antigone's, something on the morbid side, less right. Antigone is but one of the crosses Creon has to bear. Antigone's tragedy is foreseeable, and she goes to meet it at line 928; Creon has a third of the play still to suffer, for Haemon is *his* son, Euridice *his* wife, and the state which is being polluted *his* state. A sure indication of the relative importance of the state and the family in the mind of Creon is his apparently preposterous action after Tiresias has warned him of divine displeasure. Upon his request the chorus advises him (1100 f.) to free Antigone from her living burial and then bury Polynices. We should agree that the release of the living was the more pressing errand. But Creon goes first to bury Polynices, and with much ceremony (1196 ff.). Only the chivalry of a more romantic age could make one woman, and a woman who disregarded the rule of obedience appropriate to her sex, as important as the welfare of the state.

However it is read, *Antigone* is an excellent example of Sophocles' mature study of character. Not only Creon, Haemon, and Antigone, but the taciturn Euridice and the Shakespearean body-watcher are each perfect in their kind. Antigone is not only intransigent and a little in love with martyrdom, but she is pitiful. The faltering and illogical speech (904–920) in which she declares that only a brother but no other relative, not even a husband, would merit such a sacrifice (a thought plainly adopted from Herodotus 3.119) was deleted by Jebb, in spite of its being cited by Aristotle (*Rhetoric* 3.16.9) as being from Sophocles' *Antigone,* because it is inconsistent with the saintly character that Jebb conceived Antigone to be; it is, in fact, precisely suited to her character. In the tension between Creon and his son Haemon modern psychologists have perceived an underlying sexual rivalry. Whether or not there is basis for such a theory, the tense dialogue between the two, with Haemon's restraint finally bursting its bonds and Creon's hardness degenerating into bluster, is magnificently revealing. In *Antigone* also are to be found two of the best of Sophocles' choral odes, that on the power of love (781 ff.), which is an effective commentary on the Haemon scene, and that on the achievement of man, which has been mentioned above.

Trachinian Women is as puzzling to interpret as it is to date. There is not enough about Dejanira in the third of the play that follows her suicide, not enough about Heracles before his arrival, to make either the exclusive theme. If Dejanira is suitably feminine she is too much a fool, and if Heracles is suitably heroic he is too heroically self-centered for proper tragedy. The tragedy, then, is not in the persons but in their relationship and the tragic effects of that relationship on others, Iole and

Hyllus and Lichas. If the relationship itself is the theme, it is a new thing
in tragedy, and the treatment is curiously unsatisfactory. For once we
feel that a missing bit of antiquarian knowledge might illuminate the
puzzle, as puzzles in Aristophanes are illuminated. Sophocles' apparent
adaptation of the poisoned robe theme, for example, suggests that *Trachinian Women* may be a conscious "corrective" to Euripides' *Medea*.
Dejanira is a more suitable figure to attempt to win back an errant husband
by magic means, humbly and without realizing the danger; and his
daimonic stature and destiny may give Heracles better right to desert a wife.

Aristotle and most subsequent critics regard *Oedipus* (perhaps 429 B.C.)
as the model Greek tragedy. Each step in the intricate and perfectly dove-
tailed plot is motivated, and none seems contrived; the inherent improbabilities in the received story are made unobtrusive. The delinea-
tion of even the minor characters is perfect; witness the contrast between
the voluble Corinthian and the reluctant shepherd. The choral odes are
apposite and beautiful. The tragedy is centered in Oedipus and grows
out of the interaction of his own impetuous character and destiny. The
force of the tragic irony is terrific as Oedipus becomes the last person in
the whole theater to realize the devastating truth. In a drama so perfectly wrought as to make us oblivious of its author we cannot say that
this or that line expresses the author's own conviction. Yet there may
be significance in the choice of a theme which demonstrates the infal-
libility of Apollo's oracle and in which the tragic flaw is immoderate
passion.

Because *Choephoroe* and Euripides' *Electra* treat the same story Sophocles' *Electra* (perhaps 411 B.C.) affords a direct means for apprehending
his peculiar qualities. The tragedy is concentrated in the character of
Electra, which is illuminated from many angles by interaction with other
characters, who are required by the intricacy of the plot. The lament over
the urn is made the more pathetic by the presence of the living Orestes.
As the normal Ismene provided a measure for Antigone's intensity, so
does Chrysothemis for Electra's; Chrysothemis' return with cheerful news
when we have quite forgotten her and have evidence that the news is
impossible is an admirable stroke of theater. Even Electra's horrible pun-
ning to Aegisthus at the end ("They have found a way to the heart of their
hostess" and the like) contributes to the unrelieved picture of grimness.
Yet this grimness begins with a picture of a fresh dawn with birds singing and closes with the chorus singing, "O seed of Atreus, through how
many experiences have you at last emerged in freedom made perfect by
today's effort!" When Orestes emerges after killing his mother the chorus
remark (1422) that his hand drips gore, and Orestes says, in calm iambic,

"All is well within the house if Apollo's oracles spoke well." Sophocles is shutting out as extraneous to his tragedy of character any consideration of the justice of the moral order (such as occupied both Aeschylus and Euripides), or he is defending the justice of Apollo as the guardian of that order.

Philoctetes (409 B.C.) is likely to appeal to modern readers more directly than other Sophoclean plays. Here there is no bloody climax; the tragedy is in Philoctetes' renunciation of his justified hatred and even more in the death of Neoptolemus' ideals, all necessary in the cause of duty to the state. Here stark character is not paraded but rather illuminated by progressions and deteriorations, motivated by movement of intrigue within the play. The use of the god from the machine (which Sophocles had learned from Euripides) is perhaps the most skillful in all our tragedies. Only Heracles, who had used the bow to rid mankind of plagues, can admonish Philoctetes that it may not be used in a private feud but must be employed for the common good in the conquest of Troy. It is quite possible that the story of Philoctetes' reconciliation with his comrades in the Greek army is intended to prefigure the recall of Alcibiades; the date and the circumstances fit. Jebb recognizes the parallel but remarks (p. xliii of his edition): "To suppose that Sophocles intended a political allegory of this kind is surely to wrong him grievously as a poet." May not a poet have a political opinion?

The Oedipus in *Oedipus at Colonus* (produced posthumously in 401 B.C.) is ragged and blind and a beggar, but throughout this longest of Greek tragedies he is the same passionate man still, violent in resenting a slight, never compromising with his dignity for his own or his kindred's comfort, and now (possibly because Sophocles had finally accepted the *homo mensura* doctrine of the Sophists) sure of his own rightness and nobility. Is he merely an inconvenient relic, or have his deeds and sufferings given him a special stature which can confer blessing? The story of his final trials and death and heroization gives us our answer; tragic suffering is justified and made meaningful by nobility. The play reads like a conscious valedictory. It is peopled by the figures with whom Sophocles had won his greatest successes, the locale is the poet's native Colonus, and the play is filled with old memories, especially of sacred spots and cult usages. The ode in praise of white Colonus with its nightingales and narcissi (667 ff.) is justly the most familiar in Greek tragedy. In the end the tone is of reconciliation and blessing. Athens too receives comfort and praise in an hour of sorrow; chivalrous Theseus exemplifies Athens' noblest tradition of generous asylum.

The fragments of the remaining tragedies (Sophocles wrote more than a hundred plays) add little to our knowledge of him, except for *Ichneutai* ("Trackers"), some four hundred lines of which were discovered in a papyrus in 1907. This is a satyr play, of which species the only specimen hitherto known was Euripides' *Cyclops*. The subject of *Ichneutai* is the same as that of the Homeric *Hymn to Zeus,* though the order of the incidents is freely altered. The exuberant and somewhat ribald satyr play has shocked admirers of the marblelike, cool detachment usually attributed to Sophocles; in fact, it only makes obvious a vigor which Sophocles' art conceals elsewhere. As so often in considering Sophocles the analogy of sculpture suggests itself. A sensitive hand passing over a Greek marble can feel its inexhaustible energy. Sophocles has the same strength under the same perfect control; his work is at the furthest remove from the protruding and knotty muscles of an exuberant Romantic artist.

EURIPIDES

Where Sophocles was a social being, enjoying high acclaim, winning many tragic prizes, never caring to leave his city, Euripides was a brooding man who was said to write plays in a lonely, book-filled cave on Salamis, who won few prizes, whose mother, gossip said, was a greengrocer, and who left his city in his old age. But his aloofness was the aloofness of the artist; he knew and loved life, knew and propagated the new philosophy, the new music, the new ethics. He was born in 485 or 480 B.C. Fragments of his *Life* by the third-century biographer Satyrus, first published in 1912, confirm that he was a friend of the philosopher Anaxagoras and of Timotheus, the master of the new music. His perceptions of contemporary life and intellectual movements he embodied in his plays; he was an innovator, in form as in content. His chief innovation was realism, not the realism which turns a blind eye to all but the seamy side of life, but the realism which made his Admetus and Jason and Orestes, his Electra and Medea and Helen seem, despite their grandiloquent associations, contemporaries of his audience, and their problems directly relevant to the lives of his audience. He discerned abuses, social, political, and religious, and inveighed against them, but aside from a bias in favor of reason and against coercion no consistent program can be extracted from his plays. He loved Athens, but showed his bitter hatred of the Melian massacre; he was on the side of the democracy, but was prosecuted for impiety, Satyrus tells us, by Cleon, the democracy's leader. The agility of his mind appears in such plays as *Alcestis* and *Helen* and even the Aeschylean parody in *Electra,* and is distressing to sober scholars who like a clear partition between the serious and the gay—such scholars as insist that the *Republic* must be read either as a literal prescription or a long joke, or that Homer regarded the gods either with amused skepticism or with reverence.

Besides making his characters and their problems contemporary Euripides introduced more tangible innovations. His dialogue is nearer the colloquial, though it is still formal, especially in the line-for-line *stichomythia*. His choral odes are musically more elaborate and tend to be detachable from the rest of the play. His plays frequently begin with a monologue, by an actor who may or may not appear in the rest of the play, which provides necessary information about the play. Notable and, if the view here accepted is correct, highly significant is his use of the god out ᴏf the machine. When a play has so developed that its logical conclusion would be at variance with the traditional myth, a divinity appears to restore the appropriate direction for the ending. But surely the "wrong" direction was not due to accident; what the poet does, in effect, is to provide endings on two separate planes, one for the devout or for those who prefer a happy ending, and the other (always easily to be supplied by easy logic from the point where the god appears) for those willing to imagine the conclusion of the tragedy in its own terms.

So in *Alcestis* (438 B.C.), our earliest play, Admetus has allowed his wife to die for him. To Euripides' audience, who regarded women as inferior and dynastic considerations as important, Admetus' conduct was not repulsive, and the poet takes pains to show, through the hospitality shown Heracles, that Admetus conformed to the gentleman's code. Our eyes are opened to Admetus' egotism by the powerful scene with Pheres, when father and son reproach each other for letting Alcestis die; and Admetus' eyes are opened to a woman's worth when he returns from the funeral and it is too late. There is a lesson in equality of the sexes and there is tragedy, for experience teaches that death is permanent. But Heracles, whose previous appearances have inspired little confidence that he could perform such a feat, wrestles with Death and recovers Alcestis; the story and the happy ending are saved for those who wish it so.

Medea (431 B.C.) attacks contemporary injustice not only to women but also to foreigners; children by foreign wives were not regarded as legitimate citizens. Though Medea was a princess in Colchis, she gave up all for Jason, saved his life and bore him children, and now he deserts her to marry a Corinthian princess. He replies to her protests by asserting that bringing her to the civilization of Greece and making her name known there was adequate compensation. She plans to kill their children to avenge herself on Jason, but is troubled by lack of a subsequent refuge for herself. In a scene which calls attention to itself by its awkwardness

King Aegeus of Athens promises her a home; thus reassured she proceeds to cause the death of her rival and her rival's father and then to
kill her children. Jason, at the head of an angry crowd, is about to break
down the doors of the house; it appears certain that he will and that
Medea will meet the violent death which will fittingly crown the tragedy.
But she escapes, carrying the bodies of the children, on a chariot drawn
through the air by dragons. With such a chariot at her disposal, the
Aegeus scene becomes even more difficult; but if her relief at Aegeus'
promise is genuine, then perhaps the chariot is a kind of curtain to shield
queasy spectators from the lynching which logic and tragedy demand.

The *Heraclidae,* or *Children of Heracles,* which must date from the
early years of the Peloponnesian War, is, as we read it, among the poorest
of the plays. Only part of the trouble is due to gaps in the text; the real
gap is in our ignorance of some topical allusion, perhaps of some competing play which is being parodied. Athenian generosity in giving asylum
to the persecuted children of Heracles and in treatment of war prisoners
is glorified, but there is a curious tongue-in-cheek quality about the
characterization of the heroes of legend which breaks out into the openly
ludicrous when Iolaus totters off with armor he cannot carry to win
greater glory. But in Euripides we must not insist on an either-or classification of the comic and the serious; the praise of Athens is sincere,
and the self-immolation of Macaria very moving.

Hippolytus (428 B.C.) is the best single exhibition of Euripides' art,
his psychological insight, his religious outlook, and his social preachment.
Aphrodite and Artemis each represents powerful forces in life which are
scorned only at great peril. They are not gentle; part of Artemis' solace
to the dying Hippolytus is that she will retaliate by destroying a devotee
of Aphrodite. Hippolytus goes to excess in his hostility to Aphrodite and
is stiff in his social contacts (but not when he is alone) because he labors
under the stigma of bastardy. Phaedra struggles gallantly but hopelessly
against the net which life draws tighter about her. Doom is no less inevitable than in Sophocles, but unlike Sophocles, Euripides looks at both
parties to the struggle, and if he does not deny the power of divine forces
he does provoke the questions as to the justice of the moral order.

Andromache can only be understood by a generation which fought
a war against fascism. Regarded as a story with plot and characterization, no critical ingenuity can save *Andromache* from its glaring shortcomings. The stories at beginning and end are almost unrelated; probability in entrances and exits is utterly disregarded; there is no real
characterization but unrelieved white and black. The play is about a
single idea, the unprincipled ruthlessness of the Spartan way, and the or-

dinary amenities of the playwright are scorned as irrelevant ornaments in the severely functional treatment. Menelaus, Hermione, and Orestes display the facets of Spartan baseness; Menelaus is arrogant and cruel, a liar and a cheat; Hermione is luxurious and licentious, with a parochial contempt of foreigners; Orestes steals a man's wife in his absence and plots his death—at the hands of others. His patron is Apollo, whose oracle was a Spartan partisan in the Peloponnesian War. It is surely with some Spartan atrocity in the war, perhaps the slaughter of the Plataeans, that *Andromache* is to be connected.

Hecuba (perhaps 425 B.C.) is also episodic, and the fact that it is Hecuba whom the deaths of Polyxena and Polydorus touch most nearly and that it is Hecuba who punishes Polymestor is not sufficient to unify the play. Again the tragic theme is an idea, the miseries brought upon humanity by war, with which politics (the circumstances of Polyxena's death) and greed (Polymestor) are inevitably associated.

The plays of the war years deal with the subject uppermost in the minds of Athenians. If *Suppliant Women* was written when Athens rejected Spartan peace overtures after Sphacteria (424 B.C.), then certain pacifist passages scattered through the play could be regarded as indicating the theme, like anti-Spartanism in *Andromache*. "If Death were in full view when votes are cast, Greece would never be destroying itself by war madness" (484 f.). "Foolish cities, when it is in your power to avert evils by reason, you settle matters by blood, not reason" (748 f.). Athens is again praised for its justice and its championing of the weak, specifically in assisting the mothers of the Argive Seven to obtain their sons' bodies for burial from Thebes. Athens' generous concern is for all Greece.

Heracles (*ca.* 420 B.C.), like *Andromache* and *Suppliants,* is a triptych. While Heracles is absent on a mission to the underworld, Lycus, usurper at Thebes, abuses and is about to kill his family; Heracles dramatically returns to save his family, shows himself an affectionate father, boasts somewhat excessively of his real achievements, falls mad and kills his children; and Theseus, whom Heracles has saved from Hades, prevails upon him not to commit suicide but to accompany him to Athens. The tragedy is that of a great character who has shown himself a benefactor of humanity, a loyal son and affectionate father, and, eventually, brave enough to live when it is easier to die, being beaten down by the gods and reconciling himself to life through the love of a friend. Fundamentally, the tragedy is like Oedipus', but the treatment is very different, and the realism of the human characters only underscores the heartlessness of the divine. The scene of Heracles' madness is among the finest of its kind.

Ion, of uncertain date, is one of a group which includes *Alcestis, Iphigenia among the Taurians,* and *Helen,* all extremely well constructed, all comic, not only by reason of happy endings, but in general lightness of tone and in passages openly humorous, all critical of received legends concerning the gods. The plays are still tragedies, no longer of the universal type, however, but applicable primarily to the story in hand. The great step to the equally serious comedy of manners and to drama of the modern type has been taken. Ion's disillusionment is like Neoptolemus' in *Philoctetes,* and Creusa's happiness depends upon a lie being concealed, but both are relatively private tragedies, though still tragedies. Apollo is proven a rogue, without the poet having to show anger, and Hermes in the prologue and Athena in the epiphany are his amiable accomplices. Yet nowhere in pagan literature do we get a more effective representation of the beauty of holiness than in the early scenes.

The date of *Trojan Women* is important. It was produced in 415 B.C., after the Athenians had acted upon the principle of the right of might set forth in the Melian dialogue at the end of Thucydides 5 and before they set out upon the Syracusan expedition described in Thucydides 6. Its theme is the degradation and sorrow which war brings, on victor no less than on vanquished. The only cheerful person in the play is the bedizened and conscienceless Helen—for whom the war was fought. But the tone is profound sorrow rather than bitterness, and though the Melian affair had tried Euripides' patriotism sore and his gods threaten disaster at sea to a people about to sail against Syracuse, his chorus still prefers that the lot of slavery will take them to Theseus' land rather than to Sparta.

Castor's speech at the end of *Electra* suggests that the Sicilian expedition had sailed but had not yet come to grief, and the play is therefore dated to 413 B.C. Like the *Ion* group, *Electra* is well constructed, light in tone and in parts humorous, and it has the same criticism of traditional religion, but the savage characterization and the virtual denial of Apollo's existence make this an angrier play. Because the story and its persons are so familiar from *Choephoroe* and Sophocles, no play is as well suited as this to demonstrate Euripides' realism, especially in showing how the heroic deeds of legend look when carried out by contemporaries masquerading under the great names. Straightway Euripides shocks his audience by making the scene a hovel and the first speaker a peasant; further along, the parody of Aeschylus' recognition tokens proclaims the departure from the heroic. Electra is a self-pitying slattern, Orestes a timorous ruffian, Clytemnestra a suburban clubwoman, Aegisthus a courteous and popular ruler, the murders as dastardly as conceivable, Aegisthus' courtesy and Clytemnestra's mother-love being exploited to lure them to their death.

Iphigenia among the Taurians (date uncertain) is likely to be a favorite with modern audiences. The scene is a romantic country ruled by a barbarian king, the plot is intricate and exciting, the recognition scene's effectiveness has been praised by Aristotle and all subsequent critics, and the loyal friendship between Orestes and Pylades (who speaks at last) is touching. To the Greeks the scenes between these two are love scenes, and their poignancy is accordingly heightened. The noble savage puts Greek cunning in a bad light, but the weightier lesson is another attack on Apollo, who sends inconvenient protégés where they may be forgotten. The god out of the machine seems as clear an example of the alternative ending as in *Medea;* we are expressly told that a storm has prevented the Greeks' ship from leaving, and without the god the barbarians must surely have punished the Greeks' treacherous theft of their idol.

Helen (412 B.C.) is very funny. It is best read as a parody of Euripides himself, especially of the *Iphigenia*—for here too wily Greeks befuddle a barbarian king—but also of his general style. Menelaus is a bragging and whining beggar, and the recognition scene with Helen is burlesque in the conventional and in the American sense. Throughout, the comedy is broad as well as subtle, and makes us uneasy about our sober reading of certain passages in other plays. But *Helen* cannot have been presented as serious tragedy; it must have been substituted for the satyr play or given on some other occasion when serious drama was not expected.

Phoenician Women (*ca.* 410 B.C.) differs from all our other plays in being a continuous narrative, in which Euripides or his interpolators included all Theban legend rather than a concentration upon one tragic theme. The chorus connects Thebes with Cadmus and his Phoenician origin, and the subject matter of both *Oedipuses, Seven, Antigone,* is presented, with sensational elaboration, in a broad sweep which is thrilling but not, in the traditional sense, tragic. The play was extremely popular in later antiquity, perhaps because it gave so much and demanded so little, and its popularity was the cause of numerous interpolations which make the fullness even fuller.

Orestes (408 B.C.) carries on from *Electra* in all respects, in the story of what happened to the matricides of *Electra,* in the psychological treatment of their abnormal characters, in the transposition of the story to fifth-century conditions, in its comic passages, and in its attack on tradition. All these elements are intensified, and the result is a well-constructed and absorbing play. A new approach may be detected in the social criticism, for the moral shortcomings of a degenerate aristocracy are made plain. These aristocrats retain the virtues of their class, a touching loyalty between Orestes and Electra and Orestes and Pylades, but this loyalty is self-centered and disregards public law and the common good.

Bacchants, presented posthumously in 405 B.C., is among Euripides' finest in poetry, dramatic technique, and tragic concept, and it speaks more significantly to moderns than any other Greek tragedy. Pentheus wishes to govern himself and his city by the exclusive light of reason. Cadmus pays prudential lip service but also distrusts the god who represents emotion and enthusiasm. But that power is as real and exacting in human life as is Aphrodite's in *Hippolytus.* It is nonsense to say that Euripides at the end of his life recanted his rationalism. His concept of the powers which constrain human life is consistent. In *Bacchants* they are no less amoral than they have been, nor does Euripides emulate Aeschylus in attempting to force morality upon them. That is the flaw in the universe which is the foundation of tragedy.

Iphigenia in Aulis was presumably completed by Euripides' son and by him presented along with *Bacchants* and *Alcmaeon.* The text is considerably disturbed both at beginning and end. In order to retain his command by sacrificing his daughter so that contrary winds would no longer retard the expedition to Troy, Agamemnon has enticed Clytemnestra to bring Iphigenia to Aulis on the pretense of marriage with Achilles. The bearers of these grand names are, as we have learned to expect, contemporary Athenians; what is new is that they are so represented, not to debunk legend, but to tell a dramatic story, for its own sake, about ordinary people confronted by crisis. The fact that the crisis involves a marriage marks the transition to the bourgeois New Comedy of Menander. *Iphigenia* is entertaining and has scenes of high pathos, but tragedy is finished.

Rhesus is a bad play, and many critics, some ancient, have denied it Euripidean authorship. But it has come down in Euripides texts, and its various faults may individually be paralleled from genuine Euripidean plays. But a cento of faults with no apparent explanation, and no redeeming excellence of story, characterization, or dramatic idea, is hard to accept as Euripides. The story is a dramatization of *Tenth Iliad,* with a gratuitous intervention of Athena in the middle. If *Iphigenia in Aulis* proves tragedy finished, *Rhesus* shows that heroic names and legends are done. For imaginative literature, new stories and new names will have to be invented.

Cyclops is the only complete satyr play extant. Its witty and bawdy fooling turn on Odysseus' adventures with Polyphemus as told in *Odyssey* 9, where Odysseus tricks the Cyclops by giving his name as Outis ("No Man"). The rollicking satyrs and their robust humor are less startling in Euripides, who despite his moodiness and earnestness produced a *Helen*, than is the humor of Sophocles in *Ichneutai*.

The fragments of the some eighty remaining plays are, with the exception of *Phaethon* and *Andromeda* (which was particularly esteemed in antiquity), very short. The more interesting titles are: *Telephus, Philoctetes, Bellerophon, Erechtheus, Antiope, Hypsipyle, Melanippe the Wise,* and *Cresophontes* (on the Merope story). We have and know more of Euripides' work than of his predecessors' because, though he won so few prizes in his lifetime, after his death he far outstripped them in popularity. Euripides was read and loved when Aeschylus had become unintelligible and Sophocles remote. The nineteenth century disparaged him, having set Sophocles up as the standard from which deviation was counted a fault. The early twentieth grew so enthusiastic over the discovery of the philosopher on the stage with a program of reform that it neglected the artist. There can be no question of Euripides' authentic stature as artist, as there is no question of his deep concern for problems of belief and conduct. His reflections on these problems were significant to his first audiences, and they retain their significance through the generations.

Of the lesser tragedians of the fifth century B.C. five are mentioned with respect: Neophron of Sicyon, Aristarchus of Tegea, Ion of Chios—the only Greek author who wrote in several forms—Achaeus of Eretria, and Agathon of Athens. Agathon is the host in Plato's *Symposium,* and appears and is parodied in Aristophanes' *Thesmophoriazusae.* Aristotle tells us (*Poetics* 1451*b*) that Agathon invented both plot and character for a play; we know that he wrote one with the fanciful name *Anthos* ("Flower"). Aristotle also tells us that his choral songs were musical interludes (1456*a*), and in the same context that he pleased popular taste by producing tragic effects which satisfied the moral sense.

Critias, friend of Plato, leader of the Thirty, and subsequently the special hero of the Second Sophistic, wrote tragedies as well as elegies; we know of a *Pirithous* and a *Sisyphus* of his. There seem to have been three tragedians named Astydamas in the fourth century; the elder Astydamas' *Parthenopaeus* won great acclaim in 340 B.C., and his *Hector* is highly praised by Plutarch. Aristotle compares Euripides' best recognition scene, in *Iphigenia among the Taurians,* with that in Polyidus' *Iphigenia,* and gives the palm to Polyidus. Aristotle (*Rhetoric* 3.12.2) mentions Chaeremon as a poet who wrote to be read rather than acted; his fragments sug-

gest a preoccupation with sensual beauty, especially of flowers. Dionysius
the Elder, tyrant of Syracuse, was ridiculed for his efforts to write tragedy,
but won a prize in 367, the year of his death. Lucian (*The Illiterate Book-
Fancier* 15) tells us that Dionysius purchased and treasured Aeschylus'
desk, but that the desk failed to transmit genius. A sometime protégé of
the Younger Dionysius, Carcinus, wrote 160 plays and won eleven victories; he is several times cited by Aristotle. Theodectes of Phaselis, a
pupil of Plato, Aristotle, and Isocrates, was a successful orator and produced fifty plays, winning eight firsts in thirteen entries. The Cynic
philosophers, Diogenes and Crates, wrote plays, not for presentation, but
as propaganda pamphlets. Moschion, of whom little else is known, wrote
historical plays. Again we close with a satyr play. *Agen* was produced
about 324 B.C. during the Dionysiac festival celebrated in the camp of
Alexander the Great on the banks of the Hydaspes in the Punjab. Its
author, Athenaeus tells us (595*b*), was Alexander himself or one Python.
In the world which Alexander left behind the only sort of tragedy that
could be written was that of the Alexandrian Pleiad. That and the much
more vital New Comedy will be considered in its proper place. We leave
Melpomene now to sojourn a while with Thalia.

ARISTOPHANES

Pentheus in *Bacchants* came to grief because he failed to realize that
the regime of dry reason must periodically be interrupted by a season of
release, that if the sobriety of 360 days is to be kept untainted, five days
must be given over to Dionysus. It is important to realize that comedy
too was part of a religious ritual, though there was little of the solemnity
which we associate with religion. Comedies were presented in the same
theater as tragedy and at the same festivals, though on special days and
hours. Both forms told a story by acting it out in verse dialogue, with an
obviously traditional chorus for song and dance, but comedy's explosive
fantasy and boisterous bawdiness seemed calculated to put it at the farthest
remove from the somber dignity of tragedy. It is difficult to know whether,
as many scholars hold, the heroically obscene elements in comedy are
direct vestiges of a fertility rite in which comedy originated, or whether
they are there because incongruity is a capital element in the ridiculous, and
indecency is incongruous in Greek literature. All the kinds of things that
have ever moved men to laugh are to be found in Old Comedy: slapstick
and subtle word play, invective and burlesque, dialect and mumming,
and ever and again the physiological jokes, excretory and reproductive. The
mask and costume of the comic actor set the tone. He was ridiculously

padded on belly and behind, and his short jacket just fell short of the
crotch, which was decorated with a colossal phallus. Exculpations of
Aristophanic humor on the ground that it is clean dirt and not prurient
miss the mark. Every type of sex joke from the infantile to the most
sophisticated is represented; no female human or divine appears on the
stage without the suggestion being made that she be put to sexual use
forthwith. Aristophanes is not prurient because his comedy is a comedy
of pure wit, which attacks the head and not the entrails. None of the
characters engages the audience's sympathy as human beings; with none
can the audience identify itself. They are like characters in Rabelais, not
Cervantes; like the Marx Brothers, not Charlie Chaplin.

For us Old Comedy means Aristophanes. The Alexandrians joined
Cratinus and Eupolis with him to make a Comic Three as a pendant to
the tragedians, but it appears that Aristophanes towered above his rivals
by a much greater interval than any of the three tragedians was separated
from his. On the other hand, the titles and scrappy fragments of Aristophanes' rivals suggest that they differed from him in quality and degree
but not essentially in kind. Here we shall do little more than record their
names, nor can we linger over theories which attempt to explain the
origin of comedy. Aristotle's jejune sentences on the subject (*Poetics*
1449*ab*) are perfunctory and have been more vigorously disputed by
modern scholars than his fuller treatment of tragedy. It is clear that the
phallic revels which he declared the basis of comedy must have been a
large element in its origin, for they continued to be a paramount factor.
Doubtless other factors, such as beast mummeries, common to many
peoples, and iambic lampooning, which was a regular element in popular
festivals, entered in. It is also reasonable to suppose, whether or not comedy
developed from the dithyramb, that it was somehow connected with
Dionysus, almost certainly in its origin, and clearly in its developed form,
for it was presented at Dionysiac festivals.

Specific knowledge is wanting because "it was only at a late point in
its progress that a chorus of comedians was officially granted by the archon;
they used to be mere volunteers." The invention of comedy was claimed
by the Megarians (1447*b*), and the inventor's name is given by the Parian
Marble as Susarion, dated to the early sixth century. It became a regularly
established form at the Great Dionysia in 488, at which time Chionides
is said to have won the prize. The next names are supplied by Aristophanes
in the parabasis to *Knights* (424 B.C.), which complains of the bad treatment accorded comic poets when they grow old. First he names Magnes
(519 ff.) and makes allusions to titles of his plays, which the scholiast
explains as referring to *Harpists, Birds, Lydians, Gallflies,* and *Frogs.*

Epigraphical evidence records a victory for Magnes in 472. Next the parabasis mentions (526 ff.) Cratinus (*ca.* 490–470 B.C.), one of the Comic Three. Young Aristophanes speaks of his elder as a toper ruined by drink, and the very next year (423 B.C.) Cratinus' *Pytine* ("Wine-flask"), defeated Aristophanes' *Clouds*. Of the twenty-eight titles ascribed to Cratinus, most is known, due to discovery of a papyrus containing its hypothesis in 1904, of *Dionysalexandrus,* which apparently gave a rollicking account of the rape of Helen, giving Dionysus, attended by a rout of satyrs, the role of Paris. Other of Cratinus' plays were: *Nemesis* (who takes Leda's swan form and becomes the mother of Helen); *Chirons,* which Cratinus regarded as his best; *Odysses* (plural of Odysseus) on the Cyclops story; *Thracian Women,* from which Plutarch (*Pericles* 13) quotes a line calling Pericles a "squill-headed Zeus"; *Archilochoi; Nomoi* ("Laws"), in which Solon probably appeared; *Eunidai,* from which Aristophanes mentions two songs; *Boukoloi* ("Herdsmen"); *Cleoboulinai; Ploutoi; Seriphians; Busiris,* doubtless on the Heracles story; *Delian Women; Empipramenoi* ("The Ignited"); *Malthakoi* ("Softies"); *Panoptai* ("The All-seeing"); *Pylaia.*

Aristophanes next mentions (*Knights* 537 ff.) Crates, of whom Aristotle says (*Poetics* 1449*b*) that he was "the first to drop the comedy of invective and frame stories of general and non-personal nature, in other words, fables or plots." Of the fifteen titles ascribed to him *Theria* ("Beasts"), is the only one of which we have some knowledge. This play had talking animals and foresaw mechanized kitchens where all utensils worked automatically. Phrynichus (not to be confused with the tragedian of *Sack of Miletus*) wrote ten plays between 429 and 405 and is alluded to in the parabasis of *Clouds* (556 f.). Pherecrates' *Agrioi* ("Savages") seems to deal with a Golden Age, like Aristophanes' *Birds;* his *Corianno* seems to foreshadow New Comedy love intrigue. Other of Pherecrates' titles are: *Graes* ("Old Women"); *Petale; Craptaloi,* involving adventures in Hades; *Automoloi* ("Deserters"), probably political; *Myrmekanthropoi* ("Ant-Men"); *Agathoi* ("Worthies"); *Doulodidascalus* ("Slave Teacher"); *Epilesmon* ("Forgetful Man"); *Ipnos* ("Kitchen"); *Leroi* ("Trifles"); *Metalles* ("Miners"); *Metoikoi; Persians; Tyranny;* and *Chiron.* Of a number of these the authorship is disputed.

Teleclides belonged to the Periclean age and is represented by five titles: *Amphictyones; Apseudeis* ("Truth-tellers"); *Hesiodoi* ("Hesiods"); *Prytaneis* ("Presiding Magistrates"); *Sterroi* ("Stiffs"). Amipsias defeated Aristophanes in 423 and 414. Nicophon, Polyzelus, and Hermippus are little more than names. The latter, who brought Pericles' Aspasia up on charges of impiety, wrote forty plays. The third (with Aristophanes and Cratinus) of the comic triad was Eupolis, born in 445 B.C. and killed, probably in a sea action, in the Peloponnesian War. He claimed to have helped Aristophanes write *Knights,* and his *Flatterers* defeated Aristophanes' *Peace* in 421. Eupolis' *Demes* was a very highly regarded political play, conservative in tone; *Baptai* abused Alcibiades; *Flatterers* apparently ridiculed Protagoras and Callias, Protagoras' host in Plato's dialogue. *Poleis* ("Cities") probably had a chorus of which the members represented the cities of the Athenian empire, probably pleading for better treatment. *Taxiarchoi* ("Captains") is like *Frogs,* except that here Dionysus was looking for a good commander. Among other titles attributed to Eupolis are *Astrateutoi* ("Shirkers"); *Autolycus;* and *Chrysous Genos* ("Golden Age").

Plato Comicus (so called to distinguish him from the philosopher), a somewhat younger contemporary of Aristophanes, appears to have been esteemed in antiquity next after the Three. Of the some thirty titles recorded, such specimens as *Alliance, Hyperbolos, Greece or the Islands,* indicate a political interest; others suggest a parody of mythology; *Spartans or Poets,* and *Skeuai* ("Costumes") seem to deal with literary and theatrical subjects. In view of Plato's reputation his fragments are exceedingly scarce. He himself complained that because of his poverty he sold plays to others to present. Other poets part of whose career is connected with Old Comedy are Theopompus, Strattis, and Lysippus. It is a pity that we have no complete comedy except Aristophanes', but it is clear that the survival of one among the many was not accident, and we may be reasonably sure that in the eleven plays of Aristophanes we have the most representative work of the best poet. We turn, then, from barren lists to something more tangible.

Before considering Aristophanes' individual plays it will be convenient to notice certain peculiarities common to all of them. The structure of comedy, while not nearly so regular as tragedy, still maintains a pattern of its own. A prologue, either a monologue or dialogue, puts the audience in possession of the plot. Always it is based upon some wildly fantastic idea, contrary to all human experience, such as ascending to heaven to obtain peace or establishing a utopia in the clouds or descending to Hades to fetch a poet or calling a sex strike. Once the premises of this world-destroying idea are accepted, the consequences are natural. The first part of the play has to do with achieving the idea. Usually there is an *agon,* or conflict, vigorously enacted by two parts of the chorus, advocating or opposing the innovation in question. A special and wide variety of meters is employed in the *agon,* usually culminating in a kind of patter song. Somewhere about the center of the play there is a *parabasis,* where the chorus steps forward and speaks directly in the name of the poet, with little reference to the subject matter of the play. Toward the end the idea which was to be realized is shown in action. Usually the plays end with the "hero" going off for a revel and feast with some young woman, with whom there is to be a sort of marriage. Scholars have labored to show the ritual genesis of these various parts, and especially of the "marriage" at the end. Whatever validity their arguments may have, it may be remarked that the only psychologically suitable "solution" for comedy is the relaxation and renewal implicit in such a revel. Considering the nature of comedy its regularity and refinement are more remarkable than its looseness. Whatever the expectations of other Greek writers may have been, it is clear that Aristophanes was writing for a single performance and had no thought of becoming a classic. Language is used with exuberance, new formations are freely coined, liberties are taken with meter. Yet the lyrics in Aristophanes are among the most exquisite in the language.

Aristophanes' primary aim, obviously, was to give expression to his ebullient wit, to entertain, to win the prize; but he was an Athenian, and had convictions on many subjects, and it is inevitable that these convictions should appear in his writing. These convictions, in music and education as well as in politics, are consistently and pronouncedly conservative. So outspoken is he in his attacks on democratic leaders and favorite democratic policies that competent critics have gone to the absurd length of declaring that he was in the pay of the oligarchical, pro-Sparta party. On the other hand, it cannot be maintained that his ridicule of democratic leaders is a natural comedian's device, anything new or strange being an easy mark for ridicule. In fact, his audience was substantially identical with the ecclesia which voted for the leaders and policies he attacked. Time and again he claims that the poet's function is to instruct and guide, notably in several passages in *Acharnians* and *Frogs,* as for example (*Frogs* 1054 f.) : "Boys at school have a teacher to instruct them, but poets are the teachers of men."

Aristophanes disliked anything that disturbed the old-fashioned disciplines. He did not like the Sophists with their trains of eternally arguing young men. He did not like the new fashions in music, the new self-consciousness of the suppressed classes. Particularly he attacked Cleon, Pericles' successor as leader of the democracy. Ancient authorities are at one in condemning Cleon, but in this respect the impartiality of none is above question. The fact is that Cleon continued the policies of Pericles, but whereas Pericles was himself a "gentleman," Cleon was not. As against the jostling merchant and sailor class, the conservative and land-holding class had real admiration for Spartan conservatism and discipline, and little to gain and much to lose by the war. In the passions of war years there is little room for moderates. In foreign policy Aristophanes' moderation was surely on sound grounds. What he desired, as *Lysistrata* shows, was in fact the only thing that could have saved Greece: peace between Athens and Sparta and a pan-Hellenic union to present a united front against the powers of the east. The crying need for such union to avert inevitable doom is in the background of Thucydides' history, and was urgently advocated by Isocrates. But however farseeing Aristophanes' policy may have been, the fact remains that he was tender-minded to the Spartans and their friends and their friends' ideas, and opposed the representatives of those who were associated with new ideas.

Because of his concern with immediate problems and personages and their human backgrounds rather than with eternal verities, Aristophanes' teeming plays are incomparably our most important help for real knowledge of the people of Greece. He breezes through the museum hall where the majestic figures stand fixed, and they drop their poses and move about and talk, about everything that men talk about. When Dionysius, tyrant of Syracuse, asked Plato to describe the constitution of Athens, Plato sent him the works of Aristophanes. But however useful such knowledge may be, and whatever instruction the political issues in which Aristophanes took part may provide, his prime claim is as a genius of exuberant wit, a true creator who fashioned worlds in fantasy, as he fashioned man himself in Plato's charming and lifelike picture in the *Symposium*.

The first extant play is *Acharnians,* presented in 425 B.C. when the author was twenty, which won the prize over Cratinus and Eupolis. Dicaeopolis makes an individual peace with Sparta, but as he is about to celebrate the long intermitted vintage festival he is attacked by a chorus of Acharnian charcoal burners who represent the war party and wins a hearing by a parody of Euripides' *Telephus*. In a seriocomic speech he shows that the causes of the war were trifling, and wins over half the chorus, who are engaged in a violent agon by the other half. These call in the general Lamachus to assist them, but the general too is beaten in argument, and the chorus, uniting on Dicaeopolis' side, deliver the poet's parabasis. Then Megarians and Boeotians bring in for sale the good things Athens has lacked. A herald summons Lamachus to a hard campaign, and another Dicaeopolis to a wine party. Lamachus returns wounded, and Dicaeopolis reels in, having won the prize for drinking, on the arms of pretty flute girls, whom he leads out in procession. If we are astonished at the temerity of a poet who could say a word for the enemy and many words for pacifism amid the passions of war, we must be amazed at a democracy which permitted and sponsored such a play in time of war, and gave it first prize.

Acharnians shows a keen freshness, but it is in every way equal to Aristophanes' most mature work. It has the characteristic topsy-turvy fantasy of a one-man peace, beautiful lyrics, the rollicking burlesque of Euripides, vigorous exposition of an idea, tireless energy, and a reveling finale. If we admire the political tolerance of the audience, or, alternatively, their greater devotion to art, we must also admire their cultivation, for constantly Aristophanes' parodies of tragedy assume a close and wide familiarity with the poets. We have no better evidence for the general culture of the community which produced the intellectual giants of fifth-century Greece.

The fresh and mercurial inventiveness which makes *Acharnians* delightful is gone from *Knights* (424 B.C.), which is a virulent and unrelieved attack, not upon war, but upon the man Cleon. The play starts with a transparent allegory as two slaves of crotchety old Demos ("the people"), got up to resemble the generals Nicias and Demosthenes (the older editions so name the characters), complain of the bullying of Demos' new favorite, a Paphlagonian leather-seller, who represents Cleon. Among the oracles they steal from Cleon is one which foretells that Cleon shall be supplanted by a sausage-seller. The sausage-seller appears, and is persuaded that his rascality and impudence qualify him; Cleon accuses his slaves of treason, and the chorus of knights, possibly riding pick-a-back, rush to their assistance. Cleon dashes out to complain to the senate; but Sausage-seller has outdone Cleon in brazenness, and when both seek to win over Demos, Sausage-seller (now named Agoracritus) succeeds. During a second parabasis Sausage-seller (who had apparently assumed his earlier character only to out-Cleon Cleon) has rejuvenated Demos by stewing him in a pot, and he comes forth determined to abolish innovations and restore the old-fashioned ways. A few months before *Knights* was presented Cleon had brought to a successful conclusion at Sphacteria the most brilliant exploit of the war (what part he had in originating it is questionable), which caused the Spartans to propose peace (Thucydides 4.1–41). In the play Demosthenes says (54 ff.): "The other day I kneaded a Laconian cake at Pylos, but the Paphlagonian with rascally effrontery dodged in and snatched it up and himself served up the cake I had kneaded." On the other hand, a minor exploit of the knights at Corinth is glorified (595 ff.). This and the unrelieved vituperation of Cleon throughout the play are the principal evidence of Aristophanes' attachment to the oligarchical party. It is said that the mask-makers refused to provide a mask of Cleon for this play, and that Aristophanes played the part himself. Cleon doubtless sat in the front row during the performance, the right of proedria having been conferred upon him for the exploit at Pylos. The part of this play which Eupolis helped write was the second parabasis; possibly Eupolis' use of the same passage in his own *Maricas* is the basis for Aristophanes' charge in *Clouds* (553 ff.) that Eupolis' *Maricas* was a distortion of his own *Knights*.

Compared to the treatment accorded Cleon in *Knights*, Socrates is handled almost with affection in *Clouds* (423 B.C.), but readers are most offended with *Clouds* because of the reverence which has come to be paid Socrates. The play is damaging indeed (in his *Apology*, twenty-five years later, Socrates was to blame it for creating prejudice against him) and on false grounds, for he did not study natural science, did not charge fees, was not a Sophist. But a caricaturist who wished to attack the Sophists could scarcely avoid making Socrates his butt; not only was he the best known teacher (but without the aura of sanctity which generations have given him), but his physical idiosyncrasies invited caricature. It is said that when the mask-maker's art was applauded on his double's first appearance, Socrates stood up in the theater to show the likeness. It is not Socrates but science (which questioned all traditions) and the glib seekers for new knowledge which would permit them to evade responsibility that are pilloried. The contest between Just and Unjust Reason or between traditional and modern education exhibits Aristophanes' nostalgia for the old, but as in his preference of Aeschylus over Euripides the praise of the old is not unqualified. Our text of the play is a revision, which was never officially presented, and there are, consequently, serious inconsistencies in plot. The original play ran third, being defeated by Cratinus' *Pytine* and Amipsias' *Connus*.

Wasps (422 B.C.) is directed against the institution of large paid juries and their subservience to such leaders as Cleon, and incidentally against ill-founded pretenses to grand manners. The question of pay for public service was an important one in the Greek democracy, for without pay decisions would be left in the hands of those who could afford leisure. It is Aristophanes' point that with only a fraction of the state income supposedly used for such purposes (656 ff.) the demagogues purchase loyalty to themselves. The scene of Philocleon's attempted escapes when his son has shut him in is delightfully funny, as is the trial scene of the dog.

In *Peace* (421 B.C.) a farmer called Trygaeus ascends to heaven on a beetle to procure an end to the war. The gods have washed their hands of the Greeks and left War to work his will. He has buried Peace, and the chorus eventually succeed in drawing her up, to the consternation of those who profit by war and the hearty satisfaction of all others. The text as we have it is probably a conflation of two editions, but it is full of charm and high spirits. *Peace* contains what has been called the earliest idyllic poetry of the Greeks. The second parabasis (1140 ff.) which begins, in the Rogers translation,

> Ah, there's nothing half so sweet as when the seed is in the ground,
> God a gracious rain is sending, and a neighbor saunters round—

has been aptly described by Gilbert Norwood as "a blend of Hesiod, Theocritus, and Christmas as portrayed by Dickens."

There is an interval of seven years until *Birds* (414 B.C.), which attacks no specific abuse but is literally escapist, in that its heroes, wearied of the Athenian atmosphere, decide to build a utopia, which they call Nephelococcygia ("Cloudcuckoosbury"), in the sky. In fantasy, poetry, construction, good humor, *Birds* shows Aristophanes at his best, and the play is usually regarded as his masterpiece. The delegation of the gods who have come to conclude terms with the new city, which has made itself a bottleneck for sacrifices ascending from earth, is one among many delightful touches; another is the reception accorded malefactors and public nuisances who plague life on earth when they come up to exploit a virgin field. The bird lyrics are delightful, especially such a piece as the hoopoe's serenade to its mate (209 ff.):

> Awake, my mate!
> Shake off thy slumbers, and clear and strong
> Let loose the floods of thy glorious song,
> The sacred dirge of thy mouth divine
> For sore-wept Itys, thy child and mine;
> Thy tender trillings his name prolong
> With the liquid note of thy tawny throat;
> Through the leafy curls of the woodbine sweet
> The pure sound mounts to the heavenly seat.
> —B. B. Rogers

In the other plays indecency is incidental; in *Lysistrata* (411 B.C.) it is central, and yet the play is in a sense the most serious of the eleven. The debacle at Syracuse in 413 had left its mark. Now, the poet implies, no rational solution of the political problem seems possible, and only so fantastic a scheme as a sex strike on the part of the women can offer hope. The operation of the strike is excruciatingly funny, especially where the young wife teases her panting husband so unmercifully, but the play as a whole is sad. Talk of state policy in the interstices of the sexual theme is quite grave, and the political message of the whole is on a high level, being an advocacy of a pan-Hellenic union to save Greece from destruction.

The sparkle that is wanting in *Lysistrata* is to be found in fullest measure in *Thesmophoriazusae,* presented a few months later, at the Great Dionysia of the same year. At their private festival the women are to try Euripides for traducing their sex, and after applying in vain to Agathon, Euripides persuades his kinsman Mnesilochus to attend disguised as a woman and to protect his interests. The scene where Mnesilochus is singed and scraped and dressed for his role is riotous. At the women's assembly Mnesilochus is suspected when he suggests that Euripides has not revealed a fraction of women's iniquities. When he is put under guard, Euripides in disguise tries to save him by brilliant parodies of rescue scenes from his own *Telephus, Palamedes, Helen,* and *Andromeda.* If *Birds* stands first for fantasy and charm, *Thesmophoriazusae* is irresistible for its energetic and highly literate fooling.

Thesmophoriazusae is rather flattering to Euripides than otherwise. There is no ridicule in the parodies, the charges of the women are proven unjust, and Euripides is spared the broad insinuations made about Agathon. But in *Frogs* (405 B.C.) we have aspersions on Euripides (but almost as serious ones on Aeschylus) based on well-considered and legitimate critical criteria. Dionysus goes to Hades to fetch Euripides, for there are no more good tragic poets. There an elaborate contest takes place to determine whether Aeschylus or Euripides is the better poet. After tests of various elements of their art Dionysus is still at a loss and propounds a political question: What should be done with Alcibiades? Eventually, Aeschylus is chosen. It is clear that Aristophanes learned much from Euripides and knew and liked his poetry; what he objects to is the encouragement Euripides gave to the bright young men who were endlessly chattering of their new social and philosophical ideas. The adventures of Dionysus and his slave Xanthias on their way to Pluto's court are sidesplitting; the songs of the chorus of initiates in Hades are enchanting.

Ecclesiazusae ("Women Assemblymen," 392 B.C.) seems the work of an ebullient spirit grown weary. On the basis of the play alone one might surmise that something had happened to the author; what had happened was that his city had fallen and the spirit was gone out of its people. The project of women sitting in the ecclesia was almost as wildly improbable as going to Hades to fetch a poet; but the fact that it is not absolutely impossible is significant. All reasonable means had failed, and nothing could be worse than conditions as they were. The parody of the communist ideas later to be set forth in the fifth book of Plato's *Republic* shows that these ideas, including a better position for women, were being discussed. Most readers feel that Aristophanes is for the first time disgusting in the picture of the three hags who, following the new law that the least favored must come first, quarrel over and pull about a young man who is trying to make his way to his sweetheart in a balcony, with whom he sings pretty duets.

If *Ecclesiazusae* shows the old spirit crushed, *Plutus* (388 B.C.) is altogether on a humbler level. It has so far departed from Old Comedy that it is counted with Middle Comedy, of which it is, indeed, our only specimen. No individual or institution could take exception to its doctrine: good men are afflicted with poverty because Plutus (Wealth) is blind; his blindness is healed, and everything is made right. The play is entertaining enough, and there are amusing scenes when adjustments are made after the god has recovered his vision; it is respectable in moral and decent in language; and its Greek is easy to read. From antiquity it has been a favorite schoolbook, and there are at present 146 manuscripts of it. But the glory is gone. Instead of choral lyrics there is now merely the mark *chorou* indicating where a choral interlude was to be provided, as there is also in places in *Ecclesiazusae* and as there was to be in New Comedy.

Aristophanes was said to have written forty-four plays altogether, of which the genuineness of four was questioned. Of the lost plays there are almost a thousand fragments. These fragments provide some information concerning *Daitales* ("Banqueters"), produced in 427, when the poet was barely seventeen; *Babylonians* (426 B.C.), a passage of which ridiculed the eloquence of importunate ambassadors; *Georgoi* ("Farmers") (soon after 425 B.C.); *Gerytades; Nesoi* ("Islands"); *Horai* ("Seasons"); *Scenas Catalambanousae* ("Women Taking Booths"). These plays were apparently of the same general character as the eleven that are extant and would probably not alter our estimate of Aristophanes.

Production of Middle Comedy was enormous. Athenaeus says that he read more than eight hundred, and the names of thirty-four writers of Middle Comedy are known. Menander's uncle Alexis (whose life covered most of the fourth century) and Antiphanes (*ca.* 406–332 B.C.) each wrote more than two hundred. "Middle" is a proper designation, for the form looks back to Old Comedy, while the subjects—love interest, violations, recognitions—look forward to the New. These subjects derive from Euripides rather than Aristophanes, and in New Comedy were destined to form the basis for the true comedy of manners. The doubtless unjust impression of consuming interest in food and the appurtenances of dining is due to the circumstance that most of our quotations come from Athenaeus' *Doctors at Dinner*. In any case, the fragments are too slight for profitable discussion; but it is to be doubted that these plays had as much dramatic substance as the plays of the New Comedy, which we shall consider presently.

Before we seek the relief of dealing again with books which are there for us to read, mention must be made of two Sicilian figures whose work is more related to the dramatic form than to any other and who exerted a very great influence on certain subsequent writers. Epicharmus, a somewhat enigmatic figure whose name appears in connection with Pythagoras, Heraclitus, Xenophanes, and Plato was born about 560 B.C., possibly at Cos, and did most of his work in Sicily. His comedies, of which the fragments are exceedingly scanty, had such titles as *Busiris, Odysseus the Deserter, Heracles and the Girdle, The Megarian Woman.* He was esteemed as a thinker no less than as a playwright. He was said to have studied with Pythagoras, quarreled with Xenophanes, and been used by Plato; a fragment echoes Heraclitus. It is doubtful whether statements that he wrote a philosophical poem are trustworthy. Perhaps philosophical adages were collected from his works; certainly actual philosophical works were falsely ascribed to him. It is possible that the works of Epicharmus which Plato used were mimes. Another Syracusan we know wrote mimes, which long enjoyed a high reputation for their art and their wit. This was Sophron, whose mimes were classified as "of women" and "of men." Diogenes Laertius says (3.18) that Plato brought them from Sicily and imitated them; they were the models for the mimes of Theocritus and of Herodes.

Chapter 9. THE HISTORIANS

HERODOTUS

COMPARED WITH THE SPIRITUAL INTENSITY AND CONCENTRATED ARTISTIC POWER
of the dramatists or of Thucydides the wide-eyed wonder, the insatiable
curiosity and the leisurely pace of Herodotus are relaxing and entertaining, but Herodotus is no less a sophisticated and individual artist than
other Greek writers. His apparent artlessness is governed by a strict form
of its own, and his delightful and apparently trivial digressions have a
strict relevance to that form. He alone preserves and makes into literature
a genuine folk art that but for him would have disappeared, the art of
the Logos, the Thing Said, transmitted and augmented through the centuries by nameless bearers. Just as Homer is necessarily the culmination
of a long tradition for which his individual art created a new and definitive
form, so Herodotus used the mass of existing materials, adding the results of his own special inquiries and observations, for building a coherent
architectural structure to illustrate a theme as specific as the wrath of
Achilles or the homecoming of Odysseus and to convey an ethical outlook as definite as the triumph of civilization in the person of Achilles
or of justice in the slaying of the suitors. Like the Homeric bards, Herodotus
declares that his purpose is to preserve the memorable deeds of men.
His canvas is broader than Homer's, he satisfies more kinds of curiosity
and provides a greater volume of historical as contrasted with poetic
truth, but his affinities are with Homer rather than Thucydides, and
the Thucydidean material he presents is only one facet of his work among
many others to which Thucydides was wholly indifferent.

Time and circumstances favored Herodotus. He was born in Halicarnassus in Asia Minor, where streams of civilization rich in *logoi* met and left
their deposit, in 484 B.C., when the great struggle between East and West
was taking shape. He was a nephew of the poet Panyasis. He traveled
widely, whether on business or as a man of means to satisfy curiosity
and collect *logoi* we can only guess. He visited Egypt and Cyrene, Scythia
and the Black Sea regions, the countries of Asia Minor and the valley
of the Euphrates. He sojourned in Samos, knew Delphi intimately at
first hand, but he made his home in Athens. There he read from his

work in public and was on terms of friendship with Sophocles, who borrowed from his work and addressed a poem to him, and doubtless with others of the wits of Athens. He participated in the colonization of Thurii in Italy. He returned to Athens and was probably there in 430, for he shows knowledge of events of that year. He died, probably at Thurii, probably before 424 B.C., for he fails to mention at the relevant point (6.91) the destruction of the Aeginetans at Thyrea (Thucydides 4.57). The nine books of his history, which have been called by the names of the Muses, were probably composed in parts; the priority of Books 7–9 to the earlier books has been plausibly argued, and Book 2 seems to have been composed independently.

The long account of Egypt in Book 2 and similar accounts of other regions in the early books appear to be disproportionate digressions in a work which sets out to record the struggle between Greeks and barbarians, but they are rather ingressions than digressions. The history is a mighty stream, to which lesser tributaries, traced from their sources, are from time to time joined to swell the flood. The struggle involved, at least indirectly, the whole world (the ecumenical view is not the least of Herodotus' contributions), and the forces attached to each protagonist, naturally more numerous and diverse on the side of the barbarians, must be examined and appraised before they are introduced. Nor may apparently insignificant or incredible trivialities be omitted. Whether the rape of Europa and Medea by the Greeks and the rape of the Greek Io and Helen (1.1–5) was actually a cause of hostilities is not so important as that such stories were included in an inventory of grievances. Herodotus himself approves of the Persian view (1.4):

As for the carrying off of women, it is the deed of a rogue; but to make a stir about such as are carried off argues a man a fool. Men of sense care nothing for such women, since it is plain that without their own consent they would never be forced away.

Regard for the enemy's view as well as genuine respect for the merits of his culture and character constitute a most appealing aspect of Herodotus' work, for such tolerance as his has seldom if ever again been manifested in a war history. He is particularly ready to praise social institutions which seem to him superior to the Greek, and if they are unaccountably different he never scoffs. Indians and Greeks are shocked by each other's burial usages, but it is as right for the Indians to eat their dead as it is for the Greeks to burn theirs, for custom is king (3.38). Mutual recrimination among peoples is due to a belief that one's own troubles and his neighbors' vices are the worst; more careful study would convince them of error in each case (7.152). Fairness as between Athens and Sparta was more difficult than as between Greek and barbarian, yet here too Herodotus maintains his balance. Only after a judicious examination of the inevitable consequences of the Spartan proposal to yield the sea to the Persians and make a stand at the Isthmus does he reach a conclusion, to which no one can take exception (7.139): "If then a man should now say that the Athenians were the saviors of Hellas he would not exceed the truth." Here is history *sine ira et studio.*

Why, then, if the antagonists were each worthy and each fulfilling his character, need there have been war? "No one is so foolish," says Croesus after his defeat (1.87), "as to prefer to peace war, in which, instead of sons burying their fathers, fathers bury their sons. But the gods willed it so." History, no less than a fable of Sophocles, is tragedy, and it is as a tragedy that Herodotus writes his work. The stories of Croesus at the outset prefigure the tragedy, describe the nature of the conflict, indicate the tragic flaw in the character of the hero. Adrastus owed his salvation to Croesus, yet despite the best of will and the most elaborate precautions Adrastus was responsible for the death of Croesus' favorite son: destiny is inexorable. "Who is the happiest man you know of?" Croesus confidently asks Solon, after he has displayed his magnificent wealth; and Solon names an obscure Athenian who had died doing his patriotic duty. "Who next?" asks Croesus, hoping to win at least second place. Solon names two Argives, who showed dutifulness to their mother and so won the god's favor, which was prompt death: no man can be called happy until he is safely dead. Croesus' *hubris,* which led him to destruction, but prefigures the greater *hubris* and the greater destruction of Xerxes, whose pride transgressed mortal limits and drove him to lash and cross the seas in an attempt to win a prize too great for mortal man. "See how god with his lightning always smites the bigger animals," Artabanus admonishes Xerxes (7.10), "and will not suffer them to wax insolent, while those of a lesser bulk chafe him not. How likewise his bolts fall ever on the highest houses and tallest trees? So plainly does he love to bring down everything that exalts itself." It is not merely exceeding a fixed measure of prosperity that invites nemesis, be it noted, but the overweening pride and disregard of others which inevitably follow in the train of excess.

In tragedy the nobility of the characters and the gallantry of their struggle prevent the spectacle from becoming an orgy of wanton boys killing flies for their sport, and so it is in Herodotus. Xerxes is no less characteristically magnificent in defeat than in his royal progress in which he bridges the Hellespont and cuts a channel at Athos; he shows royal generosity to Pythius, who offers him his wealth, and cleaves Pythius' son in two when the father asks his release from the army. He is genuinely puzzled when Demaratus, the Spartan exile, assures him that the Greeks will fight no matter how much outnumbered, and without overseers to lash them on. In such passages Herodotus is at his happiest. When Hydarnes offers Spartan envoys wealth and preferment in return for submission they tell him (7.135):

Hydarnes, you are a one-sided counsellor. You have experience of half the matter, but the other half is beyond your knowledge. A slave's life you understand, but never having tasted liberty, you cannot tell whether it be sweet or no. Had you known what freedom is, you would have bidden us fight for it, not with the spear only, but with the battle-axe.

"It is plain from many instances everywhere," Herodotus says in his own person (5.78), "that freedom is an excellent thing; since even the Athenians, who, while they continued under the rule of the tyrants, were not a whit more valiant than any of their neighbors, no sooner shook off the yoke that they became decidedly the first of all."

Before commenting on Herodotus' techniques and historicity it will be convenient to indicate the distribution of his material.

Book 1.—The purpose of the history is to preserve a record of the great deeds of the past, in particular the causes and events of the wars between the Greeks and the Persians. Hostilities were said to have begun with the rape of women, which culminated in the Trojan War (1–5); but in historical times Croesus of Lydia was the first to commit aggressions against Greeks. His family obtained the kingdom through his ancestor Gyges, and it had been greatly increased by his father, Alyattes (6–25). Croesus is visited by Solon (26–33). He determines to make war on Persia, and after testing various oracles, trusts an equivocal oracle of Delphi; in the course of his preparations he seeks alliances with Greek states (34–55), which introduces a digression on the history of Athens and Sparta (56–70). Cyrus takes Sardis, and Croesus is saved from death on a pyre by the miraculous intervention of Apollo; the customs of Lydia are described (71–94). The Medes (95–106) were subjugated by Cyrus, whose early romantic history is recounted (107–130). The curious customs of the Persians (131–140) and the growth of their empire (141–176), culminating in the conquest of Assyria with its remarkable capital Babylon (177–200), are described. Cyrus attacks the Massagetae (whose geography and customs are described) and is defeated and killed by their Queen Tomyris (201–214).

Book 2.—Cambyses, succeeding his father Cyrus, invades Egypt, whose customs, religion, burial and other usages, are described (1–98). The history of Egypt both as reported by themselves, with numerous digressions, containing folk tales and the like (99–146), and by others (147–182) is dealt with.

Book 3.—Cambyses' expeditions (1–17), his embassy to the Ethiopians (18–25), his mad excesses (26–38), are described. The rise of Samos and the unhappy end of the overfortunate Polycrates are recounted (39–60; 120–125). Cambyses dies strangely (61–67), and the pretender Smerdis who occupied his throne is overthrown by a conspiracy of seven Persian nobles (68–79). The conspirators discuss the relative merits of monarchy, oligarchy, and democracy; and Darius, of their number, becomes king by a clever ruse (80–88). The resources of Darius' realm, especially the wonders of India and Arabia, and his conquest of Samos are recounted (89–149). The Babylonians revolt but are reconquered by a stratagem of Zopyrus, who mutilates himself for the purpose (150–160).

Book 4.—Darius leads an expedition against the Scythians, whose strange customs, especially in religion and burial, are described (1–144). Another expedition is undertaken against Cyrene and Libya, whose geography and customs are similarly described (145–205).

Book 5.—The Persians conquer Thrace (1–17) and negotiate with Macedonia (18–27). The Ionians revolt and seek help in peninsular Greece (28–38), which offers another occasion for a digression on Athenian and Spartan history (39–96), which includes a digression on the Royal Road and the countries between Sardis and Susa (49–54). The Athenians and Eretrians aid the Ionians and participate in the burning of Sardis, but the revolt is gradually suppressed by the Persians (97–126).

Book 6.—The revolt ends with the fall of Miletus (1–33); Miltiades flees to Athens before the Persian advance (34–41). Mardonius' expedition against Athens is wrecked in a storm off Athos (42–45); many Greek cities give Darius' representatives earth and water despite warnings from Athens and Sparta (46–50). The origin of the dual kingship at Sparta and the exile of their king, Demaratus (51–86), and Athens' war against Aegina (87–93) are described. The Persians take Eretria (94–101) but are defeated at Marathon by the Athenians and Plataeans alone, the Spartans being delayed by religious scruple (102–120). Though Hippias guided the invaders, the Alcmaeonids were not guilty of treasonable traffic with the enemy (121–131). Miltiades, victor of Marathon, fails in an expedition against Paros, is fined, and dies of battle wounds (132–140).

Book 7.—In the midst of preparations for a new attack Darius dies and is succeeded by Xerxes (1–4), who, after conflicting advice from Artabanus and Mardonius, determines on war (5–18), and after elaborate preparations, including digging a canal at Athos and bridging the Hellespont, marches toward Greece, with his fleet coasting along the shore, and reaches Thessaly (19–137). Athens leads in the resistance; Themistocles counsels defense by sea (138–144). The Greeks who decide to resist conclude an alliance among themselves and send embassies (which prove futile) to remote Hellene peoples, especially to Syracuse (145–171). The Persians advance through Thessaly and defeat Leonidas at Thermopylae (172–239).

Book 8.—Despite a preliminary success at Artemisium the Greek fleet retreats southward, the land forces also going south; the Persians destroy the buildings on the Acropolis (1–55). Despite sentiment for a further retreat to the Isthmus, Themistocles forces a naval battle by a ruse, and the Persian fleet is routed at Salamis (59–96). The remains of the Persian fleet and a good part of the army retreat to Sardis (97–120), and the Greeks offer thanksgiving (121–125). A Persian force operates in the Chalcidice; Mardonius, wintering in Thessaly, sends the Macedonian prince to offer the Athenians an alliance. Spartan envoys at Athens argue against such a move, and the proposals of Mardonius are rejected (126–144).

Book 9.—Mardonius thereupon advances toward Attica, but retreats to Boeotia when somewhat hesitant aid arrives from Sparta, and is overwhelmingly defeated at Plataea (1–89); at the same time, the Greek fleet wins another brilliant victory at Mycale (90–113). The following year (479 B.C.) the Athenians capture the strategic stronghold of Sestus on the Chersonese (114–120).

Judged by the canons of modern historiography Herodotus is guilty of many shortcomings. His chronology is vague and inconsistent; his statistics, as when he numbers the Persian invaders at 5,000,000, absurd; his calculations are almost all wrong; he quotes speeches which cannot have been made; he does not understand military strategy; he introduces irrelevant matter; he is uncritical; he gives too much importance to divine intervention. Some of these charges it is anachronistic to make, some ignore Herodotus' purpose, which is as different from Thucydides' as from a modern historian. Herodotus is uncritical only in the sense that he had few critical resources. He verifies where he can, and subjects everything to his own judgment of probability. "For myself," he says, distinctly enough (7.152), "my duty is to report all that is said [how else is a compiler of *logoi* to act?], but I am not obliged to believe it all alike —a remark which may be understood to apply to my whole History." Fantastic folk tales may give a more immediate sense of a people's character than statistics or lists of battles and of dynasties. The wolf never suckled Romulus and Remus, and George Washington did not cut the cherry tree down; but ignorance of these episodes would leave a serious gap in our knowledge. Geography, natural history, ethnography, sociology, anthropology, comparative religion, are surely relevant to a full understanding of history, and in these fields Herodotus is not only a pioneer, but a competent researcher. Earlier generations singled out such things as his accounts of religious prostitution or his description of Egyptian customs for special ridicule, and called him gullible or a liar. Today social anthropologists confirm his accuracy in their field, and Egyptologists say he recorded well such curiosities as would be likely to impress an intelligent and acute observer.

Besides observations and oral information Herodotus used the evidence of monuments, the writings of his predecessors, and such official accounts as were available to him. The accounts of the Persian satrapies (3.89–97), of the Royal Road (5.52–53), and of the Persian army (7.61–98) are based on official Persian documents. The material on Croesus and the oracular responses comes from the records at Delphi, and other temple records are laid under contribution in other places. The material on Athenian and Spartan history seems to derive from official sources. Herodotus regularly employs inscriptions on monuments. He probably used his predecessors Xanthos, Charon, Hellanicus, and Hecataeus. Only the last is mentioned by name, and in four passages: 6.137, to disagree with him; 2.143, as pretentious and ignorant; 5.36 and 5.125 as a prudent statesman. The ancients looked on literary borrowing much more kindly than we do, and it is probable that Herodotus made free use of Hecataeus' *Periodos* at many places. Hecataeus' parochialism at 2.143 shows that Herodotus' broader view was part of his own character. Of all historians Herodotus is the least parochial; there is no trace of the pejorative in his use of *barbaros,* which to him means simply "non-Greek." In three places Herodotus names oral informants, and in several others he reports what priests told him.

The defects of Herodotus' history are the obverse of its merits. Because he is interested in individuals rather than abstractions, in drama rather than philosophy, he tends to attribute movements to individual motives rather than to larger and remoter causes. So Plutarch (who should have learned better from Thucydides and Aristotle's *Politics*), because his concern was also with individuals, makes Pericles start the Peloponnesian War to evade a private difficulty. And because Herodotus believed that history followed a plan, his history, to modern taste, tends to be too theological. Some of his pious utterances may derive from the temples and priests who were his sources, some may be conventionally polite turns of expression, but he was clearly a pious man. He was concerned to justify the oracles—as was his friend Sophocles. He had profound respect for the religious amenities, foreign as well as Greek—as did Nicias, who allowed Athens' last hope to perish at Syracuse rather than sail when the moon was not propitious. He belonged to the generation which was horrified at the mutilation of the hermae, not to the questioning generation of young radicals who were responsible for the mutilation.

But if Herodotus' claim as a historian be discounted, his literary stature is beyond question. His story does not move in a vacuum; the canvas is full as well as broad, and the reader receives a sense of a whole wide world teeming with life. "You see, friend," says Longinus (26.2), "how he takes your spirit with him through the place, and turns hearing into seeing." There are few abstract nouns, and the grammar is almost as simple as the narrative portions of the Old Testament. But there is maturity—even, as we have noted, tragedy. A story grown to many pages in the mind will often be found, on consulting the text, to be told in a few sentences. Thucydides, to whom we now turn, dismissed Herodotus' work as an ephemeral showpiece and claimed, justly enough, that his own history was a possession for evermore. If it had proved ephemeral, the world would have remained ignorant of an entrancing area of its past, would have been impoverished of an incalculable treasure of enchantment.

THUCYDIDES

Herodotus may be read easily, for receiving pleasure; Thucydides must be pondered, for achieving understanding. Herodotus moves sympathetically among the peoples of the world and observes their manifold activities; Thucydides studies a limited segment of mankind as from Olympus or in a laboratory and formulates permanently valid laws of political behavior. The Peloponnesian War is in itself an absorbing enough subject, for it was an eventful war and its issue profoundly affected peoples whom we know almost as well and who concern us almost as much as do our own contemporaries. Without Thucydides we should know little of that war and understand less. But the importance of Thucydides' work is not so much for its record of what was, as wars are now measured, a minor incident, as for the illumination it throws upon the unchanging ways of men and nations in dealing with one another. His profound insight into the eternal verities of political behavior, combined with painstaking devotion to truth, austere detachment, and careful arrangement and disposition, may well claim for Thucydides the title of the greatest historian in our civilization.

Most of what we know of Thucydides' life comes from his own book. He was born toward the middle of the fifth century B.C., for he was of adult age when the Peloponnesian War broke out and immediately began to record its events. He was both rich and noble, being descended from Miltiades and owning rich mines in Thrace. He held a general command in that region in 424, being opposed to Brasidas, the best of the Spartan generals and indeed the only genius they produced during the war. Because of Brasidas' superior generalship or Thucydides' own negligence Amphipolis was lost to the Spartans. "For twenty years," Thucydides himself tells us (5.26), "I was banished from my country after I held the command at Amphipolis, and associating with both sides, with the Peloponnesians quite as much as with the Athenians, because of my exile, I was thus enabled to watch quietly the course of events." He apparently retained his property and traveled about unmolested, probably to Sicily as well as other places. He returned to Athens in 404 and, as the unfinished state of his work suggests, died shortly thereafter.

Thucydides starts by asserting that the Peloponnesian was the greatest war of history, and marshals political, military, social, and anthropological arguments to demonstrate that the Trojan War (whose historicity he does not question) and the Persian War were less significant. His own program he states as follows (1.22):

Of the events of the war I have not ventured to speak from any chance information, nor according to any notion of my own; I have described nothing but what I either saw myself, or learned from others of whom I made the most careful and particular enquiry. The task was a laborious one, because eyewitnesses of the same occurrences gave different accounts of them, as they remembered or were interested in the actions of one side or the other. And very likely the strictly historical character of my narrative may be disappointing to the ear. But if he who desires to have before his eyes a true picture of the events which have happened, and of the like events which may be expected to happen hereafter in the order of human things, shall pronounce what I have written to be useful, then I shall be satisfied. My history is an everlasting possession, not a prize composition which is heard and forgotten.

—Benjamin Jowett

Modern criticism has confirmed that Thucydides was faithful to his ideal of accuracy. In one important respect he departs from modern canons, and that is in reporting speeches of which he cannot have had the true text. Of this practice he himself says (*ibid.*):

As to the speeches which were made either before or during the war, it was hard for me, and for others who reported them to me, to recollect the exact words. I have therefore put into the mouth of each speaker the sentiments proper to the occasion, expressed as I thought he would be likely to express them, while at the same time I endeavored, as nearly as I could, to give the general purport of what was actually said.

In point of fact the speeches, aside from their artistic excellence, contribute substantially to the history, even from the point of view of impartiality. No exposition could set forth as clearly the disparate views of the contending parties as do the speeches at the congresses at Sparta and Corinth. For the purposes of a philosophical history, truth is better served by making a speaker say what circumstances demanded he should have said rather than by giving a verbatim report of what accident or caprice made him utter. Nor must all the speeches be dismissed as fictive; the Funeral Oration of Pericles must have been delivered substantially as reported.

Thucydides' chronology is careful. He dates the beginning of hostilities by coördinating the high priesthood of Argos, the ephorate at Sparta, and the archonship at Athens (2.1), and proceeds by summers and winters. The contents of his eight books are as follows:

Book 1.—The present is the greatest of wars, as is shown by analysis of history, and merits critical examination; its real cause was the growth of Athenian power and Sparta's consequent fear (1–23). The first alleged cause of the war was Athens' interference on behalf of the Corcyraeans in their quarrel with Corinth (24–55); the second was Sparta's interference with Athens' subject, Potidaea (55–66). A congress of the Peloponnesian League at Corinth clarifies the policies of Athens and Sparta (67–71); an Athenian embassy at Sparta fails to restrain the Spartans from determining on war (72–88). The growth of the Athenian empire and its imperialistic policy during the fifty years following the Persian War are recounted (89–117). Sparta receives assurance of success from Delphi; their allies approve military action (118–125); Spartan diplomacy strives to create dissension in Athens and make specific demands; Pericles sets forth the policy of controlling the sea and permitting the Spartans to invade Attica (126–146).

Book 2.—The Thebans attack Plataea, and Athens sends aid. Sympathy is with Sparta, as liberator from Athenian tyranny; King Archidamus makes a cautious speech at Sparta, and Pericles a confident one at Athens, listing Athens' resources and advising the rural population to move into the city (1–17). The Spartans invade Attica, and the Athenian navy makes descents on the Peloponnese (18–33). Pericles' Funeral Oration over the first casualties of the war proclaims the democratic ideal (34–46). The physical and moral effects of the plague which descended on Athens in 430 are described in detail (47–54). Pericles defends his policy before the despairing Athenians, is fined, but re-elected; his prudent policy is praised (55–70). The campaigns and events of the third year of the war are concluded (71–103).

Book 3.—Lesbos, with Spartan encouragement, revolts from Athens, but is subjugated; a decree moved by Cleon condemns the Mityleneans to destruction, but the decree is rescinded the following day and the Mityleneans saved (1–50). The Plataeans, however, who had finally surrendered to the Spartans, are massacred (51–68). At Corcyra the oligarchic and democratic parties, abetted respectively by Sparta and Athens, set the pattern for bloody civil strife for essentially selfish ends; "words lost their meaning" (69–86). The campaigns and events of the sixth year of the war, including expeditions against Melos and in Sicily and the purification of Delos, are recounted (87–116).

Book 4.—The Athenian capture of a Spartan force at Sphacteria, off Pylos, impels the Spartans to solicit terms (1–41). The Athenians gain successes in Corinthian territory, and take the Laconian island of Cythera (42–58). The Sicilians contemplate alliance in the face of the Athenian peril (59–65). An Athenian attempt on Megara is foiled by Brasidas (66–73), and the Athenians suffer reverses in Boeotia (74–101). Brasidas' military and diplomatic success in the Chalcidice induce the Athenians to conclude a truce with the Spartans and restore their captives, but hostilities are soon resumed (102–135).

Book 5.—Brasidas and Cleon having both been killed at Amphipolis, Athens and Sparta conclude peace and a fifty years' alliance after ten years of war (1–25). Though the principals refrain from invading each other's territory the treaty is violated on both sides, each encouraging hostile measures against the other; moreover, the war parties in both Athens and Sparta, with new and militant leaders, agitate for renewal of hostilities (26–83). An Athenian expedition demands submission of the Melians, who desire to remain neutral, and scorning the Melians' appeal to justice ("Of the gods we believe and of men we know that by a law of their nature wherever they can rule they will") they slaughter the Melians (84–116).

Book 6.—The project to invade Sicily, whose population is described (1–5), is discouraged by Nicias but advocated by Alcibiades (6–26), and despite the ominous mutilation of the hermae (27–29) the armada sets out with great splendor and high hope (30–32). Syracuse is dubious but prepares (33–41). Alcibiades escapes to Sparta to avoid arrest, and Nicias fails to take advantage of the energetic steps that the third general, Lamachus, counsels (42–71). The Syracusans apply for help to Sparta; Alcibiades persuades the Spartans to grant it and also to fortify Decelia, near Athens (72–93). The reinforced Athenians seize heights near Syracuse and commence circumvallation, but Lamachus falls in a skirmish, and Nicias, ill and dilatory, permits Gylippus and his Spartans to land; siege of Syracuse by land is rendered impossible (94–104).

Book 7.—Nicias requests that he be relieved, suggesting that the expedition be recalled or huge new reinforcements sent; the Athenians send Demosthenes and Eurymedon with large reinforcements (1–41). An Athenian night attack fails; Demosthenes urges immediate withdrawal of the expedition, but Nicias demurs. The Syracusans close the Athenian ships in the Great Harbor, and Eurymedon is killed (42–59). The Athenians determine to retreat by sea, if they can break the blockade, or else by land (60–68). The sea attempt (the most vivid battle piece in Thucydides) fails, the armies are captured in their hopeless attempt to retreat by land, Nicias and Demosthenes are executed and their men enslaved (69–87).

Book 8.—Despite their consternation at the news the Athenians take vigorous measures against the rebellious Chians and win over Samos (1–23), and their navy is generally successful in the Aegean (24–44). Alcibiades, grown suspect to the Spartans, joins Tissaphernes and advises him to maintain Athens and Sparta in equilibrium instead of supporting Sparta; Alcibiades intrigues for his restoration at Athens on condition that the democracy be abolished. A successful coup brings in the oligarchical Council of Four Hundred, which governs despotically and seeks terms with Sparta (45–70). The democratic forces at Samos are indignant that "the city has revolted from them" and solicit Alcibiades' help (71–89). To secure their tenure the Four Hundred appeal to Sparta (90–98). Multiplying misfortunes induce the Athenians to depose the Four Hundred and set up instead a regime of Five Thousand of the wealthiest citizens, forming a compromise between oligarchy and democracy; Alcibiades is recalled from exile (97–109).

Thucydides' book no less than Herodotus' constitutes a tragedy, but it is a tragedy of the Euripidean rather than the Sophoclean type. The tragedy grows out of the character of man rather than the character of individual men. Only so much of individual character is portrayed as is essential to understand the story; we are told a great deal about Alcibiades and Nicias, because the story requires it, but even so we have no such intimacies as Plutarch or Plato in the *Symposium* provides. In the account of the plague, symptoms, prognoses, physical and psychological effects, are detailed with clinical precision, so that we may know how to confront a recurrence. So with men; if history does not repeat itself, men do repeat themselves. The Peloponnesian War is a prolonged act of suicide, whose inevitability is not dictated by an oracle, as in Sophocles or Herodotus, but is implicit in the nature of man, as in Euripides. Thucydides shares fully in the contempt of oracles exhibited by Euripides and the rationalists; his analyses, not alone in the plague, may well have been suggested by the techniques of the Hippocratic school.

But though his distress at the moral degradation of Athens and the impending ruin of Greece and his gloomy view of man's fate are like Euripides', he has little of Euripides' pity for life's victims. Though he does not explicitly set forth a program, it is reasonably clear that his solution would be a united Greece, governed by law, presumably under the leadership of Athens. But his sympathy for Athenian democracy was qualified, and not in the direction that that democracy was itself qualified. He was a noble and owned gold mines. He admires Pericles most for his masterful control of the people; there is suspicion rather than confidence in broad democracy. For Cleon his distaste is as strong as Aristophanes', and his condemnation, because it is sober, is more devastating. He is critical of men of his own class also. His account makes Nicias' fecklessness and superstition responsible for the debacle at Syracuse, but he is curiously kind to him in his final judgment. Alcibiades was clearly odious to him, but he never questions his great competence. His charity to the Spartans may be based on historical objectivity, his own pan-Hellenic views, or upon a soldier's admiration for good soldiers. But we cannot forget that kindly feeling for Sparta was the distinguishing mark of the oligarchic party in Athens, and that Sparta was repugnant to the democracy even aside from the passions of war. The Euripides of *Andromache* at least had very different feelings about Sparta.

Thucydides' prose is the hardest we have in Greek. In many passages it is knotty and elliptical and difficult to construe. In other passages, as a scholiast says, "the lion laughs," and the style grows easier. But always it is concise and grave, in keeping with the subject matter. Many of the more difficult passages were doubtless intended to be revised. Book 8 is clearly incomplete, and the absence of speeches in it tells us something of the manner of composition of the rest of the work. But even where Thucydides is at his smoothest he cannot, as other Greek prose writers can, appear presentable in a literal version.

XENOPHON

Senses strained by the brilliance of such genius as Thucydides' or Plato's can relax in the easier atmosphere of Xenophon. No one has thought Xenophon worthy of the adulation bestowed upon Thucydides or Plato, whom he sought to rival, and indeed his emulation throws the unique power of Thucydides and Plato into clearer relief; but Xenophon has given high prowess, real or imagined, effective literary expression which has enthralled generations of readers, and directly and in passing has given useful and interesting information on Greek life and politics which we would otherwise be without. Geniuses are timeless and hence may not legitimately serve as specimens of their environment; Xenophon illustrates, as no other Greek writer can, the range of social, ethical, philosophical, and political ideals, the habits of life, interests, and capacities of an ordinary Athenian gentleman of his class. *Anabasis* remains a vivid and satisfying adventure; *Memorabilia* shows other aspects of Socrates and provides a key for distinguishing the real from the Platonic Socrates; *Hellenica* is a useful supplement to Thucydides and our fullest account of the history of its period; *Cyropedia* comes near being the first novel and contains the first proper love story in Western literature; and the shorter essays are useful for what they tell us, both directly and by implication.

Xenophon was born not long after 430 B.C., and belonged to the class of knights, who were the mainstay for the atrocities of the oligarchic regime of the Thirty in 404. He was one of the young bloods who followed in Socrates' train, and whose reactionary program and record were largely responsible for the popular feeling against Socrates. It was doubtless owing in part to the surge of popular feeling against his class after the fall of the Thirty that Xenophon accepted the invitation of his Boeotian friend Proxenus in 401 to join him at Sardis, there to take service with the Persian Cyrus. After the expedition of the Ten Thousand was well on its way into the interior it appeared that the movement was directed against Cyrus' brother Artaxerxes. At the battle of Cunaxa the Greeks were victorious, but Cyrus was killed, and the Greeks preferred to make their way back rather than surrender to the Persians or, later, establish themselves in the East. The Greek generals were enticed to a conference, where they were seized and subsequently killed, and the Ten Thousand were left leaderless in an alien and hostile country. Xenophon, impelled by a dream, Homeric in vein and in language, convoked an assembly in which new generals, of whom he himself was one, were elected. The story of the retreat through an unknown country against disheartening obstacles of terrain and weather, savage enemies, and failure of supplies gives the reader a vicarious satisfaction in the epic achievement of fellow humans of ordinary stature. Every reader shares the thrill of joyous relief when the cry *thalatta, thalatta* resounds (*Anabasis* 4.7.23 f.):

When the clamor grew louder and nearer, and each group as it came near the front began to run towards those who took up the shouting, and the volume of shouting grew as more arrived, it struck Xenophon that something serious was afoot. He mounted his horse and took Lycius and the cavalry with him and galloped forward. Soon they heard soldiers shouting 'The sea, the sea!' and passing the word along. Thereupon all began to run, even the rearguard; pack animals and horses were put to the trot. And when they arrived at the hill they embraced one another on the spot, and their generals, and their captains, weeping.

The achievements of the Ten Thousand pioneered in a sense for the conquests of Alexander and for the easy parades of Roman power led by Lucullus and Pompey. Xenophon's own resourcefulness, tact, foresight, and affability were largely responsible for the success of the march; indeed, no better demonstration could be offered of the worth of the Athenian democratic training which, as Pericles declared in the Funeral Oration, makes men resourceful to meet emergencies and competent to see them through. In his life and writings Xenophon himself is consistently and pronouncedly pro-Spartan; he approves of perpetual drill and mechanical obedience, authoritarian and secret government procedures, narrow and prescribed range of ideas such as prevailed in Sparta. Yet no Spartan we know except Brasidas could have matched Xenophon.

If Cyrus had succeeded in his designs he would surely have caused Greece, and especially Athens, great trouble. Xenophon joined the staff of Agesilaus, his beau ideal of whom he wrote an encomiastic *Life,* and with him campaigned against Artaxerxes. But in 395 Artaxerxes became an ally of Athens, and so Xenophon was fighting against his own country. He was on Agesilaus' staff when the Spartans defeated the Athenians and their Theban allies at Coronea in 394. The Athenians passed a sentence of exile upon him, which involved confiscation of property, and the grateful Spartans compensated him by giving him an estate at Scillus, near Elis, where he lived the life of a country gentleman and wrote his books.

Of these the most attractive by far is the *Anabasis,* which describes the adventures of the Ten Thousand. It was apparently written as a corrective to a rival account which was less favorable to him, and was published under another's name, perhaps for legal reasons connected with his banishment. Xenophon's longest work is the *Hellenica,* whose seven books treat of Greek affairs from 411 B.C., at the point where Thucydides left off, to 363 B.C., the date of the battle of Mantinea. The opening sentence completes, as it were, the last paragraph begun in Thucydides, and throughout the first two books the Thucydidean manner, arrangement, and impartiality are preserved, so that it has been plausibly thought that Xenophon was here working up notes left by his great predecessor. But the remaining five books, useful as they are as our only extant connected account of the period, are inferior in every respect in which Thucydides is excellent. Unreasoning prejudices in favor of Sparta and excessive admiration for Agesilaus are responsible for great distortion. The Theban Epaminondas, the authentic hero of the period, is barely mentioned, and nothing is said of his master strokes in founding Megalopolis and restoring Messene in the Peloponnese. In the account of the revolution at Thebes the democratic leader Pelopidas is not mentioned. Nor do merits of style compensate for the *Hellenica's* inadequacies as history, for the book is the dullest in the Xenophontic corpus.

Certain passages in praise of Agesilaus in his *Hellenica* are repeated in Xenophon's *Agesilaus*. Agesilaus had died, after a reign of some forty years, in 360, and it is possible that some unfavorable account of him had been published. A few years before, Isocrates had written an encomium of Evagoras, and had claimed to be the first to "praise a man's virtues in prose." The claim is unfounded, unless Isocrates means that he was first to combine an account of a man's actions with praise of his character. The first part of *Agesilaus* clearly follows the form of *Evagoras;* there is a chronological account of the subject's exploits, with comments on his character interwoven. The second part is an account of the subject's virtues, specifically his piety, justice, self-control, courage, and wisdom, in the order followed in Agathon's praise of love in the *Symposium* of Plato. There Socrates remarks that the speech reminds him of Gorgias, and it is likely that this order of virtues was established by Gorgias. The *Agesilaus* shows a pleasing if naïve exuberance in keeping with the author's enthusiasm for his subject. The measure of this enthusiasm is indicated by the opening sentences:

I know that it is not easy to write praise worthy of the merit and reputation of Agesilaus. Nevertheless the attempt must be made. For it would not be well if, because a man is perfectly good, he should on that account not receive even inferior praise.

We shall see that Xenophon's Socratic writings are conscious attempts to provide correctives for other reports of Socratic teachings, and Aulus Gellius may not be wrong in saying that the *Cyropedia,* or *Education of Cyrus,* was intended as a counterblast to Plato's *Republic.* The chief purpose of the book, which is a historical romance, is didactic; it presents an ideal monarch carrying out what Xenophon believed to be Socrates' political and philosophical ideals. The constitution and manner of life attributed to the Persians provide, in fact, an idealized picture of Sparta. Thus Xenophon's Persians crown themselves with garlands, pass a watchword down the line, sing a paean as they go into battle. Their battle arrangements and tactics are just as clearly Spartan, not Persian. Their worship of heroes, their frugal diet, and the education of their young are equally Spartan; the teacher Tigranes is clearly intended as a portrait of Socrates. Arrangements for imposing upon the imagination of the subjects mentioned at the beginning of the eighth book are reminiscent of similar devices suggested in the *Republic.*

Aside from the doctrinal elements derived from his admiration of Sparta and his concept of Socratic teaching, Xenophon used Herodotus and possibly Herodotus' predecessors, and the knowledge he gained from the Cyrus on whose expedition he served. But the divergences from Herodotus (who is of course our principal source for the hero of the *Cyropedia*) and other apparently conscious violations of historical fact indicate that Xenophon's chief concern was to produce a good story, and as a moralizing romance the eight books of the *Cyropedia,* a pioneer in its class, are very readable. The story of the Assyrian prince Abradates and his beautiful wife Panthea, who sent him to battle loyally for Cyrus clad in armor which she herself had given him and then killed herself over his dead body, is beautiful in itself and remarkable as the first love story in our literature. This story and the idealization of conventional virtue characteristic of the whole work made it a favorite in later antiquity and even through the nineteenth century, where it seems peculiarly appropriate.

In details, the picture of Socrates presented in Xenophon's specifically Socratic writings—*Memorabilia, Oeconomicus, Apology,* and *Symposium* —may well be truer than that given currency by Plato, but surely the prudent sermonizer and dispenser of practical advice which Xenophon presents falls short of the genuine Socrates. Dialogue, in Xenophon's treatises, is an effective means for eliciting answers; there is no trace of the dialectic in which ideas take shape. Plato's structure, however unSocratic, must have grown from a germ planted by Socrates; in Xenophon such a germ found stony ground. He was eager to grant Socrates the highest excellences which his own imagination was capable of conceiving, but his imagination was limited to obedience to a practical code of conduct tempered by an appealing humanitarianism; it was incapable of first philosophies or soaring aspirations. *Memorabilia* starts with a defense of Socrates against the charge of impiety proffered by one Polycrates and then, in four books apparently not composed as a unit, reports dialogues on various subjects, with none of the wit and much more grim utilitarianism than any of Plato's show. Most space is given to such subjects as would interest an admirer of the Spartan system. The peroration closes with the most eloquent praise of which Xenophon is capable (4.8.11):

For myself, I have described him as he was: so religious that he did nothing without counsel from the gods; so just that he did no slightest injury to any man but assisted greatly those who used him; so self-controlled that he never chose the pleasanter rather than the better course; so wise that he never erred in his judgment of the better and the worse, and needed no counsellor but was himself sufficient in such knowledge; masterly in defining and expounding such things; masterly also in testing others and convincing them of error and turning them to nobility and gentlemanliness. To me he seemed what a good and happy man should be. But if anyone is dissatisfied, let him compare with him the character of other men and then judge.

The very subject of the *Oeconomicus* ("Household Management"), which is a kind of appendix to the *Memorabilia,* suggests Xenophon's limitations as a Socratic philosopher. The treatise is an encomium on neatness in the household; its most delightful passage is on the proper training of an inexperienced housewife. *Apology,* unlike the Platonic *Apology,* sets forth Socrates' conduct before, during, and after the trial, and emphasizes his belief that for him death was not an evil. Like Plato's, Xenophon's *Symposium* shows Socrates in a lighter mood. Here the host is Callias (as in Plato's *Protagoras*) and the guests speak each of his own speciality; Socrates speaks of love, but love ascends no towering Platonic ladder. Enormously inferior to Plato as it is, Xenophon's *Symposium* is still the most agreeable of his Socratic writings. Though included with the essays rather than the philosophical works, *Hiero* too belongs in the latter category. It represents the King of Syracuse as discussing kingship with the poet Simonides of Ceos. The gist is that a king should be better than his subjects, and should win their affection and have regard for their interests.

It is sufficient to name the essays *On the Cavalry Commander, On the Art of Horsemanship,* and *On Hunting;* the genuineness of the last is suspected. In 355 Athens emerged from disastrous wars financially exhausted. Xenophon's *On Ways and Means (De Vectigalibus),* which borrows from Isocrates' *On the Peace,* was published in 355; it apparently supports the financial program of Eubulus, who had concluded the peace and was managing finances, and suggests certain new means of income. Xenophon deplores the dole and suggests that an income tax be used to finance state-owned merchant vessels and to erect hotels for merchants in Athens and Piraeus. The *Constitution of the Lacedaemonians* deals with constitutional matters only incidentally in the course of an enthusiastic encomium on aspects of private life in a completely authoritarian military dictatorship. No other account presents so succinctly the elements of the Spartan regime which are repugnant to the democratic tradition. Praise of Sparta was a commonplace in the Socratic circle; Xenophon took his title from an earlier work of Critias, the notorious leader of the Thirty.

Preserved among the works of Xenophon is one *On the Constitution of the Athenians,* of which considerations of style and date (probably 424 B.C.) make his authorship impossible. Its author has been christened (by Sir Alfred Zimmern) "the Old Oligarch," and that title expresses its character. It is an efficient and witty account of its subject, and despite its author's manifest repugnance to democracy it demonstrates the complete consistency with which the constitution implements the principles of Athenian democracy. "The man who, not being himself one of the People, prefers to live in a state democratically governed rather than in an oligarchical state," he says, "may be said to smooth his own path towards iniquity." The trouble with the "bad" men (i. e., the democrats) is that they are selfish and irresponsible. "This type of constitution is not to my taste," he says, "but given that a democratic form of government has been agreed upon, they do seem to me to go the right way to preserve the democracy by the adoption of the particular type which I have set forth."

A number of historians of the fourth century B.C. whose work is not extant may be mentioned here. Ephorus of Cyme, who was a pupil of Isocrates and lived during the first three quarters of the century, was the first to write universal history. His history extended to his own time and was much read in antiquity. Our fragments are from Diodorus, whom parallel papyrus fragments prove to have copied with virtually no alterations. Ephorus' thirty books were critical of the earliest periods, included matter on the "barbarian" countries, presented fictive speeches like Thucydides', but lacked Thucydides' political understanding. Assyrian and Persian history was treated in the fourteen books of Ctesias, physician to Artaxerxes, written in Ionic. Photius' epitome, made from an epitome of the age of Nero, is extant. Cratippus wrote a continuation of Thucydides; if a papyrus containing such a continuation is his, he was a better historian than Xenophon. Another continuation of Thucydides, down to the battle of Cnidos in 394, was the *Hellenica* of Theopompus, who was born in Chios in 376 B.C. His *Philippica,* in fifty-eight books, was a general history from 362 (where Xenophon's *Hellenica* ends) to the death of Philip in 336 B.C. Philistus of Syracuse, who was old enough to remember the Athenian invasion, wrote histories of Sicily from the earliest times to his own day. Other writers who dealt with Oriental history or wrote *Atthides,* or works on Athenian history and archaeology, are no more than names.

Pytheas of Marseilles sailed out from the Pillars of Hercules and to the British isles toward the end of the fourth century and brought back reports which can only be excavated from Strabo, who, like other geographers, disbelieved them. Antiphanes of Berge wrote an apparently completely fantastic account of the same regions, perhaps in parody of Pytheas. An extant short treatise on the military defense of cities, by Aeneas, called Aeneas Tacticus, dates from the end of the fourth century. It is a lively account, apparently from the hand of a professional soldier.

Chapter 10. THE PHILOSOPHERS

PLATO

REGARDLESS OF HIS STATURE AS PHILOSOPHER AND TEACHER, PLATO'S EMINENCE
as a writer places him in the very first rank of Greek literature. None has
better seized upon moments when men are most characteristically human,
that is, when they are discoursing on matters of the mind and spirit, and
fixed them in such truth and beauty. Merely as mimes, presenting to the
life interactions of interesting types, most of the dialogues would justify
completely their claim as works of art. But when the play of personalities
shapes before the eyes and ears of the audience significant truths of profound ethical and moral consequence and leads to a vision of a lofty spiritual
goal, the dialogues must be reckoned among the most sublime utterances
of mankind. To appreciate the matchless skill with which the dialogue
form is used, not to state a finished idea, but to represent its unfolding,
one need only compare the use of the form by lesser men, where the interlocutors pose questions only to make an opening for the master's ex-
cathedra answers.

It may have been by such mimes as Epicharmus' and Sophron's that Plato
was led to the dialogue form, but certainly the method was that used by
Socrates, the portrayal of whom is at least a subsidiary purpose of most
of the dialogues. How far they actually represent the content of Socratic
conversations is the intriguing subject of the Socratic problem. Socrates
himself wrote not a line, and we know of him only that he was a strikingly
ugly man, trained as a stone carver, who went about Athens asking questions and provoking discussions chiefly on ethical problems; that he was
followed and admired by a group composed for the most part of upper-class
youths; that he might be spoken of as a Sophist by a comic poet but that
he differed from the Sophists obviously in that he took no regular pupils
and received no pay; that he believed in his own mission to question
people, chiefly to the end of convincing them that an unexamined life is
not worth living; that he sometimes went into a sort of trance while pon-
dering a thought; and that in 399 B.C. at the age of seventy he was tried and
condemned to death on the charge of disbelieving in the gods of the state
and persuading others to his disbelief. In the course of time Socrates' char-

acter (like the face in sculptures of him) became idealized. Clearly, he was more than the utilitarian sage whom Xenophon represents him to be, or than the logician which he proves to be in Aristotle; clearly too, there was basis in fact for the saintly and intellectual qualities which Plato attributes to him, and the more developed doctrines which Plato puts in his mouth may be legitimate implications of actual Socratic utterances. But there is strong probability that the content as well as the form of the dialogues owes a very great deal to Plato himself.

Plato was born in 428 B.C., and so was less than thirty at the death of Socrates; the dramatic dates of the most significant of his dialogues fall in Plato's childhood. On the other hand, Plato doubtless received much Socratic doctrine from older members of the circle, among them his two older brothers, Glaucon and Adimantus, and particularly his uncles, Critias and Charmides. These latter were leading spirits in the oligarchic coup and atrocities of the Thirty in 404–403 B.C., and popular detestation of them and of others of the circle certainly played its part in bringing about the condemnation of Socrates. Plato himself was of aristocratic birth, and his political sympathies are consistently aristocratic, with the marked predilection for Sparta characteristic of the oligarchic party. He was repelled by the excesses of the Thirty, but had no taste for democracy, at least in its post-Periclean form. After the death of Socrates he, like other members of the Socratic circle, left Athens. He sojourned for a time at Megara, and is said then (but on dubious authority) to have spent some ten years in travel, to Cyrene, Egypt, and Italy. In Syracuse he met Dion, whom he found an eager and responsive student. By 387 he was back in Athens and had founded the Academy; the foundation of the Academy, which was to continue for nearly a thousand years, is a memorable event in the history of science. Isocrates had probably already established his school; but whereas Isocrates taught opinions and their elegant expression, the backbone of Plato's curriculum was hard thinking, with mathematics at its core. After some twenty years at the Academy, Plato was invited by Dion to come to Syracuse in 368, in order to make a philosopher-king of his nephew Dionysius II, who had just succeeded Dionysius I as ruler. The enterprise was construed as a scheme of Dion's to usurp power; Dion was exiled, and Plato returned to Athens in 366. In 362 he reluctantly accepted an invitation of Dionysius to return to Syracuse, without Dion, but this mission to convert the king to philosophy was also unsuccessful. The circumstances of these visits, as well as Plato's ideas on practical constitutional reforms, are set forth in his *Seventh Epistle*. Plato probably spent the remainder of his life in Athens, where he died in 347 B.C.

All of Plato's published work is extant; no ancient writer refers to writings not in our corpus as Platonic. By counting each dialogue, regardless of size, as a unit, and the thirteen epistles (now generally regarded as mostly genuine) as one unit, a list of thirty-six Platonic works was drawn up in antiquity. Extant dialogues not in this list and the collection of Platonic definitions included in the oldest manuscripts are surely spurious. Among the thirty-six there is general agreement that every dialogue of any length and interest is Platonic. There is general agreement also that *Alcibiades II, Hipparchus, Rivals, Theages, Clitophon,* and *Minos* are un-Platonic. Concerning *Alcibiades I, Ion, Menexenus, Hippias Major, Epinomis,* and *Epistles* some opinion still holds that they are spurious, but the preponderance of authority is in favor of genuineness. To arrive at a consistent picture of the development of Plato's thought it is essential that a chronology of the writings be established. It is well authenticated that *Laws* is a work of Plato's latest period, and there are good grounds for supposing that *Republic* together with *Protagoras, Phaedo,* and *Symposium* belong to an earlier period. By the application of the gauges of stylometry, that is, calculation of minute linguistic usages of whose gradual change an author is not conscious (not "style" in the usual sense), scholars working independently and employing different sets of criteria have arrived at conclusions which are virtually unanimous and in consonance with probability on other grounds. Arranged in the approximate order in which they were written the dialogues fall into three groups. In the first, so-called "Socratic" group, Socrates is the principal figure and the tone is eristic; Socrates refutes the contentions of his opponents without himself proposing positive solutions. Dialectic is gradually developed to greater precision, and is made truly dramatic by vividness of style and sharpness in character delineation. To this group belong *Apology* (which is not strictly a dialogue but a version of Socrates' defense at his trial), *Crito, Charmides, Laches, Euthyphro, Hippias Minor, Hippias Major, Ion, Lysis.*

In the second group Socrates is still the chief speaker, but more developed concepts, such as the theory of ideas, are presented; those who minimize the Socratic content of the Platonic philosophy attribute these new concepts to Plato himself, at best as development of germs in Socrates' teaching. This group is further characterized by the new use of myths, where creations of the imagination are employed to carry thought beyond the bounds of logic, as in presenting views of eschatology. Some of the dialogues of this group are directed against the Sophists, who are represented as morally inferior and unequal to Socrates in dialectic. To this group belong *Gorgias, Protagoras, Euthydemus, Cratylus, Phaedo, Republic, Meno, Alcibiades I, Menexenus, Phaedrus, Symposium, Theaetetus, Parmenides.*

In the third group Socrates is less prominent or entirely absent, and the settings are less elaborate, the myths fewer and less important. In this group are included *Sophistes, Politicus, Timaeus, Critias, Philebus, Laws, Epinomis.* Of the *Epistles* the *Seventh,* which is the most important, is almost certainly genuine, and there are no compelling reasons to doubt the genuineness of the other longer letters in the collection; the shorter letters are clearly spurious.

All the earlier dialogues seem to have at least as their secondary purpose a kind of beatification of Socrates. His pre-eminence in reason, his devotion to his mission, his selfless concern for the spiritual welfare of his fellow men, the purity of his life, even his social gifts, are underscored. The pieces dealing with his trial and death constitute a passion which is surely the second most compelling in literature. In the *Apology,* more properly *Defense,* possibly the earliest of the Socratic writings, Socrates is made to present, without coyness or swagger or unction, his own concept of his mission to sting men, like a gadfly, to self-examination and to serve as midwife to their travail with ideas.

The other dialogues of the first group present him as goad and midwife, and credit him with no positive doctrine other than the implication that the unexamined life is not worth living. Some common term of moral import, such as piety or courage or friendship or virtue, is examined with a view to determining its true meaning. The interlocutor usually offers examples of pious, courageous, or virtuous conduct, approaching but not attaining a universal definition; as far as any answer to the problem is reached it is that these various virtues are part of a single inclusive virtue, which must be the object of constant examination. If we are not given a ready definition of these qualities, at least the complacency of our imagined knowledge is shaken, and we are left with a heightened sense of the importance of unremitting application to the endeavor to escape from ignorance.

The scene of *Euthyphro,* which perfectly illustrates this pattern, is the portico of the court where Socrates has come presumably on business connected with his trial and where Euthyphro has come, because of his devotion to, and expertness in, piety, to lay charges of murder against his own father for having through negligence caused the death of a slave. The excellent characterization of the well-meaning bigot of the title and the gentle satire of utilitarian orthodoxy provide contrast for Socrates' superiority in both mind and spirit. In *Crito* Socrates' friend of that name tries to persuade him to escape from prison, where he is awaiting execution. Socrates insists that one wrong may not be righted by a retaliatory wrong, and affirms his loyalty to the laws, which he represents (and this is a Platonic myth in germ) as themselves asserting their claim upon him.

Charmides is named for Plato's uncle, who was, many years after the fictive date of the dialogue, a leader of the Thirty, and deals with sophrosyne or temperance, a central principle in the aristocratic code, in much the same manner as piety is dealt with in *Euthyphro*. *Laches* is named for a general who, with Nicias, discusses courage with Socrates. Similarly, *Lysis,* which charmingly illustrates Socrates' manner with young men, discusses friendship. In all these dialogues we are gradually led to identify the specific virtue under consideration with the knowledge of the good. The importance of correct procedure in defining the good is illustrated in *Hippias Major,* whose interlocutor, the well-known polymath Hippias of Elis, is represented as conceited on the range of his knowledge and his vogue, but uncomprehending on the true nature of the good. *Lesser Hippias* starts with a comparison of Achilles and Odysseus and turns on the Socratic principle that virtue is knowledge; the assumption always is that no one does wrong on purpose. *Ion* is a slight dialogue maintaining the position, regularly taken in Plato, that the poet is not merely a craftsman, but that poetry is produced by a combination of natural endowment and inspiration.

In *Cratylus* Socrates discusses etymology, in a rather jocular vein, with Hermogenes, a poor half brother of the wealthy patron of Sophists, Callias, and with Cratylus, a believer in Heraclitean flux. It must be noted that the dialogue assumes familiarity with the theory of ideas; realities have an independent existence, behind the words, and are alone the true objects of knowledge. *Euthydemus* is a broad farce in which a pair of minor Sophists are held up to ridicule for their fallacious logic-chopping—and their essential moral levity. The sincerity and power of Socrates' own teaching emerge as central elements in the dialogue.

Gorgias is much longer than the dialogues mentioned thus far, and its intention is plainly ethical. The master orator Gorgias himself is treated with some consideration, but opportunism (which his disciples Polus and Callicles, carrying Gorgias' own principles to their logical conclusion, are made to advocate) is shown to be immoral. The will to success, in the orators' sense, must involve wronging someone, and to do wrong is always worse than to suffer it. Popular patriotic oratory is imitated and at the same time satirized in *Menexenus*. In form *Menexenus* is Socrates' report of a funeral oration on the dead of the Corinthian War which he heard from Pericles' Aspasia. Now the Corinthian War opened in 395 B.C., four years after the death of Socrates, and Aspasia must have died even earlier; this violation of chronology, unexampled in Plato, would be sufficient ground for denying the genuineness of *Menexenus* were it not that the piece is twice alluded to by Aristotle, who could hardly be mistaken in its authorship. *Meno,* named for an interlocutor who served with Xenophon in Cyrus' expedition, deals with the question whether virtue can be taught. This dialogue introduces the theory that all learning is reminiscence, brought by the soul from a previous state. Socrates proves his point by showing that Meno's slave boy, by adroit questioning, can be made to "prove" a geometrical theorem which he cannot have learned in his lifetime.

Phaedo is the most spiritual and the most eloquent of the dialogues. In prison, during the hours preceding his death, Socrates discourses to his friends on the most timely and timeless of all questions, the immortality of the soul. The individual characters of the friends present—Simmias inclined to mysticism, Cebes more rational, Apollodorus unrestrainable in his grief, Crito the competent manager, and the others—are unmistakably indicated. The dramatic setting, the earnestness of the arguments, the eschatological vision of retribution after death which supplements the arguments, and the saintly bearing of Socrates when he takes the hemlock make *Phaedo* a great masterpiece in the literature of salvation. Cicero's reaction to reading the book is typical of readers sensitive to literature of this type at all times (*Tusculan Disputations* 1.24): "While I am reading the book I agree, but somehow, when I lay the book down and myself reflect on the immortality of the soul that agreement disperses." The use of the myth indicates that Socrates (or Plato) himself realized that logical arguments could not suffice. The best they could do was to suggest that hope of immortality is not irrational. The most persuasive argument in the treatise is the strength of Socrates' own conviction.

Plato's dramatic masterpiece, and one of his most effective encomia of the character of Socrates, is *Symposium.* A number of the fashionable wits of Athens, who are willing to make Socrates one of themselves, have gathered at the house of the tragic poet Agathon, about 416 B.C., to celebrate their host's victory in a tragic competition. Instead of the usual entertainment of flute music and enforced drinking, they decide to spend the evening by pronouncing, each in his turn, discourses on the nature of love. The first speech, by Phaedrus, sets forth the military advantages of homosexual love. Pausanias, referring to the same practice, draws a distinction between a noble and a base love. The physician Eryximachus gives love a cosmic significance by explaining it as based on natural forces of attraction and repulsion. Aristophanes, who had been prevented from speaking in his proper turn by an attack of hiccups, explains love by a peculiarly Aristophanic cosmogony. Originally, men were round, with four arms, four legs, two faces, and of three sexes: double male, double female, and male-female. These were split into halves by Zeus, and the effort of the disparate halves to rejoin their appropriate halves constitutes love. And if mankind misbehaves, Aristophanes adds, Zeus will again split mankind, so that they will have to hobble about on one leg—and incidentally the Olympians' income from sacrifices will again be doubled. Agathon next delivers an empty but highly polished encomium on love in the Gorgianic manner. By a dialectical exchange Socrates establishes that the love to be discussed is the love of what we lack, and then he reports a long discourse on love which had been taught him by Diotima, the wise woman of Mantinea. Love is to proceed from the love of one beautiful body to the love of many, and from beautiful bodies to beautiful characters, and so up the ladder of love to union with the highest goodness and beauty. It is not too much to call this speech, as A. E. Taylor does, "the narrative of the pilgrimage of a soul on the way of salvation, from the initial moment at which it feels the need for salvation to its final 'consummation.'" Alcibiades, flown with wine and bedecked with ribbons, joins the party. He is at the height of his glory, having been given the command of the Syracusan expedition but not yet having been involved in the mutilation of the hermae. Only Alcibiades, and Alcibiades drunk, could tell the story of his attempted seduction of Socrates and its utter failure, and could thus demonstrate that Socrates' life was as lofty as his professions and that he had, in fact, attained the vision of the true good. The narrator's memory of what followed is confused. He fell asleep, and when he awoke at dawn Socrates was discoursing on the nature of comedy and tragedy with Aristophanes (who could notoriously carry his liquor) and Agathon (who as host was bound to stay awake). Nowhere is Plato's art of combining the light touch with high seriousness better displayed. Even readers who find the ascent of the ladder of love a distant and romantic enterprise must enjoy an evening of informal talk with the wits of Athens.

Love figures largely in *Phaedrus* also, although its main subject has to do with literary style. Socrates, for once leaving the city haunts which he prefers because men are more communicative than nature, joins Phaedrus in a walk in the country on a summer day, and the two sit under a shady plane tree by the banks of the Ilissus. Phaedrus produces a discourse of Lysias (probably genuine), maintaining the paradoxical position that it is more expedient for a lad to be kind to a wooer who is not in love with him than to one who is. The moral implications of persuasiveness in a bad cause are discussed. Socrates' point is that a speaker must know the whole truth about his subject. In the case of love this involves knowledge of the soul, and the soul is described in a parable of a charioteer

("judgment") and a pair of winged steeds ("honor" and "appetite") forming a single whole. As they finish their conversation and leave the charming spot Socrates prays briefly to Pan "that he may become fair in the
inward man, and that the outer man may be comfortable to the inward;
that he may regard wisdom as the true riches, and that his wealth may
be such as none but the temperate can carry."

Protagoras, in which Socrates' attitude to the Sophists is most clearly
set forth, ranks with *Symposium* as a literary masterpiece. No other
dialogue is so filled with people and movement, and in no other does
Socrates' masterfulness in dialectic, here often unscrupulous, have such
free play. Young Hippocrates rouses Socrates before dawn to beg to be taken
to see the famous Sophist Protagoras, who is stopping at the house of the
wealthy Callias. There they find two other well-known Sophists, Hippias
and Prodicus, as well as Critias, Alcibiades, and many others. Protagoras
maintains the high calling of the Sophists, and explains, upon questioning by Socrates, that his art consists in teaching excellence. Socrates questions whether such knowledge can be taught. By a rather ruthless display of dialectic, in the course of which Socrates threatens to withdraw
on the grounds that he cannot remember Protagoras' long speeches, and a
detailed interpretation of a poem of Simonides is undertaken, the positions
of the two disputants are apparently changed, Socrates insisting that excellence can be taught and Protagoras dissenting. The anomaly is due to
a difference in the concept of excellence. Protagoras' excellence is the
conduct which will bring an Athenian success, and this he professes to
be able to teach. Socrates holds that all the virtues comprise a single knowledge, which is teachable, and that a single technique of goodness cannot
be isolated from the body of knowledge of all the virtues.

Republic, though somewhat shorter than *Laws,* is Plato's most considerable and most discussed work. To a greater degree than in other
of Plato's works critics have erred in taking it either as a literal blueprint
for the organization of society, or else as one long jest. It is certainly not
a jest, but neither is it a grim program to be followed to the letter. The
book is suggestive, critical, inspiring, and has high seriousness, but it is
written with agile wit and is meant for direction rather than goal. Its
declared theme is justice (not, however, in the legalistic sense connoted by
the Latin root), but the theme is enlarged so as to take in all society and
man's place in it, as well as the destiny of man's soul in a future existence.
With appropriately dramatic circumstances various definitions of justice
are offered in Book 1, as in the "Socratic" dialogues, beginning with that
of the retired businessman Cephalus and his son Polemarchus, who say
that justice is rendering every man his due, and ending with that of

Thrasymachus, who truculently maintains that justice is the right of the stronger.

In the second book Glaucon (an older brother of Plato) presents the view that moral and religious conduct are artificial human conventions followed reluctantly by tacit consent through fear and force; justice is expedient, but would cease to be so for one who, like the holder of the Ring of Gyges which made men invisible, was sure he could escape detection. Adimantus (another older brother of Plato) sets forth the position of current orthodoxy; justice is practiced for anticipated rewards, in this world or the next; wrongdoing can be atoned for by bribing the gods with sacrifice. But what is justice for its own sake? Socrates suggests that justice can be studied writ large in the community better than in the individual. One element of justice, deriving from the composition of primitive society, is division of labor, specialization of function, mutually interdependent classes, and harmonious coöperation. But as the state expands aggression must be contemplated, and a warrior class must be added. These will be the guardians of the state, and their education must therefore be rigidly supervised. This will involve careful censorship of literature, and the use of white lies where advisable, to the end of developing qualities of truthfulness, self-control, obedience, piety.

Book 3 continues the discussion of censorship of drama and music, their influence in molding character and opinion being fully realized, and prescribes a hardy physical regimen. The question of how to select the rulers from among the guardians is raised in Book 3 and continued in Book 4. Constant supervision and tests will reveal those with disinterested devotion to the commonwealth and distinguish three classes, corresponding to metals: gold, philosopher-kings or guardians; silver, soldiers and auxiliaries; iron and bronze, farmers and craftsmen. Children will normally follow the class of their parents, but elevation or demotion for merit will be possible. For the two upper classes the rule of communal living will be applied and private property will be abolished; but extremes of wealth and poverty will be eliminated in the other class also. This threefold classification applies also to the individual soul, and the respective virtues of its parts correspond to those of the classes in the state. Women are essentially equal to men, and in the two upper classes women and children will be held in common.

Book 5 expatiates on the communism, which is calculated to abolish interests for the sake of the public welfare. Though women and children are to be held in common, sexual relations are to be regulated very carefully, with a view to improving the breed. Lots for mating may be manipulated, to ensure the highest quality of children, who are then reared in state nurseries, and, along with all their elders of the upper classes, are regarded as a single family. But such an ideal society can come about, and humanity can have surcease from its troubles, only when philosophers are kings or kings become philosophers.

The qualities of the philosopher are enumerated in Book 6. He is to be a lover of all true knowledge and of abstract ideas and to be absorbed in the pleasures of the soul; he is to have such virtues as temperance, generosity, courage, justice. Current society either corrupts the philosopher or forces him to stand aside. The captain of the ship of state is chosen for irrelevant reasons, not for his competence, and is killed or drugged by the unruly passengers who wish to be pilots themselves. Sophists abet the evil by teaching the opinions of the masses rather than the truth. Society must be brought to the point where the philosopher will be esteemed and where intellectual discipline leading to the Idea of the Good may be pursued. The Idea of the Good is the end of all knowledge and is the unifying principle in the ideas of beauty, justice, goodness, and truth. It is like a divine revelation which can be mystically glimpsed, not specifically described. Progress toward the attainment of the Idea of the Good is represented by the Divided Line, at the lower end of which is knowledge in the visible world, and at the higher, apprehension of ideas.

Book 7 starts with the allegory of the cave. Men live, as it were, chained to their seats in an underground cave in such a way that they can only see shadows of reality projected upon a wall by a light of truth which is behind them. So used are they to false images that they find it hard to trust reality, but once they have accepted it and have freed themselves from the prison of the senses they have a true gauge for recognizing the counterfeit and enlightening those still imprisoned. Education to liberate from imprisonment to the senses involves a graded course in mathematics, culminating in dialectic.

The cycle of political change, and the degradation of character which accompanies each downward step, is described in Book 8. Ideal society is disrupted when the ruling class begins to acquire private property; wealth and ambition for honor then result in oligarchy. The selfishness of the oligarchy leads to revolt and the institution of democracy, whose flaw is that self-interest is checked by no sense of obligation. Professional politicians make assaults upon the wealth of the rich, who then form a reactionary party for self-defense. A demagogue arises as the champion of the people's rights, but is soon corrupted by power and becomes a tyrant. Such a tyrant represents the perfectly unjust man, as the philosopher represents the perfectly just man. Book 9 proceeds to show how the man of the tyrannical type is essentially unhappy, and sets forth the arguments for the happiness of the just man.

Book 10 resumes the attack on poetry as an art of illusion whose goal is pleasure and not truth. But truth is essential to justice, whose rewards are great, here and hereafter. The scheme of divine retribution is set forth in the best known of Plato's eschatological myths, the Vision of Er with which the book closes. Er, son of Armenius, who was slain in battle but returned to life after twelve days, tells what he has seen in his sojourn in the other world. At a place where two openings in the earth correspond to two others in heaven, souls continually arrive from heaven or earth, where they had spent a thousand years receiving rewards or punishments. Souls ready for reincarnation are given a view of the entire harmonious arrangement of the universe. Most choices are made on the basis of experience in the life already lived. When the lots have been approved by the Fates, the souls drink of Lethe, forget all their past, and are ready for a new birth. The virtuous life, therefore, is profitable in itself, and raises the standard in generations to come. Here are the closing sentences:

Wherefore my counsel is, that we hold fast ever to the heavenly way, and follow after justice and virtue always, considering that the soul is immortal, and able to endure every sort of good and every sort of evil. Thus shall we live dear to one another and to the gods, both while remaining here, and when like conquerors in the games who go round to gather gifts, we receive our reward. And for ourselves, both in this life and in the pilgrimage which we have been describing, may we fare well.

The organization of society envisaged in *Republic* is as far removed as possible from Athenian democracy, and at many points patently suggested by the constitution of Sparta, which the oligarchic party in Athens looked to as a model. As in Sparta service to the state is paramount, and overrides all individual predilections and all individual enterprise. The highest virtue for the citizen of any class is to attend to his assigned duties and concern himself with nothing else. Administration of the state is also a specialized craft, with which none but the philosopher king is to deal. This is a far cry from the ideal of democracy as set forth in the Funeral Oration of Pericles, which implies that providing opportunity for the fullest cultivation of personality is the prime aim of the state and which insists that free men can face emergencies, even of defense, as well as specialists dedicated solely to guardian duty, and that a man who does not participate in the affairs of state is useless.

Theaetetus is Plato's principal work on epistemology and the latest dialogue in which the personality of Socrates is made prominent. The interlocutors are Theodorus and the youthful Theaetetus, both mathematicians. First the usual confusion between knowledge and various applications of knowledge is cleared up; like his mother, Socrates practices the obstetric art and will assist in bringing the thoughts of the others to birth. The discussion is then made to center upon three definitions: (a) knowledge is sense perception; (b) knowledge is true opinion; and (c) knowledge is true opinion with reasoned explanation. In connection with the first definition there is an elaborate refutation of the doctrine of Protagoras that man is the measure of all things, and a more summary rejection of the doctrine of Heraclitus that all things are always in motion. This section also contains a digression, spiritual in mood and language, contrasting the contemplative life of the philosopher with the active life of the lawyer. The discussion of the second definition shows by a number of examples how opinion may be false. Memory is no better than wax tablets, which often fail to record a correct impression. Our bits of knowledge are like birds in an aviary; the birds are ours, for we caught them ourselves, but we cannot put our hand on a given bird. The third definition, after varied discussion, is found equally unsatisfactory, and the avowed purpose of the dialogue is fulfilled only in the sense that the path is cleared for the acceptance of another explanation, presumably the theory of ideas. *Theaetetus* is interesting for its dialectic, its wit, its ingenious comparisons; but the wit is more ponderous than in some of the earlier dialogues, and the dialectic is agile to the point of exasperating logicians, who find Socrates more prone than usual to dodge or browbeat.

The fictive date of *Theaetetus* is 399 B.C., when Socrates was preparing to answer the charges against him, though it was written probably some thirty years later. *Sophist* was written still later, though its fictive date is the morrow of the discussion in *Theaetetus*. The cast of characters is the same, except that this time Theodorus and Theaetetus have brought with them an Eleatic Stranger, who presently undertakes to define the philosopher, the statesman, and the Sophist. Electing to begin with the Sophist, the Eleatic illustrates his method by the simple task of defining an angler. The method is to set up a pair of alternatives, rejecting one member, and dividing the remaining member into two new alternatives, and continuing to reject and redivide until the true definition is achieved. Some of the results of the angler process are applied to the Sophist, who is satirized, more harshly than in other dialogues criticizing his class, as a juggler and deceiver. This leads to what is a digression in form but in fact the principal topic of the dialogue. Does deception involve the assumption of Not-Being? The existence of Not-Being had been denied by Parmenides and the Eleatics; and Plato shows that it has a relative existence. Not-Being is not mere negation, the opposite of Being, but denotes Difference. Of Being it is concluded that everything which can produce a change or be affected by a cause has existence and is Being. Plato's solution turns on distinguishing the use of *is* as a copula for predication and the existential use of *is*. The entire problem of assertion is involved; and in so far as *Sophist* first recognizes the functions of the copula it may claim a prime position in the history of logic. This makes *Sophist* an important dialogue; in form it is not particularly attractive.

In form *Statesman* is a continuation of *Sophist* with one change, the young Socrates taking the place of Theaetetus as the interlocutor for the Eleatic Stranger. The process of arriving at definition by classification and division is carried on, the principal examples of the method being definitions of "herdsman" and "weaver." The examples, as well as the method by which they have been defined, are applied to the main subject of the dialogue, which is the definition of the statesman. Plato is consistent with his regularly expressed view that statesmanship is a specialized craft, like medicine, and accordingly prescribes monarchy (only the monarch can parallel the physician in insisting that the patient take bitter medicine for his own good) as the best form of government. Two points of contact with other Greek thought are worth mentioning. The long myth of the time when the sun, and all life, went backward, when men were born as graybeards and "grew" backward to infancy, has many plainly recognizable Pythagorean elements; Pythagorean beliefs were associated with the old-fashioned aristocracy, and opposed by the rationalism which informed "new thought." Secondly, the doctrine that virtue and art find their standard in the absolute mean appears here for the first time, and is apparently the source of Aristotle's teaching on the subject, for *Ethics* echoes the language and examples of *Statesman*. This makes it less likely that Plato was here influenced by Aristotle, as some scholars have held.

The Eleatic philosophy is also dealt with in *Parmenides,* which is named for the great teacher of that school. Though the dialogue must have been composed at about the same time as *Theaetetus* and its companion pieces, its fictive date is about a half century earlier, for Socrates is represented as being a young man. The other persons in the dialogue are Glaucon and Adimantus, Plato's full brothers; Antiphon, his half brother; Aristotle, one of the Thirty Tyrants; and Pythodorus, who was a general in the Peloponnesian War. After an introduction setting forth the dramatic circumstances, and an exposition of the futility of the paradoxes of Zeno, Parmenides delivers a long discourse, interrupted by brief questions or expressions of assent from Aristotle, the youngest of the company. The discourse is an exhibition of the Eleatic method, not unlike that in *Sophist*. Here the discussion proceeds, not by simple dichotomies, as in *Sophist*, but by division by contraries or opposites. For illustration Parmenides deals first with the hypothesis that one exists, and then with the hypothesis that one does not exist. His conclusion is (166c):

Then let us say that, and we may add, as it appears, that whether the one is or is not, the one and the others in relation to themselves and to each other all in every way are and are not and appear and do not appear.

The reader may doubt that the interlocutor's "Very true" is said with genuine conviction. More than any other of the dialogues *Parmenides* seems to have a select audience in view, and doubtless contains elements of playfulness which we can very imperfectly follow.

The fact that *Philebus* returns to practical questions of individual morality makes its artistic decline from such masterpieces as *Protagoras* and *Symposium* the more noticeable. Socrates is again the chief speaker (a place he holds in no other dialogue later than *Theaetetus*), but his two interlocutors, Philebus and Protarchus, are otherwise unknown and do not take on clear outlines in the dialogue. The object of the discussion is to determine whether the "good" is pleasure or knowledge. It is soon agreed that a mixture of knowledge and pleasure is necessary for the most desirable life, and the proper composition of this mixture is discussed, with acute analysis of the psychological implications of pleasure and pain. Within the composition there can be no question that knowledge has the preponderance, for pleasure carried to excess makes an unseemly spectacle, as knowledge does not; on such a question the judgment of *hoi polloi* is no better than the judgment of beasts. But the arguments for the superiority of knowledge are well reasoned, with due regard for the claims of pleasure, and the dialogue does indeed have a practical ethical value higher than many of the others.

The significance of *Timaeus* is that it is the only work of Plato devoted to natural science and to a theory of the creation of the universe; furthermore, having special interest for the Neoplatonists, the greater part of it was continuously known in Western Europe in a Latin translation, being the only major work of Greek philosophy so known before the recovery of Aristotle, and therefore highly influential. The persons of the dialogue are Socrates, Timaeus (of whom nothing is known beyond what is given in the dialogue), Critias (Plato's uncle, leader of the Thirty, who appears in *Charmides* and *Protagoras*), and Hermocrates, the Syracusan leader who figures prominently in Thucydides. In form *Timaeus* is a continuation of *Republic*, and it opens (17a–29b) with a recapitulation of the first five books of *Republic*. The next section (19*b*–26*d*) relates the victory of the Athenians over the people of the lost island of Atlantis nine thousand years before. Next Timaeus sets forth his account of the creation of the universe, covering incidentally the whole field of human knowledge from astronomy to the physics of biology. God, always referred to as the Demiurge ("Maker" or "Craftsman"), who is good, created the world, which is beautiful, but according to the eternal ideas. The universe is endowed with a soul; the spherical rotation of the world is the most stable movement of the most compact form. Time is a moving image of eternity. In the human body the head is the dwelling place of the soul, and the rest of the body is designed for its tendance. Pathology, physical and mental, is dealt with; hygiene of the soul should enable it to think immortal and divine thoughts.

And now at length [the dialogue closes (92*c*)] our discourse concerning the Universe has reached its termination. For this our Cosmos has received the living creatures both mortal and immortal and been thereby fulfilled; it being itself a visible Living Creature embracing the visible creatures, a perceptible God made in the image of the Intelligible, most great and good and fair and perfect in its generation—even this one Heaven sole of its kind.

Timaeus was to have been followed, according to its preface (27*a*), by an account of the ideal citizens of primeval Athens and how they proved their excellence in war and peace. *Critias* does commence with a detailed description of primeval Athens, followed by a parallel account of the state of Atlantis, but the dialogue is broken off before the two are brought together in conflict. It has been suggested that the account of the historical struggle of Athens against the Persians related in the third book of *Laws* was intended as a substitute for the fanciful conflict.

Devotees of Plato are distressed by his latest and longest work, the twelve books of *Laws,* for the book is without literary charm and the hard authoritarianism of the political system it envisages is unmitigated. The chief speaker is an unnamed Athenian, and the interlocutors are the Spartan Megillus and the Cretan Clinias, both of states which exercised totalitarian control over the lives of their citizens. All three are old men, and age is prerequisite for membership in the Nocturnal Council, a sort of vigilante committee whose function is to control the private lives of citizens and whose guiding principle is absolute resistance to any sort of innovation. Religion is a principal means for exercising control, and for the first time it is proposed to make heretical beliefs criminal. The shocking thing here is that the rulers themselves apparently have no belief in their orthodoxies but employ them only for political discipline. The genuineness of *Epinomis,* which is a sort of thirteenth book of *Laws,* has been questioned, but on insufficient grounds. The subject is the education of the members of the Nocturnal Council. As in *Laws* obedience to the state is paramount; interest is centered on the expertness of the governors, not on the welfare of the governed.

The writings in the Platonic corpus which have been condemned as spurious derive from Plato's school and date from the fourth century B.C. *Alcibiades I* (which is defended as genuine by many scholars) is a kind of handbook on ethics, not essentially at variance with the known teachings of Plato; the picture of Alcibiades is disappointingly colorless. *Alcibiades II* is dependent on *Alcibiades I* and much inferior; its subject is prayer. *Rivals* opposes the Platonic concept of philosophy as the knowledge of the good to the shallower notion, held in the school of Isocrates, that philosophy is general culture. *Theages* relates a number of anecdotes, many borrowed from the genuine dialogues, concerning Socrates' "sign." *Hipparchus* seeks to distinguish avarice from legitimate gain. *Clitophon* is a sort of preface to *Republic;* Socrates' interlocutor of that name is a follower of Thrasymachus (whose views are set forth in *Republic* i), and is, strangely, not properly refuted. *Minos* deals with the nature of law, and seeks to show that law is not a command but a discovery of a general moral truth.

There remains the collection of thirteen *Epistles* to be glanced at. All derive from genuine traditions concerning Plato's life and were composed within a century of his time, but it is impossible that all are genuine. Criticism of the last century declared the entire collection spurious; modern scholars tend to accept as genuine all those whose contents are significant. The epistolary form for addresses to statesmen goes back to Plato's period, for we have such "open letters" of Isocrates addressed to Philip of Macedon, and being in the nature of published documents such epistles are more likely to be preserved than private letters. The longest of the Platonic Epistles, #7 and #8, are of this character, provide most of what we know of the personal history of Plato, and are almost certainly genuine. The others, being letters to Dionysius and other rulers and statesmen, may well have been "attracted" by these genuine letters to Dion.

Epistle 1 to Dionysius makes an un-Platonic parade of poetic quotations. #2 seems to be a rhetorician's composition to show how Plato ought have written Dionysius. #3 borrows from #7, and is hardly genuine if #7 is. #4, on the other hand, is inconsistent with #7 in its attitude to Dion, and in addition has a suspicious borrowing from Isocrates. #5, to Perdiccas III of Macedon, also borrows from #7; the letter shows Plato, perhaps maliciously, as a supporter of Macedon and its tyrants. #6, to Hermias of Atarneus, has marked affinity with #2 and seems to violate historical fact. #7 is the longest as well as the most important of the collection, and constitutes an elaborate defense of Plato's conduct with respect to the Syracusan rulers, possibly in answer to attacks made upon Plato in Athens; the detailed account of Syracusan politics, which would be useless for Syracusans, suggests that the "open letter" was intended for Athenian readers. The case for #8, addressed "To the relatives and companions of Dion," is less clear. The letter advises the Syracusan leaders to unite in forming a constitutional monarchy, and thus prevent continued civil war and eventual subjugation by Carthage. Plato could hardly believe that his letter would influence the course of Syracusan politics, and so the epistle must be regarded, if it is Plato's, as a kind of political manifesto, reiterating the doctrine of *Republic* and *Laws* on the desirability of the rule of law. ##9–12 are short, insignificant, and almost certainly spurious. #13 is a private letter to Dionysius, dealing with purchases, expense accounts, and other private matters, and if genuine would give us the practical side of the lofty philosopher of the dialogues who is unconcerned with petty money matters. But a number of difficulties raise serious suspicions; among these are apparent attempts to answer objections to its genuineness, as when, in the closing sentence, the writer asks that the letter be preserved, as if to forestall questions of how such a letter came to be preserved.

Because of his dualism and his antidemocratic bias Plato seems outside the main stream of Greek thought, and he has, in fact, been called "a brilliant digression." A digression he is not, for even if he were alone in his views (which he was not) his own weight is sufficient to affect the course of the stream. But certainly he diverges from the monism of the Ionian physicists, and certainly he does not represent common Athenian views: in most points, indeed, Plato is excellent evidence for what Athenians did not think. His antidemocratic bias must remain a stumbling block for those who cherish a different conception of humanity, and his unworldly idealism an annoyance to those who prefer to proceed from the evidence of the sensible world. But his literary stature cannot be questioned, and the spiritual force of his quest is undeniable. The persistent aspiration toward the ideal which his writings admonish places him among the greatest spiritual teachers of mankind.

It is interesting to observe that cynicism and skepticism, trends which insisted, respectively, on the fundamental equality of mankind and on the insufficiency of intuitive speculation to establish truth, are cognate with, though not derived from, the Academy. Antisthenes, a friend and disciple of Socrates, "inaugurated the Cynic way of life" (Diogenes Laertius 6.2) and was the teacher of Diogenes, the great exemplar of the Cynics, who denied the validity of class distinctions. None of the ten volumes of treatises which Diogenes Laertius (6.15–18) lists as being Antisthenes' are extant. The Cynics established no school, in the usual sense, nor does their doctrine show development; those of the third and fourth centuries A.D. differ from their originals only in being more acrid. Of the popular sermons of the Cynics we shall speak below.

In course of time, especially beginning with Arcesilaus (d. 240 B.C.) and the Middle Academy, Platonism itself grew skeptical, maintaining that only verisimilitude, not absolute knowledge, is attainable. The skepticism of the Academy was speculative; skepticism based on empiricism was the creation of Pyrrho of Elis (*ca.* 365–275 B.C.). After the death of Pyrrho and of Timon, the author of *Silli,* whom Sextus Empiricus calls Pyrrho's prophet, the "school" went into eclipse, partly because the Middle Academy professed a parallel doctrine. It was resuscitated in Alexandria in the first centuries A.D., when the Platonic doctrine was submerged in Neoplatonism. Skepticism has been condemned as a negative and belittling doctrine, only less vicious than Epicureanism because less insistent. Greek skepticism was, in fact, the forerunner of freedom of conscience, of rational criticism, and of the absolute right of scientific thought.

ARISTOTLE AND OTHERS

Aristotle is the first author we are called upon to treat in whose writings there is no pretense of special care for form. Cicero, who praised his golden flow (*Academica* 2.38.119), and Quintilian, who praised his sweetness (10.1.83), seem to have read an Aristotle wholly different from ours —one whose works lack even the functional beauty of a well-constructed textbook. Except for the recently recovered *Constitution of Athens* our Aristotle reads like lecture notes, frequently the disciple's rather than the master's, full of allusive, technical jargon and delightful only as a difficult intellectual game may be delightful. The separate books which comprise the longer works frequently follow no logical sequence, and some may be improved by rearrangement. To attend to Aristotle as literature is like attending to the eagle for his voice. Yet attended to he must be, for no man has left a deeper mark upon the intellect of Europe. Sometimes his influence has been for the worse, as when reverence for his authority has led to the acceptance of even his tentative conclusions as absolute truth; sometimes for the better, as when his boundless urge to know and understand has inspired emulation. For Europe he has been simply "the philosopher," or, as Dante called him, "the master of those that know." "Much of the history of civilization in the West can be and indeed has been written in the form of a debate in which the triumph of Aristotle in the thirteenth century and the defeat of Aristotle in the Renaissance indifferently herald great intellectual advances." But for what posterity did with his works Aristotle cannot be held responsible; it is enough to say that "his philosophy contains the first statement, explicit or by opposition, of many of the technical distinctions, definitions, and convictions on which later science and philosophy have been based."

Chronologically, Aristotle's life coincides with Demosthenes', but we know of no connection between the two men other than that the Antipater who ordered Demosthenes' death was chosen by Aristotle to be the executor of his will. He was born at Stagira in the Chalcidice in 384 B.C., his father Nicomachus being court physician to Amyntas II, King of Macedonia and father of Philip. At the age of seventeen he went to Athens and studied in Plato's Academy for twenty years, until the death of Plato in 347 B.C. Speusippus, who succeeded Plato, represented tendencies in the Academy—"turning philosophy into mathematics" (*Metaphysics* 992a)—which were distasteful to Aristotle. He went to Asia Minor, where for three years he was entertained by an old fellow student, the eunuch Hermias, tyrant of Atarneus and Assos, who gave him his niece in marriage. When Hermias fell into the hands of the Persians, Aristotle went to Lesbos, where he must have devoted at least part of his time to research in biology. In 343 Philip made him tutor to Alexander, in which capacity he continued for some three years. In 335 he returned to Athens, and organized the Lyceum (the school is commonly referred to as the "Peripatetic" because of its pleasant walks), which was much more professional and specialized than the Academy. For the next twelve or thirteen years he worked prodigiously, and composed most of his writings. When Alexander died in 323 B.C. and there was a sharp reaction in Athens against the Macedonians and their friends, Aristotle was prosecuted for impiety, and retired to Chalcis in Euboea, where he died in 322 B.C. Of the political upheavals of his time, in which his patrons were prime movers, his works show no evidence, though political theory was one of his favorite subjects and he collected data on the history and constitution of 158 cities. Possibly he saw in Alexander the philosopher king which Plato had desiderated, and which partisans of Alexander claim he was. But the sympathies of a man who could write "Most men are timid in danger and corruptible" (*Rhetoric* 2.5.7) or insist that some men are slaves by nature (*Politics* 1.2.5)—an odd view for a biologist—were more likely to be with Philip and Alexander than with the Athens of Demosthenes.

In antiquity Aristotle was said to have written either 1,000 or 400 books, and the titles of some 200 (possibly containing duplications) are recorded. After his manuscripts passed from the hands of his successor and legatee Theophrastus, they are said to have remained stored in a cave in the Troad for 150 years, then brought to Athens, where Sulla acquired them in 78 b.c. The editions he caused to be made are the originals of our Aristotle. The popular works, which were said to include an *Exhortation to Philosophy* and dialogues on a variety of subjects, are lost. Our corpus, as presented in the text of the Berlin Academy (by whose pages Aristotle is cited), contains, besides fragments, some forty-seven treatises, large or small, of which about two-thirds are usually accepted as genuine. The grouping is in the order of logic, natural science, first philosophy, and practical science; needless to say, this order does not represent the order of composition. Nothing could be more hopeless than an attempt to characterize the works of Aristotle in a sentence, yet some notion of their scope must be indicated; the page numbers in parentheses indicate the size of a treatise and its position in the corpus.

The collection of logical treatises called *Organon* ("instrument," "tool") is concerned with the techniques and principles of proof. It includes *Categories* (1–15), *On Interpretation* (16–23), *Prior Analytics* (24–70), *Posterior Analytics* (71–100), *Topics* (100–164), and *On Sophistical Refutations* (164–184). Roughly, the first three may be said to deal with the construction of the syllogism, and the last three to distinguish kinds of syllogism. The categories of the title are the ten principal possible classifications under which predications may be made concerning an object of inquiry, and chiefly, since he is the most differentiated of such objects, concerning man. Where *Categories* deals with isolated, uncombined terms, *On Interpretation* deals with the theory and analysis of propositions, whose function is to represent the true relationship between concepts. The first part of *Prior Analytics* (two books) enunciates and demonstrates the laws of syllogistic reasoning, and the remainder sets forth the correct use of this instrument of reasoning. *Posterior Analytics* (also in two books) carries on with methods of demonstration and definition. *Topics* (eight books) discusses the use of syllogisms and of undemonstrated but generally accepted "commonplaces" (*topoi*) in practical disputation. *On Sophistical Refutations,* sometimes regarded as a ninth book of *Topics,* shows how false syllogisms are to be refuted.

In the natural science group the longest treatise is *Physics* (184–267), which might more appropriately be entitled "Lectures on Nature." "Nature" in this sense includes, not what we understand by "physics," but all questions of movement and change, and involves psychology and, by inference, theology. Concepts of "change," "becoming," and the like are analyzed, and this involves discussion of motion, place, time, and the transformation of potentiality into actuality. Book 1 is concerned with matter and form as elements of natural body; Book 2 with various types of physical causes; Books 3–7 with movement and the notions implied in movement; and Book 8 with the prime mover, which though not itself a natural body is the cause of movement in natural bodies. The four books *On the Heavens* (268–313) deal specifically with heavenly and sublunary bodies. As conceived in this book the universe is spherical, with the sphere of the fixed stars as its circumference and the earth at its center. Successive spherical layers of different kinds of body occupy the intervening space, with ever diminishing degrees of divinity, permanence, and form as the spheres approach the center. The outermost sphere and the stars which it contains are *aither* in its purest form. This final fifth body alone is eternal and has no contrary by whose action it could be destroyed. The place of the transcendent unmoved mover is not clear from this work, for passages both implying the existence of an unmoved mover and refuting it may be cited from it. The work, then, is one of the clearest marks of transition in Aristotle's thought. The two books *On Generation and Corruption* (314–338) follow logically upon the last two books of *On the Heavens,* and show the necessary character of the cyclical sequence of transformations. In the four books of *Meteorology* (338–390) stages of composition in the constitution of things are distinguished. The first three actually deal with meteorology in the Aristotelian sense; the last, whose authenticity has been doubted, is something of an approach to physics and chemistry in the modern sense. *On the Universe* (391–401), which follows in our editions, was written centuries after Aristotle's day. By tracing the process of terrestrial change to a divine origin beyond the stars Aristotle seeks to leave a minimum of dead matter "unactualized," that is to say, without explanation of how it realizes the potentiality of its end, and hence closed to knowledge. The next step is to analyze function and form in respect to vegetable and animal life.

The form and nature to which a living body is at once matter and instrument is soul (*psyche*); plants and animals are what they are because of their ascending grades of soul, which is the efficient and final as well as the formal cause of living. Broadly characterized, the grades of soul are nutritive and reproductive, sentient, rational. These aspects of soul are discussed and the process of sensation and thought are treated at length in *On the Soul* (three books; 402–435), which lays the foundations for modern psychology. Psychological investigation is continued in the group called *Parva Naturalia,* which includes *On Senses and Sensibles* (436–449), *On Memory and Reminiscence* (449–453), *On Sleep* (453–458), *On Dreams* (458–462), *On Prophesying by Dreams* (462–464), *On Length and Brevity of Life* (464–467), *On Youth and Old Age, Life and Death, Respiration* (467–480). *On Breath* (481–486), which closes this series, knows the distinction between veins and arteries and is therefore not by Aristotle.

On the Soul and its related treatises examine one aspect of life; the treatises on natural history in our sense comprise about a fourth of all our Aristotle. The *History of* (more properly "Inquiry into") *Animals* (ten books, of which the last and parts of others are spurious; 487–638) is a classified collection of facts relating to the anatomy of the organism, and other works of the group set forth theories based on these facts. *On the Parts of Animals* (four books; 639–697) deals with morphology almost exclusively from the physiological and teleological viewpoint of function. As in other encyclopedic works in the Aristotelian corpus, the basic observations must have been accumulated by a corps of research assistants, but in the presentation the informing and systematizing influence of a single master mind is evident. *On the Motion of Animals* (698–703) deals with properties consequent upon the morphology of *On the Parts;* and *On the Progression of Animals* (704–714) deals with mechanical attributes involved in that morphology. It is a comment on the habits of professed philosophers that one of Aristotle's most impressive works, *On the Generation of Animals* (five books; 715–789), which deals with great acumen and thoroughness with the science of embryology, has been neglected, apparently because of the banausic character of its laboratory procedures. And yet, as A. L. Peck remarks in the Preface to his Loeb edition of this treatise,

It may be justly claimed that in this treatise Aristotle's thought is to be seen integrated as it is nowhere else; for in reproduction, as understood by Aristotle, not only the individual is concerned but the cosmos at large: it is a business in which the powers of the universe are concentrated and united; and it is the means whereby that eternity, with which, if he could have done it, God would have filled the whole creation from one end to the other, is attained so far as is possible by the creatures that are subject to decay; indeed, these very beings, animals and plants, have in Aristotle's view the best claim to the title of "being" (*ousia*), a much better claim than the lifeless things out of which they are composed, or the objects made by human art; and therefore they merit to an exceptional degree the attention of the student of reality.

Though Aristotle's towering achievement in the realm of speculative thought still has direct applicability while his "laboratory" science has been superseded by men with microscopes, the abiding significance of these biological treatises is not to be underestimated. When Darwin read a new translation of *On Generation* he wrote: "Linnaeus and Cuvier may have been my two gods, though in very different ways, but they were mere schoolboys to old Aristotle." It was no inconsiderable thing, to begin with, to have made the nasty business of dissection a respectable enterprise for philosophical gentlemen. In *Parts of Animals* (645*a*) Aristotle gives an apologia or exhortation to science which is worth quoting:

Of "things divine" we have already treated and have set down our views concerning them; so now it remains to speak of animals and their Nature. So far as in us lies, we will not leave out any one of them, be it never so mean; for though there are animals which have no attractiveness for the senses, yet for the eye of science, for the student who is naturally of a philosophic spirit and can discern the causes of things, Nature which fashioned them provides joys which cannot be measured. If we study mere likenesses of these things and take pleasure in so doing, because then we are contemplating the painter's or the carver's Art which fashioned them, and yet fail to delight much more in studying the works of Nature themselves, though we have the ability to discern the actual causes—that would be a strange absurdity indeed. Wherefore we must not betake ourselves to the consideration of the meaner animals with a bad grace, as though we were children; since in all natural things there is somewhat of the marvellous. . . . We ought not to hesitate nor to be abashed, but boldly to enter upon our researches concerning animals of every sort and kind, knowing that in not one of them is Nature or Beauty lacking. I add "Beauty," because in the works of Nature purpose and not accident is predominant; and the purpose or end for the sake of which those works have been constructed or formed has its place among what is beautiful.

—*A. L. Peck*

The biological treatises are followed by a number of miscellaneous spurious works: *De Coloribus* (791–799); *De Audibilibus* (800–804); *Physiognomica* (805–814). These three are Peripatetic works dating from near Aristotle's own time. *De Plantis* (815–829) is a Greek translation of a Latin translation of an Arabic translation of a Greek book probably written by Nicolaus of Damascus, a contemporary of Augustus. *De Mirabilibus Auscultationibus* (830–847) is a collection of marvelous tales of the "believe-it-or-not" type put together from earlier sources about the time of Hadrian. *Mechanica* (847–858) is an early Peripatetic work which shows a very advanced understanding of the laws of mechanics. The thirty-eight short books of *Problemata* (959–967) were put together about a thousand years after Aristotle, but mainly with Peripatetic materials. They consist wholly of numerous questions on assorted phenomena, each beginning with the word "Why," followed by suggested answers. *On Indivisible Lines* (968–972) makes direct reference to Euclid and seeks to refute the theory that every line contains a unity which is an indivisible line. *On the Situations and Names of Winds* (973) is an extract from a larger work which was called *Meteorological Signs. On Melissus, Xen-*

ophanes, and Gorgias (974-980), criticizing each of the authorities named, is, like the two works previously listed, an early Peripatetic production, but not Aristotle's.

As will have become apparent from the works listed, Aristotle felt that there must be a regular system of sciences, each concerned with a different aspect of reality. To him the theory of a universal science, as sketched in Plato's *Republic,* was unsatisfactory; but at the same time it seemed reasonable to posit a supreme science, more ultimate, more exact, more truly wisdom than the disparate sciences. The discussion of this science—wisdom, first philosophy, or theology, as it is variously called—is the subject of *Metaphysics* (fourteen books, originally ten; 980-1093), so-called simply because it was placed after (*meta-*) *Physics* in the scroll. The work starts with the sentence "All men by nature desire to know," and proceeds to discuss the nature, problems, and vocabulary of philosophy. Since philosophy is concerned with that which *is,* the meaning of the copula is first discussed, and then the meaning of *substance,* which is first in the categories of predication. The relationship of form and matter is subsumed under the four causes—material, formal, efficient, and final. From the consideration of change and motion which is involved in the actualization of potentials through these causes Aristotle proceeds to develop his theology. The continuity of processes in the universe presupposes a moving cause by which they are maintained. This cause, or prime mover, must itself be eternal and immutable, and hence entirely immaterial. It is pure form and actuality—Mind or God. Here it may be noticed that despite Aristotle's rejection of Platonic ideas his own resort to pure form as prime mover is virtually a surrender to Plato.

The remaining group in the customary division of the Aristotelian corpus is of practical sciences, and opens with the *Nicomachean Ethics* (ten books; 1094-1181), named for Aristotle's son, who was named for Aristotle's father. Together with *Politics,* with which they are closely connected, the *Ethics* are the most readable and the most generally useful of Aristotle's works. For the nonphilosophical reader the quest of the highest good of man is more engaging than classification of phenomena or speculation on first causes. And, paradoxically, because man is not so precisely definable as theories or other animals, the nonphilosophical reader may here more readily comprehend the core of Aristotle's thought —that the potential is real or intelligible only as it is actualized. Aristotle first makes the central truth of ethics, the one way to a rational existence, the proposition that the problem of practical life may be solved if we can determine the nature of a supremely good and finally desirable end or goal of all action and regard every part of our conduct as comprising means to this end, which is the standard of all human life. The essential function of the soul is discovered to be its well-being, and its well-being, activity in accordance with the highest excellence. Excellence (or virtue) is neither innate nor contrary to nature, but formed by practice and to be regulated by avoidance of excess or deficiency. The doctrine of the mean here implied is discussed with reference to such qualities as courage, liberality, loftiness of spirit. Not virtue alone but vice also is subject to will. This leads to a consideration of justice, and then to other central problems of ethics, such as pleasure and friendship. Throughout the *Ethics* (as in the biological works) the gauge for assessing values is observed nature and existing usages, and here the difference of Aristotle's approach from Plato's becomes manifest, for in Plato the gauge is not observed practice but a remote ideal to which men must aspire. *Magna Moralia* (1181–1213) follows the *Eudemian Ethics* closely but has elements of Stoic terminology and is therefore post-Aristotelian. *Eudemian Ethics* (1214–1249) is Aristotelian, but its relationship to *Nicomachean Ethics* has never been satisfactorily explained; it traverses much the same ground, and three of its books are identical with books of the superior *Nicomachean Ethics*.

In the Greek view (as we have seen from *Republic* of Plato), ethics and politics are aspects of one thing, and *Politics* (eight books, variously arranged by editors; 1252–1342) is closely connected to *Ethics*. For Aristotle himself politics is the supreme study among the practical sciences, and the incomplete state of this book suggests that he may have worked at it continuously until his death; the latest datable allusion in it is to the death of Philip (1311*b*2), which took place in 336. *Politics* has been almost as widely read, in both ancient and modern times, as *Ethics,* and is in a sense more practical. Here the opening premise is that every *community* is established to achieve some good; that good is living well, and the inquiry is directed toward whatever form of human association best serves this end. The contents of the books (their proper order is still under dispute) may be indicated as follows: (1) definition and structure of the state, slaves, property, children and wives; (2) ideal commonwealths, the best existing states, Greek lawgivers; (3) civic virtue, classification of constitutions, forms of monarchy; (4 or 6) variations in types of constitution, the best for general and special circumstance; (5 or 8) revolutions, their causes and how they may be avoided; (6 or 7) democracies and oligarchies; (7 or 4) the ideal state, its educational system; (8 or 5) the ideal education continued. It is perhaps significant of Aristotle's obliviousness to contemporary events, or of the influence of the idealist Plato, that despite Philip and Alexander he still believes that the traditional city-state can survive as an independent power and does not realize that the day of empires and great kingdoms has arrived. Of the great collection of constitutions made in the Lyceum only the damaged but valuable *Constitution of Athens* has survived, discovered in an Egyptian papyrus in 1891. *Oeconomica* (1343–1353) is a non-Aristotelian but Peripatetic conflation of *Politics* i, Xenophon's *Oeconomicus,* and other sources.

The study of literature was also assiduously pursued in the Lyceum and became a Peripatetic tradition. Research in the lives and works of the poets as carried on by the Peripatetics is the origin of the critical work done in Alexandria and of biographical writing, of which Plutarch is our best surviving example. All that we know of the dates of tragedies and comedies and the names of the victors at the Dionysia and Lenaea derives indirectly from the lost *Didascaliae* of Aristotle. Similarly, our knowledge of the early history of rhetoric derives from his lost *Collection of Treatises on the Art of Rhetoric* which Cicero used for his account in his *Brutus.* The extant *Rhetoric* (three books; 1354–1420) is a philosophical analysis of the means of persuasion. In Plato's *Gorgias* Socrates is represented as declaring that rhetoric is not an art but a mere knack of gratifying and pleasing the auditors. In the later *Phaedrus* dialectic, psychology, and genuine knowledge of the good and the true are premised as prerequisites for the respectable practice of rhetoric. Aristotle's *Rhetoric* has been spoken of as an "expanded *Phaedrus.*" The first book deals with the means of persuasion, the logical proofs based upon dialectic; and the second with the psychological or ethical proofs, based upon a knowledge of the human emotions and their causes, and of the different types of character. Style is barely touched upon in *Phaedrus;* the third book of *Rhetoric* presents a succinct analysis of questions of linguistic style, arrangement, and figures of speech, which exercised very great influence upon subsequent writers on the subject. But on principles later writers have nothing to add. Readers who smile at Aristotle's natural science and are nonplussed by his metaphysics are astonished at the perspicacity and applicability of his work on persuasion; in this field, at least, Aristotle has neither been corrected nor supplemented. Writing in 1810, Edward Copleston called *Rhetoric* "a magazine of intellectual riches . . . a text-book of human feeling; a storehouse of taste; an exemplar of condensed and accurate, but uniformly clear and candid reasoning." The warnings against the abuse of oratory and the background of logic, psychology, and ethics which render *Rhetoric* a philosophical work are absent in *Rhetoric to Alexander* (1420–1446), which merely gives instruction on how to convince an audience. The treatise has therefore been generally regarded as spurious, though some have held it to be an early work of the master.

In *Rhetoric* speech is treated in terms of purpose or end; *Poetics* (1447–1462), with which the corpus closes, deals with poetry mainly from the point of view of form and for itself. Whereas Plato had judged poetry only from the point of view of its usefulness in educating citizens for his ideal commonwealth, Aristotle deals with literature in its own terms, and is hence the first true literary critic. Plato had accounted for poetry and the other arts in terms of "imitation," but Aristotle insists not only that poetry has its origin in the instinct for imitation but that men take pleasure, grounded on recognition and learning, in things imitated. The experience of a work of art, in other words, is of the same nature as its making. In the discussion of specific forms (only the section on drama is complete) the technique is that of a biological treatise; analysis of existing specimen yields rules generally applicable to the form, which may be useful for criticism or new composition. Aristotle does not legislate what a poem must be, but classifies and describes the parts of poems as they are. Slavish adherence to what was imagined to be Aristotelian legislation (sometimes with little basis, as is the case with the "three unities") is a simple example of the harmful use to which Aristotle has been put. On the other hand, it is a testimonial to the clarity of Aristotle's insight that his general definition of tragedy—not, of course, the definition of such parts as prologue, episode, and the like—can serve as a useful criterion for Shakespeare as well as Sophocles. Any good tragedy should, in fact, be an "imitation of an action that is serious and also, as having magnitude, complete in itself; in language with pleasurable accessories; in a dramatic not in a narrative form; with incidents arousing pity and fear" (1449*b*), and its characters and incidents, as well as its psychological effects, should conform to the practices which Aristotle realized were essential to the Greek tragedies he knew.

The pre-eminence of Aristotle lies in his speculative power, his scientific method, his universality. His actual achievements are of enormous significance; perhaps even more significant are the attitudes he has shaped and the directions to which he has pointed. If, as Coleridge said, all men must be either Platonists or Aristotelians, those with whom the love of Beautiful Letters is paramount must choose Plato; others may join with Aristotle in loving Plato but loving truth better. But though the identifications of Plato and Aristotle as respectively idealist and realist are true enough, the simple dichotomy is too absolute. Plato was aware enough of the phenomenal world and his dialectic was acute enough for him to be made a lisping Aristotelian; and Aristotle was otherworldly enough to serve as a basis for a Christian theology—which neither the earlier Ionians nor the later Epicureans could have done.

Lyceum and Academy continued to function for nearly a millennium, until they were suppressed by Justinian in A.D. 529. Speusippus was followed in turn by Xenocrates, Polemo, and Crates, who form the Old Academy; the Middle and New Academies are yet to come. Fragments left by these scholarchs are insufficient to characterize their literary work. Gradually, Platonic doctrine was transformed, partly under the influence of the competing schools, more significantly by a recrudescence of Pythagoreanism, which paved the way for the mysticism of the Neoplatonists. The "inspirational" character of the school survived, and was expressed in writings of a moralizing ethical nature. The most highly regarded representative of the Old Academy after Plato, at least among the Romans, was Crantor, pupil of Polemo. Cicero speaks of his *On Mourning* as "golden, to be learned by heart," and Horace cites him as a master in morals.

The Peripatetic school retained its character as a research institution, as is suggested by the volume of non-Aristotelian writings in the corpus of Aristotle, and by the works of Aristotle's successor Theophrastus (372–287 B.C.) as head of the school. Diogenes lists about 240 titles for him, and their range suggests that he was, like his master, a polymath. Of his work there are extant (1) *History of* (more precisely "Researches in") *Plants,* in nine books; (2) *Causes of Plants,* in six books; and (3) a curious and attractive book called *Characters. History* is classification and description, showing taste as well as scholarship. To it *Causes* bears the same relation as Aristotle's *Parts of Animals* does to his *History of Animals;* that is to say, the distinctions noted in the one are explained in the other by Aristotelian "causes." Nothing in Greek literature so begs to be read aloud at a party as the thirty *Characters* of Theophrastus, and the author may well have intended such use of them. Each is only a page long. With brevity, humor, and concreteness the author represents people speaking or acting in ways which illustrate perennial social defects. Nothing is so calculated to impress a reader with the permanence and universality of human foibles as such acutely observed and neatly reported types as the Flatterer or Grumbler or Officious Man, the Newsmaker, the Avaricious Man, the Late Learner, and the rest. Despite the uniqueness of this work it is clearly its own justification, and there is no need to seek such farfetched explanations for its genesis as that it is an extract from a serious book of ethics—or (as has actually been maintained) that it was composed for Menander (who was indeed a pupil of Theophrastus) to help him in character delineation.

A number of other followers of the Peripatetic school in the late fourth and early third century B.C. must be mentioned. Aristoxenus of Tarentum was considered the best authority on music. His fragmentary *Harmonics* indicates that he studied music in its relation to words and dance and that, like Plato and Aristotle, he was concerned with the function of music in educating for citizenship as well as with its technical aspects. Among his numerous other writings was a series of biographies; the writing of biography became a regular Peripatetic pursuit, of which the biographies of Plutarch are for us the culmination. Dicaearchus of Messene in Sicily was a prolific writer of wide erudition and considerable originality; he pioneered in a number of fields which the Alexandrian scholars carried forward, and his books were respected and used by Cicero. Demetrius of Phalerum, a friend of Theophrastus, was governor of Athens from 317 to 310 B.C. He seems to have been a facile writer on philosophy, poetry, history, and politics, and is said to have been instrumental in creating the Library of Alexandria, though he was surely not responsible (as Aristeas 28 implies) for the translation of the Bible called the Septuagint. The Peripatetic biographer Satyrus deserves mention, for a large fragment of his biography of Euripides was recovered in a papyrus in 1912. Eudemus of Rhodes is said to have made a history of doctrine, and Clearchus of Soli wrote lives of the philosophers. Theophrastus was succeeded in turn by Strato, Lycon, Ariston, and Critolaus. But neither they, nor the teachers of the important provincial offshoots of the Academy, the Megarians who studied mathematics and the Cyrenaics who taught hedonism, did much to shape the thought of the new age or to merit a place in the history of literature. Popular influence incomparably broader than that of the older schools was exercised by Stoics and Epicureans. To these we shall turn after we have examined another characteristic product of the Greek genius, oratory.

Chapter 11. THE ORATORS

PERSUASIVE SPEECH, AS MIGHT BE EXPECTED FROM GREEK CHARACTER AND IN-
stitutions, was always highly regarded in Greece. When Phoenix became
Achilles' tutor his assignment was to teach him "to be a speaker of words
and a doer of deeds" (*Iliad* 9.443); and when Antenor compares Menelaus
and Odysseus he makes Odysseus pre-eminent, despite other shortcomings,
solely for his eloquence: "His words were like the snowflakes of winter"
(*Iliad* 3.204–224). In the Athenian democracy where every man had the
right to speak in the assembly (in the Roman assemblies citizens could
only vote "Aye" or "No") oratory was of paramount importance and the
principal avenue to political leadership. Oratory, in fact, comes to its
flowering with the Athenian democracy, and declines to become only a
literary ornament when that democracy declines. It is significant that
Thucydides should say of Brasidas (4.84) that "he was not a bad speaker
for a Lacedaemonian." It is natural that Themistocles should be the first
statesman the effectiveness of whose oratory is commended (Thucydides
1.138); Plutarch (*Themistocles* 11, 29) preserves some fragments of his
speeches which may well be genuine. Pericles' control of the democracy
rested largely on his eloquence; the three speeches which Thucydides attributes to him may well be fairly close representations of his actual words.
A few of the phrases ascribed to him in various authors are probably
genuine: Aegina is the eyesore of the Piraeus; the Samians are like babies
who cry when you give them their pap but take it all the same; Boeotia
is like an oak split by oaken wedges; the city has lost its youth—it is as
if the year had lost its spring.

The term "oratory," it must be noted, is not confined to eloquence;
Isocrates, who was one of the greatest of the "orators," never delivered
speeches at all. The word rather denotes persuasiveness, and hence is applicable to any effective prose style. The orators thus have a legitimate and
important place in the history of Greek literature. It is significant of the
general Greek concern for form that assembly and juries demanded an
elaborate, artistic style of their speakers; and if to us that style sometimes
seems somewhat precious, it became, in the last analysis, the pattern
for European prose.

Oratory became professional under two specific influences, that of the

Sophists and that of the rhetoricians of Sicily. The Sophists, who became prominent in the middle of the fifth century B.C., undertook to prepare men for the higher walks of civic life by instruction of various kinds. The practical character of their teaching is suggested by the famous dictum of Protagoras of Abdera, the greatest of the Sophists, who declared that "man is the measure of all things." Prodicus of Ceos, many years younger than Protagoras, paid great attention, as we can see from Plato's parody in his *Protagoras,* to the correct use of words. Hippias of Elis, who also appears in *Protagoras,* seems chiefly to have taught glibness. Forensic rhetoric originated in Syracuse, Cicero (*Brutus* 46) tells us on the authority of Aristotle, when, after the expulsion of the tyrants in 465 B.C., families who had suffered expropriation tried to re-establish their claims. At that time Corax composed a *techne,* or handbook of rhetoric, and his pupil Tisias wrote another, which Aristotle (*On Sophistic Refutations* 183*b*) thought better than his master's. Both taught the use of probability, or rather plausibility, as a device for convincing juries.

The most influential of the Sicilians by far was Gorgias, who came to Athens as ambassador from his native Leontini in 427. His virtuosity created a rage in Athens, and was widely emulated. His speeches were not written for the law courts but for display, being of the type called "epideictic." Of his compositions we have probably genuine fragments of an *epitaphios,* or funeral oration, and of encomia on Helen and on Palamedes. His mannered style can be judged from Agathon's discourse in *Symposium,* which is an imitation of it. Most of the tricks in his bag are reproduced in Professor Van Hook's skillful version of the *Encomium on Helen,* a single paragraph of which is more revealing than a page of description:

But if by violence she was defeated and unlawfully she was treated and to her injustice was meted, clearly her violator as a terrifier was importunate, while she, translated and violated, was unfortunate. Therefore, the barbarian who verbally, legally, actually attempted the barbarous attempt, should meet with verbal accusation, legal reprobation, and actual condemnation. For Helen, who was violated, and from her fatherland separated, and from her friends segregated, should justly meet with commiseration rather than with defamation. For he was the victor and she was the victim. It is just, therefore, to sympathize with the latter and anathematize the former.

—*LaRue Van Hook*

Gorgias' art won him fame and wealth, but it was not intended to sway opinion, either on political or legal questions, and Gorgias was not included in the Alexandrian canon of the Ten Attic Orators. That canon included Antiphon, Andocides, Lysias, Isocrates, and Isaeus in the first group, and Aeschines, Demosthenes, Lycurgus, Hyperides, and Dinarchus in the second group. Antiphon was born about 480 B.C., and his profession was that of *logopoios,* or writer of speeches for others to deliver. Lawyers did not plead in Athens, but a litigant might engage a professional speech writer to write his speech for him. Thucydides says (8.68) that "no one could do more for a client, whether his business lay in the law courts or the ecclesia," and praises his remarkable powers of intellect and gifts of speech as second to none. Antiphon's politics were violently antidemocratic, and it was he, according to Thucydides, who planned the conspiracy which resulted in the revolution of the Four Hundred in 411 B.C. Among the Four Hundred he was leader of the extremist group, and when the Four Hundred fell, after a short rule, Antiphon was prosecuted for treason and executed. "His defense speech," Thucydides says, "was undoubtedly the best ever made by any man tried on a capital charge down to my time."

Of the sixty speeches which were attributed to Antiphon in antiquity, fifteen are extant. All deal with cases of murder. Three Tetralogies, or sets of four speeches, present two speeches for each side of the same fictive case, and so lie on the border between theory and practice. The first Tetralogy (second in the usual numbering) deals with an accusation of murder based on the deposition of a slave who was mortally wounded at the time of the murder. In the second (#3) one boy has involuntarily killed another while practicing with the javelin in the gymnasium; the accuser charges murder, and the defendant suggests that the victim committed unintentional suicide. A third solution, suggested in a similar case elsewhere (Plutarch, *Pericles* 36), was to make the javelin guilty. The third Tetralogy (#4) deals with the death of an old man as a result of a beating by a young man.

The Murder of Herodes (#5) deals with a real case, which was tried about 416. Two men voyaging together waited out a storm on shore, and after an evening of drinking one was never seen again. The survivor, who is a Lesbian, is accused of murder. On the basis of the known politics of his party, it is to be expected that Antiphon would be eager to defend a Lesbian against an Athenian. A modern reader finds it strange that Antiphon should pass lightly over what we should regard as evidence— he makes nothing of what appears to be a real alibi—and should prefer to argue from probability; among other proofs of innocence he cites the absence of signs of divine anger, which must surely have appeared if his client were a murderer. Oration 6, *The Death of the Choreutes* (which incidentally plays upon the corruption of the officials of the democracy) defends a choirmaster against the charge of murdering a boy singer who had died as result of a drug he had taken to improve his voice. In *Against the Stepmother for Poisoning* (#1) a young man charges his stepmother with instigating the murder of his father. The authenticity of this speech has been questioned; it is less vigorous than Antiphon's other pieces, and may be a mere exercise.

Antiphon's style is characterized by poetic and rare words, circumlocutions, and a tendency to periodic (or Thucydidean) as against running (or Herodotean) sentences. He uses the usual *topoi,* or commonplaces, such as early rhetoricians had collected into handbooks; Aristotle has preserved a large assortment of such commonplaces in the first book of his *Rhetoric.* The speaker always disclaims cleverness or special eloquence: it is the strength of his case which will make him effective. The jury is always complimented for its impartiality; and deep respect is expressed for the sanctity of the laws. A tone of devout piety is maintained; as mentioned above, absence of overt signs of divine displeasure is construed as a proof of innocence. After a conventional preface (*prooimion*) possibly from a commonplace-book, there follows an introduction (*prokataskeue*) describing the crime and the circumstances under which the action has been brought. The facts, or a selection of them, are then narrated (*diegesis*), and are followed by arguments and proofs (*pisteis*). Arguments are usually from probability and display considerable casuistry and theoretical motivations. Testimony, always in the form of depositions, may be interspersed throughout the speech or reserved for the end. The peroration (*epilogos*) makes the final appeal. The artificiality of the speeches is marked, for the modern reader, not only by the somewhat precious style and the singular attitude toward evidence, but also by the fact that no attempt is made to suit the speech to the character of the person who was to deliver it. The art of realism, which was called *ethos,* was introduced by later speech writers.

The Thrasymachus who maintains that justice is the right of the stronger in *Republic* 1 and who is also mentioned in *Phaedrus* was reputed to excel in the "pathetic" style of oratory. A handbook of his is referred to by Aristotle (*Rhetoric* 3.1.7), and a fragment of one of his speeches is preserved in Dionysius of Halicarnassus (*Demosthenes* 3). Thrasymachus is not included in the canon, in which Antiphon is followed by Andocides. Andocides was born about 440 B.C. into a wealthy family; Aristophanes (*Clouds* 109) speaks of his father, Leagoras, rearing a special breed of horses. As a young man Andocides himself was a member of a hetaeria, one of the clubs which were the centers for oligarchic reaction. He was not trained for professional oratory. The central fact in his life, and the subject matter of his speeches, was his complicity in the profanation of the Eleusinian mysteries and the mutilation of the hermae which rocked Athens in 415. At the time, the two outrages were construed as attempts to subvert the democracy. Andocides apparently succeeded in clearing himself of the charge concerning the mysteries, but admitted knowledge of the mutilation. An informer had implicated a large number of persons, and to save his relatives, Andocides himself says in his *On the Mysteries,* he himself gave a true list (naming only four who were not already implicated, and presumably having given these four notice of his intention to inform against them), including his own name. His information had been given under promise of immunity, but by a subsequent decree he suffered *atimia,* which involved exclusion from market place and temples, and in consequence went abroad. His two principal speeches endeavor to procure his reinstatement in his civic rights.

About 410, on some occasion when Athenian naval reverses had endangered the grain supply, Andocides brought a shipment of grain from Cyprus and a proposal for ensuring a future supply. In the speech *On His Return* (#2), delivered before the ecclesia, he pleaded that his patriotic services during his exile and the likelihood (based on the record of his ancestors) of further patriotic services in the future should bring remission of his punishment. His plea was unsuccessful, and it was only after the amnesty of Thrasybulus (403 B.C.) that he resumed full citizenship. In 399, the year of the execution of Socrates, political passions were again aroused, and Andocides was charged with impiety on two counts, of having participated in the mysteries at a time when he was legally disqualified, and of having deposited a suppliant's branch on the altar at Eleusis during the season of the mysteries. The penalty for either charge was death, and Andocides defended himself successfully in his *On the Mysteries* (#1). It is to the credit of the restored democracy (and it makes the conviction of Socrates the more striking) that it was willing to let buried scandals remain buried.

The tone of *On the Mysteries* suggests that its audience was friendly. The man is speaking on a matter of life and death to himself, and of much greater interest to us than ordinary items on a criminal docket. Ancient critics chided him for want of polish and for neglect of rhetorical figures; these very defects, and his free and easy manner, make Antiphon seem remote and pompous by contrast. Even the conventional commonplaces, which Andocides does not disdain, have more the ring of genuineness. At the close he appeals for mercy, not only on the basis of services to the State, past and future, but also because he is the last of his line; Andocides may likely have so appealed, whether or not it was suggested by the rules of the game.

Andocides did have opportunity for further service, for in 392 he went as a delegate to negotiate a treaty at Sparta. Although the delegation was empowered to act, as he himself says, he preferred to return and set the matter before the ecclesia. He did so in *On the Peace* (#3). The speech emphasizes the advantages to Athens of accepting peace, viz., keeping its navy, walls, and certain islands, as against the reasons for rejecting it, viz., if the other Greek states have guaranteed autonomy Athenian hopes of recovering an empire become frustrated. The speech naturally lacks the personal anecdotes and the warmth which characterize the first two speeches; on the other hand, it is more stylized and has a great number of rhetorical questions. The genuineness of *On the Peace* has been suspected both in antiquity (by Dionysius of Halicarnassus) and in modern times (by, e.g., Eduard Meyer). Meyer thought it was a pamphlet circulated about 391 to vindicate the action of Andocides and members of his party against popular criticism for concluding a peace with Sparta. Others have argued for spuriousness on the bases of the confused account of history at the beginning of the speech and of the curious similarity of one passage to another in Aeschines. But historical inaccuracies are not uncommon in the orators, and Aeschines may well have borrowed from Andocides; the weight of modern opinion is accordingly in favor of genuineness.

The remaining speech, *Against Alcibiades* (#4), is certainly spurious. The speaker is represented as discussing the question whether he or Nicias or Alcibiades is to be ostracized; but the object of an ostracism was never named in advance or formally charged. The fictive date, furthermore, must be antecedent to the Sicilian expedition, at which time Andocides was a very young man; yet the speaker mentions his numerous embassies, which Andocides was too young to have held and would certainly not have failed to mention when he was reciting his services to the State in *On His Return* and *On the Mysteries*.

Lysias, third in the Alexandrian list, gives us, with Demosthenes, our best insight into Greek private life and Greek law, and is at the same time the acknowledged standard for Attic prose. He was born some time after 460 B.C.; his father, Cephalus, and his brother Polemarchus appear, very pleasingly, as Socrates' interlocutors in *Republic* 1. The family, of Syracusan descent, owned a prosperous shield factory in Piraeus, but were metics, without full citizen rights. With his brothers Polemarchus and Euthydemus, Lysias went to the Athenian colony of Thurii, which was founded in 443. After the Athenian debacle in Sicily the oligarchy in Thurii expelled Lysias and his brothers among the 300 charged with Atticizing. They returned to Athens in 412 and prospered until the Thirty, who came to power in 404, confiscated their property and put Polemarchus to death; Lysias himself escaped, and continued his services to the democracy during his exile, which lasted something less than a year. Upon his return he devoted himself to the profession of speech writing, and succeeded so well that 425 speeches were attributed to him, of which Dionysius of Halicarnassus pronounced 233 to be genuine. He died in 380 B.C.

Surviving under Lysias' name are thirty-four speeches. Most are on public cases, that is, cases involving the State; a few are on private cases, and two or three are epideictic. Oration 1 in our editions is *On the Murder of Eratosthenes* (not to be confused with #12, *Against Eratosthenes*), a defense against a charge of murder for a man who had killed his wife's lover whom he took in the act of adultery in his own home. This speech well illustrates Lysias' narrative skill and his care in making his style suit the character of the speaker; it is also a good specimen of the intimate insight Lysias provides into the private life of the Greeks. Both these features may be seen in a short passage (1.11–14):

I came home unexpectedly from the country. After dinner the baby was crying and fidgeting; the servant had been teasing it on purpose to make it cry, for that man was in the house: I learned all about it afterwards. I told my wife to go and suckle the child, to stop its howling. At first she refused, pretending to be delighted at having me back after so long; but when I began to be annoyed and bade her go, she said, "Yes, so you can have a try at the maid; once before, when you were drunk, you mauled her." I laughed, and she got up and left and shut the door, making a joke of it, and took the key with her. I thought nothing of it and had no suspicion, and cheerfully went to sleep after my day in the country. Towards daylight she came back and opened the door. When I asked why the doors had banged in the night, she said the child's lamp had gone out and she had got a light from a neighbor. I said nothing, and supposed it was true. But it did strike me that her face was powdered, though her brother had died not thirty days before.

Oration 2, *Funeral Oration for the Men Who Supported the Corinthians,* cannot have been delivered by Lysias, for he was not a citizen. Nor is it likely that an official designated to give such a speech would require the services of a speech writer. It is therefore a rhetorical specimen, closely following the Funeral Oration of Pericles and similar models, but without the appropriateness to the occasion or the sincerity of Pericles' speech. Indeed, the inflated rhetoric makes it doubtful whether the speech was written by Lysias.

Orations 3, *Against Simon,* and 4, *On Wounding by Premeditation,* both have to do with brawls over the possession of a slave girl. Skulduggery in the award of dramatic prizes is indicated in 4.3–4; the prosecutor had been nominated as judge in the Dionysia on the understanding that he would vote a certain way. The man was actually not named judge and the plan miscarried; but that the arrangement is thus publicly avowed shows that such practices were not unheard of.

Oration 5 is a fragment of a speech, *For Callias,* on a charge of sacrilege. Oration 6, *Against Andocides,* is probably not a speech, nor by Lysias. It seems to be a pamphlet, by a member of the democratic opposition, in reply to Andocides' *On the Mysteries.* Oration 7, *On the Sacred Olive,* is in defense of a man charged with uprooting the stump of a sacred olive on his farm—a sacrilege punishable by exile and confiscation of property. Oration 8, *To His Companions,* is a trivial piece, surely not by Lysias, in which the speaker abjures membership in a club because his fellow members have calumniated him and palmed a sick horse off on him. Oration 9, *For the Soldier,* is in defense of a man being prosecuted for nonpayment of a fine; its authenticity is doubtful. Oration 10 (and 11, which is an epitome of 10), *Against Theomnestus,* is a prosecution for slander. Much space is occupied in refuting a quibble of the defendant: he had asked for acquittal on the ground that he had used the word "killed," whereas the law specified that the use of the word "murdered" constituted slander.

Oration 12, *Against Eratosthenes,* is Lysias' most important speech. It was delivered by Lysias himself, probably at the public scrutiny which was held at the conclusion of an official's term of office, and illustrates Lysias' wide range of eloquence and the seamy side of the administration of the Thirty. The first part of the speech (1–37) deals with the murder of Lysias' brother Polemarchus; the latter part (37–100), with the crimes of the Thirty in general. Lysias was among the wealthy metics whom the Thirty wished to purge on the ground that they were discontented with the new constitution. He describes his own arrest at a dinner party in his house (9–12):

I asked Pison if he would save me for a price; he said he would if it was a high one. So I said I was prepared to give a talent, and he agreed to the proposal. I knew well enough that he had no regard for god or man, but circumstances being what they were I thought I could do no other than trust him. So when he had sworn, calling destruction down upon himself and his children if he did not save me when he had received the talent, I went into my bureau and opened the strong-box.

The sight of the open strongbox, which contained the value of more than six talents, was too much for Pison, and he ordered his underlings to cart it all off:

I begged him to allow me enough for my journey; but he declared that I should be glad enough to save my skin.

Lysias did escape, without Pison's help. What success the speech had is not known.

Oration 13, *Against Agoratus,* also deals with the misdeeds of the Thirty. Agoratus had been an informer and tool of the Thirty, and is now (399) brought up on the charge of murdering Dionysodorus, a victim of the Thirty, by the cousin and brother-in-law of the victim. Lysias' speech deals at length with the sinister activities of the Thirty, but only in making Agoratus responsible for many of them. The speech sticks close to the prosecution in hand, seeking to demonstrate the defendant's guilt and to refute his claim that he acted under duress and that he was exonerated by the amnesty.

Orations 14 and 15, *Against Alcibiades,* for deserting and for avoiding military service, are directed against the son of the notorious Alcibiades, who inherited all his father's vices and none of his ability. Indeed, the speaker states that he has inherited hatred of the defendant from his father's hatred of the defendant's father, and a good part of the speech is devoted to the vices of the elder Alcibiades. Isocrates (#16, *On the Chariot-Team*) defended the young Alcibiades on another charge, but could find nothing good to say of his character.

Oration 16, *For Mantitheus,* was written for delivery at the public scrutiny which preceded an official's assumption of office. Mantitheus was under a cloud for having served in the cavalry, always aristocratic, during the regime of the Thirty. He denies the charge, and proceeds to argue that his elegant affectations in dress and manner must not be taken as an index of character. The speech is admirably suited to the personality of the ingenuous dandy who was to deliver it, and illustrates Lysias' skill in ethos.

Oration 17, *On the Property of Eraton,* is the claim against the State by a creditor of Eraton whose property the State has confiscated. It is a straightforward and competent handling of a disputed claim to property. Oration 18, *On the Confiscation of the Property of the Brother of Nicias,* is a fragment, of which the greater part is an appeal to mercy, unusual in Lysias. Eucrates, the brother of the general who was killed at Syracuse, was put to death by the Thirty, and later the confiscation of his property was decreed. Eucrates' sons and nephews plead against the enforcement of this decree. A question of confiscation is also dealt with in #19, *On the Property of Aristophanes* (not the comic poet). Lysias shows great tact in handling a case jeopardized by popular prejudice. Oration 20, *For Polystratus,* is a defense of Polystratus against some charge growing out of his having held office under the Four Hundred (411 B.C.). The awkwardness of the arrangement and argument has led critics to deny Lysian authorship. Oration 21 is only the latter half of a *Defense against a Charge of Taking Bribes.* The defendant argues, by enumerating his generous expenditures for public liturgies, that he is not the sort of man who would take bribes.

Oration 22, *Against the Corn-Dealers,* is a straightforward speech which supplies interesting information on Athenian measures for control of supply and prices. Oration 23, *Against Pancleon,* proves that Pancleon, who had protested that he was a Plataean when he was prosecuted for some charge by forms used for metics, was, in fact, a runaway slave. This speech gives a vivid picture of busy street life in Athens. Oration 24, *For the Cripple,* is perhaps the best example of Lysias' realism. The cripple has been charged with collecting a disability pension unjustly, and one can almost hear his whining retorts (10–12):

He has the audacity to mention my riding. . . . If I had the means I should ride in comfort on a mule, not on borrowed horses. . . . I use two sticks when other people use one: I am surprised that he does not make that a proof of my wealth. . . . Again he asserts that my shop is the resort of numerous bad characters. . . . Every one of you calls at the barber's, the perfumer's, the shoemaker's. . . . So if you call my visitors bad characters . . . you must do the same to all the Athenians.

Oration 25, wrongly entitled *Defense against a Charge of Subverting the Democracy,* maintains that the speaker was not involved in the misdeeds of the Thirty. Oration 26, *Against Evandrus,* seeks to prove, with bitterness unusual in Lysias, that Evandrus was involved in the misdeeds of the Thirty. The occasion is the public scrutiny of Evandrus to determine his fitness for the archonship for which Leodamas has failed to pass the scrutiny. #27, *Against Epicrates,* #28, *Against Ergocles,* and #29, *Against Philocrates,* are all supplementary recapitulations of full speeches in prosecution for embezzlement of public funds.

Oration 30, *Against Nicomachus,* charges the defendant with criminal dilatoriness in carrying out an assignment to transcribe certain laws. The personal vilification, chiefly on the score of humble birth, comes strangely from the metic Lysias. Vilification, this time apparently deserved, characterizes #31, *Against Philon,* who is being scrutinized for admission to public office. Oration 32, *Against Diogiton,* is a masterly charge of malfeasance against a guardian. The characterizations of the various persons concerned possess great dramatic verisimilitude, and the details of family relationships and financial investments throw welcome light on the private life of the Athenians.

The *Olympic Oration* (#33) is unique among Lysias' speeches in dealing with large questions of international policy. Gorgias had used the occasion of the Olympic festival, where representatives from all Greek states were assembled, to plead for unification, and in 380 B.C. Isocrates was to do likewise. Dionysius of Syracuse had sent a magnificent deputation, with gold-embroidered tents to house them, to impress the assembled Greeks at Olympia. Lysias (who could speak in person, which he could not do at Athens, being a metic) urges the Greek cities to sink their private animosities and combine against the peril of foreign tyrants. Dionysius had subjugated the cities of Sicily, had defeated Carthage, and was threatening Magna Graecia. Like Artaxerxes of Persia he had a large fleet, and if the two should combine, the peril to Greece would be great indeed. In the latter part of the speech, which is not extant, Lysias is said (by Dionysius of Halicarnassus, *Lysias* 29 f.; cf. Diodorus Siculus 14.105) to have worked his audience up to a high pitch of indignation and to have called upon them to tear the Syracusans' tents down and strip them of their gold. The extant portion shows a boldness and high earnestness appropriate to the theme.

A question of high policy is also dealt with in #34, *Against the Subversion of the Ancestral Constitution of Athens,* of which only a fragment remains. When democracy had been restored after the fall of the Thirty (403 B.C.) a proposal was made that civic rights should be confined to those who possessed landed property, and it is against this proposal that the present speech was written. Dionysius (*Lysias* 32) cites the speech as a good example of Lysias' deliberative style, but doubts that it was actually delivered.

The discourse on love attributed to Lysias in Plato's *Phaedrus* is sometimes printed with Lysias' works; it may be his, but there is no cogent reason for supposing that Plato would not attribute an invented speech to Lysias. Of the 425 speeches Lysias is said (in the *Lives of the Ten Orators* formerly attributed to Plutarch) to have written, and the 233 which Dionysius pronounced genuine, 127 are known by title or small fragments. Of only six are considerable fragments preserved, and these do not alter our estimate of Lysias. In the simple and unpretentious style he remains master.

Of Isaeus we know neither his dates nor his birthplace nor his political convictions nor his tastes. For us he is only a specialized law machine, turning out highly competent speeches in a single department, that of testamentary law, in which he is our principal source for Athenian norms and practice. He is said to have been a pupil of Isocrates—which needs mean nothing more than that he emulated Isocrates in avoiding hiatus, that is, placing a word beginning with a vowel after another ending with a vowel—and a teacher of Demosthenes, who started his career by suing to recover a legacy. This would put his activity in the first half of the fourth century B.C. The *Life* by Pseudo-Plutarch says that sixty-four speeches were attributed to Isaeus, of which fifty were considered genuine. Eleven and part of a twelfth are extant. All deal with questions of inheritance, the titles in each case beginning with "On the estate of . . ." It is significant that the *argumenta* of modern editors find it necessary to provide family trees of the persons involved in several cases. His skill in dealing with such involved cases is acute, and his legal knowledge in his department encyclopedic. Dionysius denies Isaeus the charm which he finds in Lysias, but grudgingly admits his cleverness. His language too is simple and his style not ornate, though it shows the professional's touch, especially in such devices as rhetorical questions. He makes no effort, as Lysias does, to accommodate his speeches to the ethos of his clients; but he has more clearly in mind the ethos of the jury, and marshals and emphasizes his arguments so that they will be most effective. Highly competent workmanship in any field is admirable, but only fellow practitioners of Isaeus' own specialty can be expected to show enthusiasm for his achievement.

In Isocrates, on the other hand, we have a first-class writer whose range commands interest as well as respect. The political problem which concerned him throughout his long life is all but identical with the great political problem of the mid-twentieth century; his stated principles of education are those which mid-twentieth-century educators are striving to realize; and he more than any other single individual may be said to have fixed the standard for European prose style. He was born in 436 B.C., and so was a grown man when the Syracusan expedition failed, and he lived for ninety-eight years, past the subjugation of Greece by Philip at Chaeronea in 338, with undiminished power and productivity. He lost his family property—his father had been a prosperous manufacturer of flutes—as result of the Peloponnesian War; for a time he seems to have been a professional speech writer, though in his extant work he scorns that profession; and in 392 he opened a school which was singularly successful, both in bringing him wealth and in spreading his influence. Practically all the leading personages of the age were his pupils; when Artemisia, widow of Mausolus of Caria, held a great contest of eloquence, all the competitors were pupils of Isocrates. Because of physical disability, chiefly a form of nervousness, Isocrates himself never delivered speeches. His "orations" are really of the character of political pamphlets, except that they were not, and were not intended to be, ephemeral. He is said to have worked ten years on his *Panegyricus;* and if this is an exaggeration, yet it is obvious that this and similar works are carefully wrought literature, intended to endure.

Isocrates' convictions in questions of style, of education, and of politics remained singularly consistent throughout his long life, though the means he advocated for attaining the political goal he passionately desired altered with changed circumstances. He had been a pupil of Gorgias, and though he eschewed Gorgias' Pindaric distortions of language and balanced assonances, he definitely held that oratory must be as artistic as poetry and afford the same sort of pleasure that poetry does. This doctrine may well explain the virtual absence of poetry in the fourth century b.c. Attention to sound is a principal characteristic of Isocrates' work. He rigidly avoids hiatus and harsh clashes of consonants. The rhythms of cola are carefully balanced, sometimes at the expense of padding. Sentences are constructed with nice attention to their architecture, and single periods run to long paragraphs. But the architecture simplifies rather than complicates the sense. Isocrates is always artistic, but always clear.

Isocrates has much to say on the theory of education. In Plato's *Phaedrus* he is called a "companion" of Socrates, who prophesies a distinguished future for him. And he shows the influence of Socrates—Xenophon's as well as Plato's—not only in the palpable imitations of *Apology* in the *Antidosis,* which is Isocrates' apologia, and not only in such traits as aloofness from public life, critical attitude toward the democracy, and hatred of demagogues, but also in views on education. He despises the pretensions of the Sophists (although he himself taught "culture" for pay), he regards speculations on the origins of things as useless, he is deeply concerned for ethics and high morality. Exact sciences he thinks useful only as a preparatory mental discipline; and speculative philosophy he regards as worse than useless. Dialectic which pretends to attain truth in disregard of the facts of human nature (he calls such dialectic "eristic") he condemns, as he does Sophists, who aim for sensational effects. They pretend to be able to teach what cannot in fact be taught, and the practical oratory they teach deals, not with large ideas, but with petty controversies; and because its goal is success rather than truth, it is immoral. Isocrates' own theory of education is the cultivation of "the art of discourse." To him this implies reason, feeling, imagination, all that raises men above animal nature and enables them to live a civilized life—in our terms, a humanistic education. That is why he disparages both specialized and theoretical knowledge: they do not contribute to practical conduct of human relations.

Perhaps the most significant of Isocrates' convictions, certainly the one which guided his political teaching, is the view of Hellenism which exalts it to the position of a religion and which gives the character of a crusade to efforts to preserve and propagate it. Hellenism was indeed endangered by the series of ruinous wars which followed the Peloponnesian, and the only remedy was union of some sort. In the *Panegyricus,* written in 380 B.C., Isocrates calls for concord among the confederated Greeks, under the leadership of Athens, for the purpose of making war against Persia, which threatened the ruin of Hellenism. The passing years gave little hope that confederation could be achieved, and in 356 Isocrates addresses an appeal to Archidamus III, King of Sparta, to lead a Panhellenic war against Persia. In 346, in his *Address to Philip,* he appeals to the Macedonian to lead the great crusade. But other Greek patriots, and specifically Demosthenes, saw a graver peril to Greek freedom in Philip than in the Persian, and in any case Philip was an odd sort to be champion of free Hellenism. Demosthenes was right, but Isocrates was right too. He despaired of the ruinous particularism of the Greek states, and he put the precious values of Hellenism above autonomy. Half a millennium later, when Greece was completely subject to Rome, Plutarch was to find preservation of the cult of Hellenism sufficient compensation for political subjection.

In antiquity sixty orations were attributed to Isocrates, of which fewer than half were considered genuine. The twenty-one orations and nine letters we possess are probably all genuine, though question has been raised in regard to some, as will be noticed in the following brief notes. Oration 1, *To Demonicus,* and 2, *To Nicocles,* are loose treatises on ethics with detachable maxims, such as an earlier century (some of the maxims are, in fact, Theognis') would have written in verse. Shrewd, practical precepts predominate, with occasional ill-matched appeals to motives of idealism. *To Nicocles* sets forth the duties of the monarch, and its companion piece, #3, *Nicocles or the Cyprians,* deals with the obligations of subjects. Isocrates never shared Athenian democracy's horror of monarchy.

Panegyricus (#4) has always been recognized as Isocrates' masterpiece. It is probably the most carefully wrought prose in Greek, and yet it breathes high moral earnestness. Its message is that all Greece must unite, under the leadership of Athens, for war against Persia. Sparta has shown that it is not fit to lead. Athens, on the other hand, has pioneered in enlightenment; "she has brought it about that the name 'Hellenes' suggests no longer a race but an intelligence, and that the title 'Hellenes' is applied rather to those who share our culture than to those who share a common blood" (§ 50). The conquest of Persia would not only unite Greece, but would be easy (as Alexander, in fact, found it). The speech was written about 380 for circulation and reading (but not by Isocrates himself) at the festival at Olympia, where Gorgias and Lysias had spoken on kindred themes.

Some thirty-five years later, in 346, when Philip of Macedon had just concluded a ten years' war against Athens, Isocrates addressed an appeal to him (#5) to lead the expedition against Persia. From the point of view of internal Greek politics this appeal marks a complete reversal from *Panegyricus,* for the Greek states, including Athens, would have to be "reconciled" before they would accept Philip as leader; but if the expedition against the Persians was the main point (as it was for Isocrates), then there is no inconsistency:

All men will be grateful to you: the Hellenes for your kindness to them; the Macedonians if you reign over them, not like a tyrant but like a king; and the rest of the nations, if by your hands they are delivered from barbaric despotism and are brought under the protection of Hellas (154).

Archidamus (#6) shows such outspoken admiration for Sparta that critics have been inclined to dismiss it as a rhetorical exercise. Theban successes in the Peloponnese caused Sparta's allies to make overtures of peace, but Thebes insisted that the newly colonized Messene, near Sparta, remain autonomous. In the oration Archidamus is represented as speaking at the peace congress at Corinth in 366 and exhorting the Spartans to die rather than abandon Messene.

Areopagiticus (#7) was written in 355, at the close of a war in which Athens failed to recover control over certain of her former dependencies. Isocrates deplores the wrangling and dilatoriness of the democracy, which "has brought Athens the hatred of the Hellenes and the contempt of the barbarians," and calls for restoration of the constitution of Solon and Clisthenes, when qualifications upon eligibility to office made the government, in effect, an aristocracy. Specifically, he urges that its former almost unlimited power be restored to the Council of the Areopagus, for which noble birth and other tests had been requisite. Even now, when noble birth and other tests are no longer required, "we shall find that those who in all else that they do are insufferable, yet when they enter the Areopagus hesitate to indulge their true nature, being governed rather by its traditions than by their own evil instincts" (38).

On the Peace (#8) was written in 355, before the war was ended. Isocrates was certainly right in urging an immediate end of the war, even in urging Athens to abandon its ambitions for an empire which it could not afford, but his plea to Athenians to prove their pre-eminence by moral superiority seems unrealistic in the context and a surrender of the high hopes of *Panegyricus.* But perhaps moral pre-eminence involves abandonment of democracy, which would not be unrealistic. Certainly *On the Peace* contains the bitterest castigations of demagogues as unscrupulous and of those who follow them as fools.

"How is it, if indeed we are so badly advised, that we are safe and hold a power which is inferior to that of no other city?" I for my part would reply to this question that we have in our adversaries men who are no more prudent than ourselves. . . . So that if we were sensible we should supply each other with money for our general assemblies; for the oftener we meet to deliberate the more do we promote the success of our rivals (57–59).

#9, *Evagoras,* #10, *Helen,* and #11, *Busiris,* are epideictic or display pieces. *Evagoras* is a sincere encomium on the deceased King of Salamis in Cyprus, put into the mouth of his son, the Nicocles of #2 and #3. *Helen* is a tour de force, implicitly criticizing Gorgias' exuberant showpiece on the same theme. Busiris, King of Egypt, like Helen and unlike Evagoras, is a mythological personage. As *Helen* is a criticism of Gorgias, so is *Busiris* a criticism of a predecessor, named Polycrates, who had written on the same subject. Works of this character are what give "rhetoric" its pejorative connotation, but they show the importance attached to the art by serious and capable writers.

Panathenaicus (#12), is the last major work of Isocrates, begun when he was ninety-four, interrupted by illness, and completed when he was ninety-seven. It contains nothing which was not better said in earlier works —praise of Athens at the expense of Sparta in *Panegyricus,* defense of his teaching against detractors in *Antidosis,* and rebukes for extreme democracy in *Areopagiticus.* The arrangement, faulty in any case, is made worse by a puzzling epilogue (234 ff.) which retracts much of his invective against Sparta. At the other end of his career, when he first began to teach, Isocrates wrote *Against the Sophists* (#13) as a sort of prospectus for his school. Only the first part is extant, in which he criticizes his competitors, the eristics for being contentious and impractical casuists, and the rhetoricians for professing to teach what is unteachable. His own theories (as well as a full refutation of his rivals') are presented at length in *Antidosis. Plataicus* (#14) is an appeal to the Athenians, based largely on historical sentiment, to assist the Plataeans, whose city had been destroyed by the Thebans in 373 B.C., as it had once been before in 427. The speech may actually have been delivered by a Plataean in the ecclesia in 373.

Antidosis (#15), written when Isocrates was eighty-two, is his longest work. Two years before, Isocrates had been challenged to undertake a costly liturgy or, as the rules provided, accept an *antidosis* or exchange of properties. To justify his life and profession he now composes *Antidosis,* in imitation of Socrates' *Apology,* as a reply to an imaginary indictment on the charge of having corrupted the youth by teaching them habits of litigiousness. He disparages his rivals as sweepingly as in *Against the Sophists,* and proves the seriousness of his own work by reciting extracts from *Panegyricus, On the Peace,* and *Nicocles.*

Since it is not in the nature of man to attain a science by the possession of which we can know positively what we should do or what we should say, in the next resort I hold that man to be wise who is able by his powers of conjecture to arrive generally at the best course, and I hold that man to be a philosopher who occupies himself with the studies from which he will most quickly gain that kind of insight (§ 271).

—*G. Norlin*

It is the art of thoughtful speaking that leads to thoughtful action:

Therefore, it behooves all men to want to have many of their youth engaged in training to become speakers, and you Athenians most of all. For you yourselves are preeminent and superior to the rest of the world, not in your application to the business of war, nor because you govern yourselves more excellently or preserve the law handed down to you by your ancestors more faithfully than others, but in those qualities by which the nature of man rises above the other animals, and the race of the Hellenes above the barbarians, namely, in the fact that you have been educated as have been no other people in wisdom and in speech (293–294).

—*G. Norlin*

The remaining six orations are forensic speeches dating from Isocrates' salad days; later he regretted that he had occupied himself with the art. *On the Chariot-Team* (#16) defends the younger Alcibiades in an action for damages; it may be significant of Isocrates' convictions of the period that he undertook an assignment which would require him to eulogize a character like the elder Alcibiades. *Trapeziticus* (#17) is a suit to recover a deposit from the banker Pasion, who is the best known to us of Athenian bankers; the speech gives much information on Athenian banking practice. *Against Callimachus* (#18) is a defense in an action for damages. This, like *Aigineticus* (#19), which is a claim to an inheritance and the most carefully wrought of the forensic speeches, is a competent lawyer's plea. *Against Lochites* (#20) is an action for assault, and *Against Euthynus* (#21), an action to recover a deposit.

The nine letters of Isocrates are all addressed to rulers and princes and generally give ethical counsel; if they do not add details to our knowledge of Isocrates they at least show that he was on terms of familiarity with great personages of his time. *Epistle* 5, for example, is addressed to Alexander, who had probably just been placed under Aristotle's tutelage. He writes:

I hear everyone say of you that you are a friend of mankind, a friend of Athens, and a friend of learning, not foolishly, but in sensible fashion. . . . You give hope to your father and to all the world that if, as you grow older, you hold fast to this course, you will as far surpass your fellow-men in wisdom as your father had surpassed all mankind.

We can only applaud Isocrates' desire for a united Greece. But tyranny is a dear price for union, and the tyrant's peace is apt to be the peace of the cemetery. The cloistered teacher, a little suspicious of demos, called upon Philip to unite Greece and saw great promise of Alexander's becoming a friend of mankind. Demosthenes, whom we now approach, did all that one man could do to block Philip's and Alexander's designs.

With Demosthenes, questions of stylistic refinements which are all but irrelevant to a modern, nontechnical reader recede to insignificance, and there springs into clear focus a problem of momentous practical concern to modern Europeans. Almost from the beginning of our history, and with increasing urgency that makes solution imperative in our day, the question of maintaining local sovereignty as against accepting subordination to a larger complex has affected the welfare and the lives of men. No modern criticism of Demosthenes is free of its author's own predispositions in this question; Demosthenes is variously hailed as a great champion of the democratic ideal, or as a sentimental romanticist who sought, happily in vain, to block human progress. The particularism of the Greek city-states, each passionately jealous of its own sovereignty, had worked great mischief throughout Greek history and was becoming more dangerous as the edges of the world were being drawn in. Only a powerful personality could bring unity, and only by knocking the heads of the sovereign city-states together. But patriots could only look upon the powerful personality, coming not upon a white charger but with an ass load of gold, as a foreign aggressor. Demosthenes' detractors urge that Demosthenes showed an impractical romanticism in proposing for the degenerate Athens of Eubulus a program which might have been feasible in the Athens of Pericles. But it is hard to gauge degeneracy, unless by the broader rights of demos; and here it may be relevant to note that when Alexander's agent Antipater finally dictated terms to Athens in 322 B.C. not only were its democratic institutions abolished, but of its 21,000 citizens 12,000 who did not possess property to the value of 2,000 drachmas were disfranchised and deported as being a turbulent element, and the 9,000 richest citizens who constituted the "party of order" were left in possession.

Demosthenes himself (born 384 B.C.) belonged to a wealthy family, his father having owned a sword factory. The father died when Demosthenes was seven, and the guardians of the estate mismanaged it. At the age of eighteen Demosthenes laid claim to the estate, but the guardians frustrated him by various devices. Demosthenes studied under Isaeus, the expert in probate law, to such good effect that he was able to win his case when he was twenty-one. But the property had by now been squandered, and to gain a livelihood Demosthenes devoted himself to the profession of speech writing. After an early failure in an attempt to speak before the ecclesia, according to legend, he subjected himself to a severe course of training—declaiming with pebbles in his mouth, reciting speeches while running uphill, gesticulating before a mirror, copying the history of Thucydides eight times. Despite physical handicaps he became, by common consent of ancients and moderns, the greatest of the Greek orators.

The corpus of Demosthenes includes sixty-one orations, six letters, and fifty-four proems. The latter two items and about a third of the speeches have been condemned by scholars, with more or less cogency, as spurious. Of the thirty-five or forty speeches accepted as genuine (we know of no Demosthenic speeches that have not come down), the greatest number are for private cases and are not unlike similar speeches of other orators in the canon. They are carefully constructed and observe, but do not make a fetish of, the technical rules of oratorical composition. Incidentally, they provide our best single source of information concerning Greek social and legal usages. The speeches in public cases, and more particularly the deliberative speeches (*symbouleutika*), are unique for their impassioned eloquence as well as for their statesmanlike insight and patriotism. Unlike similar compositions of other orators, these speeches were actually delivered in the ecclesia, though they were doubtless revised for publication, by Demosthenes himself.

The earliest speeches, # #27–29, *Against Aphorbus* (363 B.C.), and ##30–31, *Against Onetor* (363 B.C.), deal with questions arising out of the guardianship. In #51, *On the Trierarchic Crown* (359 B.C.), one Apollodorus pleads for a crown as reward for his having furnished the best equipped ship. This speech is a prime source for matters pertaining to naval management. Oration 22, *Against Androtion* (355 B.C., Demosthenes' earliest forensic speech), again deals with a crown. Androtion had made the usual motion for a crown to be awarded the members of the outgoing boule, and it is being attacked by Diodorus for unconstitutionality on the ground that the navy had not been increased during the year. Demosthenes uses the occasion to point out the historical importance of the navy, and the corruption of the party which fails to maintain it. *Against Timocrates* (#24; 353 B.C.), was also written for Diodorus and deals with a complicated case of embezzlement. The peroration is a fine eulogy of Athenian law. In 355 Demosthenes himself makes his first appearance in a public cause with *Against Leptines* (#20). In view of the state's financial embarrassment Leptines had proposed abolition of hereditary immunities which were granted to public benefactors. Demosthenes opposes the measure on the grounds that it amounts to a breach of faith, and Athenians must not do as a state what they would shrink from doing as individuals.

The following year, at the age of thirty, Demosthenes made his first speech before the ecclesia, and thenceforward the life of Demosthenes is the history of Greece. A rumor had spread that Persia intended to invade Greece, and hotheads were calling for immediate hostilities. In *On the Naval Boards* (#14) Demosthenes calms apprehensions, but admits that trouble is to be anticipated for the future, and urges a scheme of naval reform—which was adopted fourteen years later. Demosthenes' views of international policy are clarified in the next two speeches. *For the Megalopolitans* (#16; 353 B.C.) advocates support for Megalopolis, which had been founded by Epaminondas as a makeweight against Sparta, to curb oligarchic Sparta and to win Athens friends in the southern Peloponnese. It was Demosthenes' position that Athens was bound to support democracies everywhere against oppression, and in *For the Liberty of the Rhodians* (#15; 351 B.C.) he makes this principle the basis of his advocacy of help for the democratic party in Rhodes against oppression by Artemisia, widow of Mausolus of Caria.

The same year saw the beginning of the series of harangues called *Philippics*. Philip came to the throne of Macedon in 359 B.C., and at once set about uniting and strengthening his kingdom, fostering national feeling, and creating an army. Within a few years, by a combination of force and deceit and what has come to be known as a fifth column, he became master of key points in northeast Greece—Pydna and Amphipolis, the rich gold mines of Mt. Pangaeus, Potidaea and Methone, and part of Thrace. When he began to interfere in the affairs of Thessaly, Athens was stirred to momentary activity but soon relapsed into apathy. In the *First Philippic* (#4; 351 B.C.) Demosthenes seeks to arouse the Athenians to the danger and to the need for resolute measures to meet it. Their forces must not be paper forces, their officers puppets for the market place; citizens, not mercenaries, must make up the core of the army. Their tactics had been those of a barbarian boxer, who always puts his hand where he has last been struck; "ward or look in the face he cannot nor will." People hopefully repeated the rumor that Philip was dead: even if he were, their course of inaction would soon call another Philip into being.

But nothing was done, and in 349 Philip made war on Olynthus, which appealed to Athens for help. Demosthenes' three *Olynthiacs* (## 1-3) urge prompt and vigorous help, but the Athenian forces were too little and too late. Olynthus and the other cities of the Chalcidian League were destroyed (348 B.C.) and their inhabitants sold into slavery. Athens failed in an attempt to form an alliance against Philip, and so negotiated the discreditable Peace of Philocrates, as a result of which Philip occupied the pass of Thermopylae and was able to convoke the Amphictyonic Council and pass a vote for the condemnation of Phocis. Twenty-two Phocian towns were destroyed and their votes in the Council transferred to Philip, who was also, though technically a barbarian and so ineligible, made president of the Pythian games. Athens alone sulked, and when Philip's messengers invited the Athenians to recognize him as a member of the Amphictyonic Council there was a revulsion of popular feeling. In *On the Peace* (#5; 346 B.C.) Demosthenes calmed the assembly by pointing out that the peace was an accomplished fact, which it would be suicidal to repudiate. During the six years of nominal peace which followed, Philip was careful of Athenian sensibilities, and a pro-Macedonian party was built up in Athens. But Demosthenes and such associates as the orators Lycurgus and Hyperides realized the danger. In the *Second Philippic* (#6; 344 B.C.) Demosthenes showed that Philip's benevolence to Thebes, Messene, and Argos was a ruse for using these cities against Athens; similar professions of benevolence had made Greece abandon Phocis and Thermopylae to Philip.

The anti-Macedonian party was sufficiently strong in 343 for Hyperides to effect the impeachment of Philocrates for his part in the peace of 346, and for Demosthenes to prosecute his rival Aeschines for malversation in the same negotiations. *On the Embassy* (#19), Demosthenes' longest piece, is a plausible charge that Aeschines was willfully playing into Philip's hands. Philip now looked to the Chersonese (Gallipoli), which was vital to Athens because it controlled the route of the corn ships from the Euxine. Athens sent a force thither under Diopithes (father of Menander), and Philip formally complained of Diopithes' exactions of "benevolences" in neighboring places. Demosthenes' *On the Chersonese* (#8; 341 B.C.) is a vigorous plea not to repudiate Diopithes. The *Third Philippic* (#9; 341 B.C.) again urges support of the Chersonese and speaks more fully of "the great danger which now threatens the whole of Greece. . . . If we really wait until he avows that he is at war with us we are the simplest of mortals." All Greek states must be made to realize the danger to Greek liberty; Athens must arm and put herself at the head of a great federation to preserve freedom. In the years following, Athens did succeed in forming an alliance, in reorganizing its navy and finances, and in inflicting a check on Philip at Byzantium. But Philip took the occasion of an Amphictyonic war, which his sympathizers had probably engineered, to pass through Thermopylae and fortify a strong point in Phocis. Demosthenes induced the Athenians to forget old enmities and offer Thebes all its military resources in a kind of lend-lease arrangement. But in 338 the combined forces were defeated at Chaeronea and Greek freedom extinguished. On the murder of Philip in 336 B.C., Demosthenes, now supported by Persian gold, induced the Thebans to revolt, but they were promptly crushed by Alexander, who was no less energetic and determined than his father had been.

In 330 Demosthenes delivered the great apologia of his career—and a virulent attack on Aeschines—in *On the Crown* (#18), the last and greatest of his speeches. Six years earlier Ctesiphon had proposed the award of a gold crown to Demosthenes for his services in repairing the fortifications of Athens, and Aeschines had indicted Ctesiphon for bringing up an illegal motion. Aeschines' speech will be mentioned below. Demosthenes' defense of Ctesiphon is really a justification of the policy of the anti-Macedonian party, despite its failure. The personal attack on Aeschines which fills the latter half of the speech is shocking to modern taste. Similarly disturbing is Demosthenes' apparent complicity in the affair of Harpalus, when a large sum of money was misappropriated. Demosthenes escaped prison and went into exile, from which he was fetched home in a trireme when Alexander died in 323 B.C. Athens sought to recover its independence in the Lamian War, but the Greek forces were crushed by Antipater in the battle of Crannon. Death was decreed for Demosthenes, and he took poison just as he was being arrested.

We turn briefly to the nonpolitical speeches of these years. Oration 23 (352 B.C.) is *Against Aristocrates,* who had proposed inviolability for the *condottiere* Charidemus. The speech throws light on Philip's Thracian episode and also on the law of homicide in Athens. In one instance, Demosthenes seems to have written speeches for both sides in the same case. #36 (350 B.C.) is *For Phormio,* clerk and successor to the banker Pasion, against Apollodorus, Pasion's son; #45 (349 B.C.) is *Against Stephanus,* one of Phormio's witnesses, for perjury.

In *Against Boeotus* (#39; 348 B.C.) a legitimate brother seeks to prevent an illegitimate brother from usurping his name. *Against Midias* (#21; 347 B.C.) is an indictment of a personal and political enemy who had slapped Demosthenes' face in the presence of a filled theater when Demosthenes was officiating as choregus at the Greater Dionysia. *Against Pantaenetus* (#37; 346 B.C.) has to do with damage to a mine in whose ownership six parties, owners, mortgagees, or lessees, were involved. *Against Nausimachus* (#38; 346 B.C.) seeks to enjoin certain orphans who had compromised a claim against their guardian from renewing the claim many years later against the guardian's heirs. In *Against Eubulides* (#57; 345 B.C.), Euxitheus maintains the legitimacy of his citizen status against objections which Eubulides had brought up at the revision of the citizen rolls. In #41, *Against Spudias* (date uncertain), the husband of an older daughter objects to the claim of the husband of the younger to half their father's estate on the ground that his wife's dowry had not been paid in full and that he therefore had a prior claim. *Against Conon* (#54; 341 B.C.) is an action for assault. In #55, *Against Callicles* (date uncertain), the plaintiff claims that the defendant's father had built a wall which caused the plaintiff's vineyard to flood in rainy weather.

The pieces whose genuineness has been questioned (##7, 10–13, 17, 25–26, 32–35, 40, 42–44, 46–50, 52–53, 56, and 58–61) are passed over, not because they are certainly spurious, but because the range of the Demosthenic corpus has been sufficiently indicated in the preceding paragraphs. Most of these pieces are contemporary with Demosthenes and equally valuable for their information on social and legal institutions. Two, *Halonnesus* (#7; 342 B.C.) and the *Fourth Philippic* (#10; 341 B.C.), belong in the series of *Philippics* and represent Demosthenes' views correctly. Orations 12 and 11 are a letter from Philip and Demosthenes' answer. *Epitaphius* (#60) is a funeral speech for those who fell at Chaeronea, and *Eroticus* (#61) is a very un-Demosthenic address to a boy love.

For the ancients Demosthenes was easily the first among the orators. The number of his papyrus fragments recovered from Egypt runs second only to Homer's. If we can perceive but dimly some of the merits praised by such competent critics of oratory as the author of *On the Sublime*, Dionysius of Halicarnassus, or Cicero, we are more impressed by something which the ancient critics virtually ignored. Here is earnest and far-seeing statesmanship, based on deep study of history and acute insight into men's characters and motives, shaped with exquisite care for form, not reserved for the edification of a choice circle but employed with indefatigable energy for the public good. These speeches were intended, not for display to connoisseurs, but to communicate conviction to the multitude. It is another testimonial to the taste and sobriety of the Athenian demos that Demosthenes is so careful in his use of history, so studious of form, so impatient with flamboyance. A modern, indeed, may feel that the sobriety is excessive. There is wit, in the hits at Philip and especially in the ridicule of Aeschines, but there is none of the agile humor which characterizes Plato or Euripides—and which would make so ponderous a treatment of a slap in the face as we have in *Against Midias* hard to imagine on the lips of a French or English orator of comparable standing.

Humor, as well as a physique and a voice which Demosthenes clearly envied, characterized his somewhat older rival Aeschines (born 390 B.C.). His enmity toward Demosthenes over a period of twenty years is Aeschines' chief claim to a place in history. He had had a hard life as a boy, but had made his way by study, a variety of employments, and the restless energy which is to be perceived in his speeches. His father kept a school, and his mother was a minor religious functionary. "You used to fill the ink-pots (says Demosthenes, *On the Crown* 258 ff.), sponge the benches, and sweep the schoolroom, like a slave. When you grew up you helped your mother in her initiations. . . . All night long you were wrapping the celebrants in fawn-skins, preparing their drink offerings, smearing them with clay and bran." Later he was an actor, his only income, according to Demosthenes, being the vegetables thrown at him in provincial theaters in which he performed minor roles. He had been clerk to the ecclesia, and so knew rules of procedure. He boasted of his book learning. He had a ready wit; where Demosthenes' excoriation of Aeschines is grim and sometimes suggests envy, Aeschines makes uproarious comedy of Demosthenes' foibles. He had a torrential eloquence, and must clearly have been an effective speaker. But he had no policy other than opposing Demosthenes —as Demosthenes says, because he was in Philip's pay. Whether he was as black as Demosthenes paints him may be doubted, but parts of his career which he himself recalls with satisfaction show him to have been at least irresponsible. He joined Philip in dancing the paean to celebrate the defeat of Phocis (*On the Embassy* 163), and an inflammatory speech which he made to the Amphictyonic Council in 339 led to the outbreak of the Sacred War (*Against Ctesiphon* 118).

The three extant speeches of Aeschines all have to do with Demosthenes. In his *On the Peace* Demosthenes urged that the treaty of Philocrates must be upheld, but he made insinuations against the character of Aeschines' conduct as ambassador and prepared to prosecute him for betraying his trust by accepting bribes from Philip. In this prosecution he was joined by Timarchus, and Aeschines countered by prosecuting Timarchus on the grounds that his notorious immorality debarred him from speaking in public. Throughout *Against Timarchus* Aeschines protests that his sense of propriety forbids him to deal with the long list of Timarchus' iniquities —which he carefully enumerates; Timarchus was found guilty. In his *On the Embassy* of 343 B.C. Demosthenes accuses Aeschines of treason, and Aeschines defends himself in a speech bearing the same title. Where Demosthenes' speech seems unsystematic, Aeschines is orderly and follows chronology of events; but analysis shows that this device is a red herring. Aeschines expatiates on matters not strictly relevant to the charge and glosses over the real issue. He really confesses credulity and incompetence when he defends his deception of the Athenians on the ground that he was himself deceived. But the speech is highly plausible, and Aeschines was acquitted, though by the rather small margin of thirty votes. Aeschines' longest and most interesting speech is *Against Ctesiphon,* on the charge of having illegally proposed the award of a crown to Demosthenes; Demosthenes' *On the Crown* is the refutation of this speech. The first fifth of *Against Ctesiphon* deals competently with legal points; the next three fifths enumerate instances where Demosthenes' conduct has been harmful to Athens. There are numerous hits at Demosthenes' character and habits, frequently with the *paraleipsis* or *praeteritio* which we noticed in *Against Timarchus;* but the charges are all essentially frivolous and inconsequential. There is nothing like the reasoned defense of a policy which we have in *On the Crown.* Aeschines failed to obtain a fifth of the votes, and was fined a thousand drachmas in consequence. He was unable or unwilling to pay the fine, and retired to Rhodes where he spent the rest of his days as a teacher of rhetoric.

Three other contemporary orators of the pro-Macedonian faction—Phocion, Demades, and Pytheas—are known to us only from ancient critics. The three remaining orators of the canon are still to be considered. Lycurgus was a somewhat older contemporary and ally of Demosthenes, and a living refutation of the common charge that political competence and morality or aesthetic appreciation had disappeared from Athens. He managed Athenian finances for twelve years with absolute probity and great efficiency. He completed the arsenal, enlarged the fleet, improved the harbor, built a theater and an odeon, and embellished the city with statues, in particular those of the Tragic Three. He also caused to be made the official copy of the text of the tragedians which afterward found its way to Alexandria. He built temples, encouraged religious festivals, enacted sumptuary laws. He was never a paid advocate or speech writer, but he regarded it his patriotic obligation to prosecute those who were delinquent in their duty to the state, and all of the fifteen speeches of his which were current in antiquity were indictments of this character. Of these only *Against Leocrates* is extant. The defendant had fled in the panic after Chaeronea, and had returned five or six years later thinking that his desertion would have been forgotten. The first third of Lycurgus' speech is devoted to proving the charge, and the remainder emphasizes the seriousness of the crime, with copious precedents from history and lavish citations from the poets. There is one passage of fifty-five lines from Euripides, and another of thirty-two lines from Tyrtaeus (for which Lycurgus is the only source). Lycurgus' literary leanings are revealed also in a rather curled style. He favors the periods of Isocrates, whose pupil he is said to have been, and indulges in artful antitheses. But these niceties do not detract from the severe dignity of his high moral position.

Hyperides was another contemporary and ally of Demosthenes, though his easygoing personal habits were in marked contrast to the austerity of Lycurgus. Like Demosthenes he was condemned to death after the battle of Crannon in 322 B.C., and was executed. In antiquity seventy-seven speeches were ascribed to Hyperides, of which fifty-two were thought to be genuine. All disappeared until, in the course of the last century, five were recovered in papyri, the important *Against Athenogenes* being in a papyrus of the second century B.C. and therefore one of the very oldest of our classical manuscripts. Hyperides is unique among the orators for the mercurial quality of his wit. He can be sober but also very gay, with colloquial words and expressions, startling similes, irony, and sarcasm. The fragmentary *Against Demosthenes* may have arisen from Demosthenes' policy of inactivity when, in 330, Sparta wished to fight with Antipater. The *Defense of Lycophron* defends a noble Athenian cavalry commander of that name against the charge, of which Lycurgus was one of the prosecutors, of having seduced a Lemnian woman. Euxenippus had been told off to sleep in the shrine of Amphiaraus so that his dream might determine the disposition of a tract of land in dispute between two tribes. When they reported a dream which favored their own tribe, Euxenippus was tried, Lycurgus being among the prosecutors, for reporting the dream falsely, and Hyperides' *Euxenippus* is in defense. The mutilated *Against Philippides* seems to be an indictment for illegality of a man who proposed an honorary decree in favor of Philip. The *Funeral Speech* gives an original turn to the commonplaces of its genre. Leosthenes, for whom the speech was written, had fallen in the Lamian War; he had been a close friend of Hyperides. *Against Athenogenes* is a gay exposé of an amazing and very seamy confidence game, and closes with an appeal to the judges to punish the rogue on general grounds even if the legal basis for the specific charge is weak. Apparently of the same character was the unfortunately lost *Defense of Phryne,* the famous model of Praxiteles, on the respectable charge (which she shared with Socrates) of corrupting the young. It is reported that Hyperides capped his defense by causing Phryne's robes to fall from her shoulder and revealing a person that could be guilty of no wrong.

Dinarchus, born at Corinth about 360 B.C. and therefore a metic in Athens, fitly closes the canon, for the three extant speeches of the 160 with which he was credited show clearly the decline of the art of speech writing. He was competent and composed according to rule, but the rules are now more important than the matter. There is neither originality—plagiarism is unashamed—nor moral stature. The three extant speeches, *Against Demosthenes, Aristogiton,* and *Philocles,* all have to do with the affair of Harpalus. So many of the political leaders, it appears, had become involved in the affair that it was necessary to engage a professional speech writer (as a metic, Dinarchus could not himself plead). However much or little the new tyranny may have affected other forms of literature, for political oratory it was fatal; and though speeches continued to be made we must await the rise of Rome for men again to seek to sway political behavior by the art of the spoken word.

Chapter 12. HELLENISTIC PHI-LOSOPHY, DRAMA, HISTORY

IN THE SMALL AND EXCLUSIVE CITY-STATE EACH CITIZEN WAS IMMEDIATELY concerned with the various currents, cultural as well as political, which affected his city. Pericles' *Funeral Oration* and the ethical-political writings of Plato and Aristotle make it plain that the citizen was so completely identified with his polis that his life could be looked upon as a fraction of the life of the polis. But now polis was forever gone, and men suddenly brought down from a central position of high dignity to become minute particles in an enormously expanded world—as when Copernicus showed that the earth was not the center of creation but a speck flying in space. Oppressed and reduced by unintelligible size, men could justify their existence only by turning in upon themselves and thinking of themselves as individuals. Both Stoics and Epicureans, but by a different process of reasoning, assert the dignity of the individual. Their concern was not with the discovery of truth, but with the happiness of individual men, and therefore though each had their own physical explanations of the universe these were but scaffoldings to support their doctrines of conduct. Each sought to ease the unhappiness of frustration by advocating avoidance of passion and emotion. The Stoics recommended apathy or indifference, the Epicureans ataraxy or imperturbability. Superficially, there is little difference in these words; and in fact it would be difficult to distinguish their followers by outward conduct, for each would cultivate what is vulgarly called the philosophical temper. Actually, the distinction between Porch and Garden is sharper than that between Academy and Lyceum, as even a cursory examination will show.

Epicurus, who founded his school in the Garden in 306 B.C., taught a thoroughgoing materialism. Everything is composed of atoms (he meant molecules) and void. The world is the result, not of design, but of a fortuitous concatenation of atoms. Even sense perceptions are material: a film of atoms from the object perceived strikes the sense organ of the perceiver. Gods, also composed of atoms, exist, but they have no concern with men. At death the atoms disperse. Institutions are not imposed from without, but are a natural development guided by practical considerations. There being no external imperatives and nothing to fear from the gods or death, man is independent, and his only course is to pursue his own happiness. Naturally, he will choose his pleasure by an intelligent calculus, and Epicurus and his fellows, as we can see from his will and letters in Diogenes Laertius, were abstemious in their habits and singularly kindly; the bad repute of his name is due to libertines who made "eat and drink today" a license for excess, and even more to professors of revealed religions, to whom materialism was the ultimate heresy. Actually, as compared with the partial suicide of Stoic renunciation, there is a certain dignity in a system which sets a man on his own feet and makes him master of his own destiny. "Epicurus," Diogenes Laertius says (10.26), "was a most prolific author, and eclipsed all before him in the number of his writings"; but of these all that we have to read are the summaries of his doctrines in epistles to Herodotus and others which Diogenes himself (10.35 ff.) quotes. These show how closely Epicurus was followed by Lucretius, whose *De rerum natura* is the supreme monument of the school.

To men who were lost in the suddenly enlarged world Epicurus' advice was to ignore it and go their own way. The Stoics tried to chart a course in it. Zeno, who began teaching in the Painted Porch (*Stoa Poikile*) shortly before 300 B.C., was a Semite from Cyprus; it is remarkable, and a sign of how the limits of the world were being drawn in, that many of the Stoic teachers were of Semitic origin. The ground for the Stoic teaching had been prepared by the Cynics, whose founder Antisthenes, a disciple of Socrates, taught that virtue is the only good, vice the only evil. Wealth, social position, country, are given a false value because of convention (*nomos*); nature (*physis*), before which men are equal, is satisfied with a rag and a crust. When the Cynic Diogenes (who was so little impressed with Alexander's attention that the only thing he would ask of him was to stand out of his light) was asked of what country he was, he denied the validity of all conventional distinctions by declaring that he was a *cosmopolites,* a citizen of the world. The gentler Crates, who rejected wealth and position and took up scrip and staff to follow Diogenes, softened the Cynic doctrine with something like Christian love; and Zeno was a pupil of Crates. Stoicism had a logic and a physics, but these were ancillary to, and indeed merged with, their ethics. God, providence, the world, nature, are in effect one, and the soul of man is part of the divine soul which is the motive power of the universe. Life must therefore be lived according to nature. Failure admits of no degrees; a miss is as good as a mile. Men are members one of another, and it is the duty of each individual to promote the welfare of the whole. In the period from which most of our sources derive—Seneca and Epictetus and Marcus Aurelius, the criticism of Cicero, particularly in *De finibus* 3 and *De natura deorum* 3, and especially Plutarch's *On Stoic Inconsistencies*—Stoicism had become softened and eclectic. It is natural for a lawyer like Cicero to ridicule perfectionism in observance of law; natural too that the concept of human dignity implicit in participation in the world soul should become a solace to reconcile a Roman menial to the insignificance of his station. But even a debased Stoicism contributed largely to the Roman concept of universal law before which all men are equal; its contributions to the shaping of Christianity are patent; and a renewed interest in Stoicism was a factor in bringing about the French Revolution.

Of the *Republic* which Zeno wrote we know little; we may infer its doctrine from the fact that his disciple Sphaerus of Borysthenes helped shape the program for Cleomenes' social revolution in Sparta. (Later, the Stoic Blossius of Cumae similarly advised the Gracchi.) Zeno was succeeded by Cleanthes, whose extant *Hymn to Zeus* is the noblest thing of its kind produced by paganism. Here are its opening lines:

> O God most glorious, called by many a name,
> Nature's great king, through endless years the same;
> Omnipotence, who by thy just decree
> Controllest all, hail, Zeus, for unto thee
> Behoves thy creatures in all lands to call.
> We are thy children, we alone, of all
> On earth's broad ways that wander to and fro,
> Bearing thine image whereso'er we go.
>   —*James Adam*

But this fine religious zeal could also show intolerance; when Aristarchus of Samos suggested that the sun and not the earth is the center of our system, Cleanthes declared (Diogenes Laertius 7.174) that he ought to be prosecuted "for disturbing the heart of the universe."

Cleanthes was followed by Chrysippus, who developed and systematized the Stoic philosophy (and is hence sometimes called Stoicism's St. Paul), and then by Zeno of Tarsus and Diogenes of Babylon. Probably all the Stoic teachers, certainly Zeno and Chrysippus, wrote diatribes (the original meaning of the word is simply "pastime," playful or serious)—practical moral discourses, which became the pattern for Christian homilies. The traditional schools were less responsive to contemporary spiritual needs. The Peripatetics were submerged in the scholarly research which flourished in Alexandria, and the Academy remained largely speculative until it yielded to Neoplatonism.

The circumstances which occasioned the shift in philosophy from investigation of truth and the consideration of the polis to the concern for the individual produced a similar shift in drama. Tragedies continued to be written and acted, but the paramount dramatic form, after Alexander, was New Comedy. New Comedy, it must be emphasized, derives, not from the robust exuberance of Aristophanes, but from the intrigues and the familiar characters, heroic only in name, of Euripides; its concern is not like Aristophanes', with criticism of public institutions, but like Euripides' in such plays as *Electra, Ion, Iphigenia at Aulis* with plots motivated by ordinary human emotions and with such commonplace private concerns as arranging suitable marriages. Since legend is discarded the reader tends to assume that the plots of New Comedy are intended as a realistic representation of life, and is consequently puzzled by a world which seems to be composed of seductions and unwanted children, coincidences and recognitions of long-lost daughters, irate fathers and impertinent slaves. The traditional belief in the moral decadence of Athens has been largely based on these aspects of New Comedy. But it is important to realize that despite its bourgeois cast of characters and its lack of chorus New Comedy is as conventional, in range of plot as well as in form, as tragedy or as other species of Greek literature. The limitation on the range of subjects was dictated by the history of the development of the form; the astonishing thing is that once the inhibited tourist makes himself at home in the world of New Comedy, the people who seemed at first glance undifferentiated in their uniformity take on individual and interesting characters, displaying, in fine gradations, amiable traits of loyalty, affection, high mindedness. If the reader will recognize that in sex relationships the double standard is the rule, then the moral atmosphere so far from being anarchic will prove to maintain a very high standard. The slaves, it is true, are clowns, but despite their occasional impudence they are human beings, with normal equipment of emotions and sometimes singularly generous.

Sixty-four writers of New Comedy are known to us by name; three, Philemon, Diphilus, and Menander, were more highly regarded than the others; and of the three the greatest reputation by far (after his death; he is said to have won only eight prizes) was enjoyed by Menander. Menander was born in 342 B.C. of a prominent Athenian family; his father was Diopithes, and his uncle Alexis was an esteemed comic poet whose long life and 200 plays bridged the span from Old Comedy to New. Menander served his ephebate with his contemporary Epicurus. Before he was twenty he wrote the first of his 105 (or 109) plays, *The Self-Tormenter,* which is the model for Terence's play of the same name. He was a friend of the literary dilettante Demetrius of Phalerum, who ruled Athens from

317 to 307 B.C. in the Macedonian interest, and this attachment brought Menander into some disrepute when Demetrius fell and Demetrius Poliorcetes restored a phantom democracy to Athens. We are told, too, that the kings of Macedonia and Egypt sent ships and personal emissaries to invite Menander to their courts, but that he preferred to remain in Athens, and that he was drowned in Piraeus in 291 B.C.

Throughout antiquity Menander's reputation and vogue were enormous, and he is frequently quoted, naturally mostly in single-line apothegms. Three of his lines have become English proverbs: "Whom the gods love die young"; "Evil communications corrupt good manners"; and "Conscience makes cowards of the bravest." It was on such quotations and avowed adaptations in Terence and Plautus that modern judgment of Menander was based, until papyrus discoveries—especially the Cairo papyrus which contains fragments of five plays, discovered in 1905—provided some four thousand lines, which included whole scenes. A limited selection of plays seems to have been in circulation, so that despite the great volume of Menander's work fragments of the same play are apt to recur. Enough continuous passages of three plays, *The Shearing of Glycera, The Arbitration,* and *The Girl from Samos,* have been preserved to make plausible reconstructions of their plots possible. Of the three, the most fully preserved and perhaps the best is *The Arbitration* (*Epitrepontes*), and a summary of its plot may serve to characterize the genre.

Ten months before the play begins, Pamphila, a girl of good Athenian family, had been assaulted at a night festival by Charisius, a priggish young man. Each was ignorant of the other's identity, but Pamphila had obtained Charisius' ring in the encounter. Some time later Pamphila's father, Smicrines, marries her to Charisius, as being a young man of exemplary character and frugality. Pamphila gives birth to a child in Charisius' absence, and exposes it with the usual tokens, including the ring. Charisius' loyal but officious slave Onesimus informs his master of the birth, and in chagrin Charisius leaves home and spends his time in revelry at a friend's house, employing the female entertainer Habrotonon, whom, however, he does not touch. At this point the play opens. In the first act (of which almost nothing remains) the audience is apprised of the situation, and Smicrines, concerned for Charisius' extravagance and his daughter's dowry, comes to expostulate. The continuous part of the papyrus begins with Act 2. The goatherd Davus has found the infant and given it, but without the identifying tokens, to the charcoal burner Syriscus. Syriscus, accompanied by his wife holding the baby, demands the tokens of Davus, on the grounds that they belong to the child and may some day establish its proper station; Davus holds that having freely given the baby, it is right for him to retain part of his find. Smicrines, returning from his expostulations, is appealed to, to arbitrate, and decides in favor of his grandchild, of whose identity, of course, he is not aware. As the tokens are being passed from Davus to Syriscus, Onesimus, who has entered in connection with the banquet preparations, recognizes that the ring is his master's, and prevails on Syriscus to let him have it. This act is separated from the next, as is indicated in the manuscript, by a band of revelers, who doubtless performed some pantomime; this was the usual substitute for the chorus as a division between the acts. In Act 3 Onesimus and Habrotonon plot to procure Charisius' acknowledgment of the infant as his, using the ring as evidence and Habrotonon posing as the mother. When Smicrines discovers that Charisius has acknowledged a child by Habrotonon and might therefore live with her, he is angrily determined to terminate the marriage. In Act 4 Pamphila rejects her father's arguments and insists on remaining faithful to her husband. Then she is convinced by Habrotonon that the baby is hers. Charisius has overheard Pamphila's colloquy with her father, and is so moved by contrition and self-reproach that Onesimus, who reports his conduct, is afraid for his sanity. Charisius himself soliloquizes on the injustice in condemning Pamphila for a sin so like his own. The act closes with Habrotonon convincing Charisius that the child is Pamphila's and his. Act 5 completes the story, the central part being the discomfiture of Smicrines, who has come to carry off his daughter.

Plots of other Menandrian plays can be deduced from Roman adaptations: Terence's *Andria, The Self-Tormenter, Eunuch,* and *Brothers* from Menandrian plays of the same name; Plautus' *Bacchides* from Menander's *Double Deceiver, Aulularia* probably from *Hydria,* and *Stichus* from another version of *Brothers.* Others may be inferred with less certainty from the more extensive fragments, especially *Hero* and *Farmer.* Plots of other masters of New Comedy, of Diphilus and especially of Philemon, whose wit was coarser than Menander's and who was Plautus' favorite, can be deduced from Plautus. But though *The Arbitration* is probably better than the average, from the point of view of plot, characters, and atmosphere it may be regarded as typical.

The fact that a large class can be represented even roughly by a single specimen tends to lower our estimate of the class; if only one of these plays had survived perhaps we would value it more highly. But a perhaps greater obstacle to our appreciation is their traditional classification as comedies. It is true that the sequence of highly improbable coincidences prevents our taking the plot seriously, that the exalted personages of tragedy have given way to commonplace types with names as transparent as Squire Allworthy's, that these characters are concerned, not with large problems of destiny, but with family matters, that there is a certain amount of slap-stick. But these are serious dramas, as serious as those of Molière which derive from them. Given the limits of a plot (which are hardly more in-credible, though less repetitious, than *Oedipus*) we have an illuminating exhibition of the interaction of human beings dealing with problems which concern them very nearly, not about the abstract question of man's relation to authority—what good now to speculate on authority?—but on the management of individual lives. The order of excellence is different from that of the tragedians, as a Tanagra figurine is different from a statue by Phidias; but the enthusiasm which made educated and thought-ful critics like Plutarch rate Menander in his kind with Homer in his is not without basis. The literary progeny of Menander is probably more numerous than that of any other classic author.

Tragedies too were required for the festivals, whose number was in-creased, and were produced in quantities. They cannot have been other than artificial and precious. The grandiose figures of heroic legend were grown anachronistic after Euripides; the stories which they could be repre-sented as enacting, irrelevant. In Alexandria, whither the center of gravity of Greek literary production removed in the third century b.c., no large audience which might make tragedy a living force could have the requisite education for the old type; what information we have concerning Alexan-drian tragedy indicates that it was directed to a highly select audience. Because the subject can be dealt with in a paragraph we shall anticipate the next chapter and finish our account of Greek drama here.

Seven Alexandrian writers of the early third century b.c. enjoyed enough temporary repute to be called the *Pleiad* and to bequeath that stylish title to the sixteenth-century French poets who grouped themselves about Ronsard. An attempt was made to write historical plays; Moschion (who was not in the Pleiad) wrote a *Themistocles* and a *Pheraeans,* and Lyco-phron (who was) a *Cassandria* on the recent sufferings of that place under its proletariat dictatorship. Lycophron also wrote a play on his teacher, Menedemus of Eretria; this was a satyr play, a form which the poets of the Pleiad seemed to favor. We have the outlines of *Lityerses* by Sositheus in this form. From what we have and know of these poets their loss can be borne with equanimity. One curious work of 1,474 lines is extant and must be mentioned if only as a curiosity. This is Lycophron's *Alexandra* (a collateral name for "Cassandra"), which must be classified as a tragedy because of its iambic meter but is, in fact, a single messenger's speech re-porting to Priam Cassandra's predictions on the day that Paris set out for the rape of Helen, covering a period down to six generations after Alexander. Every line of the poem is an enigma. Persons, gods, places, are almost never called by their names but referred to by the most remote and abstruse allusions; if the allusion strikes the reader as recognizable he is surely wrong, for some more remote and more paradoxical reference is intended. The separate stories and their connections are equally puzzling, though it is plain that all memorable events down to the poet's day (and perhaps beyond: an apparent allusion to Rome has puzzled scholars) are treated. To modern readers the work, happily unique in its kind, appears to be the chef d'œuvre of an erudite madman; but as we shall see in the next chapter, such madness may have had an appreciative audience in Alexandria.

The writing of history continued, and indeed was quickened after Alexander, whose conquests expanded the boundaries of curiosity as of knowledge enormously, though no substantive historical work survives from the two centuries between Xenophon and Polybius. Alexander's own career aroused natural interest, sharpened curiosity concerning remote peoples, and ultimately gave rise to a tendency to compose "universal" histories. Perhaps as a reaction to the submergence of the older local centers consequent upon the enlargement of horizons, there is an efflorescence of local histories, which included myth and legend in their chronicles. All Greek cities probably had such local histories; we know by name of a number of *Atthides,* or local histories of Athens. A precipitate of their lore was deposited in the philological work of the Alexandrians. The best known writer of an *Atthis* is Philochorus, who was put to death by Antigonus Gonatas about 261 B.C.; a considerable continuous passage is preserved in Dionysius, and new fragments have been discovered in the present century. Probably derived from Atthides is the invaluable *Marmor Parium,* a chronicle of Athens inscribed on stone at Paros in 263 B.C. and discovered in Smyrna. The Parian Marble supplies scattered dates from the time of Cecrops down to the date of its engraving, and is particularly interested in religious festivals; hence it is our principal source of information for tragic contests, sometimes supplying the names of competitors and winners as well as dates.

The compilation of the history of Alexander was a special development. A number of men in Alexander's inner circle published works based on official records and their own memories: Ptolemy, who became King of Egypt; Nearchus the admiral, and another naval officer named Androsthenes; Callisthenes, the nephew of Aristotle, who wrote a fulsome history of Alexander as well as *Hellenica* on the period 387–357 B.C. in ten books but whom Alexander subsequently put to death for plain speaking; and Aristobulus of Cassandrea. Arrian (second century A.D.) says in the preface to his seven-book *Anabasis* on Alexander that Aristobulus' account, as well as Ptolemy's, is "strictly authentic"; but Lucian (*How to Write History* 12) says that Alexander himself was so disgusted with Aristobulus' gross flattery that he threw a book of his overboard and said its author should be thrown after it. Others in the outer circle, like Onesicritus, Chares, and Ephippus, wrote books filled with trivialities or inventions. On the basis of these earlier works Clitarchus of Alexandria subsequently produced a rhetorical history which was widely read and became the authorized version of the career of Alexander. Much later a writer using the name of Callisthenes produced an early version of the *Alexander Romance* which became as influential among Greeks and non-Greeks alike as the legend of Troy.

Of the historians of the period after Alexander, Hieronymus of Cardia is described by a competent judge, but only on the basis of small fragments and citations, as "probably one of the greatest historians Greece produced." Duris of Samos is credited with innovating a pathetic, theatrical style, calculated to work on the emotions of his readers. This style was followed by Phylarchus, of whose effectiveness we get a good impression from Plutarch's *Agis and Cleomenes,* which rests largely on Phylarchus. Polybius' criticism of Phylarchus (2.56.7) tells us as much about Polybius as about Phylarchus:

In his eagerness to arouse the pity and attention of his readers he treats us to a picture of clinging women with their hair dishevelled and their breasts bare, or again of crowds of both sexes together with their children and aged parents weeping and lamenting as they are led away into slavery. This sort of thing keeps up throughout his history, always trying to bring horrors vividly before our eyes. Leaving aside the ignoble and womanish character of such a treatment of his subject, let us consider how far it is proper or serviceable to history. A historical author should not try to thrill his readers by such exaggerated pictures, nor should he, like a tragic poet, try to imagine the probable utterances of his characters or reckon up all the consequences probably incidental to the occurrences with which he deals, but simply record what really happened and what really was said, however commonplace. . . . Apart from this, Phylarchus simply narrates most of such catastrophes and does not even suggest their causes or the nature of these causes, without which it is impossible in any case to feel either legitimate pity or proper anger.

—*W. R. Paton*

Phylarchus disapproved of the policies of Aratus of Sicyon (271–213 B.C.) as being reactionary; Polybius (whose father had been Aratus' cavalry commander) approved of them. He (and Plutarch in his *Life of Aratus*) made extensive use of the *Memoirs* of Aratus, who may be mentioned as one of the numerous writers of biographies and memoirs in this period.

A number of works (none extant) dealt with lands newly won from barbarism. Two of their writers deserve mention because they were themselves newly Hellenized. Manetho, using Egyptian records, wrote a history of Egypt from the mythical age to the time of Alexander; the dynastic numeration we still use is derived from him. His fragments must be gathered from the fragments of Julius Africanus, the Armenian version of Eusebius, Josephus, and other out-of-the-way sources. Berossus, priest of Marduk at Babylon, wrote a Greek work on 468,215 years of his own country's history in three books: the first covered 432,000 years to the flood; the second went down to 747 B.C.; and the third, to the death of Alexander. Our fragments are apparently all drawn from the lost compendium of Alexander Polyhistor. In the first century A.D. Philo of Byblus adapted *Sanchuniathon,* a Phoenician work covering the period from the creation to the twelfth century B.C.; our fragments are chiefly in Eusebius. Of Greeks who wrote of exotic places mention may be made of Megasthenes, who went on embassies to the Indian King Chandragupta and wrote *Indica* in four books; long excerpts occur in Diodorus 2.35–42. The Eratosthenes who wrote on Galatia and the Hecataeus (of Abdera) who wrote a fanciful and much used account of Egypt must not be confused with their more famous namesakes. Hecataeus is the first pagan author to deal with Jews, reporting, on the basis of Egyptian sources, that they were expelled from Egypt because of a pestilential disease. The *Life of Abraham* ascribed to Hecataeus was a pseudepigraph.

Exaggerations and inventions in accounts of strange places may have been due in part to a consciously utopian intention. From *Odyssey* onward Greek writers and readers are interested in faraway places and also in the best state, and it was natural for these interests to be combined. Parts of Herodotus, for example his account of the Ethiopians, read as if they were taken from a conscious utopia, and a number of utopias were doubtless made in the Hellenistic age. Euhemerus' *Sacred Record* (*Hiera Anagraphe*) was the report of an inscription he professed to have found on the island of Panchaia in the Indian Ocean. This inscription was alleged to have recorded the deeds of Zeus and the other gods of mythology when they were still kings of earth. Hence "euhemerism" denotes the belief that the Greek gods were originally human princes who were deified out of admiration or flattery. Greater regard for fact characterized the works of the *periegetes,* or authors of travel books, of whom Polemon is mentioned favorably, and of the geographers, the greatest name among whom is Eratosthenes. On the other hand, there was a whole class of writers of *paradoxa* or marvelous tales, and of *anaischyntographoi,* or pornographers.

Other specialized subjects dealt with were the history and techniques of the various plastic arts, and agricultural matters; a *Geoponica* of the Carthaginian Mago was put into Greek in the time of Sulla.

Polybius devotes almost the whole of his Book 12 (extant only in fragments) to finding synonyms for "liar," "fool," "impertinent," and "senseless bookworm" to apply to Timaeus. And yet to later writers Timaeus was *the* historian of the West. He was born about 346 B.C. of a father who was ruler of Tauromenium (Taormina) in Sicily, had to flee at the age of thirty-four, spent fifty years in Athens, and returned to Sicily to live until ninety-six. His *History of Sicily* in forty or more books included the affairs of Carthage and Italy and long digressions on the affairs of Greece, so that despite its local patriotic coloring the scope of his work was universal. He it was who connected the early history of the West with that of the East by means of the myths of Heracles, the Argonauts, and Troy, which figured so largely in subsequent Roman tradition. Another important innovation is his dating by Olympiads, in addition to the received method of dating by archons of Athens, ephors of Sparta, and priestesses of the Argive Hera. He is used, and evidently with high respect as fragments and testimonia show, by many subsequent writers, both Latin and Greek. Even the furious criticism of Polybius admits that Timaeus possessed a deal of book learning and a high ideal of historical veracity—which, of course (Polybius charges), he consciously subverted. The fragments do show the basis of Polybius' charge that Timaeus was disrespectful of high authority, especially Aristotle's. But Timaeus can surely not have been as bad as Polybius paints him—or else Polybius displays bad judgment in devoting so much attention to so trivial an author. In any case, Polybius' Book 12 leaves a distinctly bad taste; he is indeed the second Greek historian after Thucydides, but the interval in taste is unbridgeable.

Timaeus, along with Theopompus and Ephorus, who have been mentioned in an earlier chapter, are our most considerable losses in history between Xenophon and Polybius. Lines of demarcation are difficult to draw with precision. Timaeus does deal with Rome, but it seems better to begin our account of the Greek historians of Rome with an extant classic; nor, indeed, are Timaeus and the other specialists in history alien to the scholars and scientists to whom we now turn.

Chapter 13. ALEXANDRIAN LITERATURE AND LEARNING

IT CAN NO LONGER BE NECESSARY TO REFUTE THE VIEW THAT GREEK GENIUS SO far declined in the Hellenistic age that its intellectual products are unworthy of consideration. The quest for truth took the path of exact science rather than first philosophies, the urge to create in beauty took shape in a "Venus di Milo" or "Dying Gaul" rather than in the remoter Olympians of Phidias or Praxiteles, in the high finish of Alexandrian miniatures rather than in the statuesque harmonies of fifth-century tragedy. But though the stream of Greek civilization and literature flows uninterrupted, no turning in it is as marked as that which came with the Alexandrians. We have already noticed the universalism and its corollary individualism which characterized the outlook of the Hellenistic world and which were consciously cultivated by the Stoics, who were a leading spiritual force in that world. All the world was become one *oikumene,* drawn together, not only politically, but by enormously expanded navigation, commerce, and banking; and the soul of that *oikumene* was Greek, for though the distinction between Hellene and barbarian persisted, what made a Hellene now was not race but education. The audience for Greek work was thus multiplied, and systematized procedures enabled books to be reproduced on a scale previously unknown. The number of writers increased in proportion; in the Hellenistic age the names of more than a thousand are known.

It is obvious that this expansion must have affected the character of literary production. For one thing, two separate audiences take the place of the essentially homogeneous public the Athenians addressed, one less cultivated than the Athenian and catered to by sensation mongers or mendicant moralizers like the Cynics, and the other more specialized than the Athenian, demanding work too rich for popular digestion either in finish or in erudition. Specialists dealt more and more professionally with material more and more restricted, and sometimes reached a point where display was the sole object. There was a growing tendency to write, not out of a burning compulsion, but because writing was an amusing thing to do or because it served ambition. These tendencies were crystallized and propagated by the establishment, under royal patronage, of the Museum and Library at Alexandria. The plan for these institutions is said to have been suggested to the first Ptolemy by Demetrius of Phalerum, who was a pupil of Theophrastus, when he took refuge in Alexandria after 307 B.C.; in any case, the influence of the Peripatetic school is evident. An effort was made to assemble all literature for the Library; Galen tells us that Ptolemy III kept the official state texts of the tragedians which he had borrowed from the Athenians, forfeiting his large deposit and presenting the Athenians with handsome copies, and the *Letter of Aristeas* tells us (wrongly) that Ptolemy I caused the translation of the Hebrew Scriptures known as the Septuagint to be made. By the first century B.C. the Library had grown to some seven hundred thousand rolls. The preservation of most of the classical Greek texts that we possess is due to the Library at Alexandria.

As in the schools of philosophy, the scholars were organized into a cult association. They were dedicated to the service of the Muses, and their head, appointed by the king, was priest of the Muses. The head of the Library was regularly in charge of the education of the princes, and so he was a high official of the royal household. Partly because only poets were likely to have the knowledge of the older language and dialects requisite for handling the treasures of the Library, and partly, doubtless, because the appointments were something in the nature of a prize to reward past and encourage future achievement, it was natural that the early incumbents should be poets. It was inevitable that men dependent on the court and on the court alone should develop specialization to the point of pedantry, should lose touch with the larger public and grow indifferent to their problems, in a word, should become liable to the strictures of a Timon. It is this separation from their fellow men which, in the last analysis, distinguishes the work of the Alexandrians from that of the Athenians, who were answerable, not to a patron, but to demos.

The librarians of the great period were Zenodotus of Ephesus, Apollonius "the Rhodian," Eratosthenes of Cyrene, Aristophanes of Byzantium, Apollonius "the Eidograph," and Aristarchus of Samothrace; Callimachus, whom earlier books put in the place of Apollonius, was not librarian though it was he who compiled the first catalogue. The prime achievement of these men as a group is in the field of philology. Zenodotus invented textual criticism and settled a text of Homer, expunging many interpolated lines. Aristophanes and Aristarchus worked on this text, and our vulgate text is largely the result of this work. Zenodotus also saw to sifting and arranging the books, taking care of epic and lyric himself and assigning tragedy to Alexander of Pleuron and comedy to Lycophron of Chalcis. Callimachus' *Pinakes* in 120 books was a literary history rather than a catalogue. Each writer was given a short biography and a list of works, including those lost; of each work the opening words and the number of lines were recorded, and any doubts of authenticity were noted. The whole was classified by categories such as epic, lyric, tragedy, comedy, philosophy, history, oratory. What could not be classified went into "Miscellaneous"; chance has preserved a list of authors on cake baking from this omnium-gatherum.

To us Callimachus is significant, not as a literary historian but as a poet, though his scholarship was of the first importance in shaping his own and his disciples' and imitators' poetry. He was born about 330 B.C. in Cyrene, of a family which had held high office; his father, Battus, bore the name of the legendary founder. He studied in Athens, and then became a schoolteacher at Eleusis, a suburb of Alexandria, whence he was called to work in the Library. He is credited with more than eight hundred works, in many departments of literature. We have six hymns, transmitted in a collection which contained the *Homeric Hymns;* sixty-odd *Epigrams,* chiefly from the *Palatine Anthology;* and fragments, chiefly from papyri, of *Aetia, Lock of Berenice, Hecale, Iambi,* and lesser works. We shall follow this rather than the chronological order (at best uncertain) in examining Callimachus' work.

The *Hymns* are in hexameter, except the fifth, which is in elegiacs, and are addressed to Zeus, Apollo, Artemis, Delos, the Bath of Pallas, and Demeter. Like all of Callimachus' work these hymns show great metrical skill and polish; by the new rules for the hexameter Homer commits no fewer than three errors in the first line of *Iliad.* But a more essential diference from Homer and the Homeric Hymns is that patently neither the poet nor his audience had any belief in the gods who are celebrated. The *Hymns* are not intended for cult use, but exploit antiquarian lore, not from a romantic or an anthropological but from a philological point of view; in the *Hymn to Zeus* practically every line is a refutation of some commonly held view and a defense of an alternative but less known theory. Not feeling but wit is the keynote, and the courtier always deftly introduces a compliment to his patron—in *Zeus,* by an implicit equation of Zeus with Ptolemy; in *Delos,* by having embryonic Apollo refuse to be born in Cos because another deity, Ptolemy Philadelphus, was destined to be born there. *Delos* also has an interesting reference to the Gallic invasion which threatened Delphi in 279 B.C. Contemporary events are alluded to also in *Apollo,* which is a manifesto against the threatened defection of Cyrene from the empire of the Ptolemies. Here the poet speaks in his own person, after the manner of Pindar, and closes with a rebuke to Envy,

which is taken to be an attack on Apollonius of Rhodes. The rivalry between the two is one of the famous literary quarrels in history. Callimachus'
main attack on Apollonius is thought to have been delivered in his *Ibis*,
known to us only by the supposed imitation of Ovid in a vituperative poem
of 644 elegiacs of the same title; but Ovid may have borrowed little more
than the title. *Hymn to Artemis* is a good example of the somewhat patron-
izing genre treatment which the Alexandrians bestowed on the Olympians.
Artemis is here a little girl who calls Zeus "Daddy" and cajoles him for
all the things she wants when she grows up, and he jovially promises.
But this hymn also carries the usual freight of mythological and especially
geographical erudition. In *Bath of Pallas* Callimachus attempts to communicate to his audience the emotions of devotees participating in a
lengthy ritual, in this case a procession of Argive women carrying the
image of Athena to the Inachus for a ritual ablution. In *Hymn to Demeter*,
similarly, the Procession of the Basket, an Athenian ceremony which
Ptolemy Philadelphus had introduced in Alexandria, is the theme. The
famished women waiting at the curb for the procession to pass while the
time away in chatting, and we are given a burlesque of the gruesome legend
of Erysichthon.

Most of Callimachus' *Epigrams* were written for pay, to be inscribed on
tombstones or votive offerings, before Callimachus became a courtier.
Perhaps that is why they touch the reader as none of Callimachus' other
work can do. They are among the very best in the *Anthology*, and would
justify Callimachus' title of poet if we knew nothing else of him. Cory's
famous but slightly padded version (the virtue of the epigram is of course
its economy) of the lines on Heraclitus is worth reprinting:

> They told me, Heraclitus, they told me you were dead,
> They brought me bitter news to hear and bitter tears to shed.
> I wept as I remembered how often you and I
> Had tired the sun with talking and sent him down the sky.
>
> And now that thou art lying, my dear old Carian guest,
> A handful of grey ashes, long, long ago at rest,
> Still are thy pleasant voices, thy nightingales, awake;
> For death he taketh all away, but them he cannot take.

Callimachus' principal work was his *Aetia*, which treated, in four books
of elegiacs, a variety of aetiological legends connected with history, customs, rites. The title corresponds to *Origines* of Cato, who seems to have
modeled his (prose) work on Callimachus; the subject matter is what
we might call folklore. The hundred-odd lines recovered from papyri contain material on the Athenian festival of the Broaching of Jars and on the

story of Acontius and Cydippe, known to us from Ovid. *Metamorphoses,* in fact, with its adroit linking of disparate stories, and its detached lightness of tone, is the ancient book which comes nearest *Aetia.* Callimachus' personality asserts itself more than does Ovid's. Among modern works it has been suggested that Byron's *Don Juan* offers an analogy to *Aetia.*

Another point of contact with Ovid is Callimachus' epyllion *Hecale,* of which some seventy verses are preserved on a wooden tablet (of which the reverse has a long passage from Euripides' *Phoenician Women*) which was clearly intended as a schoolbook. Just as the simple Philemon and Baucis unknowingly entertain the Olympians and receive their reward, so Hecale entertains Theseus as he sets out to slay the Marathonian bull. Part of the story seems to be told in a conversation between birds. The fragments of *Iambi,* recovered in the present century, show how much more skillful was Callimachus' use of the scazon (in which the work is mostly but not entirely composed) than was Herodes'. The lines are put into the mouth of Hipponax, who has just come up from Hades "where they sell an ox for a penny," and consist, again, of disconnected stories, witty in treatment and with a slight didactic touch. Of the work of Callimachus which is best known to moderns we have, paradoxically enough, practically no fragments. Catullus' *Lock of Berenice* (#66) is probably a fairly close version of Callimachus' poem in which the constellation newly discovered by the court astronomer Conon is identified as the lock of hair which Queen Berenice had vowed for the safe return of her husband from his expedition against the Syrian Seleucus. Similar courtly use seems to be made of astronomy in a lament for Arsinoe, fragments of which appear in a Berlin papyrus. Other fragments are of minor significance, and even new discoveries are not likely to alter our estimate of Callimachus.

If we grant that the aim of the Alexandrians was to accommodate men, not to the society of the world, but to the world of society that estimate must be very high. He is pre-eminent in mastery of form, he has taste and wit as well as learning, and inventiveness if not imagination; and so far as a bookish man addressing a polite audience may, he has a quality which may be called spirit. In this respect none of his disciples or followers approaches him. Theocritus and Apollonius are his peers, and each shows points of contact with Callimachus which may be due to direct influence; but their merits are of a different order from his. Of those who followed his lead two are spoken of by the ancients with respect. Of Eratosthenes of Cyrene (276–195 B.C.), the polymath who was called "Beta" in the Museum because he was second to the master in all subjects and whose work in geography was especially significant, we know the titles of three poems: *Hesiod,* on the story of Hesiod's murder; *Erigone,* on the origin of the vine; and *Hermes* (of which minor fragments are extant), on the birth of Hermes, with an excursus on the Milky Way. Euphorion of Chalcis (276–187 B.C.), librarian to Antiochus the Great at Antioch, had so high a reputation among the Romans that Cicero speaks (with distaste) of his whole class as "singers of Euphorion." His vogue seems to have continued, for our fragments are from a papyrus of the fifth century A.D., but it is hard to see why, for he seems to have all the vices of pedantic obscurity with none of Callimachus' merits. He seems to have been an angry man with a persecution complex. *Cup Thief* showers curses on a man who had stolen his cup; *Chiliades* prophesies misfortune for someone who had cheated him. The list of instances of inexorable though delayed punishments which he uses to frighten his adversary is supposed to have been used by Plutarch in his treatise *On the Delay in Divine Retribution.*

With the professional bookishness of the Alexandrians it was inevitable that literary quarrels should flourish; the issue whose reverberations have reached us is on the feasibility of composing epic, and the antagonists are Callimachus and Apollonius. Callimachus was opposed alike to free invention of heroic incident and to rehashing traditional material, and he hated "a big book." He favored the epyllion, treating an obscure but documentable incident of limited scope in a highly finished style. His own *Hecale* illustrates his principles; *Little Heracles* of Theocritus, who learned from Callimachus, is a fuller specimen and illustrates the characteristic treatment of the Olympians as bourgeoisie. *How Heracles Slew the Lion,* falsely ascribed to Theocritus (#25) but by a good poet nevertheless, is another specimen, and Moschus' *Europa* still another. Whether difference of opinion on the possibility of epic was the cause or a result of the bad feeling between Callimachus and Apollonius, there is no question that such feeling existed. We have seen that Callimachus spoke ill of Apollonius in the *Hymn to Apollo* and in *Ibis;* it is not unlikely that Callimachus was instrumental in procuring Apollonius' replacement as librarian (the position was usually held for life) by his own friend and pupil Eratosthenes. Apollonius retired to Rhodes (and is therefore known as "the Rhodian," though he was a native of Alexandria) and wrote *Argonautica,* apparently out of bravado, to prove that a long epic could be written. From a broader point of view the quarrel is a minor ritualistic difference between votaries of the same sect. Apollonius parades the same recondite learning, favors the same antique language, shows similar disjointedness of structure, applies the same genre treatment to gods and heroes. One thing Apollonius does have that neither Callimachus nor any of his contemporaries or predecessors has, and that is an accurate psychological description of the rise of the passion of love in the heart of a maiden; it is this which may entitle Apollonius to be called the ancestor of half of modern literature. And despite its obtruded erudition the story does march, and is much closer to Homer in spirit, despite the relatively longer interval between model and copy, than is any of the later Latin epics to Virgil. Six commentaries were written on *Argonautica* in the Hellenistic age; it was twice imitated in Latin, by Varro Atacinus and by Valerius Flaccus (only the latter is extant); it influenced Ovid in *Metamorphoses* 7. But its most enduring indirect influence was through Virgil; *Aeneid* 4, the best loved of all, is a retelling of *Argonautica* 3 with altered names, and there are other palpable influences of Apollonius in *Aeneid,* not in phrase or trope only, but in spirit.

Book 1 opens with a long catalogue of the Argonauts, the farewell of Jason and his mother, and the selection of Jason as leader after Heracles, the heroes' first choice, had declined. Jason's fecklessness is striking (a repeated epithet for him is *amechanos,* "helpless")—except when he is dealing with ladies; later, when Jason is in full glory at Hypsipyle's court on Lemnos, the poet makes a digression like Homer's describing the shield of Achilles, except that here, significantly, it is the embroidered designs on Jason's beautiful cloak that are described. At the end of the first book the poet rids himself of the man who would overshadow and embarrass his hero by leaving Heracles behind in Mysia, hallooing for his beloved Hylas who has been captured by an amorous naiad.

The second book is filled with various adventures en route, the most significant and exciting being the passage through the Symplegades or Clashing Rocks. The third and most interesting book opens with a domestic scene of the gods. Hera and Athena call on Aphrodite, who is flustered by the great ladies' visit, to ask her for Eros' assistance, and in housewifely fashion Aphrodite complains that she can never get Eros to mind. He is eventually bribed to serve, but in view of what we see going on in Medea's heart his services are as unnecessary as are Cupid's in the analogous situation in *Aeneid* 4. When her father scornfully refuses Jason's petition for the Golden Fleece, Medea is smitten by the handsome stranger in distress:

Much she brooded in her soul all the cares that the Loves awaken. And before her eyes the vision still appeared—himself what like he was, with what vesture he was clad, what things he spake, how he sat on his seat, how he moved forth to the door—and as she pondered she deemed there never was such another man; and ever in her ears rung his voice and the honey-sweet words which he uttered. And she feared for him, lest the oxen or Aeetes with his own hand should slay him; and she mourned him as though already slain outright, and in her affliction a round tear through very grievous pity coursed down her cheek (3.450–462).

—*R. C. Seaton*

She dreams that Jason has come to Colchis, not for the Golden Fleece, but to marry her and take her home. When she awakens she wishes to go to her older sister Chalcippe, but is held back by fear and shame:

Thrice she made the attempt and thrice she checked herself, the fourth time she fell on her bed face downward, writhing in pain (3.654–655).

—*R. C. Seaton*

Even in his masterly description of love become conscious of itself Apollonius never forgets his learning:

Anguish tortured her, a smouldering fire through her frame, and about her fine nerves and deep down beneath the nape of the neck where the pain enters keenest (3.761–764).

—*R. C. Seaton*

The language is technical, like a demonstration in anatomy. When Jason and Medea finally meet in the forest and Jason has made his request, Medea

cast down her eyes with a smile divinely sweet; and her soul melted within her, uplifted by his praise, and she gazed upon him face to face; nor did she know what word to utter first, but was eager to pour out everything at once . . . and her heart within grew warm, melting away as the dew melts away round roses when warmed by the morning's light (3.1008–1021).

—*R. C. Seaton*

With the aid of the charms she has given him, Jason accomplishes his tasks, and Medea flies from the palace to help him procure the Golden Fleece and to be carried off.

The fourth book describes the homeward voyage, its high points being the murder of Absyrtus who has gone in pursuit of his sister Medea, and the marriage of Jason and Medea in the land of the Phaeacians. Apollonius' attempt to reconcile divergent traditions concerning the route results in rather tiresome, and at times delirious, geographical disquisitions.

Certainly this long poem does not set forth national character and aspirations, after the manner of *Iliad* or *Aeneid*, but it tells, well enough throughout and in parts superlatively well, a fine story, and it shows an understanding of men and of nature that is both true and fresh. For the poet and presumably for his audience even the learning is fresh and still filled with the sense of wonder which is the essence of poetry—as a comparison with the tired parade of facts in other versified erudition will show.

The term "mime" is a catchall for a variety of productions. In a broad sense the Greeks designated as mimes all manner of entertainers—singers, dancers, jugglers, conjurers, pantomimes—whether they exhibited their skill at the banquet or in the market place. Literature is concerned only with such performers as recited monologues in the character of some amusing type, with dramatic and entertaining fidelity to manner and language. It may well be that persons so represented are the first fictive characters in European literature, for the persons of epic and tragedy were "historical." At a level which far transcends its origins and normal development the dialogues of Plato may be regarded as mimes, and Plato is said to have learned this part of his business from the Sicilian Epicharmus. Sicily, indeed, was always the proper climate of the mime, and left its mark in the Doricisms of their language. The mimes of the Sicilian Sophron were classified as "of men" and "of women," and we have such titles as *The Peasant, The Tunny Fisher, The Needlewoman, The Sorceress, The Mother-in-Law*. A later division, applicable to Theocritus, is of "urban" and "rural" mimes. In the Hellenistic age, if not earlier, the mime was cultivated in other parts of the Greek world, but the Sicilian tradition surely persisted, though we cannot document its history, and reached its flower in the work of Theocritus. Early criticism styled his productions bucolic idylls, but mime is a more convenient and perhaps more helpful term, not only for the clearly urban *Women at the Festival of Adonis* and the clearly rural dialogues and singing contests of shepherds and goatherds, the incantations, and the serenades, but also for such things as the autobiographical *Charites,* the *Panegyric of Ptolemy,* and *How Heracles Slew the Lion.*

Theocritus was born not earlier than 305 B.C., probably in Syracuse, though Cos, where he had connections and which is the scene of some of his mimes, is also claimed as his birthplace. All that can be said of his life is based on the internal evidence of the poems; the most significant information is that he stood in some sort of relationship with the courts both of Syracuse and of Alexandria. Such a line as "Homer is enough for all" (16.20) may be a complaint of the lack of encouragement given by patrons to new poets. Suidas names ten classes of poetry which Theocritus wrote; we possess thirty "bucolics," which derive from an edition of the bucolic poets (including Moschus and Bion) made by Artemidorus in the first century B.C., and twenty-four epigrams, preserved in the *Anthology.* In both groups the Theocritean authorship of a number of poems is dubious.

Charites (#16; 109 lines) gives some details of Theocritus' biography and may have been a dedication for a collection of his poems. Theocritus complains of the neglect he has suffered in an age which values only money, and asks for the patronage of Hiero of Syracuse. The shepherds who appear in *Harvest Home* (#7; 157 lines) probably represent real persons and allude to real events. The narrator Simichidas, who fairly clearly represents Theocritus himself, actually compliments his interlocutor and rival in song, Lycidas, on the excellence of his pastoral masquerade. The use of conventional shepherd names and custom-tailored shepherd costumes to represent actual poets in this piece has been responsible, through its adoption by Virgil, for the artificiality of the modern pastoral. The scene of *Harvest Home* is Cos, and its principal content is a singing match between Simichidas and the Cretan goatherd Lycidas. Rustic singing contests are the subject of ##5, 6, 8, 9, and 27 also. In #5, *The Goatherd and the Shepherd* (150 lines), of which the scene is southern Italy, the older goatherd Comatas and the younger shepherd Lacon each sings fourteen couplets, with the woodcutter Morson as umpire and a lamb and a goat as the prize. Number 8 (93 lines) is like #5, but probably not by Theocritus, and #9 (36 lines) seems to be an imitation of #8. In #6, called *The Country Singing Match* like# #8 and 9, Damoetas and the neatherd Daphnis each sings a song of the love of Polyphemus and Galatea. *The Lovers' Talk* (#27; 73 lines) has only one contestant's offering, in the form of a line-for-line dialogue between lovers, and the judge's decision.

Other poems contain not a contest but single songs. In *Thyrsis* (#1; 152 lines) a goatherd persuades the shepherd Thyrsis, by the inducement of a cup which he describes, to sing him the ballad of *The Afflictions of Daphnis*. In *The Reapers* (#10; 58 lines) the lovesick youth Bucaeus sings a love song, and his older friend, the reaper Milon, sings him a harvest song. In *The Herdsmen* (#4; 63 lines) we have no song but banter between Battus and Corydon, reference being made to Milo's having supplanted Battus in the favors of Amaryllis. The theme of love runs through many of the poems, and is handled with exquisite understanding in *The Spell* or *Pharmaceutriai* (#2; 166 lines), which suggests a love story such as is treated in New Comedy. Simaetha prepares a spell to recall her neglectful lover Delphis, pronounces an incantation to bring him back in ten four-line strophes, each with the refrain "Turn, magic wheel, and draw my Love to me," then utters a plaint to the moon in twelve five-line stanzas, each ending with "Bethink thee, Lady Moon, whence came my Love." *The Serenade* (#3; 54 lines) is of the type called *paraklausithyron,* or lament before a lover's locked door, and shows how absurd convention can become, for the lady lives in a doorless cave, and the lover has only to stride in. In *The Love of Cynisca* (#14; 170 lines) one speaker complains of being crossed in love, and the other suggests that he enlist in Ptolemy's army. In *The Cyclops* (#11; 81 lines) the poet offers a crossed lover consolation by telling of Polyphemus' love for Galatea. The apotheosis of

Heracles' beloved Hylas in *Hylas* (#13; 76 lines) shows the glory of love; *Epithalamium of Helen* (#18; 58 lines) and *How Heracles Slew the Lion* (#25; 281 lines) deal similarly with epic themes. These pieces are characteristically Alexandrian in their sophisticated detachment, on the one hand, and, on the other, in their concern for intimate genre details. They are, in fact, epyllia of the type which Callimachus favored.

Theocritus has a number of court poems in the Alexandrian manner. The fulsome *Panegyric of Ptolemy* (#17; 137 lines) is addressed to Ptolemy II Philadelphus, and makes play with his descent from Heracles. The story of the childhood of Heracles in *Little Heracles* (#24; 140 lines) probably had in mind the child who was to be Ptolemy III. *Hymn to the Dioscuri* (#22; 223 lines) celebrates the prowess of Castor and Pollux in the Alexandrian fashion. *The Distaff* (#28; 25 lines) in Aeolic was intended to accompany the gift of a carved ivory distaff to the wife of a friend. ##12, 29, and 30 are short love poems involving a relationship between men.

The best ancient mime we possess, and the most immediately appealing of all the work of Theocritus, is the *Adoniazusae* or *Women at the Adonis Festival* (#15; 149 lines). The stream of broad Doric chatter of these Syracusan ladies, with due attention to clothes, babies, polite and rude gentlemen, and fine needlework, as they prepare for their expedition, make their way through the festive and crowded streets of Alexandria, examine the elaborate display at the ceremony, and hear the emotional hymn, is a masterpiece in a humble style. Its most striking effect, perhaps, is its economy. So vivid a picture is given, not only of the character of the ladies, but of the gay turbulence of the streets and the emotional excitement at the service that one is amazed, on turning back to the text, to find that the whole thing is done in less than six pages.

The remaining pieces in the collection are thought to be by other hands but are nevertheless legitimate ancient examples of the class, and their titles may be listed: #19, *The Honey Stealer;* #20, *The Young Countryman;* #21, *The Fisherman;* #23, *The Lover;* and #26, *The Bacchanals.* Most of the twenty-four epigrams appear to be actual inscriptions on art works or graves, from which they were collected.

Whether his theme is rural or urban or heroic Theocritus always shows the perceptive eye of the poet. He has a sympathy for ordinary humanity based upon accurate psychological understanding, and if this is not altogether new, his equally sympathetic perceptions of the sights and sounds of nature are. It may be that this new attention to nature is a result of Cynic teaching; it may be that it is a sort of escapism from the refined elegance of the Alexandrian court, such as would appeal to the denizen of any great city today. It is true, especially in *Harvest Home,* that the rusticity has the spuriousness of a Queen Marie Antoinette masquerading as a milkmaid, or of a modern playwright who attempts to waft the bouquet of a hayfield over the footlights. Nevertheless, if the author of these poems is not a man who would choose to rise before dawn to do the chores in the barn when he could have room service, he has clearly seen and heard and smelled and felt the fields and animals and has not been repelled. The fault of the long succession of epigoni, beginning with Virgil's adaptations, whose denatured and beribboned rusticity has cloyed our taste for pastoral poetry, is that neither they nor their mouthpieces have ever got nearer to nature than the books of their predecessors. Plucked shepherds with lace cuffs have nothing to say of interest to anyone except powdered shepherdesses in hoops.

The first-century B.C. edition of the bucolics which contained Theocritus also contained Bion and Moschus, and these three have usually been printed together. None of the poems of Moschus (*fl.* 150 B.C.) is really bucolic, for the *Lament for Bion* was probably written by a pupil of Bion in imitation of Bion's own *Lament for Adonis. The Runaway Love* is an agreeable poem describing Aphrodite's search for Eros fled, and has been imitated by Ben Jonson. *Europa* is an epyllion of 166 lines, in the Callimachean manner of picturesque miniatures but in less involved language, telling how Europa dreamed she would be the object of a struggle between two continents, and describing the mythological pictures inlaid in her flower basket. There remain in the editions of Moschus three or four trifles and the longer *Megara,* of unknown authorship, which represents Heracles' wife talking to his mother, Alcmena, at Tiryns while the hero is absent on his labors.

There is really nothing to fix the date of Bion, the third of the bucolic poets. He probably lived in the second century B.C. Again, we have no real pastoral poetry from his hand. *Lament for Adonis,* familiar to English readers from the translation of Elizabeth Barrett Browning, is a fuller and richer treatment of the hymn at the end of Theocritus' *Adoniazusae;* it conveys an atmosphere of steamy emotion. The only other longer piece in the collection is the *Epithalamium of Achilles and Deidamia,* by another hand, which has the formal interest of being a unique bucolic treatment of a heroic theme.

Papyrus discoveries of texts of Menander or of Hyperides, of Bacchylides or of Aristotle's *Constitution of Athens* brought us works of whose existence we knew and of whose general nature we had some inkling. But of Herodes (also written Herondas, Herodas) there were only three or four unrevealing lines in Stobaeus, and the discovery of a remarkably well-preserved papyrus of his containing seven complete mimes and fragments of two others was a revelation. In a period of rebellion against the genteel tradition the discovery of so unmitigated a realist was hailed with enthusiasm, and Herodes pronounced the only true poet of the seamy side of life. From the point of view of form, at least, criticism is now less generous. Herodes' Loeb editor and translator, A. F. Knox, writes (p. xxii):

Where we might expect plain speech, we find a mass of literary allusions with difficulty woven into an unmetrical metre by the medium of an unreal, unstable and imaginary dialect. When Sappho wrote she turned the speech of those about her into poetry of beauty: when Herodes wrote he took the stuff of literature and converted it into a thing of ugliness.

Even if Herodes is not so bad a botcher as perfectionist criticism makes him, one point is significant for our appreciation of the mime in general, and that is that vulgar as the subject matter and coarse as the taste of the audience might be, the author nevertheless felt compelled to employ a remote and unreal dialect, a verse form dictated by canons of erudition, a mass of learned allusion, none of which he could comfortably handle. The mime, in other words, is still a *literary* form, and its conventions are so demanding as to preclude any but an initiated audience. On the other hand, for such an audience, as has been pointed out (by Headlam, on page x of his edition), Herodes' work exhibits the quality of a Dutch genre painting; it is characterized by "a small canvas, high finish, richness and precision of significant detail, and in subject the same predilection for the ugly and seamy side of life."

Herodes' date is fixed by an apparent allusion to Ptolemy Euergetes (246–222 B.C.) in his first mime, *The Bawd*. In this piece the go-between Gyllis calls upon Metriche and tries to persuade her to give up waiting for her lover Mandris, who must surely have been amusing himself in Alexandria these ten months, and bestow her favors on an upstanding young athlete named Gryllus. Metriche rejects the advances, but without being offended, and the two take a cup of wine together before Gyllis goes out to find Gryllus a more pliant beauty. Neither here nor in his other mimes does Herodes moralize or suggest indignation; his attitude, and the presumed attitude of his audience, is one of detached interest in the accuracy and skill of his representation. In the second mime, *Battarus,* a villainous brothel keeper of that name, is a plaintiff in court against Thales, a grain merchant, for having broken down the door of his establishment and abducted one of the inmates. Battarus employs all the tricks of the trial lawyer, and has even brought the abused but coy damsel to court to display to the jury. To Thales' advantage of respectability and of service to his city (Cos, as presumably in all the mimes) in importing grain in times of need, Battarus replies by declaring that the commodity he supplies is as necessary to the welfare of the city as Thales'. Lechery gives way to sadism in the third mime, *The Schoolmaster,* in which a mother brings her incorrigible son to be caned, and the schoolmaster complies willingly and bountifully. In the fourth mime, *Women Making Offerings at the Temple of Asclepius* (at Cos), two poor women, Cynno and Coccale, admire the statues and sculptures and the paintings of Apelles in the temple. The *Jealous Woman* of the fifth mime upbraids a slave for having neglected his duty as paramour. She orders him to be paraded and scourged, but at the end a slave girl begs him off. The subject of the *Chatting Women* of the sixth mime is an object manufactured by the cobbler Cerdon for the private delectation of ladies. In the seventh mime, *The Cobbler,* Cerdon himself is in his shop offering elegant footwear for sale to female clients. Mime 8, *The Dream,* is a monologue by Herodes himself, but the text is mutilated where we might get fuller information about the author; the ninth piece, entitled *Breaking Fast,* is even more mutilated.

Herodes' meter is the scazon, or limping iambic, a literary (for the tradition was certainly not continuous) reminiscence of the plain-spoken Hipponax, but like Theocritus' more dignified and far more competent hexameters, the lines were to be recited, not sung. From Aristoxenus of Tarentum, the disciple of Aristotle and authority on music, we learn (cited in Athenaeus 14, 620e) that there were two types of sung mime, *hilarody,* where the performers' costume and subject corresponded to tragedy, and *magody,* where they corresponded to comedy. A specimen of *hilarody* on a papyrus of the second century b.c. is the *Alexandrian Erotic Fragment* published by B. P. Grenfell (Oxford, 1896; reprinted in Crusius' *Herondas* and elsewhere). With great metrical virtuosity but in ordinary language a deserted hetaera laments before her lover's door and pleads to be taken back into his affections.

The moral indifference of these writers sometimes turned to something like actual ridicule of morality, and called forth a satirizing polemic from writers of a Cynic tendency. Athenaeus (13, 597) preserves a long fragment of the third book of the *Leontion* of Hermesianax of Colophon (born about 325 b.c.) in which the poet set out to teach his mistress, for whom the poem is named, that all the great men of the past had their love affairs; Homer loved Penelope; Hesiod, "Eoia," Socrates, Aspasia, and so on. Immoral flippancies of such a nature were combated, not only in the prose diatribes of itinerant Cynic preachers, but also in verse. More or less is known of five writers who used parody and satire for their moralizing. A few lines of Crates of Thebes, the disciple of Diogenes the Cynic, show that he used Homeric phrases for moralizing satire, as indeed Xenophanes had done in the sixth century. More caustic surely than the gentle Crates was Menippus of Gadara, who had the most enduring reputation of the five. It is only by this reputation that we know him: Lucian confesses his debt to him and calls him "a terrifying dog with a treacherous bite"; Marcus Aurelius says he is "a mocker of man's ephemeral existence"; and Varro calls his own (very fragmentary) satires "Menippean" after him. Menippus is not only the creator of the *spoudogeloion* type of literature—earnest jesting whose aim is *ridentem dicere verum*—but his intermingling of prose and poetry (a Semitic form which he may have learned in his birthplace) has a long progeny in European literature. Cercidas' *Meliambi* are another new contribution of the Oxyrhynchus papyri. Cercidas was a Cynic, but at the same time an intimate of Aratus of Sicyon, the leader of the Achaean League, who fought hard to suppress social revolution in the Peloponnese. In the longest of his fragments, according to the most likely interpretation, he satirizes the habits of the niggard and the spendthrift, questions divine providence, and warns the wealthy that unless they mend their ways they will be overtaken by revolution and compelled to disgorge. Phoenix of Colophon is another writer rescued by the papyri. It is doubtful whether the Cynic label attached to him is justified, but he did moralize on the failings of the rich and the undeserved sufferings of the poor. His scazons and his language are much smoother than Herodes'. In his philosophy Timon of Phlius was a Skeptic, but he was like the Cynics in his conspicuous indifference to normal manners and in his moralizing. He is credited (by Diogenes Laertius 9.110) with epics, satyric dramas, thirty comedies, sixty tragedies, obscene poems, and three books of *Silli*, besides his prose works. The *Silli*, "in which he abuses everyone and lampoons the dogmatic philosophers, using the form of parody," are for us the most significant and the source of our fragments. Homeric phrases and motifs are perverted to expose the shams and exaggerations of the pretentious philosophers. Unlike the writings of the true Cynics, the *Silli* cannot have addressed themselves to a popular audience, for they presuppose comprehensive knowledge of the history of philosophy. Timon's gibe at the Alexandrians (in Athenaeus 22*d*), that they were "well battened pedants quarreling endlessly in the fowl-coops of the Muses," might have applied as well, except on the score of dependence, to Timon himself.

Paraded erudition is characteristic of all the Alexandrian poets. If the erudition is sometimes tiresome in Theocritus, Apollonius, and Callimachus, yet their real merits entitle them to be styled poets. Learning unilluminated by excitement or insight is the characteristic of the group of long poems we now have to examine. In the earliest times verse had been used before prose, by Hesiod, Xenophanes, Empedocles, and Parmenides, to convey factual knowledge. Aristotle, in the first chapter of *Poetics* (1447*b*), distinguished between scientific versifiers and poets:

Even if a theory of medicine or physical philosophy be put forth in a metrical form, it is usual to describe the writer as a poet; Homer and Empedocles, however, have really nothing in common apart from their meter; so that if the one is to be called a poet, the other should be termed a physicist rather than a poet.

Modern taste can only agree with Aristotle's distinction, but Hellenistic taste did not. Both medicine and natural science were presented in verse, and to the hearty applause of ancient critics. Aratus of Soli (whence *solecisms* derive) in Cilicia, a contemporary of Callimachus, a pupil of Zeno, and a protégé of King Antigonus Gonatas of Macedonia, wrote *Phaenomena* in 1,154 lines on astronomy, knowing little of the subject but taking his material from the fourth-century astronomer Eudoxus, and was praised extravagantly in epigrams of Callimachus (28, *Greek Anthology* 9.507), and Leonidas of Tarentum (*Greek Anthology* 9.25), was quoted by St. Paul (*Acts* 17.28), had his picture put on the coins of his native city, was translated into Latin by Cicero, Varro, Germanicus, and Avienus, and was read in the Middle Ages when Homer was forgotten. The first two thirds of *Phaenomena* describe the heavens and the last third, weather signs. The language is simple and intelligible, and only occasionally is one of the countless opportunities for introducing mythological material used. The purpose of the book may have been in part to provide an agreeable presentation of a useful and fashionable subject, and in part to demonstrate Stoic doctrine. The exordium (1–6) echoes the magnificent Hymn of Cleanthes:

From Zeus let us begin; him do we mortals never leave unnamed; full of Zeus are all the streets and all the marketplaces of men; full is the sea and the havens thereof; always we all have need of Zeus. For we are also his offspring; and he in his kindness unto men giveth favorable signs and wakeneth the people to work, reminding them of livelihood.

—A. W. Mair

On the medical side we have two of the many didactic works of Nicander of Colophon (second century B.C.) : *Theriaca* on remedies for bites of noxious animals, and *Alexipharmaca* on remedies for other poisons, each in something under a thousand hexameters. To his distasteful subject, of which he knows little, Nicander brings on obscure, affected, and tedious style. The law of the survival of the fittest is sometimes a dead letter. These specimens are particularly regrettable, because the most resounding successes of the Hellenistic age were in the exact sciences; only in modern times has Greek work of the period been equaled.

To such a degree was poetry the medium for belles-lettres in the Alexandrian age that popularizations of scientific subjects, like Aratus' or Nicander's, were written in verse. Practically all the prose that was written was on scientific subjects, and though such things do not normally fall within the province of a history of literature, mention must be made of writers who contributed significantly to knowledge or whose works became Europe's textbooks. The Peripatetics had given an impulse to investigation in the exact sciences; what is characteristic of Hellenistic work is its complete separation from philosophy and its independent pursuit of separate disciplines. The Alexandrians' greatest lack, from the modern point of view, is in chemistry and physics, though rudimentary work was done in both. Their greatest achievement was in mathematics and related sciences, for which a foundation had been laid by the followers of Pythagoras, Plato, and Epicurus. The best known name in mathematics, because his *Elements* (of geometry) has probably been the most widely studied book in Western civilization next to the Bible, is Euclid, who lived early in the third century B.C. Besides *Elements*, another mathematical work of Euclid is extant—*Data*—and we have knowledge of others on *Divisions* (extant in Arabic), *Conic Sections, Porisms, Fallacies. Optics* dealt with perspective, *Phaenomena* with astronomy, and *Divisions of the Monochord* with music. Euclid depended largely on the work of others.

Archimedes, killed in the capture of Syracuse by the Romans in 212 B.C., contrived mechanical devices involving pulley and screw, and his earliest work, *On Mechanical Theorems,* was on applied mathematics. But he was interested in pure mathematics also, and his extant works include *On Sphere and Cylinder, On Conoidal and Spheroidal Figures, The Sand Reckoner* (on handling large numbers), *Spirals, Equilibriums, Floating Bodies,* and fragments of others. Among other authorities on mechanics mention may be made of Heron of Alexandria (first century B.C.), whose works fill four Teubner volumes. The most interesting is *Pneumatica,* which describes many ingenious inventions and toys, water organs, fountains, puppet theaters, slot machines. Heron had some rudimentary knowledge of the use of steam.

In astronomy Aristarchus of Samos (310–230 B.C.) deserves mention for suggesting that the sun and not the earth is the center of our system. As in Copernicus' day, objection was made on religious grounds, this time by the Stoic Cleanthes. All that remains of Aristarchus' works is a little treatise *On the Sizes and Distances of the Sun and Moon,* which is written from the geocentric, not heliocentric, point of view. Hipparchus of Nicaea (second century B.C.) used Babylonian material and described the precession of the equinoxes. Finally, mention must be made of Claudius Ptolemy (second century A.D.) whose *System of Mathematics* (known from the title of its Arabic translation as *Almagest*) in the thirteen sizable books with tables and diagrams held the field until Copernicus and Galileo.

In medicine the loss of the works of Herophilus of Chalcedon and Erasistratus of Antioch, both of whom worked in Alexandria in the early third century B.C., is especially deplorable. They distinguished motor and sensory nerves, and knew that arteries carried blood (not air) and pulsed from the heart. The Roman medical encyclopedist Celsus (under Augustus) says they studied from vivisections on criminals supplied by Ptolemy I. Galen, who came to Rome from Pergamum in A.D. 161, was a distinguished practitioner as well as student and author. His extant works fill twenty volumes and cover all branches of the medical art. Of the herbalists we have the *Materia Medica* of Dioscorides (first century A.D.) which describes some six hundred plants in five books. Dreams have again become a respectable object of study, and mention may be made of the *Onirocritica* of Artemidorus (second century A.D.) on the interpretation of dreams. This book, of some three hundred pages, is filled with good stories and enjoyed a wide and long vogue when it was translated into modern languages in the sixteenth century—and not wholly for its good stories.

The writers just mentioned are far outside the chronological limits of this chapter. In the chapter which follows it will be convenient to violate chronology even more drastically, for the poets of the *Anthology*, which covers the whole period, can best be dealt with continuously, and work outside the *Anthology* may therefore be included in the chapter to bring the tale of ancient Greek poetry to its end.

Chapter 14. POETRY TO THE END OF ANTIQUITY

TO DESIRE A PERMANENT RECORD OF A PHENOMENON OR EXPERIENCE IS NORMAL. In the realm of material phenomena such record was provided, before the invention of photography, by the plastic arts. With good photography available anyone who insists on oil painting by that fact proclaims that he is a person of special tastes with special requirements. Anyone who insists on reading or expressing himself in verse when prose has become the common medium for literary record similarly proclaims that he is a person of uncommon tastes and requirements. In the Alexandrian age, makers and consumers of poetry were so special a class that they seem intentionally to have erected a hedge about themselves to exclude the uninitiate. So important was the distinction conferred by verse that works of knowledge as well as of imagination were presented in that form. No one with literary pretensions could write other than poetry. But by the second century B.C., as we know from the history of the romance, imaginative works of large scope were written in prose, and verse becomes more esoteric than ever. From the Alexandrian age to the close of antiquity (the period which for convenience and in defiance of chronology will be dealt with in this chapter) all poetry is of the character of tours de force. Longer works, those of Quintus, Nonnus, Colluthus, Tryphiodorus, and Musaeus, deal with tales out of a remote heroic age. Authors like Oppian make a cultured display of wit and curious information. The functional epigram is expanded to include other vignettes which can be polished into a lapidary form. It is in this form that subjective lyric, whose fountains never run completely dry, finds expression, and in our summary survey of half a millennium of verse we turn first to the major collection of epigrams.

The *Greek Anthology* (not to be confused with modern anthologies of Greek poetry) is a collection of some four thousand short poems arranged in fifteen books according to subject matter by Constantine Cephalas, a Byzantine scholar of the tenth century A.D. Early in the fourteenth century this work was abridged, chiefly on moral principles, by

Maximus Planudes, a theologian and diplomat, and the original disappeared from view. In 1606 the youthful Saumaise (Salmasius, who became John Milton's fierce opponent) discovered the real *Anthology* in the library of the Count Palatine at Heidelberg (whence its name, *Palatine Anthology*). The manuscript went as booty to Rome in 1623 and then to Paris in 1797; at the end of the Napoleonic wars it was returned to Heidelberg. Modern editions of the *Anthology* include the fifteen books of Cephalas plus a sixteenth which contains such material as appears in Planudes but not in Cephalas.

In time, the *Anthology* ranges over almost fifteen hundred years, from the epigrams of Simonides on the Persian war; the ancient, chiefly Hellenistic, and the best material is concentrated in the fifth book, which deals with love, and the seventh, which contains the sepulchral inscriptions. The contents of the books, which are very uneven in size, is as follows: Book 1, prefaced by the note, "Let the pious and godly Christian Epigrams take precedence even if the pagans are displeased," contains 123 actual inscriptions, of indifferent merit, from Byzantine churches and their art objects dating earlier than A.D. 1000. Book 2 is a bombastic hexameter description by Christodorus of Thebes (in Egypt) of the bronze statues in a gymnasium at Byzantium in the early sixth century. Book 3 contains nineteen short epigrams on the sculptures at Cyzicus in the second century B.C. Book 4 contains the proems of collections embedded in the *Anthology:* those of Meleager of Gadara, a Hellenized Syrian poet (beginning of the first century B.C.) whose *Garland* was the first collection; Philip of Thessalonica, who made his *Garland* probably under Augustus; and Agathias, whose *Cycle* or ring was put together under Justinian (A.D. 527–565). The 309 amatory epigrams of Book 5 include the best work of its kind in Greek by some fifty authors taken from the collections named. Book 6 contains 358 dedicatory epigrams on a great variety of subjects and from a variety of sources; there is excellent ancient work here also. The 748 sepulchral epigrams, genuine or fictive, of Book 7 include the work of Simonides, Plato, and other first-rate writers. The 254 epigrams of St. Gregory (fourth century A.D., friend and peer of Basil and Chrysostom) presented in Book 8 were not part of Cephalas' collection but were included in the Palatine manuscript because of their sepulchral form. Book 9, with 827 declamatory and descriptive epigrams, is the longest and most uneven, containing very good and very poor rhetorical epigrams. Book 10 contains 126 hortatory and admonitory epigrams; Book 11 has 442 convivial and satirical epigrams, the nearest approach to the witty type of which the Roman Martial is the great master. Book 12 has a separate title: *Musa Paedica* (or *Puerilis*) of Strato (under Hadrian), and is devoted to pederasty; among its 258 pieces some passionate poems of normal love have been included by mistake. Book 13 contains thirty-one epigrams in various meters, some merely tours de force; Book 14 has 150 arithmetical problems, riddles, oracles. Book 15, entitled *Miscellanea,* has fifty-one pieces, including enigmas and figure poems, i. e., poems whose lines are so arranged as to present the appearance of an altar, an ax, a musical instrument, or the like. The Planudean Appendix (388 numbers) includes epigrams on a variety of subjects which were not included in the Palatine manuscript.

An epigram, in the original meaning of the word, is a verse inscription on hard material, gravestones or offerings, usually composed for pay by a professional poet. The conciseness and finish of the lapidary style then came to be used for expressions of similar sentiment where there was no thought of an actual inscription. Tributes to the glorious or beloved dead could take this form; indeed, composition of epitaphs for the famous dead became a kind of parlor game—hence the multiple epitaphs on a single subject found in the *Anthology*. But the lapidary style is also appropriate for other themes—love, moral observations, witty repartee —and so the epigram became a literary species. The tastes and talents of the Hellenistic age found that form particularly congenial, and some of the most appealing productions of that age are the epigrams.

Callimachus' epigrams (included in the *Anthology,* as is the work of all the poets mentioned in this chapter) have been mentioned above. Asclepiades of Samos, acclaimed under the name Sikelidas as master by Theocritus in *Harvest Home* (#7) and therefore probably an older contemporary, is represented by some forty pieces, none, curiously, in the meter which he invented and which is used so effectively by Horace. But he also invented, or has chronological primacy for us, in the short and graceful love poem. If the ladies are professional lights of love, yet their feelings as well as their beauty are understood. The poetry of love, as it appears in Asclepiades and his fellows of the *Anthology,* in *Argonautica,* in the *Erotic Fragment,* and in other Hellenistic works, may be another manifestation of concern with the individual which we noticed in the Hellenistic philosophies and which may be noticed in the new realism in sculptured portraits. Asclepiades is also represented by a number of sprightly convivial pieces, and by some pseudo-epitaphs, though he doubtless wrote real ones for pay. That to the poetess Erinna, who died at nineteen, reads more like an inscription for her book than for her grave. There is a real elegiac tone in 12.46, which starts:

> Not two and twenty, yet I tire
> Of Life and all its woe.

Closely associated with Asclepiades, first in the literary group assembled by Duris, the ruler of Samos, and then at the court of Ptolemy, were

Poseidippus of Cnidos and Hedylus of Athens. The three are linked together in Meleager's proem (4.1.45 f.) and probably published jointly; a work called *Soros* ("Heap"), was probably their joint effort. Their work is of the same general nature as Asclepiades' but inferior in spirit and grace.

Leonidas of Tarentum, born about 325 B.C. and probably the Lycidas of Theocritus' *Harvest Home,* is represented by 118 pieces, of which twenty belong to an inferior namesake. He wrote patriotic poems for the Epirot King Neoptolemus and his murderer and successor, Pyrrhus, and when Pyrrhus was defeated by the Romans, Leonidas led the life of a hungry scholar poet in the eastern Mediterranean. He wrote sepulchral inscriptions for poets ancient and modern, but his most appealing things are a series of epigrams on fishermen and other humble folk in which the tools and activities of workaday life are elevated into poetry. The kinship with Theocritus is patent. The gentle and resigned pathos of a humble life is summed up in an elegy, probably to be inscribed under the figure of a skeleton (7.472):

O man, infinite was the time ere thou camest to the light, and infinite will be the time to come in Hades. What is the portion of life that remains to thee but a pin-prick, or if there be aught tinier than a pin-prick? A little life and a sorrowful is thine; for even that little is not sweet, but more odious than death the enemy. . . . Enquire of thyself at the dawn of every day, O man, what thy strength is and learn to lie low, content with a simple life . . .

—W. R. Paton

A number of women poets are represented in the *Anthology.* Sappho is there with two epigrams, but such poetesses as Telesilla of Argos, Praxilla of Sicyon, Cleobuline of Lindus, Corinna and Myrtis of Thebes, and Erinna are passed over, and fullest representation (twenty epigrams) is given to Anyte of Tegea, whose *floruit* falls at the end of the fourth century B.C. There are epigrams for the tombs of young girls, and statues, but also for a horse, a grasshopper, a dolphin, and a cock; the latter must have been for a cenotaph, for the cock was devoured by a fox. There are two pieces on goats. But Anyte (unlike the authors of the later ingenious animal pieces) seems really to like the beasts and certainly likes the countryside, as she shows in her poems on Pan. Anyte is linked by Meleager with another poetess, Moero of Byzantium, of whom we have two good pieces. Nossis compares herself to Sappho (6.718), but the passionate poems suggested by Meleager's reference to "her tablet's wax melted by love's flame" must have been purged. The eleven poems we have are chiefly dedications, the best being on the fourth-century comic poet Rhinthon (7.414).

Dioscorides, who lived in Alexandria under Ptolemy Euergetes, is amply represented (forty epigrams) by outspoken erotic pieces, some in the

Musa Puerilis, by epigrams on ancient and modern poets, and by learned defenses, such as that of Lycambes' daughter (who was four centuries dead) against the attacks of Archilochus. Alcaeus of Messene, like his greater namesake of Lesbos, dealt with politics. In his epigrams he first glorified and then reviled Philip V of Macedonia, the opponent of Flamininus in 197 B.C.

The founder of Stoicism and many of its leading teachers who introduced into the Hellenistic world a philosophy based on religion came from the Semitic East. The Gadarene Menippus naturalized the oriental form called *maqama,* humorous causeries interspersed with verse for conveying earnest comment on men and life. Menippus' follow townsman Meleager introduced a new note in Greek poetry with sensual verses filled with the color and smell of flowers and with the bittersweet fragrance of love which is aware of the conflicting claims of body and spirit. Meleager is the best of the Syrians in the *Anthology,* of whom the earliest is Antipater of Sidon, who lived at Rome at the end of the second century B.C. and is hence a bridge from Callimachus to Catullus. Antipater's subjects are chiefly literary, though the other conventional themes are represented; among the pieces addressed to great poets of the past that on Ibycus (7.745) is the earliest treatment of the story of the cranes. Antipater is also believed to be the compiler of the collection called *Anacreontics.* When Antipater returned to Syria in 102 his place at Rome was taken by Archias of Antioch, whose citizenship Cicero defended; Archias has only two epigrams in the *Anthology.* A more tangible influence on the Latins was exerted by the Epicurean philosopher and poet, Philodemus of Gadara. Twice quoted by Horace, he was possibly a teacher of Virgil, and certainly a model for Ovid. The charred remains of his philosophical works recovered from the library of his patron (and Julius Caesar's father-in-law), Calpurnius Piso, at Herculaneum deal with rhetoric, poetics, logic, and music and are disappointing. It is something of a shock to find the dull professor also the author of luscious and lascivious titbits in the *Anthology,* though Cicero, who respects his scholarship, also alludes to the wantonness of his verses.

The voice of Philodemus' contemporary and fellow townsman Meleager is one of the sweetest and most memorable in the *Anthology.* His numerous poems (Meleager is second to Palladas in number; Antipater is third), particularly 7.417, tell us a good deal of his history, at least the history of his heart. The attachments to his fellow students at Gadara, celebrated in the *Musa Puerilis* (Book 12), were written before he went to Tyre, where he loved and wrote of a series of ladies, for one of whom —Heliodora—his passion was true and tender even by rigorous standards.

It was her death, probably, that drove him to Cos, where he spent his old age writing and putting together the *Garland* which is the basis of our *Anthology*. Even in his criticism he makes the language of flowers a short cut to heart and head; nothing could be more concise and eloquent than to symbolize Callimachus with myrtle, Anacreon with honeysuckle, Archilochus with thorn, or Sappho with the red rose.

Another contemporary Syrian who was not himself a poet but the cause of poetry in others may here be mentioned. Parthenius was brought to Rome as a prisoner and became a teacher of poets. Among his pupils were Virgil and Cornelius Gallus, who ranked with the greatest of Roman poets but whose works perished. To Gallus, Parthenius dedicated his *Love Romances,* a collection of thirty-six short love stories from unfamiliar sources baldly told for use by poets as bases for elegies. We have no specimens of Roman elegies based on these tales. The best epigrammatist in the *Garland* which Philip of Thessalonica put together under Augustus is Crinagoras, who was the "official" Greek poet as Horace was the Latin, and whose pieces are on much the same subjects as Horace's. Marcus Argentarius is also Horatian in mood. Among the satirists in Book 11 Lucilius and Nicarchus are most amply represented; they and Ammianus, Leonidas, Automedon, and Apollinides foreshadow but are inferior to Martial. The Rufinus of the *Musa Puerilis* probably lived under Trajan; his single-minded grossness must be objectionable to the least squeamish.

The extremely scanty output of Greek poetry in the period of the Roman Empire was augmented in the Byzantine period by several considerable works. These and the remaining writers of verse will be briefly discussed here to complete the tale of Greek poets before we turn back to the prose writers of the Roman period. The largest number of epigrams in the *Anthology* is credited to Palladas, a schoolmaster who lived in Alexandria about A.D. 400. Palladas is revealed in his poems as a man with a grim humor, embittered by disappointments in life, not the least of which was the victory of Christianity. Professor F. A. Wright aptly compares him to Jonathan Swift. Besides his love poems, filled with sophisticated verve and anatomical detail, which appear in Book 5 of the *Anthology,* Paul the Silentiary (the function of a silentiary was to procure silence at court ceremonies) wrote three long poems: *Santa Sophia,* in about a thousand lines, giving a brilliant description of the church and its ornaments, for recitation, at Justinian's command, at the second consecration on December 24, 563; *Ambo* (Pulpit), a description in some three hundred lines of the pulpit in Santa Sophia; and *Pythian Baths,* for the Empress Theodora, of whose elaborate train Paul was a part when she went to take the cure at the warm baths in Bithynia. In his roles both as dandified amorist and art connoisseur Paul was an artist, and he succeeds in conveying his relish to his readers. Paul's son-in-law Agathias was a lawyer and historian (five books of his in continuation of Procopius are extant), but he was also a voluminous poet and the compiler of the *Cycle* from which Cephalas made the *Anthology*. Counting by lines, Agathias himself is the best represented poet in the *Anthology;* his smooth and witty verses deal with the course of his own courtship, landscapes, literature, and many other things. Like Palladas and Paul, Agathias asks no indulgence for his date of a modern reader; his sophistication, in fact, is usually several degrees ahead of his modern reader. Besides his own and Paul's work Agathias included in his *Cycle* the work of two other officials, Macedonius the Consul and Leontius. Macedonius has fifty pieces, including some very good amatory verses, and Leontius half as many less good occasional pieces, and with these we close our view of the *Anthology*.

Of Greek poetry other than epigrams produced in the period of the Roman Empire we have to mention only the *Mythiambi Aesopei* or the *Fables* of Babrius and the *Halieutica* and *Cynegetica* of the Oppians. Babrius (second century A.D.), a Roman, judging by his name, presents "Aesop's" fables, in Greek choliambics with neatness and precision. The principal manuscript, discovered on Mount Athos in 1840, contains 122 fables arranged alphabetically in two books; the manuscript breaks off at the letter *o,* and eighteen fables from other sources, some whose Babrian authorship is dubious, have been added. The peculiarity of the meter is that it begins to show regard for pitch (as well as quantitative) accent, of the matter, that in addition to familiar "Aesopic" fables others like the "Lying Arab" and the "Ass of the Priest of Cybele" are included. The curriculum of the rhetorical schools regularly began with fables, and those of Babrius enjoyed great popularity in succeeding centuries.

Three hexameter poems, on hunting, fishing, and fowling, were ascribed to Oppian, but the problem of authorship is complicated, for *Halieutica,* on fishing, far the best as poetry and as natural science, is dedicated to Marcus Aurelius (A.D. 161–180); and the inferior *Cynegetica,* on hunting, to Caracalla (A.D. 211–217), who is said to have presented Oppian with a gold piece for every line he wrote. It looks as if a second Oppian, probably a Syrian, had followed up the work of the first. *Ixeutica,* on fowling (known only through a prose paraphrase), was ascribed to Oppian apparently only because its subject forms a natural third to the other two. *Halieutica* (five books) is written with much verve and scientific knowledge and presents with considerable wit curious information (some of it true) on the manners and morals of a great variety of fish and the methods of catching them. The author of *Cynegetica* (four books) is obviously less well founded in zoology than in wit, though his prescriptions on techniques seem sound enough to a scholar whose hunting is confined to houseflies. The competent scientist of the *Halieutica* whose descriptions of fish have been praised by ichthyologists would hardly have recorded with a straight face the old story that giraffes and ostriches are hybrids of the camel with the pard and the sparrow.

Disciples of Izaak Walton in particular and lovers of the curious in general may find *Halieutica* interesting; everyone (for of course everyone knows Homer) will find the fourteen books of the *Posthomerica* of Quintus of Smyrna interesting. What after all *did* happen after Hector was bewailed at the end of *Iliad?* This long poem tells us, and very well if what we want is a surface story with a dash of pathos but no true drama and no searching of soul. Whenever, as he frequently does, Quintus parallels an incident in Homer, whom he certainly, or in Virgil, whom he possibly, used, he regularly misses what is for us its chief excellence and flattens out his story. His characters possess all the virtues but none of the weaknesses that Homer (or the tragedians) give them, and the result is the anemic plaster perfection of story-book heroes. The story opens just where *Iliad* closes. In Book 1 the Amazon Penthesilea comes to help the Trojans and is killed in battle by Achilles. When Achilles lifts her visor he is smitten by her beauty and regrets her death, whereupon he is reviled for his weakness by Thersites. He kills Thersites, with the approval of all except Diomedes, who is a kinsman of Thersites. In Book 2 black Memnon, who has come to help the Trojans, is killed by Achilles, who is himself killed by Apollo (without Paris' help) in Book 3 and mourned by funeral games in Book 4. When his weapons, which are fully described, are assigned to Odysseus in Book 5, Ajax goes mad. Eurypylus, the grandson of Heracles, comes to help the Trojans in Book 6, and Achilles' son Neoptolemus from Scyros to help the Greeks in Book 7; in Book 8 Neoptolemus kills Eurypylus. In Book 9 Philoctetes is deserted on Lemnos. In Book 10 Paris, fatally wounded, makes his stumbling way to his first love, Oenone, who alone can help him; Oenone refuses, but when he dies she commits suttee on his funeral pyre. The Trojans fight their last battle from their walls in Book 11, the Greeks using a Roman *testudo* (358 ff.). Book 12 has Sinon, Laocoön, and the wooden horse; and in Book 13 Troy is taken and sacked, Aeneas being preserved to found the city on the Tiber. Book 14 tells how the victors sailed home and how they were tossed about by storms on the way.

If Homer is the ideal from which no deviations may be made, Quintus must be pronounced more Homeric than Apollonius, and indeed he retains a reflection of the Homeric spirit. To the modern reader the most noticeable difference is a heightened sentimentality, especially where women are involved, as in the deaths of Penthesilea and Oenone. But they too are Homeric in their timelessness, and Quintus has none of the reflections of contemporary life that *Argonautica* shows, none of Apollonius' originality. On the other hand, Quintus is free alike of the far-fetched erudition of the older Alexandrians and of the curled turgidity of the newer Egyptian school as represented by Nonnus. Indeed, *Posthomerica* is so free of mannerisms that it might have been written by any enthusiast of heroic poetry who mastered the language and meter, and only slight indications suggest the fourth century A.D. as a probable date. It is now fairly certain that Quintus used the Cyclic poets, and perhaps even preferred them to Homer, which might explain certain slight deviations from the Homeric tradition. Older writers (John Milton, for example) call our author "the Calabrian," because the manuscript (now lost) from which our texts derive was discovered in Calabria; he is now called the Smyrnaean because in an invocation to the Muse (12.310) copied from Hesiod (*Theogony* 22 ff.) he speaks of having pastured sheep in Smyrna (some use this passage to make him a Christian bishop) before his cheek was bearded.

The Hellenic restraint of Quintus contrasts pleasingly with the lush preciosity of Nonnus (fifth century A.D.), whose *Dionysica* in forty-eight books is as prodigious in language as it is in size. All that we know of the author is an anonymous epigram (*Greek Anthology* 9.198): "I am Nonnus; my native city was Panoplis [the Greek name for Egyptian Chemmis], but in Alexandria I mowed down by my vocal sword the children of the giants." The giants are the sons of Typhoeus with whom Dionysus fought. The subject of the poem is the career of Dionysus, and principally in his role of conqueror of the East, in which he had been vaguely assimilated to Alexander the Great. At 25.8 Nonnus declares that like Homer he will sing only the last year of the warfare, but he had required eight books to arrive at the birth of Dionysus, beginning with the rape of Europa, to explain Cadmus' interest. No bit of mythology that can be brought into the story is omitted, and so a story that might have had a well-constructed plot crumbles apart in digressions. The tales thus strung together are suggestive of Ovid in the *Metamorphoses,* and indeed Nonnus has something of Ovid's agile fertility. But aside from Ovid's infinitely greater deftness in making his transitions and unifying his diverse materials into a harmonious whole, there is a significant difference in the quality of disbelief which each author displays. Neither believed in the Olympians. Nonnus was presumably a Christian, and put the Fourth Gospel in the same hexameters he uses in *Dionysiaca,* while

Ovid, as far as we can see, believed in nothing. The gods for him are fit subjects for charming stories, which he tells with an urbane wit for the pleasure of witty people. Nonnus writes as if he believed the stories and expected his readers to believe them—but he doesn't, and that fact gives the *Dionysiaca* a curious unreality which is totally absent, not only from *Iliad,* but even from *Ramayana* and *Mahabharata,* which have more fantastic exaggerations than even Nonnus indulges in. The feeling that the book is "mere" literature is enhanced by the curiously wrought language with its novel epithets and a metrical scheme so strict that even Callimachus is licentious by comparison. A notion of Nonnus' Oriental exuberance, stylized preciosity, allusiveness, may be had from W. H. D. Rouse's very skillful version. At the opening of the fourteenth book Rhea musters the ranks of heaven for the Indian war:

Then swiftshoe Rhea haltered the hairy necks of her lions beside their highland manger. She lifted her wingfaring foot to run with the breezes, and paddled with her shoes through the airy spaces. So like a wing or a thought [a Homeric tag] she traversed the firmament to south, to north, to west, to the turning-place of dawn, gathering the divine battalions for Lyaeus: one all-comprehending summons was sounded for trees and for rivers, one call for Naiads and Hadryads, the troop of the forest. All the divine generations heard the summons of Cybele, and they came together from all sides. From high heaven to the Lydian land Rhea passed aloft with unerring foot, and returning again lifted the mystic torch in the night, warming the air a second time with Mygdonian fire. Now once more, ye breaths of Phoebus, after the tale of mortal heroes and warriors teach me also the host divine!

—W. H. D. Rouse

This goes on for twice the length of *Iliad,* yet the action is vigorous and the pictures telling; and a reader who finds "mere" literature satisfying will find that *Dionysiaca* will hold his interest.

The influence of Nonnus is apparent in two other Egyptian Greek writers of hexameter. Tryphiodorus (fifth century A.D.) is credited with a number of epic compositions, of which only *The Taking of Troy* (691 lines) is extant. This epyllion tells the story of the building of the wooden horse and its introduction into Troy by the stratagem of Sinon, with some minor variations of the version of *Aeneid* 2 and Quintus Smyrnaeus 12. Laocoön does not appear, but Cassandra utters a doleful though futile prophecy of the outcome. The sack is described in gory detail, and the poem closes with the sacrifice of Polyxena at the tomb of Achilles. The style is not remarkable, although we do have such strained pictures as Athena "smearing a man's voice with honied nectar" when she masquerades as a herald to counsel Odysseus.

Colluthus too is credited with a list of epics, among which the extant *Rape of Helen* (394 lines) does not appear. There is the familiar apple of discord and judgment of Paris (who is bidden to fling his milk pail away). When Cassandra sees Helen coming she tears her hair, but "Troy received her returning citizen who was the beginning of her trouble." An effective new detail is the childish distress of Hermione when she awakes in the morning to find that her mother, who had been in her bed, was gone.

Immeasurably more attractive is "the last rose of the fading garden of Greek poesy," the *Hero and Leander* of Musaeus (340 lines). Nothing from the Greek is more familiar to European readers than this tale of a lover who swam the Hellespont guided by the light of his beloved, until a storm extinguished the light and Leander's life and Hero flung herself to death on his corpse. In English the expanded version of Christopher Marlowe, finished by George Chapman, is the first of many translations; in Germany, Grillparzer made a tragedy of the story and Schiller, a ballad. Virgil had outlined the story in six lines of the *Georgics* (3.258 ff.), and Ovid wrote an imaginary letter for Hero to send to Leander (*Heroides* 19); but it is Musaeus who gives the complete story, and no one has written it with more grace and delicacy. Renaissance scholars, including the great Julius Caesar Scaliger himself, thought the author was the ancient seer who came long before Homer, and that his poem was superior to Homer's. We can see now that he must have come after Nonnus, and since his poem was known to Agathias (*Greek Anthology* 5.263) his date is probably about mid-sixth century.

Quite without indication of date but probably later than Nonnus are poems in the collection called *Orphica*. The two longest are *Lithica* and *Argonautica,* about a thousand and fourteen hundred lines respectively. In *Lithica* (which has no trace of Orphism), Theodamas, a son of Priam, recounts the virtues of precious stones to the author as they go to assist at a sacrifice to the sun. *Argonautica* is an inferior reworking of Apollonius Rhodius, with all the drama and the love interest left out and the part of Orpheus, especially in sacrifice and prayer, made prominent. The most lively section is the account of the taking of the Golden Fleece (890–1022). German romantics of the early nineteenth century valued the *Orphica* highly.

Poetry continued to be written and studied in Greek lands, but after the sixth century there was submergence which to the casual eye looks like total extinction. In any case, even when Greek poetry with a valid claim for general attention comes to be written it is no longer in the main stream of European literary production, of which the center of gravity was shifted to the West.

Chapter 15. HISTORY, TRAVEL, CRITICISM IN THE ROMAN PERIOD

JUST AS THE ELEGANT PROSE OF ISOCRATES AND THE WRITERS OF THE FIRST Sophistic was accepted as a proper substitute for poetry in the fourth century B.C. so in the first centuries of our era poetry was supplanted as the accepted medium for belles lettres by the ornate prose introduced by the writers of the Second Sophistic and their forerunners. But before the Second Sophistic subjected Greek prose to its archaizing refinements, its utilitarian virtues were employed for a series of earnest and useful works. In the centuries after Alexander poetry, for all but its makers and its special audience, was frankly an ornamental decoration to life, with little relevance to life's substance. Prose was the medium for all that was utilitarian, intellectually or spiritually, whether for setting forth the results of investigation in mathematics or astronomy or medicine, in music or literature, in history or geography, or for providing earnest guidance for the lives of men.

In the pure sciences where modern knowledge has outstripped ancient the only function of the great body of Hellenistic and Roman writings for us is to record the stages of past progress, and in such a survey as this we need only state the fact that great strides were indeed made. In other fields, where scholarship is expected to clothe itself in artistic form and where for actual facts and their interpretation contemporary accounts are directly useful, we may still go to the ancients for information artistically presented. In this category fall those writers who deal with history and geography and literary criticism, and those among them who possess special distinction merit notice. The problem of man himself and what he must do to be saved is perennially in the category of unfinished business; significant thought is timeless in its relevance, and works which record it must naturally be considered. In a word, then, whereas through the period of Demosthenes and Aristotle and for the poetry of the Alexandrian age itself the attempt has been made to touch however briefly on every work of which sufficient remains survive to make it meaningful, the pages to follow are selective; the curious may turn to the second part of Schmid-Staehlin, to Susemihl, and to other works of erudition for the names of the hundreds of writers who must be omitted here.

From the second century B.C., when Rome ceased to fight Greece and began to patronize it, until the second century A.D., when significant Roman works came to be written in Greek, the Greek writers who demand general attention (excepting, of course, the documents of Christianity) are only a handful: Polybius, who as a philosophical historian ranks next to Thucydides; Marcus Aurelius, whose *To Himself* is among the spiritual treasures of mankind; Plutarch, who summarizes and explains antiquity with learning and with charm; and Lucian, whose dialogues are pure wit, unsurpassed in their kind. During these centuries Latin writers hold pre-eminence; but it must be noted that Latin civilization, and particularly Latin literature, is not an entirely independent realm but culturally a province of Greece. Much, perhaps most, that is valuable in Catullus, Virgil, Horace, Ovid, Tibullus, and Propertius, in Sallust and Cicero and Seneca, is the specifically Roman quality, but these writers are none the less directly in the Greek literary tradition, and what is specifically Roman may be looked upon, in a larger sense, as local provincial variation. What besides language and local allusions, in a writer like Lucretius, is not in the main stream of Greek letters? In work of the first rank Latin writers are superior to the Greeks of this period, in quality and in quantity. Not only are the Roman poets without peer among contemporary Greeks, but there is no Greek historian, after Polybius, to set beside Livy and Tacitus, no orator or essayist to set beside Cicero. But in ranks below the first, in history, geography, encyclopedic compendia, it is significant that the Greeks are generally superior in scope and merit.

It will be convenient to deal with these writers by broad categories, at the expense of chronological consistency: historians, geographers, critics, and the like in the present chapter; the literature of philosophy and religion in the chapter following; the writers of the Second Sophistic in another chapter; and Lucian and the writers of romance in the final chapter. The category which first comes to attention and is most amply represented is history. We have seen above how the conquests of Alexander expanded the boundaries of historical curiosity; now the spread of Roman power made knowledge of remote peoples, and in particular of Rome itself, no longer a luxury for the curious but a necessity for all who would understand the world in which they lived. Rome was bringing ever closer to realization the ecumenical ideal which the philosophers had taught, and the Greek historians of the Roman period are increasingly informed by that ideal.

The greatest of the Greek historians of the Roman period and the first to appreciate the greatness of Rome was Polybius. Polybius' real eminence appears even loftier by reason of the depressed level of what there is to compare with him for two centuries at either side. In the field of Roman history, Mommsen wrote, "his books are like the sun; at the point where they begin the veil of mist which envelopes the Samnite and Pyrrhic wars is raised, and at the point where they end a new and, if possible, still more vexatious twilight begins." Mommsen's praise is merited, but one may surmise that it was evoked as much by approval of Polybius' politics as of his historiography. For Polybius was no more neutral in political and social questions than was Mommsen, and both, as it happens, were on the same side. Polybius was born in 201 B.C. at Megalopolis of a family which held high office in the Achaean League, his father, Lycortas, having been a close associate of Philopoemen, leader of the League and "the last of the Greeks." Polybius himself held a number of honorific and diplomatic appointments, and when, after the defeat of Perseus in 168, the Romans decided to take a thousand prominent Achaeans as hostages, it was natural that Polybius should be among them. In Italy Polybius was associated with the circle of ruling families, and especially with the Scipios. The Scipios were the leaders in the expansionist policy, promoting and exploiting philhellenism, in opposition to the "nationalist" policy, of which Cato was the spokesman. No better vantage point could be imagined for a historian who had himself practiced statecraft and whose subject was the rise of Rome from village to world empire. So attached was Polybius to the younger Scipio that he returned to his service after he was released (in 150 B.C.) and was present with him at the destruction of Carthage in 146 and the fall of Numantia in 133; he also saw the destruction of Corinth in 146. He traveled widely and took pains to inspect sites which figured in his history. He died at the age of eighty-two of a fall from his horse, and was commemorated in inscriptions in many Greek cities, especially for his service in interceding with the Romans on their behalf.

Polybius himself refers to his work on Philopoemen in three books (10.21.5; this was used by Plutarch for his *Life*) and to his *Commentaries on Tactics* (9.20.4), but all that is extant is from his forty-book *History,* which was his principal work. Of this we have the first five books complete, extensive excerpts from Books 1–16 and 18, and sundry fragments; there is nothing from Books 17, 19, 37, and 40. The main subject is one that might well fascinate any writer or reader of history—the period of fifty years during which the city on the Tiber became mistress of the Mediterranean.

This period, from the Hannibalic wars to the defeat of Perseus, is dealt with in Books 3–29. In the first two books the history of Rome and Carthage in the interval between the first two Punic wars (266–221 B.C.) is recounted by way of introduction; and in the books after Book 29, written after 146, Polybius covers the history from 168 B.C. to 144 B.C., when Rome confirmed its dominion and proved its beneficence. In the first five books the various strands are drawn together, until the climax of Cannae marks a pause. Book 6 contains the famous account of the Roman constitution. Thenceforward the story is told chronologically and dated by Olympiads and official years of Roman consuls, Strategoi of the Aetolian, Achaean, and Boeotian Leagues, and Prytaneis of Rhodes. Book 12 is an excursus criticizing other historians and setting down Polybius' own principles of historiography, and Book 34 is an excursus on geography.

Polybius' standards of veracity and impartiality are the highest; no respect can be shown to persons, he says (1.14), for history without truth is like an animal without eyes. And Polybius lives up to his principles, verifying sources, observing chronology, visiting sites of battles, and sometimes finding fault with his own friends. But he himself insists that a man whose knowledge is derived exclusively from books and who has himself had no experience in directing large affairs can only produce a book that may be entertaining, but not one that is instructive; and a history that is not instructive is nothing (12.25g). History is instructive when events are related to one another and their causal nexus pointed out. His own history, he repeatedly tells us, does so instruct; he often calls it "pragmatic." Consequently, he often intrudes into his story to draw a lesson—in contrast to Thucydides, who also wished to be useful to statesmen but who lets events speak for themselves; or to Livy, whose artful detachment from his material is almost Homeric. Rational explanations leave little room for the gods, and Polybius' only deity is, in fact, Tyche, or Fortune personified; it is the part of a strong man, as of a good historian, to limit Tyche's scope to its narrowest.

When we find this unbeliever full of praise for Roman religiosity we can see how the statesman's truth may differ from the scholar's, and how Polybius scrupulously observing the historian's rule may still (but with perfect good faith) have committed distortions. The Romans, and apparently Scipio himself, believed that Scipio was a special favorite of the gods who vouchsafed him special communications; Polybius praises Scipio by insisting that he himself had no such belief but was clever enough to exploit a popular superstition. The view of religion as a useful device for ensuring discipline is reminiscent of Macchiavelli, and there are a number of things in Polybius which recur in Macchiavelli, such as the arguments against the use of mercenaries and, significantly, the ill-concealed admiration for the infamous Agathocles. In both Polybius and the *Discourses of the First Decade of Livy,* as a comparison of the two makes clearer for each, the criterion of excellence is discipline; men and institutions are praised or blamed according as they promoted or failed to promote discipline. Here is pragmatic Polybius on religion, politics, and morality (6.56.9):

My own opinion at least is that the Romans have adopted this course of propagating religious awe for the sake of the common people. It is a course which perhaps would not have been necessary had it been possible to form a state composed of wise men, but as every multitude is fickle, full of lawless desires, unreasoned passion, and violent anger, the multitude must be held in by invisible terrors and suchlike pageantry. For this reason I think, not that the ancients acted rashly and at haphazard in introducing among the people notions concerning the gods and beliefs in the terrors of hell, but that the moderns are most rash and foolish in banishing such beliefs. The consequence is that among the Greeks, apart from other things, members of the government, if they are entrusted with no more than a talent, though they have ten copyists and as many seals and twice as many witnesses, cannot keep their faith; whereas among the Romans those who as magistrates and legates are dealing with large sums of money maintain correct conduct just because they have pledged their faith by oath.

—*W. R. Paton*

Nothing is as important for the welfare of a state (not its people) as its constitution. The "mixed" constitution of the Romans is admirable, as long as the ruling caste maintains its control. But when long prosperity makes the lives of the citizens luxurious (6.57.8–10),

they will no longer consent to obey or even to be the equals of the ruling caste, but will demand the lion's share for themselves. When this happens, the state will change its name to the finest sounding of all, freedom and democracy, but will change its nature to the worst thing of all, mob-rule.

—*W. R. Paton*

Whether or not we are made uncomfortable by Polybius' analyses, it is evident that we have to do with a well-stocked, active, and truthful mind, and the unadorned sobriety of his style enhances the reader's feeling that he is dealing with a serious and mature work. We have ampler remains of other Greek historians who dealt with Rome, but none approaches Polybius' quality. The only one who did offer a thoughtful appraisal of the career of Rome in terms of human society was Posidonius, whose remains are exceedingly fragmentary.

Though Posidonius is known only from fragments (the longest in Strabo and Athenaeus), he merits attention as the most influential mind

in the first century B.C. He was born at Apama in Syria about 135, studied
in Athens under the Stoic Panaetius, traveled very widely, became head
of the Stoic school at Rhodes, and represented the Rhodians diplomatically
at Rome, where he spent the last year of his life. Posidonius' encyclopedic
and restless knowledge touched and refreshed all branches of intellectual
activity. He wrote on astronomy, meteorology, geography, mathematics,
history, and especially ethics, and unlike the bulk of the scientists and
philosophers of the Hellenistic and Roman age, his writings were artistic
and readable. He thought the sun was many times the size of the earth
(but made the earth much too small); he knew that the oceans all joined,
and thought that a man sailing due west from Cadiz would find India (a
millennium and a half later a man followed his suggestion, transmitted
through Roger Bacon, of sailing west from Cadiz, but what he thought was
India was really America). Logic, Posidonius regarded as the bones of
philosophy, physics its flesh, and ethics its soul, and some of his numerous
ethical essays are the originals of some of Cicero's (both Cicero and Pompey
attended his lectures) and were read by St. Jerome. Because his influence
is known to have been very great and his remains are few, modern scholars
have tended to attribute all the intellectual currents of the first century to
him and have left him an inconsistent figure. His teaching seems to have
been an eclecticism based on a diluted Stoicism with a dash of Oriental
mysticism. He did teach that the universe was a harmonious whole, mutually sensitive in all its parts, and sought to remove barriers between
earth and heaven, man and god, East and West, barbarian and Greek,
slave and freeman, philosopher and layman; to the Romans he was the
transmitter of the ecumenical idea which their empire did much to realize.
Posidonius' *History* in fifty-two books was a continuation of Polybius,
and covered the period from 144 to 86 B.C. He seems to have favored
Pompey and the senatorial party. Through Timagenes, Livy, Nicolaus of
Damascus, Diodorus, Strabo, Josephus, Plutarch, and Appian, all of whom
use him, he is the source of most of our knowledge of the history of the
period. But his philosophical approach to history seems to have been followed chiefly by Sallust (who was of Caesar's party); Sallust himself is
unfortunately fragmentary, but was the chief source for Roman history
in St. Augustine's *City of God*.

As Rome approached political realization of the ecumenical ideal set
forth by the Stoics, it was natural that the affairs of each people should
interest all and that writers should undertake to produce universal histories. Of several such works which were produced in the first century
B.C. we have most extensive remains of the *Bibliotheca* ("Library") of
Diodorus Siculus, who wrote because he believed (1.3.8) that "a history

of this nature must be held to surpass all others to the same degree as
the whole is more useful than the part and continuity than discontinuity."
He was born, he tells us (1.4.4), at Agyrium in Sicily, and learned Latin
and spent thirty years in travel and research for the task of composing a
history from the beginning of human society to Caesar's Gallic war and
the archonship of Herodes Atticus in 59 B.C. The first six of his forty
books dealt with prehistory, down to the Trojan War: Book 1, after an
introduction, with Egypt; Books 2 and 3 with the remaining barbarian
peoples; and Books 3–6 with the legendary period of the Greek peoples.
In the historical section Books 7–17 dealt with the period from the Trojan
War to the death of Alexander, and 18–40 carried the story down to Julius
Caesar. Books 1–5 and 11–20 are extant in their entirety (the preservation
of ancient works in groups of five or ten books, as in Polybius and Livy,
is due to their being reproduced in decads or pentads); of the remainder
there are fragments. Though he seldom names his sources directly it is
clear that Diodorus leaned upon certain authors very heavily for certain
sections, as, for example, Hecataeus of Abdera for Egypt, Ctesias for
Assyria and Persia, Megasthenes for India, Ephorus and Theopompus for
Greece, and Timaeus for Sicily, for which he shows a local patriotism.
Nineteenth-century criticism dismissed Diodorus with impatience as a
scissors-and-paste compiler, valuable only for the better men he embalmed.
But Diodorus deserves credit for the largeness of his concept, and in a
measure for its execution. He did use his head (not, to be sure, a first-class
critical implement) and his pen. In some places where he can be compared with his source, for example Polybius, it appears that Diodorus
shortened and adapted; he had the good taste to omit the rhetorical speeches
which all historians after Thucydides inserted in their books. In keeping
with his Stoic professions he wished to make his work instructive. He
chooses matter for inclusion by a criterion of usefulness, and he makes it
a practice to praise good and censure evil men. For uncritical readers in his
own age (but only the Elder Pliny seems to cite it) the *Library* was a
useful book; and for us it is useful as showing what uncritical readers
believed and for filling in gaps even for the early period of which Thucydides wrote.

An even more ambitious *Universal History* was the 144-book work of
Nicolaus of Damascus, secretary and political adviser to King Herod
(40–4 B.C.). Nicolaus' *History* also began with the earliest times, and it
continued to the death of Herod; the first 120 books were mere compilation,
but the remainder is the original work of a competent writer who had
first-hand knowledge of the events he describes. Josephus' dramatic account
of the family history of Herod (*Antiquities* 14.1–17.12) is drawn from Books

123 and 124 of Nicolaus. In addition, there are copious excerpts of Books
1–7 made by order of the Byzantine Emperor Constantine Porphyrogenitus
(A.D. 912–959), and quotations in Strabo, Plutarch, and Athenaeus. Nicolaus
also wrote a highly encomiastic work on the youth of the Emperor
Augustus, whose excerpts are useful, and an even more encomiastic auto-
biography. He is more of a stylist than Diodorus as well as a more competent historian, and the loss of the bulk of his work is regrettable. Of two
other encyclopedic writers, much more freely used by their successors than
either Diodorus or Nicolaus, there are practically no remains; these are
Alexander Polyhistor of Miletus and King Juba II of Mauretania.

Strabo, born at Amasea in Pontus in 63 B.C., was known to later antiquity
as the geographer par excellence. Strabo was a convert to Stoicism and
thoroughly convinced of the beneficent role of Rome as the unifier of the
ecumene. The Romans, he says (127), civilized savage and remote peoples
and made them useful parts of the society of mankind. Because of its size
the empire must be administered by one man as by a father (288):

Never in fact have the Romans and their allies had such abundance of peace
and prosperity as Caesar Augustus gave them, from the time when he assumed
absolute rule, and as Tiberius, his son and successor gives them now.

Strabo's principal work is his *Historical Commentaries* in forty-three
books, in which he treated the periods before and after the history of Polybius; this work is lost, but it was much used by subsequent writers, and it is
plain that Strabo was in agreement with Polybius' political views. What
we have is the seventeen-book *Geography,* which is rather an encyclopedia
of information known in the first century B.C. concerning the various
countries of the ecumene; through it, indeed, we get our last unified view
of the ecumene before it began to disintegrate. Geography to Strabo was a
sphere of philosophy, demanding broad and expert knowledge and critical
acumen. His style is plain and direct, with none of the ornate decoration
favored by his contemporary Dionysius. He inserts no fictive speeches,
though he may have done so in the lost *History.* His work marks a decline
from the scientific level of his predecessors (whose books he studied during
a long sojourn in Alexandria), but is at the same time our chief source of
information on those predecessors. The earth is of course spherical for
Strabo, and the oceans continuous; but the universe is geocentric.

The first two books of the *Geography* are a general introduction, including a defense of Homer as a geographer (in keeping with the orthodox
view of the Stoics, for whom Homer, generously allegorized, was a bible),
and a criticism of Eratosthenes, Hipparchus, Crates, Polybius, and
Posidonius. Books 3–10 deal with the geography of Europe, 11–16 with
Asia, and Book 17 with Africa. Space is allotted to various countries accord-

ing to the amount of information Strabo had available, though he insists that he employed principles of selection. He includes careful notes on the history, economics, natural lore, and especially the names of distinguished writers or scientists associated with places he mentions. Aside from useful information Strabo offers high entertainment value, being the most avid collector of curious lore and the most picturesque since Herodotus. His book is filled with accounts of strange customs, from Ireland to Nubia; strange religious practices, from those of Gallic druids to those of Indian fakirs; strange techniques of hunting and fishing, from ostriches to sword-fish. But throughout this omnium-gatherum he remains the thoughtful Stoic. The ecumenical idea meant something to him, and he recurs to it and to other Stoic doctrine, especially that of life according to nature; the latter doctrine is especially prominent in the passages on Egypt in Book 17. It is probable, incidentally, that Strabo wrote his book not for Romans, but for Greeks of Asia Minor, and in the first instance for Queen Pythodoris of Pontus. His flattery of the Romans may have been to some degree timeserving, but only to some degree. He wished to do his part toward making all the world known to all the people in it, to help make the world one.

Better understanding between peoples is the avowed aim of Dionysius of Halicarnassus' *Roman Antiquities,* though the book dealt only with Roman history from its legendary beginnings to the First Punic War, where Polybius began. By showing that the Romans and their institutions orig-inally derived from the Greek—he tells us, with an air of bestowing the supreme compliment, that Rome is a Greek city—Dionysius hopes to reconcile the Greek world to Roman rule, and perhaps to make Romans conscious of the responsibilities of kinship. Dionysius wrote under Au-gustus; of the twenty books of his *Antiquities* the first ten and most of the eleventh are extant, and extracts of the others are in the collection made for Constantine Porphyrogenitus. Dionysius tells us that he learned Latin and spent twenty-two years of research in preparation for writing his book, and he speaks of the historian's obligation to choose a noble sub-ject and to follow truth. But the value of his own work is vitiated by his premise that the Romans started with complete civilization at once in-stead of advancing from crude beginnings, by his tendency to make plaster saints of all Roman heroes, and by his faulty understanding of Roman institutions. He never fully realizes the difference between patricians and senators, for example, possibly because of the word *patres* in *patres conscripti.* He was himself a teacher of rhetoric at Rome, and illustrates the vices of the rhetorical school of historiography; speeches, none show-ing imagination or understanding or carrying the story forward, occupy almost a third of his space. He makes us realize the merit of Polybius as an intellect and of Livy as an artist. Using the same sources as Livy (but not Livy himself) for such stories as those of Romulus and Remus, the Horatii and Curiatii, Tullia, or Coriolanus, Dionysius takes ten times Livy's space and confuses the reader with useless names and details. Livy trims the superfluities and tightens the whole into dramatic vignettes. In religion and politics too Dionysius is naïve compared with the other two. All three favor Rome and the senatorial class and think religion is at least expedient, but only to Dionysius are the patrician great without flaw and the official religion immaculate.

If Dionysius could not himself write a good history his judgment of the work of others puts him in the first rank of literary critics. Aristotle had written his bony *Poetics,* and the Peripatetic epigoni, as we have seen, industriously assembled the facts of literary history; but for literary criticism in our sense, in which chronology and the apparatus of higher criticism are observed, but in which details of style are studied as a basis for aesthetic appreciation, Dionysius is our first writer, and a writer of masterly competence. Dionysius' critical writings are included in a corpus generally called *Scripta rhetorica.* The most important piece is *On the Arrangement of Words,* in which the details of a fine style by which prose could be given the attractions of poetry are discussed. Such matters as structure, rhythm, choice of words, harmonious arrangement, are dealt with competently. A special interest that attaches to this treatise is that it has preserved two of the finest gems of Greek poetry, Simonides' *Danae* and Sappho's *Aphrodite. On Imitation,* in three books, is fragmentary. Only three of the six essays *On the Ancient Orators* is extant, those on Lysias, Isaeus, and Isocrates. This was a literary history in the modern sense, giving, in the case of each author, a short life, critical comments, and then specimen extracts to illustrate these comments. *On the Style of Demosthenes* is enthusiastic but reasoned praise of Demosthenes as the supreme master of eloquence. *On Dinarchus* is a more matter-of-fact account of that orator, with a list of his authentic speeches. *On Thucydides* discusses the historian from a rhetorical point of view. Thucydides is accounted inferior to Herodotus (possibly because Herodotus was a fellow Halicarnassian, partly because Dionysius was an inferior historian) and Plato to Demosthenes in the *Letter to Cn. Pompeius.* The *First Letter to Ammaeus* refutes the Peripatetic claim, on chronological grounds, that Demosthenes learned what he knew from Aristotle's *Rhetoric;* the *Second Letter to Ammaeus* is a detailed study, in response to his correspondent's request, of the style of Thucydides. His example, as well as his precepts, make Dionysius a forerunner of the Second Sophistic. In all his works Dionysius favors a "classic" as against a florid "Asianic" style, and his partisanship and didactic aim detract from his criticism.

The critic whose only criterion is excellence, who is acute in recognizing it and determining its elements, and who is able to communicate his enthusiasms to his readers is the author of the treatise *On the Sublime,* called "Longinus," formerly thought to be the friend and adviser of Queen Zenobia of Palmyra in the third century B.C., and now left anonymous and dated to the first century. There is no mention of this treatise in ancient sources, but since it was published in 1554, and especially since Boileau translated it in 1674, it has probably been the most influential single work of literary criticism. "Till now," Gibbon wrote of this work in his *Journal,*

I was acquainted only with two ways of criticizing a beautiful passage, the one to show by an exact anatomy of it the distinct beauties of it and whence they sprung; the other an idle exclamation or a general encomium, which leaves nothing behind. Longinus has shown me that there is a third. He tells me his own feelings upon reading it, and tells them with such energy that he communicates them.

Longinus' object is to define true grandeur in literature as opposed to sophomoric turgidity and frigid pretentiousness. Of the five sources of the sublime, he decides, two are mainly innate, to wit, full-blooded ideas and vehement emotion. The other three depend on skill, and are figures, noble diction, and elevated composition. He is catholic in his choice of examples, and is the first pagan to quote the Old Testament (9.9):

So too the Jewish lawgiver, no ordinary man, having formed a worthy conception of divine power, gave expression to it at the very threshold of his *Laws* where he says: "God said"—what? " 'Let there be light,' and there was light. 'Let there be earth,' and there was earth."

His knowledge of the Hebrew Scriptures Longinus may have obtained from Caecilius of Calacte, a Jew who taught rhetoric at Rome in the time of Augustus and whose work Longinus mentions.

The third in the group of works of literary criticism attributed to the first century is the treatise *On Style* by Demetrius, once thought to be the famous third-century Demetrius of Phalerum but now identified as Demetrius of Tarsus, friend of Plutarch and teacher of Greek at York about A.D. 80. *On Style* is a systematic handbook on prose composition, following Peripatetic models, especially Aristotle himself and Theophrastus, and citing a wealth of examples to illustrate the various technical points made and terms used. The four types of style treated are the elevated, the elegant, the plain, and the forcible. *On Style* is workmanlike and useful, but it has nothing of the special quality of *On the Sublime.*

From this excursion into the literature of criticism we return to the historians, and to the most widely read, in modern times before our own, of all ancient historians. Josephus, the Jewish historian par excellence, was born of a priestly family in A.D. 37. He mastered the tenets of the various Jewish sects at an early age, and associated himself with the Pharisees, whom he compares to the Stoics. In 64 he visited Rome, to secure the release of certain priests, and was so impressed with its might that on his return to Palestine he sought to convince his countrymen of the futility of resistance to Rome. Nevertheless, when hostilities broke out he was given an important command against the Romans in Galilee. At Jotapata he contrived to be the sole survivor ("Should one say by fortune or by the providence of God?"—*Jewish War* 3.391) of a garrison which cast lots for the order of their suicide. As a prisoner of war he won Vespasian's favor when he prophesied Vespasian's elevation to the purple, and he continued to be a client of the Flavians in Rome, where they provided him with living quarters and sponsored his work. The books which he wrote during his long sojourn in Rome (he lived until after A.D. 100) were much admired; Eusebius says (*Ecclesiastical History* 3.9.2) that they were deposited in the public libraries and that a statue was erected in their author's honor.

The four works of Josephus which have come down to us are *Jewish War, Jewish Antiquities, Life,* and *Against Apion.* Of these the best both as history and as literature is the *War,* in seven books. Josephus wrote the first draft of this work in Aramaic, for "the barbarians of the interior . . . not so much to extol the Romans as to console those whom they have vanquished and to deter others who may be tempted to revolt" (3.108). It has been suggested, with no great probability, that the account of Jesus in the Slavonic version is from the original Aramaic or an earlier Greek version of it; the only mention of Jesus in our Greek text of Josephus (*Antiquities* 18.63) is a later interpolation. The Greek version (certainly not merely translation) of *War* was made for the benefit of "the subjects of the Roman Empire" (1.3). It is in good classical style, with no traces of Semitic phraseology; it was written with the assistance (only in *Antiquities,* not in *War,* does Josephus admit he used such assistance, "for the sake of the Greek") of Greek secretaries, whose personalities modern criticism has been able to distinguish. The "Sophoclean" is a lover of good poetry and of Sophocles in particular; the "Thucydidean" is a more commonplace hack. The first two books are introductory, and present the history of Judaea from the time of Antiochus Epiphanes (170 B.C.) to Vespasian's campaign of A.D. 67. Books 3–6 carry the story down to the capture of Jerusalem by Titus in 70. Book 7 describes the return to Rome, some final operations in Palestine, and the triumph over the Jews cele-

brated in Rome. Josephus' taste in describing the triumph over his com-
patriots with such apparent relish has been questioned; here and elsewhere
it is plain that he is seeking to please his victorious patrons. Aside from
efforts to ingratiate himself with the Romans and to put himself in a most
favorable light Josephus' account is generally trustworthy. He had access
to Vespasian's and Titus' own memoirs, he used the competent work of
Nicolaus of Damascus (especially for Herod), and he was himself an
active participant in the events he describes.

Much less valuable as history is Josephus' *opus magnum*, the twenty
books of *Antiquities*, of which the title, scope, and number of books were
suggested by the work of Dionysius of Halicarnassus. *Antiquities* covers
the history of the Jews from creation to the reign of Nero; its purpose is
to acquaint the gentile world with the venerable respectability of Jewish
history and institutions. The main source for the earlier portion is Scripture,
both in the original and Septuagint, supplemented by interpretations from
rabbinical literature and Philo. Where possible Josephus cites sources outside Jewish tradition, such as Berossus, Manetho, and others; but the fact
that lists of external authorities so often conclude with Nicolaus of Damascus suggests that the citations may have been taken over from Nicolaus.
For the period between the close of the Old Testament record and his own
War Josephus' account is very thin. The style of *Antiquities* is less careful
than that of *War;* as in *War* the hands of the Greek assistants may be
detected. The weakness of *Antiquities* (as of Josephus' other writings) as
apologetics is the natural tendency to regard Greco-Roman usages as the
norm; the best that Josephus can do for Jewish institutions is not to show
such substantive worth as they may have but to point to their similarity
to Greco-Roman institutions. Where analogies are possible, Josephus
expatiates; things that might be distasteful to Romans he glosses over.

Josephus is least credible in his own *Life*, which is chiefly a defense
against the damaging criticism of a rival historian, Justus of Tiberias. His
account of his relations with the Romans is inconsistent with what he had
himself said in *War*. The only parts which are autobiographic in the
usual sense are the early sections on his youth in Palestine and the end
on his life in Rome; and in these his boasting is offensive. The style is as
crude as the matter; *Life* shows that the "Sophoclean" and the "Thucydidean" earned their salt when they worked. The most attractive of all
Josephus' works are the two books *Against Apion*, a reasoned, and well-
planned, and well-informed defense of Jews and Judaism against the
slanders of hostile critics, of whom Apion was only one. Here Josephus
shows sincere zeal for his people, as well as knowledge both of their
literature and thought and that of the Greeks. Like *Antiquities* and like

the writings of Philo, *Against Apion* is a defense which accepts the prosecution's rules of procedure. But the works of these men and of others show that the rules were being slowly broadened, and the ecumenical ideal, with interludes of hot rebellion and of intolerance and suppression, was proceeding toward realization.

The best account of the career of Alexander the Great is the *Anabasis* of Arrian (*ca.* A.D. 95–175). Arrian was born in Nicomedia, and by 131 had so distinguished himself as to be raised to the high office of Governor of Cappadocia. In 147, we know from an inscription, he was Archon Eponymus of Athens. Arrian consciously modeled himself on Xenophon. Epictetus was his Socrates; his *Discourses* and *Enchiridion* are virtually stenographic reports and belong in a discussion of Epictetus. To match Xenophon's *Anabasis* Arrian wrote a work of the same title and size (seven books) on Alexander. *Anabasis* is a straightforward account, perhaps intended as a corrective to the rank growth of the Alexander romance. Arrian conscientiously follows critical principles, though these may not be strict enough for modern requirements. The official histories of Aristobulus and King Ptolemy are accepted without question, and there is a certain gullibility about oracles and portents. But though Arrian is partial to his hero to the point of giving him superhuman stature, he conveys no sense of the demonic drive of the man and the demonic implications of his achievement. Arrian wrote a number of other works: *Indica,* a sort of annex to *Anabasis,* based on the *Periplus* of Alexander's admiral Nearchus; *Periplus of the Euxine Sea; On Tactics,* and *Plan of Campaign against the Alans; Cynegetica,* a supplement to Xenophon's essay on hunting; and biographies (lost) of Timoleon and Dion and perhaps others.

Another provincial, roughly contemporary with Arrian, who attained a high position in the Roman administration and wrote history is Appian of Alexandria, whom Hadrian made procurator; a letter from Fronto recommending Appian to a post is extant. Appian wrote his *History of Rome* in the leisure of retirement, about 160. His plan was to divide the whole of Roman history into segments defined by geography or logic. Photius knew of twenty-four books: Book 1, *Royal* (beginning with Aeneas); Book 2, *Italic;* Book 3, *Samnite;* Book 4, *Celtic;* Book 5, *Sicilian and Island;* Book 6, *Spanish;* Book 7, *Hannibalic;* Book 8, *Libyan* (or *Numidian*); Book 9, *Macedonian and Illyrian;* Book 10, *Greek and Ionian;* Book 11, *Syrian;* Book 12, *Mithradatic;* Book 13–17, *Civil;* Book 18–21, *Egyptian;* Book 22, *Hundred-year;* Book 23, *Dacian;* Book 24, *Arabian.* Besides fragments of others we have eleven of these almost complete: one each of *Spanish, Hannibalic, Libyan, Syrian, Mithradatic,* and *Illyrian,* and five of *Civil Wars*. As Arrian fails to convey a feeling of the real power of the Alexander story, so Appian, partly due to his division, fails to convey the romance of the story of Rome. But he is a careful workman, and for stretches of history where we have no other continuous account, his work is indispensable to historians. This is especially true of *Civil Wars* 1, which covers the period from the Gracchi to the defeat of Spartacus. He is more appreciative of the honorable motives of the Gracchi and the highhandedness of their senatorial opposition than Plutarch in his comparable *Gracchi*. So in the third book Appian takes no pains to whitewash Octavian and gives Antony his due; he is critical of Cicero's role in 44 B.C., but moved by Cicero's death in the proscriptions. He says he visited Gaieta "to gain knowledge of this lamentable affair" (4.19), and his account of the proscriptions in general is moving without being rhetorical.

Pausanias is the archaeologist's bible, and a prime source for the student of Greek religion. His *Description of Greece* (in ten books) was written, as we learn from an allusion at 5.1.2, in the latter part of the second century A.D.; nothing is known of the author himself, except that he is not to be identified with others of his name. The tours he describes are exactly those that a lay visitor to Greece with antiquarian interest would take today. In his opening sentences he starts, as a voyager from the Aegean would, at Cape Sunium and covers *Attica* (Book 1); then come Book 2, *Corinthiaca* (including Argos, Mycenae, Tiryns, Epidaurus); Book 3, *Laconica;* Book 4, *Messeniaca;* Books 5 and 6, *Eliaca* (Olympia); then back to the mainland, Book 9, *Boeotica;* and Book 10, *Phocica*. He locates buildings, monuments, and paintings, especially those of antiquarian interest (which was very lively in the second century), and in the framework of this account he inserts all manner of legends, myths, folklore, prophecies, scraps of history. The latter, which an analogous modern work would relegate to an appendix, disturb the harmony of the whole. Since his sites, and especially such places as Olympia and Delphi, are predominantly of a religious character, his material is especially valuable to the student of religion. He frequently refers to ciceroni (*exegetai*), and his incidental remarks are like the patter of a competent guide. Apparently he used books also; much of his detail, as for example the inscriptions of monuments and offerings, may have come from written sources. He does not indulge in art criticism; he tells his reader what is worth seeing for size or historical interest, tells him something of its history, precisely how to find it, and then leaves him to make his own aesthetic judgment. His locations have proven very precise; the Hermes of Praxiteles, for example, was found exactly where he said it was. He deals with topography, where

his narrative demands it, but does not, as a modern guidebook is likely
to do, expatiate on natural scenery. Nor is he interested in economic or
industrial questions. He never misses a chance to include a name; artists,
builders, dedicators of votive offerings, figures in history or legend, genealogies, swell his *index nominum* to heroic proportions. He is honest,
shows no interests outside his specialty, and has no ax to grind in politics
or philosophy. His attitude on a question of literary history, which is
characteristic of his approach generally, may be cited (9.30.3):

Though I have investigated very carefully the dates of Hesiod and Homer, I
do not like to state my results, knowing as I do the carping disposition of some
people, especially of the professors of poetry at the present day.

Pausanias' style is commonplace; his occasional attempts at elegance are
unfortunate. His book is ideal for an armchair tourist; the assorted information with which he spices sight-seeing has much of the quality of
Herodotus, but without Herodotus' charming naïveté.

Pausanias' mythological material is incidental and unsystematic. A
completely systematic handbook of Greek mythology is the *Library* of
Apollodorus, which is so objective that it gives no clue at all to its author's
time and place, though it was probably written in the first century A.D.
The author used books and added nothing of his own except the arrangement; he scrupulously avoids indulging either in philosophical interpretation or rhetorical embellishment, but gives a straightforward and uninspired account. Classes in Greek mythology today may well use Apollodorus as their principal textbook. Apollodorus devotes his first chapters
to a theogony, and then proceeds by families—Deucalion, Inachus, Agenor,
Pelasgus, and the like—with whom all the figures of mythology are connected. Of the original seven books only the first three (carrying the account through Theseus) are extant in their original form; for the remainder we have an epitome discovered in modern times.

A group of what appear on the surface to be technical handbooks shows
the blight that descended on science when "philosophers" undertook to
teach everything and so displaced specialist students. *Tactics* of Asclepiodotus, a pupil of Posidonius, *The General* of Onosander (first century A.D.), and the *Stratagems* of Polyaenus, who dedicated his work to
Marcus Aurelius and Verus, are all literary rather than professional, and
draw their examples from a remote period whose practices were long
antiquated. *The General* is the most rhetorical of the lot. The principal
manuscript of Asclepiodotus (tenth century A.D.) is of special interest
for its reproductions of the author's original diagrams. Polyaenus' 900
Stratagems (in eight books) do cite instances otherwise unknown, but
despite the author's protestations of the labor he expended upon it his work

is careless. He repeats the same stratagem from different sources, and he confuses different persons who bore the same name. None of his examples is nearer than two centuries to his own time. Educationists of the first centuries of our era anticipated the theory that mastery of subject matter is secondary to the art of presentation—and were unfortunately not particularly effective in presentation.

The most important historian of the empire was Dio Cassius Cocceianus (ca. A.D. 155–235), and his *Roman History* in eighty books was the most complete history of Rome. Dio came from Nicaea in Bithynia (Dio Chrysostom was of the same family), attained consular rank in Rome, and held important posts in Asia Minor, North Africa, Dalmatia, and Pannonia. He retired from public service and heeded what he believed was a divine call to write the history of Rome. His first forty books carried the story from the arrival of Aeneas in Italy down to the war between Caesar and Pompey, the next twenty to the death of Claudius, and the remaining twenty to 229. Books 36–60 (with slight losses at the beginning and end) and epitomes of Books 88–90 are extant.

For the large lacunae at the beginning and end we have a considerable number of excerpts and two epitomes. John Xiphilinus (eleventh century A.D.) made an epitome from Book 36 onward, using some material not in Dio, and divided his work according to the emperors from Augustus to Elagabalus; the material on Marcus Aurelius, at Books 70 and 71, was already lost. For the lacuna at the beginning we have the history of Zonaras (twelfth century A.D.), who followed Dio mainly but used other books, especially Plutarch, in addition. Dio's own sources are difficult to determine precisely; he used Livy (but along with the Roman annalists), Sallust and Caesar (probably through an intermediary), and Tacitus (possibly directly). He mentions the memoirs of Augustus, Hadrian, and Severus. For long stretches of Roman history Dio is our only continuous source. For the period from Marcus Aurelius onward he is a first-hand authority; he is a first-class source also for the period of the decline of the republic, though here Appian is superior. His arrangement is annalistic, rather than according to subject or location. Like Dionysius of Halicarnassus Dio feels that a history must be given dignity; this and his rhetorical tendencies are the chief weaknesses of his history. He will shift emphasis, assign new motives, expand speeches, so that events familiar from Caesar's *Commentaries* and for which Caesar must have been his principal source are hardly recognizable. A speech like the well-known discourse of Maecenas to Augustus in Book 52 is valuable as a statement of the theory of the principate, though it contains much that is patently anachronistic. Dio's political sympathies are senatorial and aristocratic; he has a poor opinion of the common people, and he resents the power of the praetorian guard. With the accession of Commodus, he himself says, his history makes a steep descent from a golden to an iron age.

We close our list of secular historians with the Syrian Herodian (early third century A.D.) whose work was long a schoolbook for ancient history in Europe, until history developed a critical sense. Like Dio, Herodian was an imperial official, though of not nearly so high a rank. His *History of Events after Marcus* in eight books covers the period until the rise of Gordian III (A.D. 238). Herodian is superficial; he speaks at length in a moralizing tone of the succession of palace revolutions and military dictatorships, but is unaware of the significance of such developments as the spread of Christianity or of Roman citizenship under Caracalla. Despite his professions of accuracy he is unreliable for facts, chronology, topography. Herodian is typical of the rhetorical historian; not facts and understanding, but an artistic book with a moralizing tone is the objective he has in mind. Such a book is an eloquent example of the divorce between life and letters which we shall notice in the next chapters.

Chapter 16. LITERATURE OF RELIGION

THE MOST WIDELY QUOTED SENTENCE IN GIBBON IS WRONG. AFTER DESCRIBING the constitution of Rome in the second century Gibbon says (ch. 3, end): "If a man were called to fix the period in the history of the world, during which the condition of the human race was most happy and prosperous, he would, without hesitation, name that which elapsed from the death of Domitian to the accession of Commodus." Instead, as modern scholarship has shown, the burden of life was especially grievous for the common man at this period, and hope for improvement, on this earth, exceedingly faint. Larger and larger numbers of people were separated from any share in political or economic control. It is against a background of depression rather than happy confidence that the intellectual and literary manifestations of the empire must be seen and can be explained. The compensatory mechanism which men devised was to deny the hopeless world which engulfed them and create a different abode for their spirits. For those who were secular minded the substitute was a retrojection into the past. The chief characteristic of the so-called "Second Sophistic," which was the paramount literary movement, is its irrelevance to life. Its archaizing and elaborately polished language aims to be as different as possible from the language of living people. Matter is of secondary importance; its chief requirement, one is tempted to say, is that it should have nothing to do with questions in which people are deeply concerned. With the writers who used this shallow channel to escape from reality we shall deal in the chapter following.

Another route was to substitute a new reality, of which the apparent reality of the phenomenal world was only shadow or preparation. The predominance of spiritual concerns over material was manifested in a deepened inwardness in philosophy and in the rapid spread of otherworldly religions. Oriental cults which promised salvation without distinction of class exerted an enormous mass appeal. Of these the most successful was Christianity, whose rapid propagation might well seem miraculous. The basis of hostility to Christianity was at least as much social as intellectual. Its appeal to individualism was completely foreign to the main line of Greek tradition, but that tradition could only be maintained by the ruling classes. And as society continued to disintegrate, the ruling classes finally adopted Christianity as a state institution.

Christianity was a new dispensation; perhaps a clearer indication of the direction which men's minds were taking can be seen in the deviations from their traditional doctrine which became evident in the established philosophical sects. The Academy, to begin with the oldest, had given way to Neoplatonism, and whatever paths of rationalism Neoplatonism preserved were destined to wander off into byways of emotional mystical experience. In the early third century A.D. Plotinus, as the first sentence of Porphyry's biography tells, seemed ashamed of being in the body. Plotinus' one goal was to liberate men's souls from the ties of the world. The most chacteristic attitude of the early Stoics had been their sense of community and the fine zeal with which they sought to initiate the kingdom of heaven on earth. Now their social aims and the rigid sense of duty which the Romans had admired were diluted. The impersonal deity of Cleanthes' hymn has become personalized and shows a father's feeling toward good men, whom he dearly loves (Seneca, *De Providentia* 2.6). What is now emphasized is Stoic "indifference"; that is the burden of Epictetus' teaching, and he even shows impatience with disciples who continue to con the doctrinal Stoicism of Chrysippus (*Discourses* 1.4.7). Only the Epicureans, because their doctrine was mainly negative, remain consistent. In a philosophical discussion in Plutarch (*On the Delay of Divine Retribution* 548B) the Epicurean says his say and departs; for him there is nothing to argue about. Not only the ethical preachers but the literary gentlemen of the Second Sophistic, and, indeed, more feelingly, disapproved of serious thinkers. Dion Chrysostom, before he was himself converted to philosophy, was denied his merited place in Philostratus' list of rhetoricians. Philistinism toward philosophy becomes more striking when we realize how weak a claim the "philosophers" of the empire had to that title. But even if they were not original thinkers the "philosophical" writers of the empire produced a quantity of effective work. It is with these writers that the Christian apologists and polemicists show the closest affinity. We proceed then to consider the work of Stoics and Cynics and Skeptics, of Neoplatonists and Jews and Christians.

The philosophical schools in vogue at Rome were the Stoic, the New Academy, and the Epicurean; and our best source for their teaching are the philosophical essays of Cicero, who admitted (*Ad Atticum* 12.52) that these essays were "copies of the Greek to which I contribute only words, of which I have a great plenty." If the recovered treatises of the

Epicurean Philodemus are a fair specimen, only the words which Cicero possessed could make the Greek philosophical treatises of the Hellenistic and Roman periods presentable as literature. Cicero himself professed to be a follower of the New Academy, which held that only verisimilitude but not knowledge was attainable. This skeptical turn was introduced by Arcesilaus (d. 240 B.C.), who begins the Middle Academy, and expanded and given currency by Carneades (214–129 B.C.), the most gifted of the followers of Plato, who came to Rome on an embassy in 155 B.C. The Stoa had been represented in Rome by Panaetius (180–111 B.C.) and Posidonius, in whose hands it had grown relaxed and eclectic, though even in the empire enough of its pristine vigor seems to have been retained for emperors with autocratic tendencies to begin their reigns by expelling the "philosophers," who were usually Stoics. What philosophical literature we have from Rome after Lucretius and Cicero is Stoic—the Latin essays of Seneca and the Greek works of Epictetus and Marcus Aurelius.

Epictetus (ca. A.D. 50–120) was a Phrygian slave who had belonged to Epaphroditus, freedman of Nero. He studied under Musonius Rufus, the most prominent Stoic teacher of his day, and must have attained some standing as a philosopher to be banished when Domitian (in A.D. 89 or 92) expelled philosophers from Rome. He settled at Nicopolis, across the Adriatic from Brundisium, and there taught philosophy. Like Socrates he wrote nothing. What we have are Arrian's notes, virtually stenographic, as is shown by their differences from Arrian's own books in such unconscious matters of style as use of prepositions. Four of the original eight books of his *Discourses* are extant, and also the *Enchiridion* or handbook, which is a concise summary of Epictetus' doctrine. The center of that doctrine is reconciliation to the inevitable:

> Behave in life as at a banquet: a dish comes to you—stretch out your hand and take a portion politely; it passes on—do not detain it; it has not yet reached you—do not anticipate it in desire. (*Enchiridion* 15.)

> Stop admiring your clothes, and you are not angry at the man who steals them; stop admiring your wife's beauty, and you are not angry at her adulterer. (*Discourses* 1.18.11.)

If this is a slave morality and as unsocial as suicide, yet it satisfied the pathetic longing of tired men for a passive kind of happiness. Epictetus' own honesty, strength, and zeal are transparent. His language, unique among our books in not having been subjected to literary treatment, has a fresh vigor, and his pages are larded with pictures from daily life. A man who could not bear to stay at home when his beloved child was sick, for instance, is like "a certain man in Rome who covered his head when the horse which he backed was running—and then, when it won un-expectedly, they had to apply sponges to him to revive him from his faint" (*Discourses* 1.11.27). His forthrightness and sincerity make Epictetus a tonic even for those who question the premises out of which his teaching grew; that he answered and answers a real need is shown by the enormous popularity his work has always enjoyed.

When we read the twelve books *To Himself* of the Emperor Marcus Aurelius Antoninus (A.D. 121–180) we feel that we might at any moment be embarrassed by the author's looking up to find us peering into the window of his private chamber which he had forgotten to shutter, for the books were written only for his own eye and not meant for publica-tion. Yet Marcus Aurelius in undress has nothing to be ashamed of, and no peering could be more rewarding. Here is Stoicism at work, not in display to the world, but in the inward life of a sensitive and conscientious spirit, who happened to possess the highest secular power in the world. *To Himself* is as difficult to analyze as inspirational works are; its value, besides the inspiration which the reader shares with the author, is in the picture of the author himself. He reminds himself to be grateful to his benefactors, to be content with his lot, to "retreat into this little plot that is thyself" (4.4), and ever and again to do his duty. It was duty which compelled a peace-loving man to spend his winters fighting in the cold north (from where his twelve books are dated), a charitable man to order the burning of Christians, a man who sensed beauty in the cracks of a loaf or the slaver of a boar to speak of a fine dinner as a pig's corpse or of a fine robe as sheep's covering steeped in shellfish blood. If we sometimes suspect that the slave's asceticism is sour grapes raised to a philosophy, no one can question the utter sincerity of the emperor's code. We might deplore the retreat from reality, wish that the sense of duty were not fenced in but spread abroad as Zeno's immediate disciples sought to spread it abroad; but then we should not have Marcus Aurelius' *To Himself,* which remains one of the abiding spiritual treasures of the race.

Marcus Aurelius addressed himself, Epictetus his school and those who consulted him; many others spoke admonition and instruction to all who would hear. Some were the vain artistes of the Second Sophistic, of which we shall speak presently; some, as we should surmise and as Lucian warns us, were charlatans who exploited the philosopher's garb; but many were earnest teachers and the legitimate forerunners of Christian sermonizers. Far the most distinguished of this group is Dion of Prusa (A.D. 40–120), called Chrysostom ("golden-mouthed") for his eloquence, like the more famous Bishop of Constantinople. Dion was originally a rhetor and hos-tile to philosophy, but he was converted to Stoicism by Musonius, who was also Epictetus' teacher. In 82 he was involved in the downfall of a Roman patron, and for fourteen years he led the life of a wandering Cynic preacher, with staff and scrip. He continued as an apostle of the Cynic-Stoic way of life after he was recalled from exile and received Trajan's imperial favor. He enjoyed the enormous popularity bestowed upon the shining lights of the Second Sophistic (with whom he should be included but for his moral earnestness); he employed and was, in fact, an innovator in the archaizing style they affected, being the first to use the antiquated dual number. But neither in style nor matter nor in personal habits does he descend to the preening artificiality of a Polemon. Dion's extant works include eighty *Orations* and an essay in *Praise of Hair* quoted in its entirety in Synesius' *Praise of Baldness,* in addition to fragments; works on philosophy and history ascribed to him are lost. But even in antiquity Dion's reputation rested chiefly on his *Orations,* of which many more were extant than appear in our collection. Of those we have, two (#37 and #64 belong to Dion's pupil Favorinus, and the text of the others is confused. The ordinary arrangement follows no principle of chronology, but we learn from Synesius what we should guess in any case, that the sophistical pieces come first, the political next, and the moral discourses last.

Besides *Praise of Hair* and similar lost works (we know, for example, of a *Praise of a Parrot*) some dozen *Orations* (##11, 21, 26, 28–29, 58, 60, 61, 66, 74, 76) are ascribed to Dion's sophistical period. The long *Trojan Oration* (#11) seeks to prove, perhaps to gratify the Romans, that Homer was wrong in saying that the Greeks took Troy. This piece, incidentally, is a good and full exposition of contemporary Homeric criticism. Related to this group are a number of other literary pieces. *On Training for Public Speaking* (#18), like Quintilian's *Education of an Orator,* prescribes a program of reading—a sort of "Hundred Best Books"—for some high official, perhaps a Roman emperor. Dion shows a predilection for Plato and Xenophon. The best known of the literary pieces is #52, which compares the tragedies on Philoctetes written by Aeschylus, Sophocles, and Euripides; #59 is merely a stylized paraphrase of the beginning of Euripides' *Philoctetes.* Socrates' debt to Homer is discussed in #55. The long and carefully wrought *Rhodian Oration* (#31) is shown by its expressed regret for Nero to belong to the reign of Domitian and therefore to Dion's sophistical period. Dion reproves the Rhodians for their habit of altering inscriptions on old statues to satisfy the lucrative demand for honorary monuments.

Dion's political *Orations* (roughly, ## 38–51) are concerned with the affairs of the Greek cities of Asia Minor, on which they throw welcome light. Dion uses his prestige and his good sense to warn against turbulence and to reconcile quarrels; he accepts or declines honorary awards for his services. His guiding principle, like Plutarch's, is that the Greek cities must accommodate themselves to Roman rule, as a means to preserving the values of Hellenism. An ethical rather than political note characterizes a number of pieces similarly addressed to communities. *To the Alexandrians* (#32), for example, begins as follows:

My friends, would you kindly be serious for a brief while and give heed to my words? For you are forever being frivolous and heedless, and you are practically never at a loss for fun-making and enjoyment and laughter—indeed you yourselves are naturally inclined to laughter and jollity, and you have many who minister to such tendencies—but I find in you a complete lack of seriousness. And yet there are those who praise you for your wisdom and cleverness, asserting that, although you assemble here in thousands, you not only can conceive what is fitting but at the same time are quick to put your conceptions into words. But I for my part should prefer to praise you as being slow to speak, indeed, and self-restrained enough to keep silent, and yet correct of judgment.

—*H. L. Crosby*

Similar pieces, combining seriousness with a tone of banter, are addressed to the people of Tarsus (##33–34), of Celaenae (#35), and of Borysthenes (#36). The *Olympian Oration* (#12) which belongs to this group is important for its statement of a theory of art. Phidias is represented as discoursing on the functions and limitations of the plastic arts; poetry is pronounced as superior to sculpture for portrayal of character.

Dion is easily at his best in his moral treatises, which belong to his last period. Many are short and deal with ethical commonplaces, chiefly on the various emotions, frequently in dialogue form. Some, for their elevation and earnestness, are gems of homiletic literature. The first four orations, probably addressed to Trajan, set forth the Cynic-Stoic ideal of kingship. "Not every king but only the good king derives his royal prerogative from Zeus [with reference to *Iliad* 2.24–25], and he receives it on no other title than that he should plan and study the welfare of his subjects" (1.12). Similarly, in #2, which is in the form of a dialogue between Philip and Alexander, quotations from Homer are used to demonstrate the high responsibility of the kingly office. Oration #4 is a dialogue between Alexander and Diogenes; the true king, Diogenes says, proves that he is a son of Zeus by qualities of mind and character, not by power and wide dominion. Events in the life of Diogenes, as the Cynic prototype, are dealt with in another group (##6, 8, 9, 10). In a *Libyan Myth* (#5) the tale of a seductive and cruel mermaid supplies a moral on the control of passions.

Dion's single most delightful work, as charming as it is edifying, is the *Euboean* (#7). When he was shipwrecked off the coast of Euboea, Dion tells us, he was saved and entertained by a family of hunters who led an idyllic life in the interior. The central scene is a trial conducted in a city theater, where one of the hunters has been cited on charges of evading taxes. When the simple-minded and wholehearted rustic by his very naturalness outfaces the cunning city lawyer the moralizing intent is plain, but the scene is nevertheless dramatically effective. The lesson of the corruption of civilization and of the nobility of the Cynic's natural-ness is eloquently enforced. The piece closes with a fine assertion of the dignity of poverty and of humble callings, and an attack on the exploita-tion of human beings, and especially on the degradation of prostitution. The spectacular trial scene with its "recognition," the flawless virtue of the protagonists, and the marriages at the end are characteristic elements, as we shall see, of the Greek romance. But none of the romancers, and very few other writers of the period, thought so deeply or wrote so effectively of the problems of men in society. Dion is less intellectual than Plutarch, and more concerned with men's day-to-day conduct; indeed, he tells us more about habits of life and thought at the turn of the first and second centuries than does any other author. His earnestness and humor are sufficient to redeem him for his rhetorical excesses, which are, in any case, less offensive than those of other writers of the Second Sophistic. For the agreeable picture they give of the author himself and of his world, and for their own worth as entertainment and edification, Dion's works are second only to Plutarch's among the pagan writers of this period.

Maximus of Tyre (late second century A.D.) is a lesser figure than either Dion or Plutarch; but like Dion, his moral tone and his respect for philoso-phy entitle him to a place with the thinkers rather than with the declaimers, where he is usually classified. Maximus counted himself a Platonist, and the Platonic influence is very apparent in his work, but he is manifestly influenced by Stoicism also, and he speaks approvingly (especially in #36) of the Cynic way of life. His forty-one extant Orations, quite superficial but earnest and persuasive and filled with good examples and anecdotes, deal mostly with ethical commonplaces. They do not give so vivid a picture of contemporary life as Dion's, but are of perhaps greater value as illustrating the scope of intellectual interest and the religious probings of Maximus' age. In his discussion of prayer (#5), for example, he concludes that prayer should be a "conference" rather than petition; the function of images in worship (#2) is only to recall the deity to the mind of the worshiper. There are discussions also on such questions as whether one who injures should be injured in return (#12); whether virtue is ever

a free gift of fate (#38); whether poets or philosophers are more authoritative teachers of religion (#4); whether oracles have value (#13); and
on the origin of evil, seeing that the deity creates only the good (#41).
There are comparisons of the practical and contemplative life (#16);
between diseases of the body and the spirit (#7); between friends and
flatterers (#14); between the merits of farmers and warriors (#23-24).
Others are more clearly in the Platonic tradition: learning as recollection
(#10); whether virtue can be taught (#37); on Socratic love (##18-
21); whether Socrates did well in not defending himself before the judges
(#3); on Socrates' "demon" (##8-9; a subject treated also by Plutarch
and Apuleius). Maximus' manner is that of an extempore speaker, each
thought being repeated in many various forms and with many examples.
His language is the archaizing Attic of the Second Sophistic, but his
verbosity is characteristic of the Asianic rather than the Attic style.

In both Dion and Maximus the Platonic tradition is manifest, and it
will be found even more striking in Plutarch. But it is significant that
the tradition is no longer spoken of as Academic but as Platonic. The
skepticism associated with the Academy after Arcesilaus and Carneades
had fallen into disfavor as Platonism approached Neoplatonism, and to
fill its place the Skepticism of Pyrrho, which had been submerged in the
Academy, was resuscitated. The great teacher of Skepticism in the Pyrrhonic tradition in the first century A.D. was Aenesidemus of Alexandria,
who has been called the last original thinker of antiquity. Aenesidemus,
and the entire Skeptic tradition from Pyrrho onward, is known to us
from the work of Sextus Empiricus, who is dated to the late second century
by his quarrels on medical questions (his own medical works are not extant) with Galen. Sextus' Pyrrhonic *Hypotyposes* or outlines, based on
a work of the same title by Aenesidemus, is a complete summary of Pyr-
rhonism and its relations to Academic Skepticism and to other schools. His
Against the Mathematicians is a combination of two works comprising
eleven books under the title of the first of the two. *Against the Mathematicians* proper contains treatises against *Grammarians, Orators, Ge-
ometricians, Arithmeticians, Astrologers,* and *Musicians. Against Dogmatic
Philosophers,* which is combined with *Against the Mathematicians,* contains two books *Against Logicians,* two *Against Natural Philosophers,*
and one *Against Teachers of Ethics.* All dogmatists are shown to present
such inconsistencies that both speculation and perception are futile as
guides to truth and to distinctions between good and evil. Hume was able
to recover his cheerfulness only by forgetting his own arguments, and the
ancient Skeptics attained their ataraxy, or freedom from perturbation,
in much the same way, as Sextus tells (Pyrrhonic *Hypotyposes* 28-29):

What is told of Apelles the painter has in fact happened to the Skeptics. The story goes that he was painting a horse and wished to show its foam but could not and flung the sponge upon which he wiped the colors off his brush at the picture. When the sponge hit the picture it produced the likeness of a horse's foam. The Skeptics hoped to gain ataraxy by forming some decision on the discrepancy of things as they appear to the eye and to the mind, and when they could not they suspended judgment—and upon this suspense as if by accident ataraxy followed, as a shadow follows a body.

Skepticism yielded to the positive teachings of Christianity and of Neo-platonism. From the point of view of any positive doctrine Skepticism must be scorned as leading only to futility and negation. On the other hand, Greek Skepticism was one of the last voices raised in antiquity for freedom of conscience, of criticism, of rational and scientific thought.

Because of its easy Greek and high moral tone, and because its author was supposed to be Socrates' Theban friend of that name, Cebes' twenty-page *Tablet* was long a favorite schoolbook in Europe. But though the *Tablet* uses Platonic dialogue and a myth, its author clearly knows Stoicism, and it probably belongs to the first century A.D. The tablet of the title is a symbolic picture hanging in the vestibule of a temple of Cronus, and an Old Man explains to a Stranger how the picture symbolizes life with its virtues and vices. The use of a picture for a text upon which to enlarge on a story or a description is common in the Second Sophistic, and was employed by Lucian, Callistratus, and Longus, among others.

No better summary of the intellectual stock of antiquity after it had attained its fullest development can be found than the amiable sage of Chaeronea. Plutarch (*ca.* A.D. 45–125) was no master spirit whose attainments or inclination put him in opposition to the world about him or outside it; he participated fully in the intellectual and active life of his environment, and he summarizes his world in a more copious body of writings than has been left us by any readable ancient author. He had read all the literature (most of it was as "classic" to him as it is to us, except that it was part of a living tradition); he had studied, with greater or less sympathy, all the current philosophies and theologies, native and exotic; he had seen and appreciated the masterpieces of plastic art; and he was a connoisseur of music and mathematics. He knew Athens and Rome very well, and probably Alexandria also. He had been entrusted with important diplomatic missions and was on terms of intimacy with powerful Romans. He might undoubtedly have remained at Rome in a position of honor, but he preferred to return to provincial Chaeronea, "a small place that would be even smaller if I did not live there" (*Demosthenes* 2), there to become a petty local magistrate and a priest of Delphi. The return, the magistracy and priesthood, the writing of essays and especially *Lives,* were all consistent with a reasoned program of adjustment to life in the empire which we shall consider when we have glanced at his works.

Plutarch's works are as diverting as they are edifying. They provide quotations or anecdotes for any situation. Plutarch loved literature and he loved anecdotes; when he speaks of Pericles' Aspasia he must tell of another woman whose lover called her Aspasia, and then he apologizes for his irrelevance by saying "it were inhuman to pass the story by" (*Pericles* 24). Most but not all of Plutarch's writings have come down to us; many titles in the catalogue called Lamprias' are not in our corpus; and undoubtedly genuine pieces in our corpus are not in the catalogue. What we have are the more familiar *Parallel Lives* and the misnamed *Moralia,* essays in the form of dialogues, lectures, or letters on a wide variety of subjects. To list the seventy-seven pieces in *Moralia* is tedious, but will serve to indicate the scope and something of the direction of Plutarch's thought. (The numerals in brackets are the universally cited folio pages of the 1570 Xylander edition; they will serve to locate the essays and indicate their size.) The moral aspect of education is emphasized in the first three: *Education of Children* (1*A*), *How to Study Poetry* (17*D*), and *Listening to Lectures* (37*B*). All have shrewd and pertinent remarks on education; its numerous quotations make *How to Study Poetry* virtually an anthology. *How to Tell a Flatterer from a Friend* (48*E*) has good remarks on psychology. *How One Recognizes Progress in Virtue* (75*A*) is a polemic against the impractical perfectionism of the Stoics. *How to Profit by One's Enemies* (86*B*), *On Having Many Friends* (93*A*), *Chance* (97*C*), and *Virtue and Vice* (100*B*) are all agreeable ethical sermons. Quotations in *Condolence to Apollonius* (101*F*) are so numerous as to render Plutarchian authorship suspect. *Advice about Keeping Well* (122*B*) illustrates Plutarch's special interest (and competence) in medicine; and *Advice to Bride and Groom* (138*B*), his concern for people's happiness. *Dinner of the Seven Sages* (146*B*) is a literary tour de force in which the sages are made to repeat doctrine ascribed to them in easy conversation. *Superstition* (164*E*) is the best statement of Plutarch's own religion: "Some persons, in trying to escape superstition, rush into a rough and hardened atheism, thus overleaping true religion which lies between."

Sayings of Kings and Commanders (172*A*), *Sayings of Spartans* (208*A*), *Spartan Customs* (236*F*), *Sayings of Spartan Women* (240*C*), and *Bravery of Women* (242*E*) are all collections (in which Spartan virtue especially is idealized), possibly for use in lectures or *Lives*. *Roman Questions* (263*D*) and *Greek Questions* (291*D*) deal respectively with 113 and 59 Roman and Greek problems in ancient religion. *Greek and Roman Parallel Stories* (305*A*) is an inferior matching of instances from Greek history with instances from Roman. *The Fortune of the Romans* (316*B*), *The Fortune or Virtue of Alexander* (326*D*), *Were the Athenians More Famous in War or Wisdom?* (345*C*) are epideictic pieces. A series of first-class essays showing the spiritual worth of traditional religions and explaining away their apparent crudities are *Isis and Osiris* (351*C*), *The E at Delphi* (384*C*), *The Oracles at Delphi* (394*D*), and *Obsolescence of Oracles* (409*E*). There follows a series of ethical treatises: *Can Virtue Be Taught?* (439*A*), *Moral Virtue* (440*D*), *Control of Anger* (452*E*), *Tranquillity of Mind* (464*E*), *Brotherly Love* (478*A*), *Affection for Off-spring* (493*A*), *Whether Vice Be Sufficient to Cause Unhappiness* (498*A*), *Whether the Affections of the Soul Are Worse than of the Body* (500*B*), *Talkativeness* (502*B*), *Curiosity* (515*B*), *Greed for Wealth* (523*C*), *False Shame* (528*C*), *Envy and Hatred* (536*E*), and *Self-Praise without Incurring Envy* (539*A*).

Of highest importance for Plutarch's theology are *On Delay of Divine Retribution* (548*A*), *Fate* (568*B*), and *Socrates' Daimon* (575*A*); the latter sets forth Plutarch's doctrine of intermediary powers, which explain how a perfect deity may govern the world imperfectly and also serve as intermediary for prayer. *Exile* (599*A*) says that a good man is at home everywhere. When Plutarch's little daughter died in his absence he sent his wife the very appealing *Consolation* (608), exhorting her to remember the child's playfulness and generosity which the pressure of time might have spoiled. The nine books of *Symposiacs* (612*C*) show Plutarch as an effective teacher, discoursing to his provincial disciples on all subjects that a cultured Greek gentleman was expected to know. But the most attractive picture of the teacher himself is in *Eroticus* (748*E*), which does not quite succeed as a Platonic dialogue, which it evidently seeks to be, partly because of the large number of interlocutors. *Love Stories* (771*E*) are five brief pieces, such as might have been expanded into novels. The series which follows has to do with the responsibility of rulers: *A Philosopher Ought to Converse Especially with Men in Power* (776*A*), *To an Uneducated Ruler* (779*C*), *Whether an Old Man Should Engage in Public Affairs* (783*A*), *Precepts of Statecraft* (798*A*), *Monarchy, Democracy, Oligarchy* (826*A*). *That We Ought Not to Borrow* (827*D*) speaks for itself. *Lives of the Ten Orators* (832*B*) is surely spurious. The fragmentary *Comparison of Aristophanes and Menander* (853*A*) is impatient with Aristophanes' boisterousness and prefers Menander's comedy of character.

On the Malignity of Herodotus (854*E*) chides the historian for his treatment of Plutarch's native Boeotia. The five books of *Preferences of Philosophers* (874*D*) are certainly spurious. *Natural Questions* (911*C*) show Plutarch's characteristic interest in medicine and in animals.

The *Face Which Appears in the Moon* (920*A*) illustrates Plutarch's demonology and eschatology. The subjects of *The Origin of Gold* (945*E*), *Whether Water or Fire Be More Useful* (955*D*), *Whether Land or Water Animals Be Cleverer* (959*A*), *Reasoning of Brute Animals* (985*D*), and *On Eating Flesh* (993*A*) are self-evident. Sympathetic interpretations of Plato, but with more concern to save theology than to save Plato, are to be found in *Platonic Questions* (999*C*), *On the Creation of the Soul in the Timaeus* (1012*A*), and an *Epitome* of the latter piece (1030*D*). Stoic philosophy is attacked in *Stoic Inconsistencies* (1033*A*), *Stoics More Absurd than Poets* (an epitome; 1057*C*), and *Common Arguments against the Stoics* (1058*E*); Epicurean in *Pleasant Life Is Impossible According to Epicurus* (1086*C*), *Against Colotes* (1107*D*), and *Whether "Live Apart" Is Well Said* (1128*A*). Our best information concerning ancient music comes from *On Music* (1131*A*).

Other works of similar nature are cited as Plutarch's, and a number in our list, besides those mentioned as such, are doubtless spurious. It is significant of Plutarch's character that a good modern critic could make the apt if unscientific criterion of the genuineness of doubtful pieces the answer to the question, "Would an amiable and sincere Protestant pastor in a provincial Dutch town have written such a piece?" Plutarch was certainly not directly affected by Christianity, but his "humanitarianism" (*philanthropia* is one of his favorite words), his consideration for animals and for children, his exaltation of women, do introduce a new and softer note into Greek literature.

Ethical teaching is obviously one of the main objects of the *Parallel Lives;* Plutarch himself insists (*Alexander* 1) that he is not writing history but devoting himself to "the signs of soul in men." Concern with the individual does result in curious distortions, as when Pericles is made to precipitate the Peloponnesian War merely to free himself of an embarrassing lawsuit growing out of his patronage of Phidias. On the other hand, focusing on an individual can produce such moving delineations of character as those of *Agis and Cleomenes;* the description of their passion, especially Cleomenes', deserves a place with the world's best in this kind. Our collection contains fifty biographies—twenty-three pairs, in which a Roman is bracketed with a Greek and the two then form the subject of a *Comparison,* and four separate Lives. Except for Demosthenes and Cicero, who were writers as well as doers, the list is confined to generals and politicians. If a modern amateur of antiquity finds it odd that a man of Plutarch's culture makes no room for Socrates or Euripides or Phidias, the explanation may throw light on a new response to the challenge of making life under Rome livable. The *Lives* were written, not to introduce Greeks to Romans or Romans to Greeks, but to show Greeks that their own past could boast statesmen and warriors (there was no need to press the point for artists and philosophers) that were easily comparable to those of their Roman masters. If the demonstration seems to us unnecessary, we must remember that the Greeks had now been under Roman domination for centuries and might be inclined to accept the contemptuous attitude of the Romans toward themselves. For Plutarch to question the continuance of Roman domination would be as fantastic as it would be for him to question the institution of slavery. Though such *Lives* as *Marcus Cato* and *Marius* reveal Plutarch's contempt for the "barbarism" of individual Romans plainly enough, he believed that the Romans were the divinely chosen instrument for preserving security and order (602E; 408B). Plutarch's answer was to elevate Hellenism to a cult. The pride in Greek achievement and the loyalty to Greek institutions which he inculcates are aspects, not of patriotism, but of religion. In the Greek city-state man and citizen were indistinguishable, and there were no other loyalties; now Hellenism is a church in a larger political structure.

The concept of Hellenism as a cult is the key to Plutarch's life as well as to his *Lives*. To sit at a symposium and discourse urbanely of subjects in the liberal arts curriculum is to do service to that cult, and so is being a petty magistrate and pretending to be a Greek statesman, or being a priest of an obsolescent shrine. Like other cults Hellenism was eager for proselytes, but it demanded full surrender. Much has been written of Plutarch's syncretism and cosmopolitanism; the fact is that his syncretism never involves mingling but rather the assimilation of an alien God to Greek ideas. All the exotic religions except the Egyptian, for whose antiquity he had a reverent regard and to whose identity with the Greek Herodotus had already pointed, he looked upon as barbarous superstitions. For example (169C):

Because it was the Sabbath day the Jews sat in their places immovable while the enemy were planting ladders against the walls of Jerusalem and capturing the defenses, and they did not get up, but remained there, fast bound in the toils of superstition as in one great net.

—*F. C. Babbitt*

It is the same with all peoples *in partibus infidelium* who are not assimilable to the Greek way of life (799D):

The Carthaginians are bitter, sullen, subservient to their rulers, harsh to their subjects, most abject when afraid, most savage when enraged, stubborn in adhering to decisions, disagreeable and hard in their attitude towards playfulness and urbanity.

—H. N. Fowler

When Jerusalem fell in A.D. 70 a contemporary of Plutarch, named Johanan ben Zakkai, took a course exactly parallel to Plutarch's by willingly surrendering sovereignty to the Romans and removing his disciples to Jamnia, there to form a religion out of a way of life. But the Jews of the Dispersion, who are calculated to have comprised 7 percent of the population in Greek-speaking lands, sought to assimilate themselves to their environment in all but religion. The Alexandrian community was the oldest and largest, and for its use the translation of the Hebrew Scriptures called Septuagint was made; the statement in *Letter of Aristeas* (perhaps the first century B.C.), which describes the making of the Septuagint, that it was made by royal order for the Alexandrian Library is to be discounted along with the miracles which were said to attend the work. Of the Septuagint, the Pentateuch, which is very literal, was surely completed early in the third century B.C.; the remaining books, some of which (e. g., Jeremiah) show wide divergences from the received texts, may have been done somewhat later. In addition to the books in the Hebrew (or Protestant) Bible, the Septuagint contains certain other books and additions to older books, which are called the Apocrypha. Language, style, and matter would make the Septuagint a difficult and puzzling book for Greeks to read, and there is no indication that anyone but Jews and proselytes looked at it. To assert their cultural claims both in their own community and to the gentile environment Alexandrian Jews—Demetrius, Eupolemus, Artapanus, Aristeas, Cleodemus Malchus—wrote accounts of early Hebrew history; their fragments are cited in Eusebius and Clement. Aristobulus seems to be the first to propose the idea, adopted by the Greek Fathers, that Pythagoras and Socrates studied from Moses; Origen thought Musaeus was a corruption of Moses. There was a whole literature of forgeries; lines containing Jewish, and later Christian, doctrine were fathered on Aeschylus, Sophocles, Menander. The 230 lines of pseudo-Phocylides have been mentioned; a *Life of Abraham* was attributed to Hecataeus of Abdera. Oracles were a favorite form; a great part of the extant *Sibylline Oracles* are of Jewish or Christian origin. Independent works were also produced. Some of the Apocrypha is doubtless of Hellenistic origin. II Maccabees is avowedly an epitome of the history of Jason of Cyrene. Wisdom of Solomon, which is an impassioned assertion of immortality, shows marked influence of Greek poetry and was probably written by an Alexandrian. Philo (called "the elder" to distinguish him from the philosopher) and Theodotus wrote epics on Biblical history, and considerable fragments survive (in Eusebius) of a drama on the Exodus by Ezekielos. In the fourth century, it may be noted, when Julian forbade Homer to Christian teachers, a father and son, both called Apollinaris, made a new Homer out of the Pentateuch and a Plato out of the Gospels.

But the greatest and most characteristic monument of Alexandrian Jewry are the works of Philo, which are in polished Greek and show complete familiarity with Greek literature and thought, but are concerned with interpreting Jewish tradition. Of Philo's wholehearted devotion to his own traditions there can be no question, and he clearly has no thought of dealing unfairly with his texts when he so allegorizes them as to make them acceptable by the norms of Hellenic culture; but the fact that Hellenic culture is the norm, with the Jewish tradition molded to that norm, is significant. The bridge which Philo constructs is thus a bridge to Hellenism, and that bridge was later used, with finger posts turned, by Christian writers. Their only complaint is Philo's want of Christianity; though he lived through Jesus', John the Baptist's, and most of St. Paul's lifetime, he shows no knowledge of Christianity. The main body of his writings is devoted to what he conceives to be the inner and spiritual meaning of incidents and texts in Scripture; but just as the Epicureans used physics mainly as a scaffolding to support their ethics, so Scripture, indispensable as it appears in Philo and literally inspired even in the Septuagint (it is doubtful whether he knew Hebrew), is only a basis for discovering the history of the human soul in its relation to God. Philo's attitude of ecstatic contemplation of God made him useful, not only to Christians, but in an even greater degree to Neoplatonists. Plato's *Timaeus*, which was their central document, absorbed Philo also; and though Philo drew from all the schools, and especially the Stoic, his chief philosophical resource was Plato, and his assimilation of other doctrine to Plato also contributed to Neoplatonism. But the greatest significance of Philo for Western thought is not in any single item but rather in the direction which he initiated and which dominated philosophy, Arabic and Christian as well as Jewish, until the time of Spinoza; it was Philo who first recognized that there were two sources of truth, resting in revelation and the human intellect, which must somehow be brought into consonance.

Most of what we know of Philo's life (and that of the Jewish community in Alexandria) comes from his *Embassy to Gaius,* an account of the official abuses which the Jewish community in Alexandria suffered and the activities of their delegation to Emperor Caligula at Rome which Philo headed when he was an old man. We know from this that he belonged to a prominent Jewish family; that his education was very complete is plain from his works. These works, very voluminous though much has been lost, may be divided into three groups: philosophy, Biblical exegesis, and history. The first group, probably the work of Philo's youth, is by far the best known and at the same time the least significant. It includes *On the Eternity of the World, Every Good Man Is Free, The Contemplative Life* (a highly eulogistic account of the mystical sect of Therapeutae settled near Alexandria), *Hypothetica* (a defense of the Jews, known only from extensive fragments in Eusebius), and *On Providence* (known from fragments in Eusebius and a complete Armenian version). Philo's interlocutor in the last-named piece is his nephew Tiberius Alexander, who subsequently apostatized from Judaism and became governor in Jerusalem.

The exegetical works are of quite a different order. They appear to be rambling, one allegorical fancy following another, and the second suggesting a third, so that the impression is sometimes given that an ingenious game is being played, both in finding allegorical meanings and in stringing them together. But Philo's high moral earnestness makes it clear that this is no game. Form is, in fact, carefully regarded, not only in elegance of language, but even in structure, which was traditional (though not in Greek) for Philo's subject. Philo used rabbinical material, as he avows, and concatenated discursiveness is the characteristic form in which both *halakhah* and *haggadah,* regulatory and expository interpretation, were written. This division is reflected in the two parts of Philo's writings on the Bible (really only on the Pentateuch), one part of which deals with laws while the other is expository. And just as in rabbinical tradition the normative *halakhah* takes precedence over *haggadah,* so Philo's exposition of the early chapters of Genesis is really an introduction to his treatment of the laws, for creation is thought of as establishing God's title as lawgiver.

The exegetical works originally constituted a complete *Allegorical Commentary on Genesis.* What we have preserved are parts of this commentary in separate sections, each dealing extensively with a single passage or incident. The scale is very generous, and only a few passages from the first eighteen chapters of Genesis are covered; on the episode of Noah's drunkenness, for example (Genesis 9.20–27), we have four pieces: *On Husbandry, On Noah's Work as a Planter, On Drunkenness,* and *On Sobriety.* The exposition of the laws is introduced by biographies of the principal lawgivers, *Abraham, Joseph,* and *Moses;* the last, more than Philo's other Biblical writings, seems to envisage a gentile audience, which is to be convinced of Moses' priority to the Greeks. There follow a long book *On the*

Decalogue and four on *Special Laws* in the Decalogue. Finally, but also in connection with laws, are treatises *On the Virtues* and *On Rewards and Punishments.*

The historical works are the *Embassy to Gaius,* mentioned above, and *Against Flaccus,* who was the governor of Alexandria against whom the Jews complained. Even this treatise is a theodicy of God's providence and justice: He visited retribution upon Flaccus, and He will always watch over His own. But such justifications of providence were not a new thing in Greek letters; Plutarch's *On the Delay of Divine Retribution,* though written somewhat later, repeats instances collected by earlier writers. What is new is Philo's repeated assertion of direct experience of God. One typical passage among many may be cited (*On the Migration of Abraham* 34):

I feel no shame in recording my own experience, a thing I know from its having happened to me a thousand times, after making up my mind to follow the usual course of writing on philosophical tenets, and knowing definitely the substance of what I was to set down, I have my understanding incapable of giving birth to a single idea, and have given it up without accomplishing anything, reviling my understanding for its self-conceit, and filled with amazement at the might of Him that IS to Whom is due the opening and closing of the soul-wombs. On other occasions, I have approached my work empty and suddenly become full, the ideas falling in a shower from above and being sown invisibly, so that under the influence of the Divine posssession I have been filled with corybantic frenzy and been unconscious of anything, place, persons, present, myself, words spoken, lines written. For I obtained language, ideas, an enjoyment of light, keenest vision, pellucid distinctness of objects, such as might be received through the eyes as the result of clearest shewing.

—*F. H. Colson and G. H. Whitaker*

Confessions like this, of which there are many in Philo, might be and indeed later were made by a number of Christians and Neoplatonists. With the Christians Philo has this in common, that he relies ultimately on a specific revelation which recounts a series of historical events, though Philo was unaware of the Christian revelation; and with the Neoplatonists, that he claims a rational basis for his convictions. Of the Neoplatonists, to whom Philo makes the natural transition, it must be understood that they were from first to last rationalists, as ready as any philosophers to expound their reasons for their convictions. In Neoplatonism there is no supernaturalistic dualism, no divine episodic drama operating in the world but outside it. The world is spiritual through and through, and not divided into nature and supernature. There is no dichotomy between thought and devotion, faith and reason, rationality and mysticism. But like all ethical theories, beginning with Plato's, and to a greater degree than the others, the foundation for conviction in Neoplatonism is mystical experience. Ammonius Saccas (the surname suggests that he was a porter) was spoken of as *theodidaktos* ("taught of god"), which implies that he had no instructor in philosophy. Ammonius was born of Christian parents in the reign of Commodus (A.D. 180–192). Like Socrates or Epictetus he was a teacher of humble social position but great gifts of personality who himself wrote nothing. He taught at Alexandria, and among his pupils were Origen and (for eleven years) Plotinus.

Plotinus (A.D. 204–270) is to Ammonius as Chrysippus to Zeno or St. Paul to Jesus. He was a successful and revered teacher in Rome, and enjoyed the patronage of the Emperor Gallienus and his Empress Salonina. His personal life was saintly; Porphyry begins his *Life of Plotinus* by telling us that:

Plotinus the philosopher, our contemporary, seemed ashamed of being in the body. So deeply rooted was this feeling that he could never be induced to tell of his ancestry, his parentage, or his birthplace. He showed, too, an unconquerable reluctance to sit to a painter or sculptor.

—Stephen Mackenna

The *Life* tells us further (7):

I myself, Porphyry of Tyre, was one of Plotinus' very closest friends, and it was to me he entrusted the task of revising his writings. Such revision was necessary.

—Stephen Mackenna

The writings which Porphyry put into such shape as they have are the *Enneads* (Nines), which are the written monument of Neoplatonism. The *Enneads* comprise six sections of nine discussions each, setting forth, but in extremely unsystematic form, the metaphysical basis of the system. Each of the fifty-four essays presupposes a large body of doctrine common to the writer and his audience, and proceeds at once to illuminate some particular aspect of it which had been discussed in the seminar or to examine some difficulty which has been raised. Questions of ethics, psychology, metaphysics, cosmology, and aesthetics are expounded one by one, as they arose in the school. The general principles of the system are referred to only incidentally, and their structural significance becomes clear only upon a comparison of a number of different passages. Though Plotinus is not the founder but rather the culmination of Neoplatonism, the school owes more to him than to any individual thinker except Plato. Modern critics have called him "the greatest individual thinker between Aristotle and Descartes," "the greatest metaphysician of antiquity," "the most deeply spiritual of all philosophers." Plotinus left his successors a powerful and delicate dialectical instrument and a vivid tradition of personal mysticism. The object of the entire discipline was to enable the soul to attain spiritual ecstasy, "the flight of the Alone to the Alone" (*Enneads* 6.9). During the period of his association with Porphyry, Plotinus is said to have achieved a vision of the Absolute four times.

Porphyry (the Greek adaptation of his Semitic name Malchus; A.D. 233–301), though less original than Plotinus, is a better scholar, indeed the last great scholar of paganism, and also more concerned with practical religion. But along with his sober scholarship and emphasis on practical religion Porphyry was also a mystic who preached the ascetic life and valued oracles. His prolific writings included works on grammar, chronology, history, mathematics, Homeric criticism, vegetarianism, psychology, and metaphysics. His fifteen-book *Against the Christians* (burned by imperial order in 448) has been pronounced, on the basis of copious quotations in the Latin Fathers, a most thorough and scholarly critique, written in a judicial temper. His fairness is illustrated by his *Letter to Anebo,* an Egyptian priest, on divination, in which he is completely frank in exposing the chicaneries of polytheist priests. His *Life of Pythagoras* and *On Abstaining from Animal Food* (four books) exhibit the Neo-Pythagorean elements in Neoplatonism, and the Neoplatonists' high regard for animal life as well as their ascetic tendencies. *On the Cave of the Nymphs in the Odyssey* (on *Odyssey* 13.102–112) is a specimen of allegorical interpretation of Homer as pursued by the Stoics. *On Statues,* extant in fragments, opposes worship of images. *Auxiliaries to the Perception of Intelligible Natures* is a sort of anthology, with comment, from Plotinus. The most generally attractive of Porphyry's surviving work is the *Letter to Marcella,* a friend's widow whom Porphyry had married. The spiritual tone of this little work, at once lofty and warm, is unsurpassable. The following paragraph (18) from this treatise illustrates the Neoplatonist attitude toward conventional religion:

The chief fruit of piety is to honor God according to the laws of our country, not deeming that God has need of anything, but that He calls us to honor Him by His truly reverend and blessed majesty. We are not harmed by reverencing God's altars, nor benefited by neglecting them. But whoever honors God under the impression that He is in need of him, he unconsciously deems himself greater than God. 'Tis not when they are angry that the gods do us harm, but when they are not understood. Anger is foreign to the gods, for anger is involuntary, and there is nothing involuntary in God. Do not then dishonor the divine nature by false human opinions, since thou wilt not injure the eternally blessed One, whose immortal nature is incapable of injury, but thou wilt bind thyself to the conception of what is greatest and chiefest.

—*Alice Zimmern*

In Iamblichus (d. *ca.* A.D. 330), another Syrian and head of the Syrian school of Neoplatonists, the system becomes more a theology and less a philosophy. He was far inferior to Plotinus as a thinker, being rather a mystagogue and thaumaturgist, but he also contributed to the doctrines and the dialectical principles of the school. Eunapius (§ 457 ff.) represents him chiefly as a wonder worker; this, the fact that Iamblichus' disciple Maximus converted Julian to paganism, and Julian's reverent adulation of him have darkened Iamblichus' reputation. But he appears to have possessed singular gifts of mind and spirit. The five extant works which are certainly his (*On the Pythagorean Life, Exhortation, On Common Knowledge of Mathematics, On the Arithmetic of Nicomachus,* and *On Theology of Arithmetic*) together with others that are lost formed a *Collection of Pythagorean Dogmas.* The treatise *On the Mysteries of the Egyptians* (whose authorship has been questioned, but on insufficient grounds) is the loftiest and most moving defense of spiritual religion from the pen of any pagan. Here is Iamblichus on prayer (*On the Mysteries of the Egyptians* 5.26):

To spend a long time in prayer nourishes our spiritual understanding, makes a far wider room in our souls for the reception of the Gods, opens the things of the Gods to men, gives us familiarity with the flashings of the Light, little by little perfects us internally for the Divine contact, till it leads us upward to the highest height, gently uproots the habits of our own minds and plants instead those of the Gods, awakens trust and communion and indissoluble friendship, increases the Divine Love, kindles what is Divine in the soul, purges away from the Soul everything of contrary quality, eliminates so much of the shining aether-stuff round about the Soul as disposes us to physical reproduction, perfects good hope and faith in the Light: in sum, Prayer makes those who employ it, if I may use the word, familiars of the Gods.

—Edwyn Bevan

As will be apparent from this quotation, the central deity in Iamblichus' pantheon, as in Julian's, was Mithra. Iamblichus is also credited with having systematized the methods of exegesis of Plato, which were followed by his successors. Of these such as are represented by considerable literary remains are associated with the Second Sophistic and will be glanced at in the next chapter. The only remaining philosophical teacher who merits our attention is Proclus.

Proclus (A.D. 410–485) is important because his systematization was the principal vehicle for transmitting Platonic and Neoplatonic teaching to the West and became the textbook for various Neoplatonist revivals. Coleridge, for example, wrote of him (*Memorials of Coleorton II, January 1810*):

The most beautiful and orderly development of philosophy, which endeavours to explain all things by an analysis of consciousness, and builds up a world in the mind out of materials furnished by the mind itself, is to be found in the *Platonic Theology* of Proclus.

Proclus' writings fall into five groups: (1) Extant commentaries, apparently in the form of lecture notes, on *Republic, Parmenides, Timaeus, Alcibiades I,* and *Cratylus* (excerpts only); his commentaries on a number of other Platonic treatises are lost. (2) *Platonic Theology;* of *Orphic Theology* and *Harmony of Orpheus, Pythagoras, and Plato,* both lost, Proclus was probably editor rather than author. (3) A group of lost works on religious symbolism, against the Christians. (4) A number of occasional essays, three extant in medieval Latin versions. (5) Two systematic manuals, *Elements of Theology* and *Elements of Physics.* The most useful and influential is the *Elements of Theology.* Proclus' chief virtue is as systematizer of previous doctrine, and even as such his merits are not high. Within a generation of Proclus' death some unknown eccentric Christianized his *Elements,* introducing the minimum of change, and presented it as the work of Dionysius the Areopagite, under which style it enjoyed enormous vogue; the original came to be regarded as a pagan imitation of the Areopagite's work. Proclus was a considerable factor in the Neoplatonist revival during the Renaissance; there are over forty fifteenth- and sixteenth-century manuscripts of the *Elements of Theology.* One was written by Marsilio Ficino (1433-1499) who translated Plotinus into Latin and interpreted *Symposium* according to Plotinus; another was owned by Pico della Mirandola. From Italy the movement moved north, and was the source of the Neoplatonism in the English poets of the sixteenth and seventeenth centuries and in particular of Edmund Spenser.

Proclus worked in Athens, whither the seat of Neoplatonism removed from Alexandria. In the fourth century, particularly, Athens flourished as a university town, and received as students not only the masters of the Second Sophistic, but also the most distinguished of the Greek Fathers, Julian and his teachers as well as the Cappadocian triad who opposed him. The university was closed by order of Justinian in 529. Among those deprived of their chairs was Simplicius, the commentator of Aristotle as well as of Epictetus. Simplicius closes his commentary on *Enchiridion* with a prayer with which we may fittingly take leave of the pagan philosophers:

I beseech thee, O Lord our Father and Guide of our reason, make us mindful of the dignity which Thou hast deemed us worthy. Grant unto us moral freedom, that we may be cleansed from the contagion of the body and of all irrational passions; may we overcome and master them, and, as is fitting, use them properly as our instruments. Assist us to a proper direction of the reason within us and its harmony with all Reality by means of the light of Truth. Thirdly, I beseech Thee, my Savior, remove completely the mist from our eyes that, as Homer says, we may know God and man.

—S. Angus

Philosophical paganism had curiously changed places with Christianity. By the beginning of the fourth century a section at least of the ancient world had, independently of Christian influence, attained an exalted moral and religious standard. Though retaining external veneration for an official creed, philosophical heathenism, by the time of Porphyry, had grown as unworldly as Christianity in its purest days. The Neoplatonists write like teachers in a conventicle, addressing a chosen congregation of the devout. Their prohibition to seek after riches practically excluded the commercial classes from their influence. Their prohibition to enter into controversy practically barred expansion by missionary effort. More significant still, they had lost confidence in the state. "The conventional law," Porphyry writes to Marcella (§ 25), "is subject to expediency, and is differently laid down at different times according to the arbitrary will of the prevailing government." All of this is very like the beliefs of the primitive Christians, except that they were animated by the expectation of a supernatural renovation of the world in their own time. But the standards of the small sect altered when it grew into an extensive and authoritative society, and as doctrines and practices inevitably broadened to suit Christianity's new and official position, it came about that philosophical paganism entered the cloister as Christianity emerged from it.

But before Christianity's scope and secular authority were enlarged by its being made the official state religion the main concern of the Christian teachers was like that of the other writers dealt with in this chapter, to provide men with a spiritual resource wherewith to face life. In all of them, and in ascending scale, the prescription is unworldliness. Their direction may be regarded as being toward man's fullest realization of his spiritual potentialities. But if the direction was toward one thing it was also away from another—from a world in which improvement of economic or social conditions seemed hopeless. The rather copious pre-Christian apocalyptic literature, as an analogy, can be dated with considerable precision from external circumstances: when history grew particularly oppressive men were more inclined to look away from this world. It was against a background of material hopelessness and widespread spiritual quest that Christianity with its positive doctrine of salvation based upon a specific revelation appeared and made rapid conquest. We proceed then to a brief sketch of Christian writings from their first appearance as an exotic phenomenon on the periphery of Greek literature until they mastered and adopted Greek forms and themselves became the main stream of Greek literature.

The first genuinely popular writing we encounter in Greek is to be found in the basic monuments of Christianity. The twenty-seven pieces which were collected into a New Testament toward the end of the second century envisaged a much simpler and infinitely wider audience than had ever been addressed in writing before. Like the Judaism which the earliest Christians rebelled against, Greek literature's preoccupation with form tended to choke substance, and early Christian writers disregarded forms which limited both expression and audience and wrote as ordinary people spoke. If influence is a legitimate factor in appraising the worth of a book, that factor alone would make the New Testament immeasurably the most important work in Greek literature. Of the source of the book's power and of its doctrine this is not the place to speak; it came into a world which hungered sore for such doctrine, and its form was exactly right for those who hungered most, which meant the population of the Roman Empire outside its ruling class.

The oldest writings in the New Testament are the Epistles of Paul (born about the beginning of the Christian era); their purpose was to spread the gospel among the gentiles. Some, like Romans, both Corinthians, Galatians, are of the nature of treatises; others, like Philippians and Philemon, have a more personal character. Except for the closing formulas the Epistles were dictated; hence imperfect periods and anacolutha occur. The Pauline authorship of Hebrews is questionable. Besides the fourteen Pauline Epistles there are seven so-called "Catholic" Epistles: James, Peter 1 and 2, John 1, 2, and 3, and Jude. Of the Synoptic Gospels, which employ a common source, the oldest (about A.D. 65) and the simplest in thought and language is Mark; the latest is Matthew, which is addressed to an audience presumably familiar with Hebrew Scriptures and has a more controversial tone. Luke is fullest of narrative pictures and parables and is in a better Greek style. Whereas the Synoptics report the career of Jesus, the Gospel according to John, which is dated to the early second century, considers that career as a mystery, in the Greek sense, which the reader is to experience. Acts is in effect the second part of a single work of which Luke is the first. It envisages a cultivated audience, and follows Greek usage in employing invented speeches. Revelation is an example of an old and continuing class of apocalyptic writings (from which it borrows freely) which foretell the future in highly colored symbolic imagery. The New Testament was born of a protest against the tyranny of a canon, and was itself canonized through an increasing demand for external authority. Quantities of other writings of the same classes, some extant in part, gospels, epistles, acts of the several apostles, apocalypses, were produced but not included in any canon.

From the end of the first and the second centuries we have epistles of the five Apostolic Fathers, Clement, Barnabas, Ignatius, Polycarp, Hermas. Clement (called "of Rome" to distinguish him from Clement of Alexandria) is the earliest, Ignatius the most vigorous, and Hermas (or the composite authors of *Shepherd*) the most agreeable in its mixture of fancy and instruction. We pass over many works important for doctrinal reasons and come to the early apologetes, of whom the greatest was Justin Martyr, who addressed an *Apology for the Christians* to Antoninus Pius and Marcus Aurelius. A notable genuine piece among the mass of his pseudepigrapha is his interesting *Dialogue with Tryphon the Jew*. Athenagoras similarly addressed Marcus Aurelius and Commodus with an *Appeal for the Christians*. Justin and Athenagoras were both styled "philosopher" and were not nearly so hostile to Greek thought as was the Syrian Tatian. But though none of the Greek Fathers was as bitter against Greek thought as, for example, the Latin Tertullian, who condemned Greek philosophy as the root of all heresy, nevertheless the two views of life were mutually contradictory. If the contradiction had been allowed to become unbridgeable, Hellenism on its part could not have embraced and become leavened by Christianity, and Christianity might have continued an exotic and humble sect instead of rapidly becoming a world religion.

The importance of the work of Clement of Alexandria (*ca.* 150–212) in effecting a symbiosis can therefore hardly be exaggerated. Clement was born a pagan in Athens, and had a complete secular education before he was converted. He succeeded his teacher Pantaenus as head of the catechetical school at Alexandria, and produced many writings of which we have, besides fragments, four works. *Exhortation to the Greeks* points to the follies of paganism and urges acceptance of Christianity. The account of the Greek mysteries in the second chapter is one of our best sources on the subject, and makes it appear that Clement himself was an Eleusinian initiate. To those who have been converted, Clement writes the *Pedagogue,* as a guide for their new conduct. Thirdly, we have *Stromateis* (Miscellanies) in eight discursive books which show the use that devout Christians may make of Greek philosophy. Clement recognized that philosophy had stood in the same relationship to the Greeks as prophecy to the Hebrews, and accordingly believed that devout Christians need cut themselves off from the one no more than from the other. In *The Rich Man's Salvation,*

Clement relaxes, by use of Philonic allegory, another early Christian belief by insisting that rich men can accept Christianity and retain their wealth. Clement is perfectly aware of his role as innovator and reconciler. He starts his *Stromateis* by defending the writing of books—else what are letters for?—and pointing out that if good books are not written the field is left to bad writers, among whom he names Epicurus, "the fountain-head of impiety."

Aside from his significance as innovator, Clement merits a place in Greek literature, both for his own effective writing and because he is a mine of information on previous writers. He mentions some three hundred writers (perhaps largely from secondary books) whose works are lost. Among the Greek poets and philosophers he quotes, along with the Old and New Testament, on every page, he shows special affection for Homer and the highest esteem for Plato. Quotations, moreover, are brought in with aptness and are made the subject of enlightening comment; *Stromateis* (which is literally "mattress ticking") is no such unassorted, if not so well-stuffed, rag bag as the *Deipnosophists* of Clement's contemporary Athenaeus.

When Clement fled Alexandria during the persecutions of Septimius Severus in 202 his eighteen-year-old pupil Origen took charge of the school. Origen was indubitably the greatest scholar and most productive writer of early Christianity; he employed seven stenographers who worked in relays and a battery of copyists, all of whom were provided by a wealthy patron named Ambrose. Of the 6,000 books he is said to have written most have perished, though a great deal is left. Origen is of greater interest to the historian of dogma than of literature. Among his extant Biblical commentaries, homilies, and letters, mention may be made of the apologetic *Against Celsus* and the dogmatic *On Principles. Against Celsus* is a very long reply to the rationalist criticisms leveled against Christianity by the pagan Celsus. Celsus was a Platonist of the late second century, and his *True Word* appears to have been the earliest literary attack on Christianity. Celsus' argument, and a good bit of his actual language, can be reconstituted from Origen's refutation. He apparently satirized Christianity on the grounds of absurdity; it seemed to him a denial of reason that God should favor one people above others, that He should take human form, that religion should be elevated above civic obligations. Origen's *On Principles,* whose four books are extant only in a Latin version and in fragments of the Greek, is a systematic, subtle, and profound exposition of Christian theology. An important textual work of Origen, early lost, is his *Hexapla,* an edition of the Old Testament in six columns giving the Hebrew text, its transliteration into Greek, and four Greek versions. As we should expect from his personal history, Origen is a more intense writer than Clement as well as a more original thinker, and his style is less careful.

In 313 Constantine's edict made Christianity a tolerated religion, and the change in worldly position affected literature as well as life. There is no longer need for a defensive tone, no longer an awkward appropriation of alien forms. The Greek manner becomes so thoroughly assimilated in Christianity that it is now used by Christian Fathers in their intestine quarrels over the Arian heresy, and these quarrels and their literary expression move into the main stream of Greek letters. There is no feeling of anomaly when a bishop writes elegant Greek, no tension between the Christian and the Greek in such authors as Synesius or John Chrysostom. The transition is marked by Eusebius (ca. 260–340) of Caesarea in Palestine, whose literary activity falls after 313. Eusebius was not an original thinker like Origen (whom he greatly admired, though Origen's teaching gave some comfort to the Arians); he justifies Christianity on scholarly grounds, without raising his voice. He deals with Church history as a secular scholar would deal with philology. His merit is that he systematically recorded events, facts, and texts of preceding generations. In connection with his work in Biblical exegesis, for example, he wrote a geography of the Old Testament in four books; the fourth book, called *Onomasticon,* which identifies place names in the Old Testament, survives. A work of similar character is the *Chronicle,* in which, after brief introductory histories of Chaldaeans, Assyrians, Hebrews, Egyptians, Greeks, and Romans, he presents chronological tables of all ancient history, with the object of showing the priority of the Hebrews. This work is extant in Armenian and in Jerome's Latin.

Eusebius' most useful scholarly work is his *Ecclesiastic History* (in ten books, the last two being added to an original eight), which records Christian successions (not development, for it was believed there was none) from the Crucifixion to his own day. His opening paragraph states that his work will record Church leaders and transactions, heretics, penalties visited upon the Jews for the Crucifixion, persecutions, and martyrdoms. The method is that of literary scholarship, and long passages of earlier works are cited. Eusebius' other principal extant works are *Evangelical Preparation* (fifteen books) and *Evangelical Demonstration* (twenty books, of which 1–10 are extant). *Preparation* is an answer to the pagan charge that Christians had forsaken their own religion and adopted Judaism, which they then corrupted; and *Demonstration,* an answer to the Jewish charge that the Christians demanded participation in the promises vouchsafed to the Jews without accepting the obligations those promises involved.

Preparation is particularly valuable for its bountiful quotations from earlier literature, pagan as well as Christian and Jewish. The books are well written by pagan standards, but perhaps their greatest significance lies in the fact that the three faiths are not conceived of as in separate compartments; the historical manifestations of all are regarded as a unit. Besides his theological works Eusebius wrote a fulsome *Life of Constantine* (extant in four books), and addresses to Constantine on the occasion of his thirtieth anniversary as ruler and of his consecration of the Church of the Holy Sepulcher in Jerusalem. The single-minded devotion to Christianity credited to Constantine is surely an exaggeration in a prince who showed himself ruthless in securing his own power and whose acceptance of Christianity was more than a little a matter of political expedience. What Eusebius here did was to embody the Christian ideal in Constantine as a kind of mirror of princes, and thus to assert Christianity's place in the broader world. Even more clearly than Eusebius' style and the character of his other works, these productions show that Christianity was fully naturalized in the Greek environment.

The century after Constantine is, in fact, the golden age of patristic literature. Julian made an abortive attempt to restore paganism (361–363), but a few decades later Theodosius made Christianity the state religion, and paganism was on the defensive until it was extirpated. Christian writers appeared in parts of the world hitherto unrepresented in literature, though Alexandria continued to hold a kind of primacy. The voluminous writings of the Copt Athanasius are chiefly interesting for their anti-Arian doctrine; perhaps the best known of his works is the *Life of Antony* (the eremite), which shows resemblance to such pagan "Lives of the Saints" as Philostratus' *Apollonius of Tyana*. Of all the patristic writers the one who best illustrates the blending of cultures, whose personal thoughts and habits are best known, and who is capable of charming a nonspecialist reader is Synesius (*ca.* 370–412), born of a pagan family in Cyrene which claimed descent from the Heraclids of Sparta, and subsequently bishop of Ptolemais. He farmed, studied philosophy, fought brigands, hunted, dabbled in Neoplatonism, married a Christian wife. All of this we know from his 156 attractive letters, addressed to various friends, among them the intelligent and ill-starred Hypatia. Besides the letters we have a number of other works, equally worth reading. As a young man Synesius was sent to Constantinople to plead for a remission of taxes for Cyrene, and the address *On Kingship* which he delivered before Arcadius in 399 is a thoughtful and outspoken "Mirror of Princes," altogether free of adulation. Here is his complaint that kingship has been orientalized (§ 10):

Nothing has done the Romans more harm in past days than the protection and attention given the sovereign's person. . . . This majesty and the fear of being brought to the level of man by becoming an accustomed sight, caused you to be cloistered and besieged by your very self, seeing very little, hearing very little of those things by which the wisdom of action is accumulated. You rejoice only in the pleasures of the body, and the most material of these, even as many as touch and taste offer you; and so you live the life of a polyp of the sea. As long as you deem man unworthy of you you will not attain man's perfection.

—Augustine FitzGerald

The *Egyptian Tale; or, On Providence* is a kind of philosophical romance. The struggle between Osiris and Typhos represents the conflict between good and evil, and events in a contemporary history at Constantinople are allegorized. His voyage home from Constantinople is described in one of his most charming *Letters* (#4). In Cyrene he is severely criticized, both by the men in white and the men in black, and he voices his disapproval of the excesses of both sophists and monks in his *Dio* (on Dion Chrysostom), which he sends to Hypatia with a covering letter (#154). His *Praise of Baldness,* a piece of ingenious fooling which must still provoke smiles, is suggested by Dion's *Praise of Hair,* which he quotes. *On Dreams* pleads for intercourse with the divine in sleep. His searchings of heart on his elevation to the episcopacy of Ptolemais are revealed in a letter to his brother (#104). As a bishop he gave up hunting, but not fighting for his flock, nor did he give up his attachment to Neoplatonic thought nor pride in the Hellenic heritage. In the seventh of his nine hymns, in Doric dialect and ancient meters, Synesius avows that he is the first to compose hymns to Christ for lyre accompaniment. The opening lines of the first hymn will show the strands that went to form Synesius, and how he wove them into a single skein:

Sound forth, clear-tongued lyre, after the Teian cadence, after the Lesbian movement; sing to me in more time-honored strains a Dorian ode, not one for dainty love-laughing girls or for the adolescence of flowering youths that compelleth desire; for it is a sacred travail of divine wisdom and one unsullied that prompts me to strike the strings of my lyre to divine refrain, and bids me flee from the honied infatuation of earthly loves. What is force and what beauty, what is gold or renown, and what are royal honors as compared with meditations upon God?

—Augustine FitzGerald

With Synesius such designations as "Greek Christian" or "Christian Greek" become futile; the two are become one flesh.

Cappadocia was made illustrious in the fourth century by a great trinity: Basil the Great; his close friend, Gregory of Nazianz; and his younger brother, Gregory of Nyssa, all of whom were educated in the Second Sophistic at Athens. Basil the Great gave eastern orthodoxy its permanent form. Many of his *Homilies* and 365 *Letters* (some falsely ascribed) are extant, and exhibit a cultivated literary style. He quotes freely from the poets, from Plutarch, and especially from Plato. The *Letters* are frequently admonitions, addressed to friends or congregations; many are intended to confirm resistance against Arianism. Whereas Basil's style is Attic, Gregory of Nazianz uses the florid Asianic style and is fond of rhetorical tropes. He is less the churchman and more the literary man. He is represented by 458 *Homilies*, 243 *Letters*, bitter *Invectives* against Julian, and many poems. The letters are highly polished and intended for publication. Some of the poems are theologic, some autobiographic; the latter are *On His Own Life*, in 1,949 iambic lines; *On His Own Matters*, in 600 hexameters; and *Dirge on the Suffering of His Own Soul*, in 175 distichs. It is thought that these poems may have suggested St. Augustine's *Confessions*. Book 8 of *Palatine Anthology* consists of 254 of Gregory's epigrams. His poems are in quantitative verse, except for two hymns, *Evening Hymn* and *Admonition to Virginity*, which are accentual. The long tragedy *Christus Patiens*, which is a cento of Euripidean verses reproduced so faithfully that the play can be used for the textual criticism of Euripides, is falsely ascribed to Gregory; it is, in fact, later by several centuries. Gregory of Nyssa, brother of Basil, is less forceful and less artistic than his Cappadocian peers, but more scholarly and a better philosopher. He is capable of carrying a line of philosophical reasoning up to the point where it might interfere with orthodoxy, and then stopping short and bridging the gap by a Q.E.D. based on the will to conform to orthodoxy. Gregory of Nyssa's writings include commentaries, dogmatic treatises, homilies, and letters.

The best beloved as well as the most voluminous writer of the fourth century was John Chrysostom (344-407). There was some irregularity in his elevation to the episcopacy of Constantinople, and his advocacy of simplicity brought him the enmity of the Empress Eudoxia and part of the population, so that he was the cause of serious riots and was banished. As his name "Golden-mouthed" suggests, he was greatest as a preacher. His sermons were loudly applauded (as custom then allowed) and became the richest mine for subsequent preachers. They show him to be well read, but he seems to make an effort to conceal his erudition; the great merit of the sermons are their numerous effective pictures and analogies from daily life. These and some 240 letters, written to many friends from his exile, reveal a real and sympathetic figure, with pronounced likes and dislikes.

One of John's many pupils was Theodoretus, who is one of the three church historians who carried Eusebius' work forward; his *History* (five books) extends to 428. The greatest of the three is Socrates, each of whose seven books covers the reign of one emperor; Socrates is valuable for his verbatim reports of official documents. Socrates was one of the chief sources for Sozomen, the fullest of the three. The first part of his work, from the Assumption to 323, is lost; the nine extant books (with a lacuna at the end) cover the period from 425 to 439. For John's other successors, as for many contemporaries and predecessors, room cannot be found here. In 379 and the years following, a series of decrees had made dissident forms of Christianity as well as paganism illegal. The age of quest and controversy was over; the authority of the Church Catholic was complete. By the middle of the fifth century the great period of patristic writing had come to its close. Philosophy continued to be taught at Athens until the schools were closed by Justinian in 529. This gesture has been correctly taken to mark the end of antiquity, and hence must be the limit of our survey. But two sixth-century works must be mentioned—the one, because it gives the history of Justinian's own reign, is the most readable history since Appian, and, most of all, shows what the end of antiquity meant politically; and the other, because it makes crystal clear what the end of antiquity signified in the history of the human spirit.

Procopius of Caesarea held high office under Justinian and Belisarius, but was involved in a conspiracy in 562 and died shortly thereafter. He wrote successively, as Gibbon (ch. 40) put it, "the *history,* the *panegyric,* and the *satire* of his own times." His *History* in eight books, is divided (after the model of Appian) into two books on the Persian, two on the Vandal, and three on the Ostrogoth wars, with a final book to cover the period from 551 to 554. The *History* is based on critical first-hand knowledge of events, places, men, and politics. Procopius consciously imitates both Herodotus and Thucydides, and inserts fictive speeches in his work; but his style is straightforward and clear and inspires confidence in the author's competence. Possibly because the outspokenness of the *History* was not well received Procopius filled his six-book *On the Buildings* [*of Justinian*] with fulsome adulation. *On the Buildings* provides valuable information on the history of art and on Byzantine administration. The adulation was apparently insufficient to restore Procopius to imperial favor, and he took his revenge in *Secret History,* which could naturally not be published until after his own death and the end of Justinian's dynasty. There is no reason to doubt Procopius' authorship of *Secret History,* nor the essential truth of the work. Though some of the more lurid passages concerning the habits of the Empress Theodora (of which Gibbon said they "must be veiled in the obscurity of a learned language") may spice the naked truth a little, the picture of the scandals, intrigue, and debauchery of the court must be essentially just. We have here, then, the testimony of an intelligent and experienced observer recording the transformation of the Eastern Roman monarchy into Byzantine despotism.

The implications of this transformation for the life of the intellect become clear in the work of Cosmas Indicopleustes. His *Christian Topography,* written in the sixth century, conceives that the earth is patterned after the Tabernacle of Moses. It is therefore a flat plain with high walls enclosing it on each of its four sides. The sky is a semicylindrical lid which rests on the walls and thus makes a cover for the plain. Motive power for the heavenly bodies is supplied by the angels, who produce night and day and other phenomena by carrying the heavenly bodies round a high mountain that lies to the north of the plain. Perhaps it is a comfort for man not to trouble himself about the nature of the universe, as the Ionian physicists had done more than a millennium before, and not to seek an answer in the nature of the universe itself. But when men turned their backs on the eager inquiries of the Ionians and their successors in the Lyceum and the Museum a vital part of their nature went into a coma, and almost another millennium was to pass before they could rouse themselves from it.

Chapter 17. ORATORS AND ENCYCLOPEDISTS OF THE SECOND SOPHISTIC

THE TEACHERS OF PHILOSOPHY AND RELIGION DEALT WITH IN THE PRECEDING chapter sought relief from the unsatisfactory world about them in a different and ideal reality, and their efforts command respect if not assent. The reality in which the writers of the Second Sophistic took refuge was the reality of Cloud-cuckoo-land. "Your sophist," Dion Chrysostom (4.35–36) represents Diogenes as saying to Alexander in a gross but telling figure, "does not differ one whit from a lecherous eunuch." When Alexander asked why, Diogenes replied:

Because the most wanton eunuchs, protesting their virility and their passion for women, lie with them and annoy them, and yet nothing comes of it, not even if they stay with them night and day. So too in the schools of the sophists. . . .
—*J. W. Cohoon*

The renaissance which began under Hadrian and continued for two centuries was classicism at its worst; never has concern for form so overshadowed matter, and seldom have literary figures received such adulation from their admirers. Next to the actual rulers outstanding Sophists were the most powerful figures in society. They held high official positions, accumulated great wealth, were the darlings of crowds of devotees; cities vied for the honor of harboring them, and of giving them burial. They were the ruin of philosophy and science and history, all of which they scorned. Their actual performances were subject to intricate rules, which their audiences were expert in, but which we cannot hope to know. One of these rules was to confine language and forms to fifth- and fourth-century models; with the matter of their models the Sophists were unconcerned, except to refute slurs on Sophists wherever they found them. Their subjects were trivial or preposterous—Demosthenes defending Aeschines, for example. A similar phenomenon appeared in another renaissance, when Cardinal Bembo found himself unable to mention the Holy

Ghost in a sermon because the words do not occur in Cicero. To balance the canon of the Ten Attic Orators, of whom Isocrates was naturally the supreme model, a new canon was drawn up. Of the composition of this canon there is greatest agreement on the names of Dion Chrysostom, Nicostratus, Polemon, Herodes Atticus, Philostratus, and Aelius Aristides. Our knowledge of these individuals and of the whole movement depends largely on the second Philostratus' *Lives of the Sophists,* which covers the period from Hadrian to Gordian III, and on Eunapius' *Lives of the Philosophers and Sophists* (late fourth century) which is important for the Neoplatonists.

Philostratus' account (*Lives of the Sophists* 25) of the fantastic honors and fees heaped upon Polemon (*ca.* 88–145) and of Polemon's arrogant "temperament" tells us something of the adulation these virtuosi enjoyed. The titles and extant scraps of his work exhibit the belabored emptiness we should expect. Some effective expressions of his, as, for example, "Rome the epitome of the oecumene," are quoted. A more sympathetic figure is the enormously wealthy Herodes Atticus (101–177), who was the most brilliant and successful of the earlier Sophists, and held high political offices. The nature of his princely benefactions (the surviving Odeon at Athens is an example) is evidence of his genuine admiration of the ancient culture and his desire to revivify it. Of his considerable literary productions (he was called "tongue of the Greeks, king of words") only one doubtful and colorless piece remains. Herodes' most distinguished pupil, Aelius Aristides (129–189), provides us with our completest specimens of the Sophists' art. Aelius was born in Mysia, traveled widely, and settled in Smyrna, which counted him its next most important citizen after Homer. His fifty-five *Orations* were intended, like Isocrates', for reading and for posterity; he failed as improviser and as teacher. The speeches include rhetorical exercises, eulogies, condolences, birthday addresses, appeals for imperial assistance for his city, attacks on Plato and Herodotus for speaking lightly of rhetoric, fulsome praise of Athens (in a speech entitled *Panathenaicus,* like Isocrates', but with no political meaning), the same of Rome, with apparently real feeling, and six *Sacred Discourses* which discuss with elaborate art Asclepius' treatment of a disease from which Aelius had been suffering for thirteen years. Aelius is not content to glorify humbuggery, but must disparage real science.

The remaining Sophists of Philostratus' list who limited themselves to declamation we may pass over, but mention must be made of certain writers of the school who made compilations useful for literary study, such as Philostratus himself. The earliest of these still to be named (Dionysius of Halicarnassus, Dio Cassius, and Appian really belong to the school) is Favorinus, an epicene from Arles in Gaul, teacher of Herodes, friend of Plutarch, rival of Polemon, bitter enemy of Galen, honored by public monuments at Athens and Corinth—which were pulled down when Trajan withdrew his favor. Favorinus' two speeches in the corpus of his teacher Dion, *On Fortune* (#64) and *Corinthiaca* (#37; the longest extant specimen of "Asianic" prose of the second century) show the emptiness and excessive ornamentation of their genre. But the collections of anecdotes and miscellaneous jottings in Favorinus' lost *Notebooks* and *Miscellaneous Histories* (in twenty-four books) are the progenitors of a class of encyclopedic compilations rich in gossip which includes Aulus Gellius and Diogenes Laertius (who used them), Athenaeus, Aelian, and Clement of Alexandria.

Lives of the Sophists of Philostratus is one such gossipy compilation. In the second and third centuries four Philostrati of the same Lemnian family are known to have been practicing Sophists, and scholars are not yet perfectly agreed as to how the items in the Philostratean corpus are to be distributed among them. Of Philostratus I, Suidas gives a long list of works; the only title which coincides with anything in the corpus is a *Nero*. Philostratus II (*ca.* 170–248) is the author of the *Lives,* and necessarily (for he alludes to the work in *Lives*) of *Apollonius of Tyana,* and so of the two most important works in the corpus. He is also the author of *Erotic Epistles* and a brief discourse *On Nature and Law*. Philostratus III and IV wrote on art criticism, and will be dealt with presently. The author of *Lives* and *Apollonius* was a member of the salon of Julia Domna, Septimus Severus' Syrian empress, who affected an interest in philosophy and mathematics. It was at her request that he wrote the *Apollonius,* but it was published after her death in 217. *Lives* is dedicated to Gordian, and was therefore written between 230 and 238. Its chief purpose is to glorify the triumphs of the sophistic tribe, to which Philostratus himself belonged; the book reads like nothing so much as the effusions of a public relations expert in a movie magazine. Philostratus purposely avoids anything like systematic order in the arrangement of the *Lives* as a whole or in the treatment of individual Sophists; the style is conversational, and only what is sensational is mentioned. The biographies of Eunapius, who imitated Philostratus, are equally exasperating.

In the reign of Diocletian, when the struggle between Christianity and paganism was most bitter, it occurred to a certain Hierocles to argue that Apollonius of Tyana was as remarkable a sage, miracle worker, and exorcist as Jesus of Nazareth. Christian refutations have left Apollonius with a bad reputation as a wizard and charlatan. To judge from Philostratus' *Life,* Apollonius, who was born at the beginning of the Christian era but lived to Nerva's reign, was a good and earnest man (though hardly as good as Philostratus paints him) who in another century would have become a saint; and Philostratus surely had no thought of presenting him as a rival to Jesus, though Julia Domna may have thought of him in that light. It was she who gave Philostratus the memoirs of Apollonius collected by his disciple Damis, which he used along with a life written by another admirer and letters and treatises of Apollonius himself. The framework is a travel narrative; Apollonius' counsels, miracles, and discussions are told in connection with his movements from place to place. He was a very rigid ascetic, observing a vow of complete silence for five years, he divested himself of all property, he believed in metempsychosis and other Pythagorean doctrines, he consorted with the Gymnosophists of the Thebaid and with Brahmins, he rebuked evil doers and composed quarrels, he opposed bloody sacrifices, he performed miracles, and his career was closed by a translation rather than by ordinary death. However the legend came to grow (and diverse elements are recognizable in it), there can be little doubt that there is a man behind it; and even if it is of whole cloth it is not only edifying reading but shows one kind of quest which concerned men of the second century. The nearest analogue to *Life of Apollonius of Tyana* is Athanasius' *Life of Antony.*

A less well-known production of the same syncretistic, mystical, religious character is Philostratus' *Heroicus,* a dialogue in which a humble Greek of the Thracian Chersonese seeks to convert a Phoenician seaman to belief in the cult of the hero Protesilaus and of other Greek heroes. The piece is interesting evidence of an upsurge in the second century of popular beliefs, which must always have persisted but of which our formal literature shows little trace. In *Gymnasticus* (known only through testimonia until a century ago), Philostratus seeks to revive interest in another aspect of the ancient culture by producing a handbook on the practices of the gymnasia. Only the first sixty-four of the collection of seventy-three *Love Letters* are of an erotic nature, being addressed to both boys and girls, and though letter writing was a regular sophistic practice these do not show the elaboration characteristic of Philostratus, and are probably not his. Many of their conceits are like those in the Latin elegiasts, and both may derive from a common Hellenistic source. Epistle 33, it may be noted, was the original of Jonson's *Drink to Me Only with Thine Eyes.* There is no reason to doubt the genuineness of the remaining nine letters, which are addressed to specific persons, one to the Empress Julia Domna. A brief discourse on *Law and Custom,* an old sophistic commonplace, is attached to the *Letters.*

Imagines, a series of sixty-five short talks on a collection of paintings represented as hanging in a portico facing the bay of Naples, is probably by Philostratus III. The talks are addressed to a ten-year-old boy who is standing at the head of a group of visitors as they move from picture to picture. They are exercises in literary expression rather than art criticism as we understand it. Though technical matters, such as perspective, use of shadows, intensity of coloring, are mentioned, elaboration of the subjects of the paintings receives most attention. It is doubtful whether the pictures actually existed or are imaginary; but students of ancient painting find them useful, nevertheless, for the descriptions have been shown to be of the classes of pictures which actually were painted. Another *Imagines* dealing with seventeen pictures, based upon, and inferior to, the first, is ascribed to a grandson of Philostratus II, called the Younger Philostratus or Philostratus IV. Usually printed with *Imagines* are fourteen *Descriptions of Statues* by Callistratus (third or fourth century). The treatment is like that of the Philostrati, and whether or not the statues described actually existed, others like them certainly did.

Another work frequently bracketed with Philostratus', of whose *Lives of the Sophists* it is an imitation, is *Lives of the Philosophers and Sophists* of Eunapius (346–414). The want of system in his *Lives* is more exasperating than Philostratus', but just as Philostratus is valuable for showing the figure which Sophists cut so Eunapius tells us more about the behavior of Neoplatonists than we could otherwise have known. Some of his striking omissions seem purely capricious; so, for example, when he mentions names of his predecessors who wrote lives of philosophers he fails to mention Diogenes Laertius.

The date of Diogenes Laertius, author of *Lives of Eminent Philosophers,* is unknown but can hardly have been later than the third century, for he does not mention Neoplatonism, though he is particularly interested in the Platonic succession. Diogenes Laertius was not a clever man, and his book is badly put together, but in default of any similar work from antiquity it is indispensable for the information it preserves, some surely derived from preceding handbooks but some doubtless from Diogenes' own reading. After an introductory book dealing with ancient "barbarian" philosophies and the Seven Sages, the material is arranged according to an Ionian succession (Books 2–7), beginning with Anaximander, and an Italian succession (Book 8), beginning with Pythagoras; a scattered group outside these successions is treated in Books 9 and 10. The long tenth book on Epicurus is extremely valuable for its original Epicurean documents. Besides our *Lives of Eminent Philosophers* Diogenes also wrote a book of *Epigrams in Various Meters,* and the complacency with which he cites his own wretched verses in the *Lives* is a measure of his judgment. He was not a student of philosophy but a literary man, and like other biographers we have dealt with he is more interested in a piquant anecdote than in philosophical dogma. Yet he knows the kind of facts that a user of such a book would seek, and his pieces on Socrates, Plato, and Aristotle, on Zeno and Chrysippus, are competent summaries. Diogenes' influence on European education has been out of proportion to his intellectual merit; he not only introduced the study of the history of philosophy but was himself much read, for example, by Montaigne.

If the *Lives of the Eminent Philosophers* is indispensable to students of philosophy, the *Deipnosophists* (Doctors at Dinner) of Athenaeus of Naucratis (third century) is equally indispensable to students of literature, being our single most important source for Greek literary gossip and quotations from lost works. About seven hundred writers who would otherwise remain unknown are quoted. As a book in its own right, *Deipnosophists* is much weaker than other fictive literary parties. The dinner is too long (apparently it lasts three days), the guests are too numerous, and though grammarians, philosophers, musicians, and physicians participate, their characters are not precisely limned. But if the whole does not make a credible drama, the details about food and drink, cooking and serving, dinner entertainments and furniture, parasites and hetaerae, and above all the literary gossip and quotations, apt or funny or just too good to pass over, make Athenaeus as good a bed book as Burton's *Anatomy of Melancholy* as well as an encyclopedic guide to late Greek manners and tastes and literary stock. As with all books of this kind it is impossible that Athenaeus should not have used previous collections of quotations and anecdotes, but for the modern reader the only drawback to such composition is that anachronisms in representation of customs may sometimes be involved. It appears that the book was originally much larger than the fifteen books we have. In our texts, Books 1, 2, and the beginning of 3 are only an epitome, made in antiquity, and there are gaps in Book 11 and at the end of Book 15.

Reality can be dodged by a fund of piquant anecdotes as surely, if not so well, as by conscious archaizing or by a quest for otherworldliness. A man or age which derives sustenance from entertaining anecdotes, to use a figure suggested by Athenaeus, is like a host who covers an undistinguished *pièce de résistance* with elaborate *hors d'oeuvres*. Claudius Aelianus, the third (not necessarily in time) of our third-century encyclopedists, seems conscious of the frivolity of anecdotes as pure art and seeks to give his a moral, or rather to choose anecdotes to which a moral has been attached. His *Nature of Animals* (seventeen books) illustrates the marvels of nature in endowing dolphins with music, elephants with docility, dogs with loyalty, bees with mechanical dexterity, and uses these animals, after the Cynic fashion, to rebuke the corruption of mankind. Not all the stories are edifying; there is a long series on the love life of animals, some of which indeed convey lessons of loyalty and devotion to death but others of which can only be intended to titillate. There is just enough pretension to science to make the reader deplore the decline from the Aristotelian level in zoology. The first fifteen chapters of Aelian's other work, *Various History* (imperfectly preserved in fourteen books), also deal with animal life, but the remainder is filled with anecdotes of figures historical or otherwise. The *Various History* is sometimes cited for historical data otherwise unknown, but mostly the stories which display the utmost variety in subject and are generally very well told have no other value than to entertain by relating curious, paradoxical, or amusing incidents. Plutarch, who must have used some of the same sources as Aelian used, usually seeks to give his versions ethical meaning. Aelian's remaining surviving item is a collection of twenty fictive *Rustic Epistles,* of which the material is drawn from the orators and comic poets of the fourth century. It is of interest to note that Aelian, who is praised by Philostratus (2.31) for his perfect Attic, was born at Praeneste, near Rome. This is additional proof, if proof were necessary, of the complete control of letters that the Second Sophistic had acquired. We turn now to glance at the outstanding representatives of the movement in the fourth century, Himerius and Themistius, Libanius and Julian.

There is no better key to the life and letters of the fourth century than the voluminous works of Libanius (314–*ca.* 393). Libanius was born of a wealthy family at Antioch, educated in sophistic at Athens, opened a school at Constantinople in 342 and was forced to leave it by the intrigues of rivals in 346, and eventually settled in Antioch. His pupils included Basil the Great, Gregory of Nazianz, Theodore of Mopsuestia, and John Chrysostom, whom he would have liked to make his successor "if the Christians had not snatched him." The central fact in his career was the friendship of Julian; Julian's death meant to him the loss of a friend and a defender of Hellenism. Seven of his orations have to do with Julian; in one, delivered sixteen years after Julian's death, he hints that Christians were indirectly responsible. If Julian had survived, Libanius would certainly have been given some high public office; as it was, Libanius' influence was enormous, quite comparable to that of the second-century Sophists. But whereas Libanius, like his predecessors, retreated to the classics for forms and examples, he was deeply concerned for contemporary men and events, had a program, and was personally less arrogant. His program was the preservation of Hellenism, for reasons like Plutarch's. In matters of faith he was perfectly tolerant; cultured Christians were among his close associates. What he objected to (as in #28, *On Sanctuaries*) was the break with old traditions of culture and the barbarization of art, poetry, and eloquence that must result from the ascetic tendencies of the Christians. It is a testimonial to his own tolerance and sense of responsibility that he writes on behalf of Christians as well as pagans, and that he intercedes with Christian emperors on behalf of pagans.

Libanius' popularity is attested by more than five hundred manuscripts, none, naturally, containing all his works. These may be divided into three groups—exercises, orations, and letters. In the first group are some fifty school *Declamations,* on mythological, historical, or dramatic (an appropriate speech for a given character in a given situation) subjects, and also 143 *Practice Models,* including descriptions, dramatic situations, and the like. To this group also belong the introductions and argumenta of the orations of Demosthenes, who was Libanius' favorite author. The *Orations* number sixty-five. A few are on fictive subjects ("an apology for Socrates"), some on ethical commonplaces ("greed," "wealth," "boasting"), but most are on contemporary affairs, and afford an insight into the life of the schools, aspects of a great eastern Greek metropolis, imperial administration, or the personalities of the emperors. Each adds substantially to our knowledge, and altogether they present a favorable picture of an educated Greek gentleman seriously concerned to fulfill the obligations laid upon him by tradition. This picture is made clearer by the largest corpus of letters that has come down from antiquity. These number 1,607, besides 400 Latin letters which are spurious. These letters thank, praise, condole, intercede, recommend, and introduce; among the addressees are all the important personages of the age, Christian as well as pagan. Libanius' reputation in his own day was so high that it was considered a prize to obtain a letter from him. Libanius was not a forceful intellect, and for all his care in composition and generous use of figures, he is not a great writer. But surely Bentley was unfair in calling him "a dreaming pedant, with his elbow on his desk." Conservative opponents of revolution can only be called dreamy romantics—when the revolution succeeds.

Himerius (315–386), who was born at Prusa and taught at Athens throughout his adult life, shows no awareness of religious or political currents of his day. The twenty-four (out of eighty known to the Byzantines) *Orations* are school pieces or addresses to students at opening or closing exercises, birthdays, recoveries from illness, and the like. He is the perfect Sophist, for whom meaning is immaterial and who is only concerned with pretty sounds and pretty words, which he borrows generously from lyric and, especially, pastoral poetry. And yet men of much greater force could apparently learn from him, for Basil the Great and Gregory of Nazianz were among his pupils.

Quite a different picture is presented by Themistius (*ca.* 317–388). He was educated in part by his father, who was a country gentleman and a student of philosophy in Paphlagonia, and when Themistius removed to Constantinople in 337 and opened a school there in 345 he refused to accept salary or fees and continued his interest in philosophy. For his own use (he says they were published without his consent) he made *Paraphrases of Aristotle*, expanding Aristotle's knotty language and inserting occasional explanatory excursuses. Aristotle had already been much commented upon, but this treatment was a new and useful departure. Themistius' paraphrases on *Analytics, Physics, On the Soul*, and some of the *Parva Naturalia* are extant. If these show the seriousness of his intellectual interests, his *Orations*, of which thirty-five are extant, show him to have been a man of spirit with a sense of responsibility to society. He was, in effect, the official public orator of Constantinople, and the five speeches addressed to the emperors on various occasions are among his best. None are adulatory; his complimentary language is really a courteous vehicle for conveying the philosopher's ideal of the responsibilities of kingship. Oration 1, addressed to Constantius, bears the collateral title *On Philanthropy*. In #2 he finds no higher praise for Constantius than that he has realized Plato's ideal of the philosopher-king. Oration 5, *To Jovian on His Assumption of the Consulate* (A.D. 364) is a forceful plea for religious tolerance, which the Christians were eager to end:

He who uses force in these matters robs us of a possession which God has vouchsafed. . . . The law of liberty neither confiscation nor crucifixion nor torture can crush. You can master the body and kill it, if so be, but the soul will go its way, carrying with it its own thought along with the law of liberty, even if its tongue be constrained.

There are other passages also which illustrate Themistius' austere liberalism. If he cannot be called an original thinker either in philosophy or politics, yet he is a demonstration of what the abiding influence of Greek democratic culture could produce.

Concerning Julian, called the Apostate (332–363), it is hard to be temperate, for those who refuse to believe that he was in league with Satan are apt to exalt him beyond his merits. For stories of his persecutions of Christians we must go to Christian polemicists, who may have been right but were certainly prejudiced. On the basis of his own writings and the contemporary Latin historian Ammianus Marcellinus his anti-Christian activity consisted, not in placing disabilities upon them, but in withdrawing special privileges they had enjoyed. Of his anti-Christian measures the one that seems pettiest, and is at the same time characteristic of his temperament, was his prohibition to Christian teachers to use the pagan classics in their teaching. Julian was the first Caesar after Julius to attain eminence as a writer. His extant work includes orations, satires, and letters.

Julian was nephew to Constantine the Great, after whose death the Emperor Constantius, fearing rivals to his power, put Julian's father and half brother to death and interned Julian in a castle in Cappadocia. Having no sons to succeed to his power Constantius made Julian "Caesar" in 355 and assigned him the task of pacifying the Gallic provinces. Julian's impressive and unexpected success, especially in a battle at Strasbourg, aroused Constantius' jealousy, whereupon he ordered the best part of Julian's troops to be transferred to the East. The troops, who were supposed to serve only in the West, demurred, and at Paris in 360 proclaimed Julian "Augustus." While Julian was at Nish, on his way to contest the empire with Constantius, Constantius died, and Julian became emperor, in November, 361. In February, 362, he issued his edict of tolerance for paganism and restored the rights of Christian heretics who had been banished. In June, 363, he fell, by a wound said to have been inflicted by one of his own soldiers, fighting against the Parthians under their King Sapor. It was on receiving his death blow that Julian is reported to have said (the story is doubtless apocryphal), "Thou hast conquered, Galilaean."

Julian ceased being a Christian in 350, but did not openly profess paganism until 361. After that date his writings all have to do with his religious reforms. The first oration in our collections is an encomium to Constantius, written before he undertook the Gallic command. The second is another, drawing comparisons favorable to Constantius between himself and the heroes of Homer, written at Paris. The third expresses thanks to Eusebia, Constantius' first wife; Eusebia had shown him great kindness, when he was an awkward youth at Milan, and had given him books to take with him to the wars. Oration 4 is a prose *Hymn to Helios,* written probably for Helios' birthday festival on December 25, 362, and dedicated to Sallustius, the principal theologian of paganism. For Julian, Helios is virtually the sole deity; the other gods of paganism are intermediary powers. Oration 5 is a similar prose *Hymn to the Mother of the Gods.* #6 is addressed *To Uneducated Cynics,* and #7 *To the Cynic Heraclius, on Composing Myths.* In their asceticism and rejection of myths contemporary Cynics were close to Christians, and both these pieces are indirect attacks on Christianity. Oration 8 is a *Consolation to Himself on the Departure of Sallustius,* who had been ordered by Constantius to leave Julian's company in Gaul. *Caesars* or *Kronia* is a satire in which Romulus is represented as entertaining various outstanding emperors who set forth their claims to distinction; Christianity is satirized as offering easy absolution for sins, no matter how often repeated. *Misopogon* (Beard Hater) satirizes the inhabitants of Antioch for their frivolous pursuit of pleasure and their cool reception of his pagan austerities.

Among Julian's eighty-seven *Letters,* which are the fullest source for information concerning his career and convictions, some are personal and some of a more formal nature. Among the latter are *To Themistius; To the Athenians,* written from Nish, to justify his acceptance of the title of Augustus; and the fragmentary *To a Priest,* encouraging pagan priests to emulate Christian in teaching morality. Letter 25 (Wright 51) addressed *To the Community of the Jews,* relieves the Jews of discriminatory taxation and repressive ordinances and promises that

when I have successfully concluded the war with Persia, I shall rebuild by my own efforts the sacred city of Jerusalem, which for so many years you have longed to see inhabited, and may bring settlers there, and, together with you, sanctify the Most High God therein.

Julian's motive here was rather anti-Christian than pro-Zionist, and similar manifestations appear in other letters. His principal anti-Christian work was *Against the Galilaeans,* known only from extensive excerpts from its first book in Cyril's refutation. Like Porphyry, from whom he borrowed, Julian rebukes the Christians for being degenerate Jews, and the Jews for worshiping an exclusive tribal God, as opposed to the universal deities of the pagans. Julian, who was only thirty-two at his death, had not named a successor, and his army hailed Jovian as emperor. It was this Jovian to whom Themistius had addressed his plea for tolerance, but Jovian restored Christianity as the official religion, and Julian remained, not only the last champion of Hellenism, but for many centuries the last secular writer. With his death the Middle Ages may be said to begin.

There remain to be mentioned, as an offshoot of the work of the Sophists, a number of lexicographical works which have been of great importance in the history of scholarship. Julius Pollux of Naucratis dedicated his ten-book *Onomasticon* of Attic words and phrases, a kind of thesaurus of rare words for the use of orators, to the Emperor Commodus (180–192). The work is arranged by subjects, and doubtless leans heavily on earlier works; Book 4, on music, dancing, and theater, is the most valuable. The scholiast on Lucian's *Lexiphanes,* and on *Rhetorician's Vade Mecum,* says that the satire in these pieces is aimed at Pollux. The biography of Pollux and criticism of his oratory are given in Philostratus' *Lives* 2.12. The most extensive of our ancient lexica (and even so it is an abridgment) is that of

Hesychius of Alexandria, probably of the fifth century. The work of Hesychius is a glossary rather than a lexicon, and it has enabled critics to restore an original word in an ancient text where its place has been taken by an explanatory synonym. The *Geographical Lexicon* of Stephen of Byzantium was so large that the articles before *S* covered fifty volumes. It included notices of historical events and important personages and extracts from ancient authors. A few entries, chiefly at the end of *D,* are preserved, as well as abridgments of some of the remainder. There were a number of compilers of chrestomathies; the Proclus whose *Chrestomathy* is the ultimate source of our knowledge of the Cyclic poets is almost certainly not the Neoplatonic philosopher. The only chrestomathy which has come down in approximately complete form is that of John Stobaeus (of Stobi in Macedonia), probably of the sixth century. Its four books contain 206 sections which present extracts, many of which would otherwise be unknown, from some 500 authors. Finally, a word must be said of Photius, patriarch at Constantinople in the years 858–867 and 878–886, two of whose numerous works are important for the history of ancient literature. His *Lexicon,* preserved in a single Cambridge manuscript, is based on good ancient sources. Far more important is his *Bibliotheca* or *Myriobiblon,* which summarizes, criticizes, and excerpts 280 separate works. The 280 chapters fill 545 double-column, printed quarto pages. He is interested, and a competent critic, in all the arts and sciences, but especially in history; he is weakest in poetry. Photius is extremely valuable for the many authors he has preserved from oblivion, but valuable too for his shrewd and terse critical remarks.

We shall now take our last sweep backward to assemble and consider a group of imaginative writers in prose, all of whom may in some sense be styled writers of romances.

Chapter 18. LUCIAN, THE NOVEL

OF MANY OF THE RELIGIOUS AND PHILOSOPHICAL TEACHERS OF THE SECOND CEN-
tury and those following, the sincerity cannot be questioned, and not all
the Sophists were vain popinjays. But it is evident that professional specialization would lead to hypocritical posturing in religion and to mere virtuoso
preciosity in letters. The favored status and official countenance which
professional practitioners in both departments enjoyed tempted to charla-
tanry and made lay criticism difficult. It wanted a questioning mind to
probe into pretensions, an agile but detached wit to perceive their ab-
surdities, a sharp and deft pen to expose them and prick their dupes into
thinking for themselves. These gifts Lucian of Samosata (*ca.* 120–190)
possessed in measure so abundant as to make him the most stimulating
and amusing (but not the most original thinker or the most substantial)
Greek writer since the decline of Athens. Even the shortest list of Greek
classics with a direct claim on a modern reader's attention must find room
for Lucian.

If that claim has often been disputed the reasons are easy to see. Those
who cherish tradition are made uncomfortable when even a Tartuffe is
exposed, for it is hard to set limits to a probing wit. Nor is Lucian's good
faith as a satirist beyond question. No one believed in the Olympians he
derides, in the Tartuffes he unmasks; rather than demonstrating the folly
of superstition he may simply be exploiting an existing mass of disbelief
—and being careful not to go beyond it—for his own profit. He has no
positive doctrine to offer to balance his ridicule of the spurious. He is
neither as bold nor as constructive in his milieu as Rabelais or Swift (with
both of whom he shows marked affinities) were in theirs. And yet in an
age when convention has hardened into an impervious shell it is a whole-
some thing to crack through to reality. It is significant that many of
Lucian's best dialogues represent the interlocutors as dead, and so surely
stripped of trappings which conceal men's true nature. When values are
distorted by Panglosses and baronial quarterings and inquisitions and
Pococurantes, then "Cultivate your garden" acquires a special meaning.

Negative and frivolous as he may be, the implication of the best of Lucian is not very different from the teaching of Socrates: the unexamined life is not worth living.

But it is as a creative literary artist rather than as a profound thinker that Lucian makes his special claim. He has a rich imagination, an agile wit, and a style whose verve perfectly suits his matter. Dialogue is his most successful form, but his art is nearer Aristophanes' than Plato's. He is all head and no bowels. His wit is bright and hard, capable of thinking the familiar world away and substituting another operating on different laws. His characters are never psychologically delineated so as to engage a reader's sympathy or antipathy; as in Aristophanes they are pure mathematical symbols, useful only to make a demonstration explicit and to create fun. Lucian learned from his predecessors, of course, from Plato, from Comedy Old and New, from Menippus, whom he specially mentions. But surely scholars go too far in making his work merely an adaptation of Menippus. In the Lucianic dialogue Lucian is not only the master but unique.

The instability which critics ancient and modern have charged against Lucian is a reflection of his maturing intellect, and admirable rather than otherwise. He was born in Syria of a humble family which could not afford secondary education for him, and so was apprenticed to an uncle who was a statuary. The basis for the choice was his childish habit of scraping the wax from his school tablet and making little figures of it; Lucian's writings do, in fact, show a marked appreciation for works of art. On the first day of his apprenticeship Lucian spoiled a block of stone, was beaten, and ran home. At night he saw a vision (all this he tells us in his autobiographical *Dream*) in which two female figures, Statuary and Culture, set forth the attractions of the careers they offer. Lucian decided to follow Culture (or Rhetoric), learned Greek so perfectly as to reveal no trace of his native Syrian, probably practiced law for a short time in Antioch, and achieved great success as a practicing Sophist in Greece, Italy, and Asia Minor. For a time he held a lucrative chair of rhetoric in Gaul. But about the age of forty he wearied of the emptiness of Rhetoric and deserted her for Dialogue. In *The Double Indictment,* also autobiographic, he answers Rhetoric's charge that he was ingrate and disloyal (§ 31):

Gentlemen, all that the plaintiff has said is true. She educated me; she bore me company in my travels; she made a Greek of me. She has each of these claims to a husband's gratitude. I have now to give my reasons for abandoning her and cultivating the acquaintance of Dialogue: and, believe me, no motive of self-interest shall induce me to misrepresent the facts. I found, then, that the discreet bearing, the seemly dress, which had distinguished her in the days of her union with the illustrious demesman of Paeania (Demosthenes), were now thrown aside: I saw her tricked out and bedizened, rouged and painted like a courtesan.

—*H. W. and F. G. Fowler*

His rejection of Rhetoric must have branded Lucian a renegade among the Sophists; Philostratus pointedly fails to give him his merited place in *Lives of the Sophists*. The change meant, not that Lucian was now to turn philosopher in any precise sense, but that he would lead a simple life, forsake the pursuit of wealth, and free himself of the degrading restraints depicted in *The Dependent Scholar*. But toward the end of his life he realized, as he tells us in the *Apology*, that it was not degrading to receive pay, and accepted a highly remunerative official post in Egypt. His conversion to philosophy by the Platonist Nigrinus, of which he tells in *Nigrinus*, was not very serious. What he admired in the Academy was its suspension of judgment and its use of dialogue, and he was also sympathetic to the Cynics for their contempt of convention; but he was impatient with the speculations of the one, and with the pride in humility of the other. His only real interest in philosophy was to express contempt for its contemporary practitioners. The only philosopher of whom he speaks with genuine admiration is Epicurus. In the last paragraph of *Alexander the Oracle Monger* he explains that he had composed the work

to strike a blow for Epicurus, that great man whose holiness and divinity of nature were *not* shams, who alone had and imparted true insight into the good, and who brought deliverance to all that consorted with him.

—*H. W. and F. G. Fowler*

There is no sure method of testing the genuineness or establishing the chronology of most of the eighty-two pieces (besides epigrams in the *Anthology*) ascribed to Lucian. It is probable that the rhetorical pieces come from his early period, the philosophical pieces next, and the satires last. Some of his work falls into groups, presumably deriving from the same period, according as it is influenced by New Comedy, by Menippus, or follows a certain pattern. The usual classification is by categories, as follows:

1. *Rhetorical pieces.*—These differ in merit but not in kind from the usual sophistic productions. To this class belong *Tyrannicide, Disinherited, Phalaris I* and *II* (the tyrant of Acragas sends his brazen bull to Delphi: should the Delphians accept it?), *Dipsas, Praise of a Fly,* and others. *A Slip of the Tongue in Salutation,* on the other hand, clearly belongs to his last period, and shows the uncertainty of dating any of the pieces.

2. *Literary pieces.*—In this group mention may be made of *Lexiphanes*

and *Trial in the Court of Vowels,* both of which ridicule extreme Atticizing, and *How to Write History,* which is an acute criticism of rhetorical and imitative historians and may still be used as an elementary text in historiography. *How to Write History* is, in effect, an introduction to *The True History,* which is a fantastic and delightful account of an adventurous journey involving a flight to the moon and a voyage inside a whale whose interior accommodated whole warring cities. *True History* may have been intended as a parody of certain Hellenistic utopias. Certainly it is to be classed as a romance. Its moralizing is negligible, especially in comparison with the voyages of Cyrano or Gulliver which it helped inspire, but it is sufficiently justified by its exuberant fancy and high adventure. Rostovtzeff has shown that Lucian must have used a Greek romance with a Scythian background for his *Toxaris.*

3. *Satires of philosophy.*—This group contains some of Lucian's most mature and most amusing work. The most ambitious, perhaps, is *Hermotimus,* which ridicules the pretensions of all the schools, but especially the Stoic. Much the same thing is done in *Cock, Sale of Lives, Icaromenippus, Demonax, Charon, Fisher, Zeus Cross-examined, Voyage to the Lower World.*

4. *General satires.*—These are not very different in manner or spirit from the previous group but are directed against classes other than philosophers. The most outspoken attacks on religious humbuggery are *The Liar, Alexander the Oracle Monger,* and *Peregrinus.* The vanity of conventional values is satirized in a series of *Dialogues—Of the Gods, Of the Sea Gods, Of the Hetaerae.* False pretensions to scholarship and the degradation of the "kept" scholar are pilloried in *The Illiterate Book-Fancier* and *The Dependent Scholar.*

5. *Miscellaneous works.*—These include *Tragopodagra* (Tragic Gout) and *Ocypus* (Swiftfoot) in verse. The style of *Lucius; or, The Ass* is coarser than Lucian's usual style, but there is no sufficient reason to deny his authorship, or to call it, as is often done, a reworking, retaining the original style, of an older work by Lucius of Patrae, which was also the model for Apuleius' *Metamorphoses.* It is most probably an epitome, by another hand, of a romance written by Lucian himself and called *Metamorphoses.*

With any satirist, even with one as angry as Juvenal seems to be, there is always a question whether the indignation is genuine or part of a literary convention. But even if Lucian's moralizing is sincere it remains true that his function as teacher is secondary to his function as entertainer. His work is of the highest significance in restoring to Greek letters literature's chief province, the artistic presentation of works of creative imagination.

The tradition of artistic imaginative works produced for pleasure is naturally very old. The presence of conscious romance in Greek literature is one of the attributes which distinguishes that from other surviving ancient literatures, and notably from the Hebrew. No history of romantic fiction can do other than begin with *Odyssey*. The stories of Candaules' wife, of Rhampsinitus' treasure, and of Xerxes' love in Herodotus (1.8–12; 2.121; 9.108–113) are complete novelettes combining love and adventure and are part of a continuing Ionian tradition of the art of the logos. Xenophon's *Cyropedia* is fictionalized and romanticized biography; the story of Abradatas and Panthea which it contains has been called the first love story in European prose. Aristides of Miletus wrote a collection of lascivious *Milesian Tales* in the second century B.C.; some of these were translated into Latin by Cornelius Sisenna in the first century B.C. and have doubtless left their mark in Petronius' *Satyrica* and Apuleius' *Metamorphoses*. Parthenius' short *Love Romances* present unfamiliar tales of well-known mythological figures, usually against a background of war. Certain works classified as "travel" were doubtless utopian romances; the *Hiera Anagraphe* of Euhemerus probably belonged to this class. A utopian or moralizing motive is responsible for moralizing embellishments in such works as Dion's *Euboean Discourse* or Philostratus' *Life of Apollonius of Tyana* and perhaps Athanasius' *Life of Antony*.

The practice cases of the rhetorical schools sometimes involved romantic plots, like those of New Comedy. New Comedy characters and situations are the subject matter of the delightful *Letters* of Alciphron, who was a contemporary and, according to Aristaenetus, correspondent of Lucian. The 122 letters of Alciphron's collection are divided into two larger groups, each subdivided into two smaller sections. The country letters involve *Fishermen* and *Farmers;* the town letters, *Parasites* and *Hetaerae*. All are amusing, even those that are pathetic; all are offered as spectacle; there is no attempt to engage the reader's sympathy for the characters, as there is in the romance. Alciphron is only the best known of the letter writers; Hercher's edition of the epistolographers contains 1,600 letters of sixty different authors. For our purpose only Aristaenetus (sixth century) need be mentioned. His sixty-one *Letters* are really short stories, humorous or coarse, culled from such collections of anecdotes as the encyclopedists of the Second Sophistic compiled.

Erwin Rohde's classic work on the Greek romances (*Der griechische Roman und seine Vorlaeufer*, 1876) postulated the Second Sophistic as the origin of fiction of that type. The better known surviving romances, Chariton's *Chaereas and Callirhoe*, Xenophon of Ephesus' *Habrocomes and Anthia*, Heliodorus' *Theagenes and Chariclea*, Achilles Tatius' *Leu-*

cippe and Clitophon, and Longus' *Daphnis and Chloe,* do plainly show the effects of the Second Sophistic, but the discovery in the 1890's of the fragments of the *Ninus Romance,* which is dated on good grounds to the first century B.C., proved that the genre existed long before the Second Sophistic came into being. It may well be that a prime impulse to romance was a desire on the part of peoples who had lost their political independence to assert the dignity of their national traditions, to impress the dominant Greek environment as well as to bolster their own self-esteem, by making some great national figure of the remote past into a romantic hero. The Assyrian Semiramis, the Egyptian Sesostris, the Phrygian Manes, the Hebrew Moses, as well as Ninus, seem to have become romantic bearers of patriotic traditions which had grown faded in the Greek environment. Very early in the Hellenistic period Berossus, priest of Bel, dedicated his *Babyloniaca* to Antiochus I Soter, and Manetho, high priest at Heliopolis, his *Aegyptiaca* to Ptolemy Philadelphus. We have noticed above that much of the Alexandrian Jewish writing was similarly motivated.

The remains of the *Ninus Romance* consist of two extensive separate fragments. In the first, the sixteen-year-old hero Ninus and the heroine, daughter of Derceia but herself unnamed, each approach the other's mother, declare their love, and ask for a speedy marriage. In the second, the young couple seem to be together at the beginning, but Ninus is soon marshaling an Assyrian army of 70,000 foot, 30,000 horse, and 150 elephants against an Armenian enemy. Ninus is doubtless the mythical founder of Nineveh, and Derceia is a variant of Derceto, mother of Semiramis, Ninus' consort. The tale then might be taken as an illustration of the progress from the semi-historical to the purely fictional romance. The tendency is best illustrated by the evolution of the *Alexander Romance.* The oldest extant version is that of Pseudo-Callisthenes, dated about A.D. 300, but papyrus fragments indicate that a large part of the material goes back to the period shortly after the death of Alexander the Great. New fragments of other romances (which show, incidentally, that the genre was much more copious than was suspected) illustrate the same tendency of using an increasingly disguised historical background for fiction.

The *Ninus Romance,* then, is typical of the genre in resting ultimately on a "historical" background, and it is typical also in the character of the hero and heroine. The youthful heroes are gallant and impulsive but strictly honorable; the heroines are supremely beautiful and chaste and continuously conscious of their chastity. The lesser characters are not so immaculate a white or unsullied a crimson, but most of the reader's attention and all his sympathy are pre-empted by hero and heroine. They are not types to be apprehended intellectually like characters in drama, even New Comedy, but they demand emotional identification of the reader, who is to agonize over their perils and exult in the sudden improvement of their fortunes. Style and use of literary allusions suggest an educated audience. The moral premises are very like those which govern the production code of the American moving picture industry: vice is never made attractive, and virtue is always rewarded. Other patent affinities with moving pictures are the rapidly shifting scenes, the patterned plots, the interest in the spectacular, such as shipwrecks, courtroom scenes, and the courts of foreign potentates, and in a constant tendency toward the melodramatic. But despite the conventional moralizing and marked attention to the observance of religious usages, these stories are in the fullest sense romances, a literature of escape. They thus constitute the logical and final step in the direction we have seen illustrated by individualistic philosophy, by archaizing rhetoric, and by otherworldly religion.

The earliest complete extant romance is Chariton's *Chaereas and Callirhoe,* dated to the second century A.D. The hero and heroine (their fathers are historical characters of the fifth century B.C.) fall in love at a festival in Syracuse and marry. Jealous rivals contrive to make Chaereas suspicious of his wife's fidelity; he kicks her into a deathlike swoon, and she is elaborately entombed with much treasure. Pirates who plunder the tomb kidnap and sell her to Dionysius, an Ionian prince, who respects her beauty and her sad history (but she neglects to tell him she is married) and woos her honorably. When she finds that she is two months pregnant she decides to marry Dionysius to give her child a father, being persuaded by her maid that Dionysius will believe it a seven-months child. Chaereas has discovered that Callirhoe is alive and with his friend Epicharmus goes to recover her, but is captured and sold to Mithradates of Caria. Mithradates has also seen and fallen in love with Callirhoe, and sends her a letter from Chaereas together with one of his own. Dionysius intercepts the letters, and procures that the (historical) King Artaxerxes should summon Mithradates to trial. The trial scene is highly spectacular; Artaxerxes, who has also fallen in love with Callirhoe, postpones decision as to which of her husbands shall have her. He is summoned to suppress an Egyptian revolt, and takes with him his queen, in whose charge he has put Callirhoe, who rejects his advances. Dionysius, who is serving with King Artaxerxes, deceives Chaereas into thinking that Callirhoe has been awarded to him, and Chaereas in despair joins the Egyptian army with his faithful friend. He is prodigiously successful and eventually captures an island upon which the King's suite has been placed for safety. Chaereas and Callirhoe thus reunited sail back to Syracuse, after Callirhoe has persuaded to return to the King his queen, who had been kind to her, and has surreptitiously sent Dionysius an affectionate letter bespeaking his kindness for the son he still believes is his. At the end we are given to understand that Chaereas and Callirhoe will live happily ever after. The narrative is rapid and artful. The hairbreadth escapes are varied with descriptions of rich pageantry, and the attention of the reader, if he is willing to lend himself to such a tale, is never permitted to flag.

Involved as this curtailed outline of Chariton's story shows it to be, its plot is simple compared to Xenophon's or Heliodorus'. The *Ephesian Tale; or, Habrocomes and Anthia* of Xenophon of Ephesus (second or third century) seems to show direct borrowing from Chariton. There are in Xenophon more and stranger journeys, more pirates, shipwrecks, dreams, more unsuccessful but trying attempts to assault the lovers' virtue and to keep them apart, more of all the elements (including a more exciting premature burial) that make for thrilling love romance than in Chariton, but they are so compactly and unpretentiously told that many scholars believe that the work as we have it is an epitome. So crowded is the book that an adequate summary must be nearly as long as its thirty-five pages, and would fail to induce the suspension of disbelief which the book somehow succeeds in doing. The lovers are finally united against what seem to be even more hopeless odds. Though there is the same interest in exotic courts and pageantry the tone seems more bourgeois. Where a succession of princes tries to marry Callirhoe, almost a dozen lesser characters try to rape Anthia, and she is actually in the hands of a brothel keeper and a slave merchant. But her loyalty is more austere than Callirhoe's, who after all, though under the constraint of pregnancy, did marry a second husband—and then secretly write him an affectionate letter. The multiplication of peril and calcination of virtue would seem to make the story less credible and less meaningful, but it is, in fact, easier to accept than Chariton's. In part, this is due to the fuller attention given to lesser characters. All are sympathetically conceived as human beings; even the bawd and the slave dealer are kindly people who are only following their trade but whose sympathies can be engaged by a story of misfortune, and the intending rapists are clearly helpless before the shattering beauty of the heroine. There is less of war than in Chariton, but more of religion. Hero and heroine are constantly praying to Aphrodite and Artemis, who do, in fact, watch over their wards. There is a general sense that the world and its people are controlled by a providence whose workings are sometimes inscrutable and painfully dilatory but in the end always benevolent.

The fullest and best known of the Greek romances is Heliodorus' *Aethiopica; or, Theagenes and Chariclea* (third century), whose author is said (but demonstration is impossible) to have been bishop of Tricca.

Aethiopica shows a maturer art than its predecessors; there is conscious imitation of the structure of *Odyssey* and of the theatrical effects, especially recognitions, of drama. There is interest in history, and geography, as in the earlier romances, but a very marked and adult interest in comparative religion. The plot is as crowded as Xenophon's, and has as large a cast of characters, but the manner of telling is less kaleidoscopic. The opening is stunningly effective. A band of pirates on a hill near the mouth of the Nile look out upon a laden ship with no one aboard, a field strewn with dead bodies and the remains of a banquet, and a wounded young man being tended by a superlatively beautiful young woman dressed as a priestess or goddess. There follow thrilling adventures involving pirates and brigands, with a parallel subplot whose characters show what Theagenes and Chariclea might have been if they were not so impregnably virtuous. In course of their wandering in Egypt they meet their foster father, Calasiris, a priest of Isis, who in a flash back which requires two days to narrate tells the story from its beginning to the point where the book opened: An Ethiopian merchant had given an infant with its rich tokens to Charicles, a philosopher of Delphi, to rear. Charicles had named the child Chariclea, had brought her up carefully, and betrothed her to a young man of Delphi. She and Theagenes (who is a descendant of Achilles) met at a religious ceremony in which each had a prominent role and fell in love. Charicles consulted his friend Calasiris, who was in Delphi on a self-imposed exile, to know why Chariclea was languishing, and showed Calasiris the tokens, which included a letter which Calasiris was able to read. In this letter Persinna, Queen of Ethiopia, declared that her daughter (our Chariclea) had been born white, because at the time of conception she had been looking at a picture of Andromeda, and that she was exposing the infant with tokens and jewels to avoid imputation of adultery. Prompted by a vision, Calasiris had spirited Theagenes and Chariclea away, Theagenes binding himself by an oath not to force Chariclea's love. A series of adventurous voyages, separations, kidnapings, and escapes brought the story down to date. Direct narrative is resumed with more exciting adventures, involving separations, disguises, the masquerade of hero and heroine as brother and sister, frustrated assaults on their virute, an accidental substitution of a poisoned potion, Chariclea being sentenced to burn at the stake and the miraculous refusal of the flames to touch her—all against a background of sieges and war between Ethiopians and Egyptians motivated in part by Chariclea's beauty. The ending, involving a test of chastity by fire, through which Theagenes and Chariclea naturally pass triumphantly, the sensational recognition of Chariclea as princess as she is about to be publicly sacrified, the liberation of Theagenes after an extraordinary exhibition of prowess, and the marriage, is as stunningly effective in its kind as the opening.

From the start there is never a doubt that blood will tell and virtue be rewarded, but the reader's anxiety is kept tense. His attention is occasionally relieved (or distracted) by a wide variety of matter on geography and ethnology and zoology, and particularly by details of religious customs and beliefs. The *Aethiopica,* indeed, is an extremely interesting and sympathetic reflection of the religion of Isis, of the Sun God, and of the Gymnosophists, who figure prominently at the end. The narrative itself is varied, not only by descriptions, some of which may well be commonplaces from the novelists' files, but by stretches of dialogue and by soliloquies. The style is markedly "literary"; epic and drama not only furnish structural techniques but provide numerous verbal expressions, and the language is further ornamented by the rhetorical devices of the Second Sophistic.

As a story of love and adventure well told *Aethiopica* probably has the best claim of all the Greek romances on the modern reader's attention. On the Elizabethans its influence was very great, only rivaled or perhaps surpassed by that of the *Daphnis and Chloe* of Longus (third century). *Daphnis and Chloe* has no great weight but is surely one of the most charming stories ever told. Here too there are the alarums of war, hairbreadth escapes, kidnapings, and reunions; here too hero and heroine are eventually recognized to be of noble blood. But background and atmosphere reflect, not the sophisticated metropolitan life of New Comedy, but the pastoral rusticity of Theocritus. The actual influence of Theocritus is palpable, in names and incidents as well as atmosphere. Hero and heroine had each been exposed as infants, had been adopted and reared by neighboring shepherd families, tended their flocks together, frolicked and played their pipes together, together worshiped the rustic deities and escaped the perils that came with visitors from the city. The sympathetic description of their awakening love is without parallel in the other romances. Their goodness somehow seems more natural, less constrained than the hard virtue paraded in the other romances. The wicked tempters (except for one amiable oaf who tries to rape Chloe) and fighters are city folk. Even after they are recognized as gentry and are married, Daphnis and Chloe insist on following the rustic life. The sounds and sights and smells and religiosity of country life are authentic and described *con amore,* but described, nevertheless, by a highly sophisticated author and addressed to an educated audience. In his proem the author declares that he was moved to write by a picture he had seen representing such a story. He has Theocritus and similar bucolic writers at his tongue's end, and expects his readers to recognize his allusions. There is at least one reminiscence of Sappho, when Daphnis plucks Chloe the lone apple from the topmost bough.

In Achilles Tatius' *Leucippe and Clitophon* (about A.D. 300) sophistication is carried to a point where the author himself parodies the absurd conventions of the romance and produces what looks like a tongue-in-cheek treatment of the conventional theme of chastity. Achilles Tatius' attitude toward his predecessors has been compared to Euripides' toward his; the comparison is apt, for though each was patently critical of his predecessors, each was a sincere artist in his own form and did not debase that form to a mere vehicle for criticism. When the author is admiring works of art in a temple at Sidon (enthusiastic appreciations of pictures occur throughout the book) he remarks, of a statue of Eros, "Think of such a brat being lord of earth and sea!" Clitophon, a young Greek of Tyre, offers to testify to the power of Eros from his own experience, and tells his story sitting under a plane tree by a brook. The adventures of Clitophon and his beloved Leucippe include the various vicissitudes recounted in the earlier romances but exaggerated to a point where the author's intent can only have been ironic. Once Clitophon sees Leucippe disemboweled and buried before his eyes, once he sees black pirates decapitate her, once her murder is circumstantially described to him, but each time she has, in fact, escaped by a sleight. In the matter of chastity Achilles Tatius' tongue is even further in his cheek. Leucippe retains her physical virginity, though she is willing enough, and with no great crisis involved, to arrange an assignation; the broad scenes with Melitta, who vigorously, single-mindedly, and withal humorously sets about to seduce Clitophon, show what Leucippe would be if she were not restrained by the requirements for a heroine of Greek romance. Melitta's every thought is of sex; the filled sails on a ship, for example, she compares to the belly of a pregnant woman. Indeed, the entire caste is a set of rogues worthy of any picaresque novel. And yet, gross-minded as our author is, he presents in the story of Callisthenes and Calligone (2.13–18; 8.17–19) the first foreshadowing of chivalry, when the insolent profligate is transformed into a model citizen, brave and courteous, through the power of love.

The romances which have survived are but a fraction of those written; we cannot tell how many perished, except for their shadows in *Gesta Romanorum* or elsewhere. *Pericles Prince of Tyre,* for example, is a Greek romance, which Gower took from the *Gesta* and Shakespeare changed but little. The romances were widely read, and even by Christians. The Byzantines, who were extremely fond of the romances and began to write them anew in the eleventh century, thought that both Heliodorus and

Achilles Tatius were bishops. Julian, it may be noted, thought they were frivolous and forbade his priests to read them (Letter 49). Christians not only read romances but wrote them. The perfectly orthodox *Acts of Xanthippe and Polyxena,* first printed a half century ago and dated to the third or fourth century, has all the thrilling kidnapings, deliveries, and surprises of the typical Greek romance. *The Descent into Hell,* now embedded in the *Acts of Nicodemus,* is a vigorous and imaginative piece of fourth-century fiction, and shows the effects of Greek models.

If the philosophers and poets of an earlier age did more to shape the substance of European thought, these later writers of romance did as much to fashion the molds and conventions of literary form. On the Elizabethan prose writers their influence was very great, and through these writers they affected the drama, even such works as *King Lear* or *The Winter's Tale.* And through the Elizabethans and directly their influence continued. Tom Jones and his Sophia follow, and quite within sight of their trail blazer, the path marked by Theagenes and Chariclea; Paul and Virginia *are* Daphnis and Chloe. Among ourselves the art form which has the largest popular following is the cinema, and the techniques and social and moral premises of the cinema story find their closest parallel in the Greek romance. The Greek experience of some 1,500 years which we have surveyed is so broad as to provide analogy, close or labored, for any new situation. Does it mark a rise in our own spiritual stature and institutions that we find ourselves spiritually at home in the dreariest centuries of those 1,500 years?

BIBLIOGRAPHICAL NOTES

GENERAL

THE FOLLOWING NOTES ARE INTENDED PRIMARILY FOR READERS OF ENGLISH; A handful of books in other languages are listed because readers interested in the subject should know of their existence or may find them of use in locating bibliographical information on a special author or subject.

For each Greek author it is to be assumed that texts are to be found in one of the series listed below; the volumes in the *Loeb Classical Library,* to which the reader will have most frequent recourse, regularly provide bibliographies, and therefore only text editions whose introductions and commentaries have special value for the English reader will be mentioned. For the later period some editions will be listed mainly to show the extent of an author's extant remains and the date at which his text has last received critical attention.

Abbreviations are self-explanatory, except that "LL" means *Loeb Classical Library,* now published by Harvard University Press, Cambridge, Massachusetts, and "ODGR" refers to the series called "Our Debt to Greece and Rome," now published by Longmans Green, New York. In the case of books published by Harvard University Press the word "Harvard" is used instead of "Cambridge"; "Cambridge" means Cambridge in England.

Histories of Greek literature.—The fullest history of Greek literature, invaluable for its bibliographical information, is that included in the series of philological handbooks called "Iwan Mullers Handbuch der Altertumswissenschaft" (Beck, Munich). The three volumes of the newest revision of the first part, by W. Schmid and O. Staehlin, cover the period through Euripides (1929, 1934, 1940); the two volumes of the second half, by W. von Christ, W. Schmid, and O. Staehlin, cover the Alexandrian and Roman periods. More readable and more stimulating for its critical judgments is the *Histoire de la littérature grecque* of Alfred and Maurice Croiset, 5 vols. (Paris, 1909–1928).

Encyclopedias and dictionaries.—The standard reference work for all classical disciplines is the *Real-Enzyklopaedie der klassischen Altertumswissenschaft* (Stuttgart), edited by A. Pauly, G. Wissowa, and W. Kroll. The prestige of this work is enormous and deserved. A much simpler work is the *Dictionnaire des antiquités grecques et romaines,* edited by C. Daremberg and E. Saglio, 9 vols. (Paris, 1877–1919). The excellent *Oxford Classical Dictionary* (Oxford, 1949) will cover the needs of ordinary students; P. Harvey, *The Oxford Companion to Classical Literature* (Oxford, 1937) is useful. *Smith's Classical Dictionary* in the "Everyman" series is useful for its size.

History.—*The Cambridge Ancient History* (all but the twelfth and final volume have been published) is standard and provides excellent bibliographies. The twelve-volume *History* of George Grote is very readable and more "modern" and penetrating in social and political questions than books written seventy-five years later; the first volume has, of course, been antiquated by archaeological discovery. A dependable and full one-volume *History of Greece* is J. B. Bury's (now a Modern Library Giant); G. W. Botsford and C. A. Robinson, Jr.'s *Hellenic History* (New York, 1939) is a good modern textbook.

Texts and Translations.—The standard series of classical texts are the *Teubner* (*Bibliotheca Scriptorum Graecorum et Romanorum Teubneriana,* Leipzig), which includes almost all ancient authors, and the less full but more attractive *Oxford* (*Scriptorum Classicorum Bibliotheca Oxoniensis*). A number of authors, with parallel Latin translation, appear in the older *Didot* series (Paris). The reader of this book is likely to find all that he requires in the volumes of the *Loeb Classical Library* (LL), which offer text and translation, introductions, bibliography, and an occasional note; virtually all the significant works mentioned in this book are included. An analogous French series, generally superior but not so full, is the *Budé* (*Collection des universités de France, publiée sous le patronage de l'Association Guillaume Budé,* Paris).

A key to available translations is F. S. Smith, *The Classics in Translation* (New York, 1930). There are numerous anthologies. The latest and fullest is W. J. Oates and C. T. Murphy, *Greek Literature in Translation* (New York, 1946); a shorter book but with fuller and more spirited introductory material is R. W. Livingstone, *The Pageant of Greece* (Oxford, 1924).

For Greek (and Roman) influences on Western literature a palmary work is G. Highet, *The Classical Tradition* (Oxford, 1949).

CHAPTER 1. THE NATURE OF
GREEK LITERATURE

Characterizations of Greek "genius" as expressed in literature are numberless. Interesting aspects are suggested in R. W. Livingstone, *The Greek Genius and Its Meaning to Us* (2d ed.; Oxford, 1915) and *Greek Ideals and Modern Life* (Harvard, 1935); G. Lowes Dickinson, *The Greek View of Life* (16th ed.; London, 1929); M. Hutton, *The Greek Point of View* (New York, n.d.). More relevant to this chapter are F. R. Earp, *The Way of the Greeks* (Oxford, 1929) and E. E. Sikes, *The Greek View of Poetry* (New York, 1931). T. B. L. Webster, *Greek Art and Literature* (Oxford, 1939) shows the affinity between literature and the other Greek arts. W. C. Greene, *Moira: Fate Good and Evil in Greek Thought* (Harvard, 1944) presents some basic concepts that run through Greek literature. An ambitious and suggestive but potentially misleading work is W. Jaeger, *Paideia: the Ideals of Greek Culture,* translated by G. Highet, 3 vols. (New York, 1939–1944); those using this work should consult the reviews of G. M. A. Grube in *American Journal of Philology,* LXVIII (1947), 200–215, and

R. K. Hack in *Classical Philology,* XXXVII (1942), 197–206. A thoroughgoing Marxist interpretation of Greek history and literature is Margaret O. Wason, *Class Struggles in Ancient Greece* (London, 1947).

CHAPTER 2. ORIGINS AND TRANSMISSION

ORIGINS AND EARLY CIVILIZATION: A. R. Burn, *Minoans, Philistines, and Greeks* (New York, 1930) and *The World of Hesiod* (London, 1936); G. Glotz, *Aegean Civilization,* translated by M. R. Dobie and E. M. Riley (New York, 1927); A. Jarde, *The Formation of the Greek People,* translated by M. R. Dobie (New York, 1926); H. R. Hall, *The Civilization of Greece in the Bronze Age* (London, 1928) and *The Ancient History of the Near East* (London, 1932); W. R. Halliday, *Indo-European Folk-Tales and Greek Legend* (Cambridge, 1933); J. L. Myres, *Who Were the Greeks?* (Berkeley, Calif., 1930); H. J. Rose, *Primitive Culture in Greece* (London, 1930).

RELIGION: M. P. Nilsson, *A History of Greek Religion* (Oxford, 1925) and the much fuller *Geschichte der griechischen Religion* (Munich, 1939); O. Kern, *Die Religion der Griechen,* 3 vols. (Berlin, 1926–1938); U. von Wilamowitz-Moelendorff, *Die Glaube der Hellenen,* 2 vols. (Berlin, 1931–1932).

LANGUAGE: B. F. C. Atkinson, *The Greek Language* (London, 1931) is interesting and informing even to those with no Greek.

WRITING AND BOOKS: F. G. Kenyon, *Books and Readers in Ancient Greece and Rome* (Oxford, 1932).

CARE AND TRANSMISSION OF TEXTS: J. E. Sandys, *A History of Classical Scholarship,* 3 vols. (Cambridge, 1903–1908; Vol. I, 3d ed.; 1921).

CHAPTER 3. HOMER

For the nature of early epic see H. V. Routh, *God, Man, and Epic Poetry,* Vol. I, "Classical" (Cambridge, 1927); H. M. Chadwick, *The Heroic Age* (Cambridge, 1912). For Homeric origins, T. W. Allen, *Homer, Origins and Transmission* (Oxford, 1924); Rhys Carpenter, *Folk Tale, Fiction, and Saga in the Homeric Epics* (Berkeley, Calif., 1946); M. P. Nilsson, *Homer and Mycenae* (London, 1933). The best refutation of theories of disparate authorship is J. A. Scott, *The Unity of Homer* (Berkeley, Calif., 1921); see also his *Homer* (ODGR, 1925). C. M. Bowra's excellent *Tradition and Design in the Iliad* (Oxford, 1930) carries conviction of unity on reasoned aesthetic as well as philological grounds. A fine appreciation of Homer as a poet by a non-Hellenist poet and critic is Mark Van Doren, *The Noble Voice* (New York, 1946), chs. 1 and 2, pp. 1–87. An illuminating and more technical study is S. E. Bassett, *The Poetry of Homer* (Berkeley, Calif., 1938); a similar work on *Odyssey* is W. J. Woodhouse, *The Composition of Homer's Odyssey* (Oxford, 1930). A persuasive presentation of theories of nonunitary authorship (but not entirely orthodox separatism) is Gilbert Murray, *The Rise of the Greek Epic* (4th ed.;

Oxford, 1924). A volume of attractive studies on special points is A. Shewan, *Homeric Essays* (Oxford, 1935). T. D. Seymour, *Life in the Homeric Age* (New York, 1907) is still useful for "background."

Numerous translations of Homer will be found listed in any library catalogue. The prose versions of Samuel Butler are vigorous and accurate (except for the unfortunate use of Roman names for Greek divinities), as is the *Odyssey* of G. H. Palmer or T. E. Lawrence; none of these is as mannered as the versions of Lang, Leaf, and Myers and Butcher and Lang, which have become almost the "authorized" version. In verse the new line-for-line hexameter translation of W. B. Smith and W. Miller (New York, 1944) is quite successful, but the hexameters in H. B. Cotterill's *Odyssey* (London, 1911) are more musical and more vigorous. A good blank verse translation is W. Marris's *Iliad* (Oxford, 1934). Other good verse translations are A. S. Way and W. C. Bryant (both *Iliad* and *Odyssey*), Edward, Earl of Derby (*Iliad*), and W. Cowper and W. Morris (*Odyssey*). Every reader of Homer should also look into Pope as well as Chapman.

CHAPTER 4. CYCLIC POEMS, HOMERIC HYMNS, OTHER HOMERICA

Texts and testimonia of all the works discussed in this chapter are to be found in Vol. V of T. W. Allen's Oxford *Homer* (1911), and almost as fully, with bibliographies, in H. G. Evelyn-White's LL *Hesiod, Homeric Hymns, and Homerica.*

HOMERIC HYMNS: T. W. Allen, W. R. Halliday, and E. E. Sikes, *The Homeric Hymns* (2d ed.; Oxford, 1936) has full introduction and commentary, and is a model of scholarship and taste. The only other translation of hymns that need be mentioned is Andrew Lang's (London, 1899), which discusses points of folklore.

CHAPTER 5. HESIOD AND HESIODIC SCHOOLS

HESIOD: H. G. Evelyn-White's LL *Hesiod* is excellent. T. A. Sinclair, *Hesiod, Works and Days* (London, 1932) has useful introduction and commentary. A. W. Mair's complete translation of Hesiod (Oxford, 1908) has useful remarks on agriculture and Biblical parallels. For the Greek "Middle Ages" see A. R. Burn, *The World of Hesiod* (London, 1936).

"Prudent clown," "sordid aims in life": see J. A. Symonds, *Studies of the Greek Poets* (3d ed.; London, 1920), p. 108.

ORPHICS: The fragments are collected in O. Kern, *Orphicorum Fragmenta* (Berlin, 1932). W. K. C. Guthrie, *Orpheus and Greek Religion* (London, 1935); Jane Harrison, *Prolegomena to the Study of Greek Religion* (3d ed.; Cambridge, 1922); E. Rohde, *Psyche,* translated by W. B. Hillis (8th ed.; New York, 1925).

XENOPHANES *et al.:* Xenophanes and Empedocles are in H. Diels, *Poetarum*

Philosophorum Fragmenta (Berlin, 1901), and Parmenides in his *Fragmente der Vorsokratiker* (5th ed.; Berlin, 1934). William Ellery Leonard, *The Fragments of Empedocles* (Chicago, 1908) includes a verse translation. Concise accounts of the lives and doctrines of all the philosophers mentioned in this book are to be found in standard histories of philosophy, and especially in F. Ueberweg-K. Praechter, *Grundriss der Geschichte der Philosophie,* Vol. I (12th ed.; Berlin, 1926). Translations of the pre-Socratics, together with chapter 1 of Theodor Gomperz's *Greek Thinkers,* are conveniently presented in M. C. Nahm, *Selections from Early Greek Philosophy* (New York, 1935). See also under "Pre-Socratics," chapter 7.

CHAPTER 6. LYRIC

The standard texts of the Greek lyric poets are E. Diehl, *Anthologia lyrica Graeca,* 2 vols. (Leipzig, 1925), and T. Bergk, *Poetae Lyrici Graeci* (latest revisions, by other hands, 1923, 1915, 1914). Bergk is the older, and citations are usually by his numbering. J. M. Edmonds' LL collections, Greek *Elegy and Iambus with the Anacreontea,* 2 vols., and *Lyra Graeca,* 3 vols., are quite complete, with new fragments, testimonia, and parallel numbering for reference to older editions. Edmonds's "Account of Greek Lyric Poetry" printed at the end of *Lyra Graeca* (3.583-679) is an admirable introduction to the subject; the long introduction of H. W. Smyth, *Greek Melic Poets* (London, 1900) is also useful. *The Oxford Book of Greek Verse* (OBGV) is a good anthology, and is admirably translated in *The Oxford Book of Greek Verse in Translation,* ed. T. F. Higham and C. M. Bowra (Oxford, 1938); the introduction to the latter is entertaining as well as informing. Two older but still stimulating works are J. A. Symonds, *Studies of the Greek Poets* (3d ed.; London, 1920), and J. W. Mackail, *Lectures on Greek Poetry* (2d ed.; London, 1926).

ELEGY: An excellent analysis is C. M. Bowra, *Early Greek Elegists* (Harvard, 1938). The best edition of selections, with English introduction and commentary, is T. Hudson-Williams, *Early Greek Elegy* (Cardiff, 1926). Callinus quotation: OBGV.

SOLON: I. M. Linforth, *Solon the Athenian* (Berkeley, Calif., 1919) and Kathleen Freeman, *The Life and Work of Solon* (London, 1926), each contains translations and commentary. See also under "Athenian polity," chapter 7. Solon quotation: LL.

THEOGNIS: Text and commentary in T. Hudson-Williams, *The Elegies of Theognis* (London, 1910). Besides Edmonds's in LL *Elegy* there is a prose version by J. Banks and verse by J. H. Frere in a Bohn volume. Theognis quotation: LL.

ARCHILOCHUS: A. Hauvette, *Archiloque, sa vie et ses poésies* (Paris, 1905). Archilochus and Simonides quotations: OBGV.

LYRIC POETS: See especially the perceptive analyses in C. M. Bowra, *Greek Lyric Poetry* (Oxford, 1936).

SAPPHO: E. Lobel, *The Fragments of the Lyrical Poems of Sappho* (Oxford,

1925). D. M. Robinson, *Sappho* (ODGR, 1924) is one of the fullest volumes in that series and useful for directing the reader to other works; its own view of Sappho is somewhat quaint. An imaginative reconstruction of Sappho's life is Margaret Goldsmith, *Sappho of Lesbos; a Psychological Reconstruction of Her Life* (London, 1938).

ALCAEUS: E. Lobel, *The Fragments of the Lyrical Poems of Alcaeus* (Oxford, 1927). There is a fine Budé volume of Alcaeus and Sappho, with French introduction and translation, by T. Reinach and A. Puech (Paris, 1937). Alcaeus quotation: OBGV.

Anacreon quotation: Bowra, *op. cit.*

Simonides quotation: Symonds, *op. cit., 207.*

PINDAR: The fullest English edition, with translation and literary and critical commentaries, is L. F. Farnell, *The Works of Pindar,* 3 vols. (London, 1930–1932). Of other editions, B. L. Gildersleeve, *Pindar, the Olympian and Pythian Odes* (New York, 1885) is memorable for its fine and spirited introduction. Richmond Lattimore, *The Odes of Pindar* (Chicago, 1947) is a version both poetic and faithful. An illuminating criticism of Pindar's art is G. Norwood, *Pindar* (Berkeley, 1945). For the games which Pindar celebrated see E. N. Gardiner, *Athletics of the Ancient World* (Oxford, 1930). Polybius quotation: LL; Pindar quotation; Lattimore, *op. cit.*

BACCHYLIDES: Text, translation, and commentary in R. C. Jebb, *Bacchylides, the Poems and Fragments* (Cambridge, 1905); verse translation with good introduction, A. S. Way, *Bacchylides* (London, 1929).

Longinus quotation: From edition of W. Rhys Roberts (2d ed.; Cambridge, 1907).

Timotheus quotation: Jebb, *op. cit., 49.*

CHAPTER 7. PROSE BEGINNINGS: THE RISE OF ATHENS

Fragments of all the Greek historians mentioned in this book are collected in C. and T. Muller, *Fragmenta Historicorum Graecorum,* 5 vols. (Paris, 1841–1870), and F. Jacoby, *Die Fragmente der griechischen Historiker* (in progress; Berlin, 1923–). For the Ionian historians, with full treatment of Hecataeus, Xanthus, Charon, and Hellanicus, see L. Pearson, *Early Ionian Historians* (Oxford, 1939). J. A. K. Thomson, *The Art of the Logos* (London, 1935) is a charming book; a more technical work is W. Aly, *Volksmaerchen, Sage, und Novelle bei Herodot und seinen Zeitgenossen* (Goettingen, 1921).

Dionysius quotation: Pearson, *op. cit.,* p. 3.

AESOP: The Budé editions of É. Chambry, *Ésope Fables* (Paris, 1927), has a good introduction and commentary. The latest critical edition is A. Hausrath, *Corpus Fabularum Aesopicarum* (Leipzig, 1940); Hausrath's article in Pauly-Wissowa-Kroll is the best treatment of the subject.

PRE-SOCRATICS: The standard text is H. Diels-W. Kranze, *Die Fragmente der Vorsokratiker,* with German translation, 3 vols. (5th ed.; Berlin, 1934–1937);

see also works listed under "Xenophanes" in chapter 5. For the atomists see especially C. Bailey, *The Greek Atomists and Epicurus* (Oxford, 1928). A well-informed and suggestive book is L. Robin, *Greek Thought and the Origins of the Scientific Spirit,* translated by M. R. Dobie (New York, 1928); see also J. Adam, *The Religious Teachers of Greece* (Edinburgh, 1908) and J. Burnet, *Early Greek Philosophy* (4th ed.; New York, 1930).

HIPPOCRATES: E. Littré, *Oeuvres completes d'Hippocrate,* text, French translation and commentary, 10 vols. (Paris 1839–1861), is still very useful though both the text and understanding of it have improved. These improvements are taken account of in the excellent LL *Hippocrates* of W. H. S. Jones and E. T. Withington (4 vols.); Jones' General Introduction and the introductions to the separate treatises give all the information the ordinary student needs. See also A. I. Brock, *Greek Medicine* (New York, 1929); C. Singer, *Greek Biology and Medicine* (Oxford, 1922); H. O. Taylor, *Greek Biology and Medicine* (ODGR, 1922).

ATHENIAN POLITY: In addition to histories listed under "General" see W. J. Woodhouse, *Solon the Liberator* (London, 1928) and the works on Solon in chapter 3; P. N. Ure, *The Origin of Tyranny* (Cambridge, 1922); A. E. Zimmern, *The Greek Commonwealth* (5th ed.; Oxford, 1931); G. Thomson, *Aeschylus and Athens* (London, 1941).

CHAPTER 8. DRAMA

A convenient and comprehensive book on ancient drama, with good bibliographies, is P. W. Harsh, *A Handbook of Classical Drama* (Palo Alto, Calif., 1944). This work is more concerned with criticism of the individual plays, while a work like R. C. Flickinger, *The Greek Theater and Its Drama* (4th ed.; Chicago, 1936) deals more with "antiquities." G. Norwood, *Greek Tragedy* (Boston, 1928), gives an adequate account of the antiquities and penetrating (though sometimes extreme) analyses of the plays; his *Greek Comedy* (Boston, 1932) is somewhat more specialized and more indispensable, for it has no rival. A. E. Haigh, *The Tragic Drama of the Greeks* (Oxford, 1896) is still a sound and useful book. Translations of all extant plays (including Menander's), but by no means always the best available, are to be found in W. J. Oates and E. O'Neill, Jr., *The Complete Greek Drama* (New York, 1938).

ORIGINS: Besides chapters in other works, see A. W. Pickard-Cambridge, *Dithyramb, Tragedy, and Comedy* (Oxford, 1947). See also A. M. G. Little, *Myth and Society in Attic Drama* (New York, 1942).

GREEK THEATER AND ANTIQUITIES: A. W. Pickard-Cambridge, *The Greek Theatre of Dionysus at Athens* (Oxford, 1946); M. Bieber, *The History of the Greek and Roman Theater* (Princeton, N.J., 1939); J. T. Allen, *Stage Antiquities of the Greeks and Romans* (ODGR, 1927).

AESCHYLUS: G. Murray, *Aeschylus the Creator of Tragedy* (Oxford, 1940) and G. Thomson, *Aeschylus and Athens* (London, 1941) are too much concerned with irrelevant anthropology and archaeology, the latter with anachronistic social questions. H. W. Smyth, *Aeschylean Tragedy* (Berkeley, Calif., 1924) is a good book, and his LL prose translation the safest guide to what Aeschylus said, though there are many good verse translations, e. g., E. D. A. Morshead.

SOPHOCLES: The editions of the individual plays with full introductions, commentary, and distinguished prose translations by R. C. Jebb (Cambridge, 1887–1907) are still the best tool for the student of Sophocles; the translations are published separately in a single volume. C. M. Bowra, *Sophoclean Tragedy* (Oxford, 1945), like all Bowra's criticism, is acute and stimulating. T. B. L. Webster, *An Introduction to Sophocles* (Oxford, 1936) shows the social implication of the plays. W. N. Bates, *Sophocles Poet and Dramatist* (Philadelphia, 1940) gives a rather pedestrian analysis of the plays, but is more useful for the fragments. Paul Shorey on Athena in *Ajax:* Martin Classical Lectures (Harvard, 1931), I, 59 f. *Antigone* misinterpreted: Bates, *op. cit.* pp. 73 ff. For Jebb's deletion see his commentary *ad loc.*

EURIPIDES: The beautiful and widely read versions of Gilbert Murray, the reader must be warned, are not Euripides. There are no good prose versions to compare with Jebb's Sophocles or Smyth's Aeschylus; a bald translation of ten plays is M. Hadas and J. H. McLean, *The Plays of Euripides* (New York, 1936). The best book on Euripides is G. M. A. Grube, *The Drama of Euripides* (London, 1941). G. Murray, *Euripides and His Age* (London, 1913) is stimulating but to be taken with reserve. W. N. Bates, *Euripides, Student of Human Nature* (Philadelphia, 1930) is uninspired but useful for reference. Of earlier interpreters mention must be made of A. W. Verrall, whose series of studies culminating in *Euripides the Rationalist* (Cambridge, 1895), though sometimes bizarre, led to a new appreciation of Euripides as artist and social thinker.

ARISTOPHANES: The best complete Aristophanes for the English reader is still B. B. Rogers, whose individual plays, with full introductions, commentary, and sprightly translations, were published separately beginning in 1852. Rogers's introductions and commentary are antiquated; the translation is reprinted, with a minimum of helpful notes, in LL. W. J. M. Starkie's *Acharnians* and *Clouds* (London, 1909 and 1911) have good introductions and notes as well as a faithful prose translation. M. Croiset, *Aristophanes and the Political Parties at Athens,* translated by J. Loeb (London, 1909) shows the extent of Aristophanes' partisanship. G. Murray, *Aristophanes, a Study* (Oxford, 1933) has some good things but is generally disappointing; L. E. Lord, *Aristophanes* (ODGR, 1925) is also limited. V. Ehrenberg, *The People of Aristophanes* (Oxford, 1943) uses the plays for a sociological study; W. M. Hugill, *Panhellenism in Aristophanes* (Chicago, 1936) analyzes a central political conviction in Aristophanes. F. M. Cornford, *The Origin of Attic Comedy* (London, 1914) is eccentric. The most useful work on all the comedians is G. Norwood, *Greek Comedy* (Boston, 1932). Norwood on *Peace* parabasis: *ibid.,* pp. 213 f.

CHAPTER 9. THE HISTORIANS

Chapters on the Greek historians are to be found in J. T. Shotwell, *The History of History* (New York, 1939) and J. B. Bury, *The Ancient Greek Historians*

(New York, 1909); see also Pearson and works on history listed under chapter 7. F. R. B. Godolphin, *The Greek Historians*, 2 vols. (New York, 1942) contains G. Rawlinson's Herodotus (debowdlerized); B. Jowett's Thucydides; H. G. Dakyns's Xenophon's *Hellenica, Anabasis, Ways and Means, Constitution of the Spartans*, and *The Constitution of the Athenians* ascribed to the "Old Oligarch"; E. J. Chinnock's Arrian's *Anabasis* and *Indica;* and F. G. Kenyon's Aristotle's *Constitution of Athens;* plus introduction, indices, and other subsidia.

HERODOTUS: W. W. How and J. Wells, *A Commentary on Herodotus*, 2 vols. (Oxford, 1912) is of use even to Greekless readers. T. R. Glover, *Herodotus* (Berkeley, Calif., 1924) is a charming, long essay on Herodotus; J. E. Powell, *The History of Herodotus* (Cambridge, 1939) a short one. Besides Godley's LL tr. (4 vols.) and Rawlinson's (in Godolphin's collection or "Everyman"), there is a translation by C. G. Macaulay, 2 vols. (London, 1890).

THUCYDIDES: LL is unreadable; much better are B. Jowett, 2 vols. (2d ed.; Oxford, 1900), or in Godolphin, or Richard Crawley ("Everymans" or Modern Library). A. W. Gomme's commentary—so far only one volume—(Oxford, 1944) is a full and fine performance. There are many good books on Thucydides: G. F. Abbott, *Thucydides, a Study in Historical Reality* (London, 1925); C. N. Cochrane, *Thucydides and the Science of History* (Oxford, 1929); J. H. Finley, *Thucydides* (Harvard, 1942); G. B. Grundy, *Thucydides and the History of His Age* (London, 1911); B. W. Henderson, *The Great War between Athens and Sparta* (London, 1927); L. E. Lord, *Thucydides and the World War* (Harvard, 1945).

XENOPHON: LL volumes provide bibliography; for *Cyropedia* the introduction and notes of H. A. Holden's four-volume edition (Cambridge, 1887–1890) are useful.

OLD OLIGARCH: Translated by J. A. Petch (Oxford, 1926) and by Dakyns in Godolphin's collection.

EPHORUS: G. L. Barber, *The Historian Ephorus* (Cambridge, 1935).

CTESIAS: J. Gilmore, *The Fragments of the Persika of Ktesias* (London, 1888).

PYTHEAS: See H. F. Tozer, *A History of Ancient Geography,* revised by M. Cary (Cambridge, 1935); M. Cary and E. H. Warmington, *The Ancient Explorers* (London, 1929); J. O. Thomson, *History of Ancient Geography* (London, 1948).

AENEAS TACTICUS: L. W. Hunter-S. A. Handford, *Aeneas on Siegecraft,* text, translation, commentary (Oxford, 1927); LL (with Asclepiodotus and Onosander) by Illinois Greek Club.

CHAPTER 10. THE PHILOSOPHERS

PLATO: B. Jowett's translations, 5 vols. (Oxford, 1892 and reprints) is the "authorized" version but vitiated by Jowett's Victorian prepossessions about his author. The single most useful work for the student is A. E. Taylor, *Plato the Man and His Work* (New York, 1927); but Taylor too is a devoted disciple who will see no flaw in his author. The extreme of derogation is Warner Fite, The *Platonic Legend* (New York, 1934). A. D. Winspear, *The Genesis of Plato's Thought* (New York, 1940) is a realistic work. Trustworthy analyses are G. M. A. Grube, *Plato's Thought* (London, 1935), and P. Shorey, *What Plato Said* (Chicago, 1933). Among the numerous other books on Plato mention may be made of: E. Barker, *Greek Political Theory, Plato and His Predecessors* (London, 1925); J. Burnet, *Platonism* (Berkeley, Calif., 1928); G. C. Field, *Plato and His Contemporaries* (London, 1930); Paul Shorey, *Platonism Ancient and Modern* (Berkeley, 1938); J. A. Stewart, *The Myths of Plato* (London, 1905) and *Plato's Doctrine of Ideas* (Oxford, 1909); A. E. Taylor, *Platonism* (ODGR, 1924). For possible Indian influence see E. J. Urwick, *The Message of Plato* (London, 1920). Editions of individual treatises frequently have excellent introductions; special mention may be made of Burnet's *Euthyphro, Apology, Crito,* and *Phaedo;* A. E. Taylor's *Timaeus* and *Critias;* and R. Hackforth's *Philebus,* under the title *Plato's Examination of Pleasure* (Cambridge, 1945).

SKEPTICS: see Mary M. Patrick, *The Greek Sceptics* (New York, 1929).

ARISTOTLE: The standard translation is *The Works of Aristotle* translated into English, edited by J. A. Smith and W. D. Ross, 11 vols. (Oxford, 1908–1931). The greater part of these are available in a single volume, *The Basic Works of Aristotle,* with an introduction by R. McKeon (New York, 1941). The most useful single work on Aristotle is W. D. Ross, *Aristotle* (London, 1930); a good shorter work is G. R. G. Mure, *Aristotle* (London, 1932). Others are: W. Jaeger, *Aristotle,* translated by R. Robinson (Oxford, 1934); J. L. Stocks, *Aristotelianism* (ODGR, 1925); A. E. Taylor, Aristotle (2d ed.; London, 1919). Quotation on Aristotle's influence: McKeon, *op. cit.,* p. xi. Separate treatises: LL (over 20 vols.) is generally excellent and provides bibliographical information; only a few editions with special literary interest will be mentioned here. *On the Soul:* R. D. Hicks, *De Anima* (Cambridge, 1907). *Parts of Animals* quotation: A. L. Peck, LL. *Ethics:* besides H. Rackham's LL mention may be made of the edition of J. Burnet (1904), the *Notes* of J. A. Stewart, 2 vols. (1892), the translations of D. P. Chase, F. H. Peters, W. D. Ross, and J. E. C. Welldon. *Politics:* E. Barker, *The Politics of Aristotle* (Oxford, 1946) is a superb work. There are numerous essays on special points in the edition of W. L. Newman, 4 vols. (Oxford, 1887–1902). Translations, besides Rackham's LL, by B. Jowett (available, without notes, in Modern Library), and J. E. C. Welldon, *Constitution of Athens:* text and commentary, J. E. Sandys (2d ed.; Cambridge, 1912); translated by F. G. Kenyon (Oxford, 1920) and in Godolphin. *Rhetoric:* edited, with commentary, by E. M. Cope-J. E. Sandys, 3 vols. (Cambridge, 1877); translators, besides J. Freese in LL, R. C. Jebb and J. E. Sandys (Cambridge, 1909) and J. E. C. Welldon (London, 1886). Lane Cooper has an expanded translation (New York, 1932). *Poetics:* S. H. Butcher, *Aristotle's Theory of Poetry and Fine Arts* (4th ed.; London, 1927); I. Bywater, *Aristotle on the Art of Poetry* (Oxford, 1909). See also Lane Cooper, *The Poetics of Aristotle* (ODGR, 1924).

THEOPHRASTUS: R. C. Jebb-J. E. Sandys, *The Characters of Theophrastus* (London, 1909) contains full introduction, commentary, and translation. The *Metaphysics* are edited by W. D. Ross and F. H. Fobes (Oxford, 1929).

ARISTOXENUS: Edition and translation of *Harmonics,* H. S. Macran (Oxford, 1902).

CHAPTER 11. THE ORATORS

A good short work is J. F. Dobson, *The Greek Orators* (London, 1918); selections with full introductions and commentary are given in R. C. Jebb, *The Attic Orators,* 2 vols. (London, 1876). LL contains all except Lycurgus, Hyperides, and Dinarchus. For legal questions involved in the private orations see G. M. Calhoun, *The Business Life of Ancient Athens* (Chicago, 1926), and R. J. Bonner, *Lawyers and Litigants in Ancient Athens* (Chicago, 1927).

GORGIAS quotation: LaRue Van Hook, *Greek Life and Thought* (New York, 1923).

LYSIAS: The school edition of E. S. Shuckburgh (London, 1882, and reprints) is useful.

ISAEUS: W. Wyse's ample edition (Cambridge, 1904) discusses the legal questions fully.

ISOCRATES: see Jaeger's *Paideia, passim,* and G. Mathieu, *Les Idées politiques d'Isocrates* (Paris, 1925).

DEMOSTHENES: There are a number of good annotated editions, particularly those of Sandys and Goodwin; translations, besides LL (7 vols.), are those of C. R. Kennedy in the Bohn series, 5 vols., (one volume of selections in "Everyman"), and A. W. Pickard-Cambridge, *Demosthenes, Public Orations,* 2 vols. (Oxford, 1912). On Demosthenes' life, policy, and influence see: C. D. Adams, *Demosthenes* (ODGR, 1927); Georges Clémenceau, *Démosthène* (Paris, 1926); W. Jaeger, *Demosthenes; the Origin and Growth of His Policy* (Berkeley, Calif., 1938); A. W. Pickard-Cambridge, *Demosthenes and the Last Days of Greek Freedom* (New York, 1914). For the political history in which Demosthenes was involved the twelfth volume of Grote is still excellent.

LYCURGUS: A. Petrie, *Lycurgus; the Speech against Leocrates* (Cambridge, 1922); F. Durbach's Budé *Lycurgus* (Paris, 1932) is excellent.

Historians: fragments in Müller and Jacoby (see under chapter 7).

Hieronymus: the high opinion is expressed by W. W. Tarn, *Hellenistic Civilisation* (2d ed.; London, 1930), p. 250.

CHAPTER 12. HELLENISTIC PHILOSOPHY, DRAMA, HISTORY

For the Hellenistic Age, besides the histories mentioned under "General," see W. W. Tarn's excellent *Hellenistic Civilisation* (2d ed.; London, 1930) and a fine series of essays by J. B. Bury and others in *The Hellenistic Age* (Cambridge, 1925).

EPICURUS AND ZENO: Cyril Bailey, *Epicurus, the Extant Remains*, text, translation, and notes (Oxford, 1926). The standard collection of the Stoic fragments is H. von Arnim, *Stoicorum Veterum Fragmenta*, 4 vols. (Leipzig, 1903–1924). Translations of Stoic and Epicurean classics are conveniently collected in W. J. Oates, *Stoic and Epicurean Philosophers* (New York, 1940). See also: R. D. Hicks, *Stoic and Epicurean* (New York, 1910); E. P. Bevan, *Stoics and Sceptics* (Oxford, 1913); E. V. Arnold, *Roman Stoicism* (Cambridge, 1911); R. M. Wenley, *Stoicism* (ODGR, 1924); C. Bailey, *The Greek Atomists and Epicurus* (Oxford, 1928); P. E. More, *Hellenistic Philosophies* (Princeton, 1923).

NEW COMEDY: P. E. LeGrand, *The New Greek Comedy*, translated by James Loeb (London, 1917). F. G. Allinson's LL Menander is very good, and provides bibliography. Other translations are L. A. Post, *Three Plays of Menander* (London, 1929; reprinted in Oates and O'Neill) and G. Murray, *Two Plays of Menander* (Oxford, 1945). A. W. Gomme has a fine essay on Menander in his *Essays in Greek History and Literature* (Oxford, 1937), pp. 249 ff. New Comedy is treated in the books on Alexandrian literature mentioned in the next section.

LYCOPHRON: A. W. Mair in LL volume with Callimachus; verse translations by G. W. Mooney (London, 1921) and Lord Royston (Cambridge, 1806).

CHAPTER 13. ALEXANDRIAN LITERATURE
AND LEARNING

General accounts of Alexandrian literature: A. Koerte, *Hellenistic Poetry*, translated by J. Hammer and M. Hadas (New York, 1929); A. Couat, *Poetry under the First Three Ptolemies*, translated by J. Loeb (New York, 1931).

CALLIMACHUS: Mair's excellent LL edition (contains Lycophron and Aratus also) provides good bibliography. E. Cahen has a good Budé edition (Paris, 1922) and also *Callimaque et son oeuvre poétique* (Paris, 1931). See also G. M. Young, *The Epigrams of Callimachus* (Oxford, 1934).

APOLLONIUS: Besides Seaton's LL prose (from which quotations in the text are taken) there is a good verse translation by A. S. Way (London, 1901). William Morris's *Life and Death of Jason* romanticizes the story. See also J. R. Bacon, *The Voyage of the Argonauts* (London, 1925).

THEOCRITUS, BION, MOSCHUS: Besides J. M. Edmonds LL *Greek Bucolic Poets*, there is the prose translation of A. Lang (London, 1901) and verse translations of C. S. Calverley (London, 1892), J. H. Hallard (London, 1924), and A. S. Way (Cambridge, 1913). H. H. Chamberlin, *Last Flowers* (Harvard, 1937) contains translations of the *Leontium* of Hermesianax as well as Moschus and Bion. The introduction and notes of R. J. Cholmeley, *The Idylls of Theocritus* (London, 1919) are helpful.

HERONDAS: The best edition is W. Headlam, *Herodas; the Mimes and Fragments*, edited by A. D. Knox (Cambridge, 1922); Knox's LL edition, which is quoted in the text, is bound with Edmonds's *Theophrastus' Characters*. A verse translation of Herondas is H. Sharpley, *A Realist of the Aegean* (London, 1906).

ALEXANDRIAN EROTIC FRAGMENT (Grenfell): S. Gaselee in his LL *Achilles Tatius;* verse version in Koerte, *op. cit.,* pp. 348 ff.

HERMESIANAX: translated by Chamberlin, *op. cit.*

CERCIDAS AND PHOENIX: With Knox's LL *Herondas.*

GREEK SCIENCE: M. Cohen and I. Drabkin, *A Source Book in Greek Science* (New York, 1948).

ARATUS: besides G. R. Mair's LL ed. (quoted in the text; bound with A. W. Mair's *Callimachus and Lycophron*) there is a verse translation with notes: E. Poste, *The Skies and Weather-Forecasts of Aratus* (London, 1880).

EUCLID: J. L. Heiberg and H. Menge have edited all the extant works, with Latin translations, 8 vols. (Leipzig, 1883–1916); translation and English commentary of the *Elements* in three volumes by T. L. Heath (2d ed.; Oxford, 1926). For all the mathematicians see Heath's *History of Greek Mathematics,* 2 vols. (Oxford, 1921) and *Manual of Greek Mathematics* (Oxford, 1931).

ARCHIMEDES: text and Latin translation, 3 vols., J. L. Heiberg (2d ed.; Leipzig, 1910–1915); T. L. Heath, *Archimedes* (London, 1920).

HERON: text and German translation, W. Schmidt, H. Schoene, and J. L. Heiberg, 6 vols. (Leipzig, 1899–1914).

ARISTARCHUS AND OTHERS: T. L. Heath, *Aristarchus of Samos, the Ancient Copernicus: a History of Greek Astronomy to Aristarchus,* with text, commentary, and translation (Oxford, 1913). Heath has a good chapter for the layman in R. W. Livingstone, *The Legacy of Greece* (Oxford, 1923), pp. 97 ff., and a collection of passages in translation with comments in *Greek Astronomy* (Library of Greek Thought: New York, 1924).

GREEK MEDICINE: See under "Hippocrates," chapter 7.

ARTEMIDORUS: a fourth edition of Robert Wood's translation was published in London in 1644.

CHAPTER 14. POETRY TO THE END OF ANTIQUITY

PALATINE ANTHOLOGY: W. R. Paton's five-volume LL edition is excellent and lists previous translations down to 1916. J. W. Mackail, *Select Epigrams from the Greek Anthology* (3d ed.; London, 1911) is the most useful single book. F. A. Wright, *The Poets of the Greek Anthology* gives an account with translations of the principal poets in the Anthology, and his *Girdle of Aphrodite* has a good general introduction and bright translations of all the love poems (both volumes in "Broadway Translations," London, n.d.).

ASCLEPIADES: William and Mary Wallace, *Asklepiades of Samos* (Oxford, 1941).

LEONIDAS: Edwyn Bevan, *The Poems of Leonidas of Tarentum* (Oxford, 1931).

MELEAGER: W. Headlam, *Fifty Poems of Meleager* (London, 1890).

PARTHENIUS: Gaselee in LL (with his *Daphnis and Chloe*).

PALLADAS: T. R. Glover, *Life and Letters in the Fourth Century* (Cambridge, 1901), pp. 303 ff.

PAUL THE SILENTIARY: Text and commentary on *Santa Sophia* and *Ambo* in Paul Friedlaender, *Johannes von Gaza und Paulus Silentiarius Kunstbeschreibungen Justinianischer Zeit* (Leipzig, 1912).

BABRIUS: W. G. Rutherford, *Babrius* (London, 1883).

OPPIAN: A. W. Mair's LL, containing also Colluthus and Tryphiodorus.

QUINTUS: A. S. Way in LL; T. R. Glover, *op. cit.*, pp. 77 ff.

NONNUS: W. H. D. Rouse's fine LL version (4 vols.) is the source of the quotation.

MUSAEUS: Tr. E. E. Sikes (London, 1920).

CHAPTER 15. HISTORY, TRAVEL, CRITICISM
IN THE ROMAN PERIOD

POLYBIUS: The quotation from Theodor Mommsen is from his *History of Rome* (Everyman ed.), 3.439. T. R. Glover has a good, but too generous, chapter on Polybius in *Cambridge Ancient History*, IX, 1 ff. (1930). The quotations from Polybius are from Paton's LL ed. (6 vols.).

POSIDONIUS: I. Heinemann, *Poseidonios' metaphysische Schriften*, 2 vols. (Berlin, 1921–1928); K. Reinhardt, *Poseidonios* (Munich, 1921) and other studies.

DIODORUS SICULUS: LL, to be completed in twelve volumes.

NICOLAUS OF DAMASCUS: C. M. Hall, *Life of Augustus*, with translation (Northampton, Mass., 1923). Excerpts: U. P. Boissevain *et al.*, *Excerpta historica Jussu Imp. Constantini Porphyrogeniti Confecta*, 4 vols. (Berlin, 1903–1906).

STRABO: LL; T. R. Glover, *Greek Byways* (Cambridge, 1932), pp. 223 ff.; H. F. Tozer, *A History of Ancient Geography*, revised by M. Cary (Cambridge, 1935); M. Cary and E. H. Warmington, *The Ancient Explorers* (London, 1929).

DIONYSIUS OF HALICARNASSUS: *Roman Antiquities* in LL. *Scripta rhetorica*: W. Rhys Roberts, *Dionysius of Halicarnassus; the Three Literary Letters* (Cambridge, 1901), and *On Literary Composition* (London, 1910); S. F. Bonner, *The Literary Treatises of Dionysius of Halicarnassus* (Cambridge, 1939).

LITERARY CRITICISM: J. W. H. Atkins, *Literary Criticism in Antiquity*, 2 vols. (Cambridge, 1934); W. Rhys Roberts, *Greek Rhetoric and Literary Criticism* (ODGR, 1928); C. S. Baldwin, *Ancient Rhetoric and Poetic* (New York, 1924).

LONGINUS: In W. H. Fyfe's LL volume which contains Aristotle's *Poetics* and Demetrius also; with translation and commentary, W. Rhys Roberts (2d ed.; Cambridge, 1907); translation by A. O. Prickard (Oxford, 1906).

Gibbon quotation: from Roberts' ODGR volume, p. 141.

CAECILIUS OF CALACTE: The fragments are collected in a Teubner volume by E. Ofenloch (Leipzig, 1907).

JOSEPHUS: LL (8 vols.) by H. St. J. Thackeray and Ralph Marcus; Marcus's appendices in the latter volumes are especially useful. See also H. St. J. Thackeray, *Josephus the Man and the Historian* (New York, 1929). Lion Feuchtwanger's novels on Josephus use the sources conscientiously.

ARRIAN: E. Iliff Robson in LL; E. J. Chinnock's version, with notes (London, 1893), or in Godolphin's *Greek Historians*.

APPIAN: H. E. White in LL (4 vols.).

PAUSANIAS: J. G. Frazer's great six-volume edition (2d ed.; London, 1913) is a mine of information; LL (6 vols.) by W. H. S. Jones and H. A. Ormerod is also very useful.

APOLLODORUS: J. G. Frazer's two-volume LL is unique in that series for the fullness of its commentary.

ASCLEPIODOTUS AND ONOSANDER: with Aeneas Tacticus in LL by Illinois Greek Club.

DIO CASSIUS: nine-volume LL by E. W. Cary; Book 53 with commentary, H. T. F. Duckworth (Toronto, 1916).

HERODIAN: The translations are old—Nicholas Smith (1629) and J. Hart (1749).

CHAPTER 16. LITERATURE OF RELIGION

Besides histories and reference works on religion see S. Angus, *The Religious Quests of the Graeco-Roman World* (New York, 1929); C. N. Cochrane, *Christianity and Classical Culture* (Oxford, 1940); and the collection of passages in the translation in E. R. Bevan, *Later Greek Religion* (New York, 1927). The later representatives of the schools are dealt with in the standard histories of philosophy; complete and concise treatments are to be found in, e. g., F. Ueberweg-K. Praechter, *Grundriss der Geschichte der Philosophie* (12th ed.; Berlin, 1926).

PANAETIUS: Modestus van Straaten, *Panétius, sa vie, ses écrits, et sa doctrine,* including edition of fragments (Amsterdam, 1946).

EPICTETUS AND MARCUS AURELIUS: W. A. Oldfather's two-volume LL *Epictetus* and C. R. Haines LL *Marcus* have excellent introductions and bibliographies; see also the works on Stoicism listed under chapter 12. W. J. Oates, *Stoic and Epicurean Philosophers* (New York, 1940) includes translations of Epictetus and Marcus Aurelius.

DION CHRYSOSTOM: J. W. Cohoon and H. L. Crosby in LL (5 vols.); H. von Arnim, *Leben und Werke des Dion von Prusa*, 2 vols. (Berlin, 1898), and L. François, *Essai sur Dion Chrysostome* (Paris, 1921).

MAXIMUS OF TYRE: Translated by Thomas Taylor, *Dissertations of Maximus of Tyre,* 2 vols. (London, 1804).

SEXTUS EMPIRICUS: R. G. Bury, LL (3 vols.); Mary M. Patrick, *The Greek Sceptics* (New York, 1929).

CEBES: School edition, C. S. Jerram (Oxford, 1878 and reprints).

PLUTARCH: LL has eleven volumes of *Lives* (B. Perrin) and will have fourteen of *Moralia* (F. C. Babbitt and others); the *Lives* are hardly an improvement on the so-called "Dryden-Clough version," available in one volume (Modern Library Giants), the *Moralia,* an enormous improvement on *Plutarch's Morals Translated by Several Hands,* revised by W. W. Goodwin, 6 vols. (Boston, 1898), in which the best thing is Ralph Waldo Emerson's introduction. There is a translation of a good selection of the *Moralia* by T. G. Tucker and A. O. Prickard, 2 vols. (Oxford, 1913–1918). For ancient biography see D. R. Stuart, *Epochs of Greek and Roman Biography* (Berkeley, Calif., 1928).

Dutch pastor argument: J. J. Hartmann, *De Plutarcho Scriptore et Philosopho* (Leyden, 1916), pp. 662 ff. Hartmann is worth quoting on Plutarch's use of earlier writers (p. 6): *Rembrandtius ubi linteum suum oleumque emere sit solitus quis curat?*

SEPTUAGINT: H. B. Swete, *Introduction to the Old Testament in Greek* (Cambridge, 1900) contains the text (with introduction) of *Letter of Aristeas* by H. St. J. Thackeray, who also translated it (London, 1917). See also H. G. Meecham, *Letter of Aristeas* (Manchester, 1935), and C. H. Dodd, *The Bible and the Greeks* (London, 1935). Convenient introductions and commentaries to the books of the Apocrypha are to be found in *A New Commentary on Holy Scripture Including the Apocrypha,* edited by C. Gore, H. L. Goudge, and A. Guillaume (New York, 1929); this volume contains many good essays relevant to the subject matter of this chapter.

HELLENISTIC JEWISH WRITERS: The fragments are collected, chiefly from Eusebius and Clement, with inadequate introductions and notes, in W. N. Sterns, *Fragments from Graeco-Jewish Writers* (Chicago, 1908). The *Sibylline Oracles* are edited, with a German introduction, by J. Geffcken (Leipzig, 1902), translations of Books 3–5, H. N. Bate (London, 1918).

PHILO: LL to be completed in ten volumes by F. H. Colson, G. H. Whitaker, and Ralph Marcus. A prime work on Philo is H. A. Wolfson, *Philo; Foundations of Religious Philosophy in Judaism, Christianity, and Islam,* 2 vols. (Harvard, 1947); see also E. R. Goodenough, *By Light, Light: the Mystic Gospel of Hellenistic Judaism* (New Haven, Conn., 1935).

NEOPLATONISM: T. Whittaker, *The Neoplatonists* (Cambridge, 1918).

PLOTINUS: Translated by S. MacKenna, 5 vols. (London, 1917–1930); K. S. Guthrie, 4 vols. (London, 1918–1928). W. R. Inge, *The Philosophy of Plotinus,* 2 vols. (New York, 1918); Grace H. Turnbull, *The Essence of Plotinus* (New York, 1934); A. H. Armstrong, *The Architecture of the Intelligible Universe in the Philosophy of Plotinus* (Cambridge, 1940).

PORPHYRY: Translation of *On Abstinence, Cave of the Nymphs, Auxiliaries to Perception* in Thomas Taylor, *Porphyry; Selected Works* (London, 1805). Porphyry quotation: from Alcie Zimmern, *Porphyry to Marcella* (London, 1896).

IAMBLICHUS: Newest text, L. Deubner, *Iamblichi de Vita Pythagorica Liber* (Leipzig, 1937). Iamblichus quotation: Edwyn Bevan, in his *Later Greek Religion,* p. 226.

PROCLUS: E. R. Dodds, Proclus, *The Elements of Theology* (Oxford, 1933) has a full introduction and commentary as well as text and translation; other translations are K. S. Guthrie, *Proclus, Life, Hymns, Works* (New York, n.d.); Thomas Taylor, *Proclus, on the Theology of Plato, etc.,* 8 vols. (London, 1792–1833).

NEOPLATONIST INFLUENCES IN ENGLISH POETRY: J. S. Harrison, *Platonism in English Poetry of the Sixteenth and Seventeenth Centuries* (New York, 1903); Appendix to Turnbull, *op. cit.*

Simplicius quotation: Angus, *op. cit.*, p. 9; there is a translation of Simplicius' commentary on Epictetus in G. Stanhope, *Epictetus His Morals with Simplicius His Comment* (London, 1704).

NEW TESTAMENT: Good introductions are very numerous; E. F. Scott, *The Literature of the New Testament* (New York, 1932) and E. J. Goodspeed, *An Introduction to the New Testament* (Chicago, 1937) are scholarly and readable.

PATRISTIC LITERATURE: Texts of all patristic authors, with Latin translations, are in the 161 volumes of J. P. Migne, *Patrologia Graeca* (Paris, 1854–1866); there are, of course, separate (and better) texts of many. There are three great series of translations: *The Ante-Nicene Christian Library,* 24 vols., edited by A. Roberts and J. Donaldson (Edinburgh, 1867–1872); *The Select Library of Nicene and Post-Nicene Fathers,* 28 vols., edited by P. Schaff (Edinburgh, 1890–1908); and the older collection of E. B. Pusey, *The Fathers Anterior to the Division of East and West,* 50 vols. (Oxford, 1839 ff.). Standard critical works are O. Bardenhewer, *Geschichte der Altchristlichen Literatur,* 5 vols. (Freiburg, 1913–1932); A. Puech, *Histoire de la littérature grecque chrétienne* (to the end of fourth century), 3 vols. (Paris, 1928–1930); F. Ueberweg-B. Geyer, *Die patristische und scholastische Philosophie,* 11th ed., which is the second part of the *Grundriss der Geschichte der Philosophie* (Berlin, 1928). Shorter introductions are: E. Leigh-Bennett, *Handbook of the Early Christian Fathers* (London, 1920); E. J. Goodspeed, *A History of Early Christian Literature* (Chicago, 1942); J. M. Campbell, *The Greek Fathers* (ODGR, 1929).

APOSTOLIC FATHERS: Text, translation, commentary by J. B. Lightfoot, *The Apostolic Fathers,* 6 vols. (London, 1890); LL, 2 vols., K. Lake; see also A. C. McGiffert, *The Apostolic Age* (New York, 1897).

CLEMENT: *Exhortation to the Greeks, Rich Man's Salvation,* and *To the Newly Baptized* in LL, G. W. Butterworth; see also B. Tollinton, *Clement of Alexandria; a Study in Christian Liberalism,* 2 vols. (London, 1914).

Origen *Against Celsus:* for Celsus' *True Word* see R. Bader, *Der Alethes Logos des Kelsos* (Stuttgart, 1940).

EUSEBIUS: *Ecclesiastical History,* K. Lake and J. E. L. Oulton in LL (2 vols.), or translations alone by H. J. Lawler and J. E. L. Oulton (London, 1927); E. H. Gifford, *Eusebius, Preparation for the Gospel* (Oxford, 1903); W. J. Ferrar, *Eusebius, the Proof of the Gospel,* 2 vols. (London, 1904).

SYNESIUS: Augustine FitzGerald has translated, with introductions and notes, *The Letters of Synesius* (Oxford, 1926) and *The Essays and Hymns of Synesius,* 2 vols. (Oxford, 1930). See also Alice Gardner, *Synesius of Cyrene* (London, 1886); W. S. Crawford, *Synesius the Hellene* (London, 1901); and T. R.

Glover, *Life and Letters in the Fourth Century* (Cambridge, 1901), pp. 320 ff. Charles Kingsley's novel *Hypatia* (1853) sticks to the sources.

ST. BASIL: Letters in LL by R. J. Deferrari (4 vols.); W. K. L. Clarke, *The Ascetic Works of St. Basil* (London, 1925).

GREGORY OF NYSSA: H. F. Cherniss, *The Platonism of Gregory of Nyssa,* University of California Publications in Classical Philology No. 11 (Berkeley, Calif., 1934), is an illuminating monograph.

JOHN CHRYSOSTOM: J. F. D'Alton, *Selections from St. John Chrysostom* (London, 1940) is a good introduction. The translations in the *Nicene Fathers* and the Pusey collection (15 vols.) are quite readable. See also A. Puech, *John Chrysostom,* translated by Mildred Partridge (2d ed.; London, 1917).

THEODORETUS, SOCRATES, SOZOMEN: All three are translated in volumes of the Bohn series.

PROCOPIUS: H. B. Dewing in LL, 7 vols.

COSMAS INDICOPLEUSTES: E. O. Winstedt, *The Christian Topography of Cosmas Indicopleustes* (Cambridge, 1909); see especially B. Farrington, *Science and Politics in the Ancient World* (London, 1939), p. 21.

CHAPTER 17. ORATORS AND ENCYCLOPEDISTS OF THE SECOND SOPHISTIC

A good brief essay on the Second Sophistic is W. C. Wright's introduction to her LL *Philostratus and Eunapius*. For reference see W. Schmid, *Der Atticismus in seinen Hauptvertretern von Dionysius Hal. bis auf den zweiten Philostratus,* 2 vols. (Stuttgart, 1887–1897). W. W. Capes, *University Life in Ancient Athens* (London, 1877) has a good chapter on the fourth century. For the period as a whole see the early chapters in the *Cambridge Medieval History,* Vol. I (1911); J. B. Bury, *History of the Later Roman Empire,* 395–565, 2 vols. (London, 1923); and Bury's revision of *Gibbon's Decline and Fall of the Roman Empire.* Dion quotation: Cohoon in LL.

AELIUS ARISTIDES: With Latin commentary, W. Dindorf, 3 vols. (Leipzig, 1829); A. Boulanger, *Aelius Aristide et la Sophistique dans la Province d'Asie* (Paris, 1923).

PHILOSTRATUS: *Lives of the Sophists* (with Eunapius), LL by W. C. Wright; *Life of Apollonius of Tyana,* LL (2 vols.), W. C. Conybeare; also translation by J. S. Phillimore, 2 vols. (Oxford, 1912).

PHILOSTRATUS, JR., AND CALLISTRATUS: A. Fairbanks in LL.

DIOGENES LAERTIUS: Useful introduction and bibliography in R. D. Hicks, LL (2 vols.).

ATHENAEUS: G. B. Gulick in LL (7 vols.); with Latin translation and commentary, J. Schweighaeuser, 14 vols. (Strassburg, 1801–1807).

AELIAN: Text, 2 vols., edited by R. Hercher (Leipzig, 1864–1866); *idem,* with Latin translation (Paris, 1858).

LIBANIUS: R. Foerster, 13 vols. (Leipzig, 1903–1927).

HIMERIUS: F. Duebner (Paris, 1849).

THEMISTIUS: G. Dindorf (Leipzig, 1832).

JULIAN: W. C. Wright in LL (3 vols.). There are many lives of Julian, e. g., Alice Gardner, *Julian* (New York, 1895).

SALLUSTIUS, friend of Julian: A. D. Nock, *Sallustius, concerning Gods and the Universe,* edited with prolegomena and translation (Cambridge, 1926); translated by T. Taylor, (London, 1793).

POLLUX AND OTHER LEXICOGRAPHERS: J. E. Sandys, *A History of Classical Scholarship,* Vol. I (Cambridge, 1921); J. H. Freese, *The Library of Photius* (London, 1920).

CHAPTER 18. LUCIAN, THE NOVEL

LUCIAN: Besides Harmon's excellent LL version there are the sprightly translations of H. W. and F. G. Fowler, *The Works of Lucian of Samosata,* 4 vols. (Oxford, 1905); Elizabeth H. Haight, *Essays on the Greek Romances* (New York, 1943), pp. 144–185; M. Croiset, *Essai sur la vie et les oeuvres de Lucien* (Paris, 1882); F. G. Allinson, *Lucian* (ODGR, 1926). Allinson's introduction to his *Lucian's Selected Writings* (New York, 1905) is also useful. *True History:* see P. G. Gove, *The Imaginary Voyage in Prose Fiction* (New York, 1941). TOXARIS: evidence cited in Haight, *op. cit.,* p. 128. *Lucius; or, The Ass:* see B. E. Perry, *The Metamorphoses Ascribed to Lucius of Patrae* (Princeton, 1920).

IONIAN LOGOI: see J. A. K. Thomson, *The Art of the Logos* (London, 1935).

ALCIPHRON: Translated by F. A. Wright, *Alciphron; Letters from the Country and the Town* (London, n.d.).

ARISTAENETUS: J. Brenous, *Aristénète; lettres d'amour* (Paris, 1938).

GREEK ROMANCES: E. Rohde, *Der Griechische Roman u. seine Vorlaeufer,* with Appendix by W. Schmid (3d ed.; Leipzig, 1914); Elizabeth H. Haight, *Essays on Greek Romances* (New York, 1943); F. A. Todd, *Some Ancient Novels* (Oxford, 1940): R. M. Rattenbury in *New Chapters in the History of Greek Literature, Third Series* (Oxford, 1933); S. Gaselee, "Appendix on the Greek Novel" in his LL *Daphnis and Chloe;* M. Braun, *History and Romance in Graeco-Oriental Literature* (Oxford, 1938). Texts: *Erotici Graeci,* Didot (with Latin translation) edited by G. A. Hirschig and others (Paris, 1856) contains Achilles Tatius, Antonius Diogenes, Apollonius Tyrius, Chariton Aphrodisiensis, Eustathius Makrembolites, Heliodorus, Iamblichus, Longus, Nicetas Eugenianus, Parthenius, Xenophon Ephesius; the two-volume Teubner, edited by R. Hercher (1858–1859), does not contain Apollonius Tyrius or Heliodorus, but does contain Constantius Manasses and Theodorus Prodromus. There is a Bohn translation of three romances by Rev. Rowland Smith, *The Greek Romances of Heliodorus, Longus, and Achilles Tatius* (London, 1855).

NINUS ROMANCE: in S. Gaselee's LL *Daphnis and Chloe,* pp. 387–393.

ALEXANDER ROMANCE: Adolf Ausfeld, *Der Griechische Alexanderroman* (Leipzig, 1909).

CHARITON: Text, W. E. Blake (Oxford, 1938); translated *idem, Chariton's*

Chaereas and Callirhoe (Ann Arbor, Mich., 1939); Aristide Calderini, *Le Avventure di Cherea e Calliroe* (Torino, 1913).

XENOPHON OF EPHESUS: G. Dalmeyda's Budé *Xenophon d'Éphèse, les Ephésiaques* (Paris, 1926).

HELIODORUS: Budé text and translation by R. M. Rattenbury, T. W. Lumb, J. Maillou, 4 vols. (Paris, 1935–1938); Aristides Colonna, *Heliodori Aethiopica* (Rome, 1938). Thomas Underdowne's sixteenth-century translation is revised by F. A. Wright (London, n.d.).

LONGUS: Text translation, commentary by W. D. Lowe, *Daphnis and Chloe* (London, 1908); Budé by G. Dalmeyda (Paris, 1934). George Thornley's 1657 translation is available with introduction by George Saintsbury (London, n.d.); George Moore, *The Pastoral Loves of Daphnis and Chloe* (London, 1924) is a beautiful piece.

ELIZABETHANS: S. L. Wolff, *The Greek Romances in Elizabethan Prose Fiction* (New York, 1912).

CHRISTIAN NOVELS: see T. R. Glover, *Life and Letters in the Fourth Century* (Cambridge, 1901), chapter 15, "Greek and Early Christian Novels," pp. 357–386.

INDEX

Figures in italics indicate the principal passage for the rubric. Titles of individual works and contents of quoted or summarized material are not as a rule indexed.